Jonathan Conlin is Senior Lecturer in History at the University of Southampton. His books include *Tales of Two Cities: Paris, London and the Making of the Modern City* (2013), *Evolution and the Victorians* (2014) and *Adam Smith* (2016).

Great Economic Thinkers

from ADAM SMITH *to* AMARTYA SEN

Edited by
Jonathan Conlin

SPEAKING TIGER

Speaking Tiger Books LLP
125 A, Ground Floor Shahpur Jat, Near Asiad Village
New Delhi 110049, India

Great Economic Thinkers edited by Jonathan Conlin was first
published in London, UK, by Reaktion Books 2018
Published in India in paperback by Speaking Tiger 2018

ISBN:978-93-88326-16-2
eISBN: 978-93-88326-17-9
10 9 8 7 6 5 4 3 2

Printed at Nutech Print Services - India

CONTENTS

INTRODUCTION

D'Maris Coffman

To speak of Great Economic Thinkers, let alone to provide pen portraits of their lives and works, as the authors of these essays have done, is to assert that the writings of economists matter in the formation of economic policymaking. Perhaps what most strongly unites the subjects of these biographies (with the exceptions of Milton Friedman and John Nash) was a conviction best articulated by Keynes:

> The ideas of economists and political philosophers, both when they are right, and when they are wrong, are more powerful than is commonly understood. Indeed, the world is ruled by little else. Practical men, who believe themselves to be quite exempt from any intellectual influences, are usually the slaves of some defunct economist. Madmen in authority, who hear voices in the air, are distilling their frenzy from some academic scribbler of a few years back.[1]

All of the economists discussed in this volume rose above the ranks of ordinary 'academic scribblers', and each had a profound influence on attitudes towards market intervention and regulation, taxation, trade and monetary policy. Likewise, their theories – division of labour, comparative advantage, surplus value, marginal utility, the tax state, aggregate demand, rational choice theory, quantity theory of money, the Nash equilibrium, cognitive biases and prospect theory, social choice theory and information asymmetry, to name but a few of the most influential – have come to structure the way in which we talk about economic and social life. How then should economists and historians approach these authors and their works? One answer is given by the writer who forms the subject of Chapter Six.

Joseph A. Schumpeter's distinction between 'history of economic thought' and 'history of economic analysis' is often neglected but offers helpful guidance. In Schumpeter's schematic, the former is associated with a focus of interest on the content of economic theories rather than their formal structure, the relationship between economic thinking and its historical context and the relationship between economic ideas and the intellectual influences acting on them. The latter is primarily concerned with the internal history of the discipline, the axiomatic structure of theory and the evolution and development of specific theoretical formulations. The two approaches may lead to radically different views of scientific revolutions in economics. History of economic thought tends to see theory 'in context' so that multiple and not always mutually compatible influences come into play. In this case, and somewhat paradoxically, a fundamental continuity of developments is often assumed and ruptures are often seen as a consequence of external history rather than as a result of internal dynamics.

On the other hand, the history of economic analysis tends to recognize continuities within any given research line but neglects discontinuities across different research lines and intellectual traditions. In other words, the relative autonomy of the discipline is acknowledged, and ruptures ('scientific revolutions', such as those posited by Thomas Kuhn[2]) are seen as emerging from paradigm switches taking the discipline from one research line to another. In particular, those switches are turning points at which one structural specification of the economy gives way to another, thereby changing the main focus of attention and the explanatory domain of theory. The widely acknowledged need for a new approach to the study of economics points to the fact that specifications of the economy that could be appropriate at one time could miss causal processes and interdependencies that are central at a different time, after a regime change (of the sort specified in mathematical models) has occurred.

An economist dealing today with the historical evolution of economic literature is much more likely to encounter the history of economic thought than the history of economic analysis. This means that he or she will often meet a descriptive account of the theories of the past (often seen as anticipations of one strand or another of current economic theory) but only rarely an analytical account of the logical (formal) structure of past theories. This will only reinforce a Whig conception of the evolution of economic ideas and a rather naive attitude to the possibility of progress in economics that might ultimately make historical awareness redundant, providing a teleological view of scientific progress leading to the 'end of history' in economics, which is what has happened to the discipline in the last forty years. Advocates of the 'efficient-markets' hypothesis thought they had the 'last word' and that their predecessors were thus necessarily unworthy of attention.

It is increasingly acknowledged that fresh economic thinking requires a thorough grounding in historical understanding, but for the latter to be fully effective it is necessary to explore in depth the analytical structure of the theories of the past, which are often as logically demanding as current theories. Only in this way will a proper comparison between different theoretical frameworks be possible, and the economist will be able to draw from the full range of economic theories – past and present – suitable to the specific historical context in view.

A strength of this collection of essays is that it brings together a group of economists and historians who offer a mix of these two approaches, thereby enriching the reader's appreciation of both the continuities and discontinuities in economic writing, the extent to which the thinkers profiled share common intellectual interests and offer us genuinely original insights, that are the product of the particular problems of their age.

Forerunners of Adam Smith

Any history of classical economic thought will have a somewhat arbitrary starting point, as antecedents of many of these ideas can be traced back to antiquity. In a more immediate sense, in Renaissance and Reformation Europe, the literary genre of 'advice to princes' flourished, where courtiers sought to counsel their sovereigns on matters of policy and politics more generally. By the sixteenth century, the 'mirror for princes' conceit (of offering either examples for emulation or object lessons in misgovernment) had given way to more or less explicitly polemical writing, often inspired by engagement with Machiavelli's *The Prince* (1532). In England particularly, this tradition flourished alongside 'projecting', whereupon a large number of newly educated commoners proposed potentially lucrative 'projects' to the king, which ranged from fisheries and draining swampland to land banks and even new colonies.

Projects to encourage trade and reform taxation were frequently proposed, often with elaborate and well-reasoned justifications, which emphasized the public benefits. A minority of their authors are typically called the mercantilists, because they argued forcibly that England should maintain a positive balance of trade in order to remain prosperous and to ensure that the king had sufficient supplies of metallic coin in his treasury. Their writings occurred against the twin backdrop of the rise of the great parastatal joint-stock trading companies, of which the East India Company was paradigmatic, and of the financial demands of the Military Revolution, which increased the scale and expense of keeping armies in the field. Securing realm and religion depended on the means with which to pay mercenaries to battle the mercenary armies of other great powers and to ensure that British ships could safely voyage across the globe.

Thomas Mun's *A Discourse of Trade from England Unto the East Indies* (1621) and *England's Treasure by Foreign Trade, or the Balance of Forraign Trade is the Rule of Our Treasure* (1620s) are typical examples of Jacobean mercantilism, and contain both general advice to James I about how to respond to the economic slowdown occasioned by the Thirty Years War (1618–48) in continental Europe, as well as an apologetic for the East India Company, of which he was a director. Thomas Mun held firmly to the need for a positive balance of trade, and greatly admired the mercantile Dutch. Mun's *England's Treasure* was printed for the first time in 1664 (the 1620s editions had been circulated at court in manuscript form), sparking renewed debate. Sir Josiah Child's *Brief Observations concerning Trade and the Interest of Money* (1668) and his *A New Discourse of Trade* (1668) engage directly with Mun's ideas.

While Child was an advocate of protectionism (and a defender of the Navigation Acts), he disagreed with Mun's opposition to the export of precious metals and even advocated a limited version of the free-trade doctrine more commonly associated with Adam Smith. A later mercantilist author, Charles Davenant, who served the Crown first as an excise commissioner and then as an Inspector-General of Customs, also favoured a positive balance of trade, but was principally concerned in his early works, such as *Two Discourses on the Public Revenues and Trade of England* (1698), with the sustainability of the growing national debt. Yet in *An Essay on the probable means of making the people gainers in the balance of Trade* (1699), Davenant anticipates a doctrine not unlike Ricardian comparative advantage. In any case, unlike early mercantilist writers, Davenant held that 'trade is in its nature free, finds its own channel, and best directs its own course.'[3]

Two additional English authors bear mentioning. An ambitious 'projector', who undertook the Down Survey in Ireland on behalf of Charles II, William Petty was a man of both commercial and intellectual interests. He was arguably the grandfather of political economy. Trained in Caen in medicine by the Jesuits, the young Petty became

Thomas Hobbes's personal secretary upon his return to England. As an economic writer, Petty blended the empiricism of Francis Bacon with Hobbesian rationalism, giving his 'political arithmetik' formal rigour and a strong evidentiary base. Each of his major works – *Treatise of Taxes and Contributions* (1662), *Verbum Sapienti* (1655) and *Quantulumcunque concerning Money* (1682) – can be profitably read today. Petty's calculations of national income anticipated and inspired the more detailed work of Gregory King, while Petty's ideas about compensatory taxation, the circulation and velocity of money, market rates of interest and economic policy inspired both Smith and Marx and were admired by Keynes. Petty's theories of value gave rise to his system of national accounting (formally developed in the French context by François Quesnay). Turgot and Smith were sufficiently impressed by Petty's *Treatise on Taxes* to adopt its structure and contents list as a template for their own writings. The relative obscurity into which Petty has fallen is probably a product more of the diversity of his writings and the challenge of pinning down his field (historical demography, geography, economics, economic policy, political philosophy and so forth) than of the quality of his thought.

David Hume likewise towers above contemporaries and defies classification within modern disciplinary boundaries. His monetary theories within his *Political Writings* are especially important, as they expound Locke's quantity theory of money, establish a price–specie flow mechanism and provide a strong argument for a mildly inflationary monetary policy. Equally Hume's concept of 'equilibration' anticipated modern economic models. Hume was Smith's friend and literary executor, as well as a correspondent of the leading French Physiocrats.

The founder of the Physiocratic School, François Quesnay was, like Petty, trained as a physician and even served the French court in that capacity. His *Tableau économique* (1759) established the first formal macroeconomic model, dividing the economy into two sectors: agriculture and manufacturing. For Quesnay and his followers, a kingdom's wealth was the 'net product' of its land, as their model assumed that manufacturing merely transformed inputs into outputs, without adding value. From this the Physiocrats derived two principal policy objectives: to remove internal barriers to trade in agricultural products and to abandon France's fiscal mix of direct (land) and indirect (commodity) taxation, most of which had been farmed to private parties at great expense to the king, in favour of a single tax on land, which they called 'l'impôt unique'. Their attempts to abolish medieval regulations and privileges, including the requirement that peasants perform the *corvée* (forced labour, usually road-building), and their attack on monopolies and chartered trading companies earned them the approbation of *laissez-faire économistes.*

Quesnay died in 1774, before the publication of his admirer Adam Smith's *The Wealth of Nations*, but Turgot, who was allied with the Physiocrats, if perhaps more widely remembered for his activities as Comptroller-General of Finances, built on Quesnay's model in important ways in his *Réflexions sur la formation et la distribution des richesses* (1769) (*Reflections on the Causes and Distribution of Wealth*). His distinctions between agricultural labour, artisanal labour and rentiers are familiar to nineteenth-century political economy, and his commitment to Lockean notions of natural law made him a favourite with his English correspondents, including Hume and Smith. His concern about how to best regulate (or deregulate) the 'corn' trade (meaning the agricultural commodities markets) was typical of late eighteenth-century writers in both France and England, as well as Italy and Prussia. Turgot's attempts to introduce 'l'impôt unique' made him the enemy of powerful tax farmers, who eventually brought about his downfall. For the purposes of this volume, however, it might be worth noting for readers the very great similarities between the organization of his *Réflexions* and *The Wealth of Nations.*

Profiling Thirteen Great Economic Thinkers

No summary of influences on Adam Smith and his followers can do justice to the full range of European Enlightenment economic writing. This discussion has necessarily omitted the Prussian and Swedish Cameralists, the writers of the Neapolitan Enlightenment (as well their forefather, Antonio Serra) and those around the court of Joseph II in Austria. These authors, while important, are less obvious antecedents of the economic writers contained in this volume.

Choosing only thirteen economists from Smith to Stiglitz equally requires hard choices, as the six Nobel laureates profiled in the second half of the volume are chosen from nearly fifty such awards. What unites these thirteen economists as Great Economic Thinkers is not their radical projects or their novelty, but rather the extent to which they have contributed to the intellectual furniture of modern economic thinking, as most readers would recognize it. Even so, many readers may find at least some fault with the selection: If this is about economics as most people learned it, where is Paul Samuelson? If Nash is included as a mathematician who influenced the course of mainstream economics, why not Léon Walras, the architect of general equilibrium theory? Given the focus on macroeconomic policymaking, surely John Hicks, who developed the IS-LM model familiar to undergraduates, deserves inclusion? The best defence we can offer is that these are not necessarily the thirteen greatest economic thinkers, but they are hopefully representative of great economic thinking.

Jonathan Conlin's biography of Adam Smith in Chapter One offers a concise survey of the varied intellectual influences on his subject. He situates Smith's economic writings alongside his treatises on moral philosophy (*Theory of Moral Sentiments*) and his eighteenth-century preoccupations. Conlin blends histories of economic thought and economic analysis to illustrate for the reader how Smith gave us the categories of modern microeconomics without sharing the assumptions of modern micro theory. Smith's ideal of economic life was far removed from that of *homo economicus.*

In Chapter Two, Helen Paul examines how Ricardo built on Smith's division of labour to elucidate his theory of comparative advantage in international trade, which she identifies as his main contribution to modern economics in a conceptual sense. His methodological contribution consisted of his development of a 'corn model', which he could use to critique the Corn Laws and which arose out of his correspondence with Malthus about the extent to which the kingdom's agricultural production could support its demographic regime. As Paul tells her readers, Ricardo's posthumous reputation was re-established by Piero Sraffa's edition of Ricardo's works and letters. Ricardo's other principal contribution to modern economics lies in the concept of Ricardian Equivalence, for which he was given credit 150 years later by Robert J. Barro, who wanted to claim Ricardo as a forerunner of Friedman's monetarism. The attribution was born of a throwaway remark in which Ricardo observes that taxpayers are likely to be indifferent to a choice between immediate tax increases to fund a war and longer-term tax increases to fund government borrowing to finance a war, because they will anticipate the future increases and reduce their consumption accordingly. This was a concern shared by Davenant, writing over a century earlier, who could equally claim to have anticipated many of the debates about how far the establishment of parliamentary supremacy over crown finance created a 'credible commitment' to probity in public finance. The monetarism of Barro, Robert Lucas and the Lucas Critique, and Finn E. Kydland and Edward C. Prescott's 'time-inconsistent policymaking', in which economic agents would anticipate economic planners so as to frustrate the process, would have been unrecognizable to Ricardo. His liberalism, as Paul shows, was born of different preoccupations.

In Chapter Three, Joseph Persky explores how John Stuart Mill's economic writings were informed by his attempts to understand the structural economic changes engendered by the Industrial Revolution, which Mill could observe around him, and which represented a rupture with the economic and social life of the past century. As Persky argues, Mill is usually neglected as an economic writer, dismissed as derivative of Malthus, Ricardo and even Smith. Persky aims to rehabilitate Mill's reputation by illustrating his beliefs about property and the ability of the state to redistribute it, his theories of accumulation and economic growth, and his ultimate desire for a post-capitalist communitarian society, which together amounted to a coherent economic programme and a 'political economy of progress'.

Paul Prew takes on the Herculean task of introducing Karl Marx in Chapter Four. He wants to demystify Marx, on the one hand, and on the other to offer something new to readers already familiar with Marxian economics. The first part of the essay concentrates on Marx's historicist method, locating it within the context of Marx's university education in Germany and his anthropological orientation. Prew's elucidation of the Marxian theory of the 'alienation' of labour from the means of production in capitalist societies is thus grounded in a discussion of Marx's interpretative strategy. Marxian notions of commodity exchange and accumulation are thus presented as foundational blocks of Marx's theory of surplus value. In Prew's account, *The Communist Manifesto* is presented as an afterthought, dashed off as it was during the Revolutions of 1848. A proper account of Marx's legacy is beyond the scope of a biographical sketch, yet Prew alludes to the many different ways one might approach such a question.

Katia Caldari's sketch of Alfred Marshall forms the basis of Chapter Five. In Caldari's account, Marshall's chief motivation was to understand and solve the problem of poverty (alongside housing and environmental conditions in which workers lived), a project to which his mathematical economics was hitched. She describes how Marshall deliberately founded the discipline of economics as practised in Cambridge, and how he reformed the Moral Sciences Tripos. Caldari contends that in contrast to many of his followers, Marshall wore his mathematical reasoning lightly, relegating his formulae, tables and figures to scholarly para-text in his main works. As Caldari recognizes, Marshall's most enduring contributions to modern economics appear to rest primarily in the analytical tools he bequeathed to it, particularly demand and supply curves, diminishing marginal utility, partial equilibria and elasticities of supply and demand. These are the fundamentals of neoclassical microeconomics. Caldari will have achieved her main aim if her readers are moved to read Marshall less for those recognizable concepts than for his wider commentary on late nineteenth-century Britain, which, as she argues, is subtle yet riddled with contradictions.

In Chapter Six, Mário Graça Moura introduces Joseph Schumpeter as the man who identified innovation and entrepreneurship as the engines of capitalism, and who inaugurated the discipline of economic analysis. In Schumpeter's scheme, a complete history of economic analysis required a mastery of four sub-fields: economic history, statistics, economic theory and economic sociology. In Schumpeter's account, innovation is endogenous, providing economic systems the wherewithal to adapt to exogenous shocks. Schumpeter's views remain influential, inspiring the likes of Bill Janeway and Mariana Mazzucato, who want to understand the role of the state in fostering innovation. Graça Moura also identifies Schumpeter's theory of business cycles as a significant advance upon his predecessors, which include figures beyond the scope of this volume such as Clément Juglar, Jean Lescure, Albert Aftalion and even A. C. Pigou. Graça Moura examines Schumpeter's socioeconomic theories, which follow a logic notably different from Marx's economic determinism where social class is determined by relationship to the means of production. If Schumpeter is less read today than Keynes or Marx, then it is again largely because he defies classification within modern universities. He would have been at home with Braudel in the French Annales school.

Victoria Bateman introduces John Maynard Keynes in Chapter Seven by noticing that despite his heroic intellectual and practical achievements, her subject is heavily criticized both by free-market capitalists and by Marxian socialists. His aim is to save capitalism not to abolish it, as he finds the alternatives, in the form of the totalitarian regimes of interwar Europe, unpalatable. While Keynes made many contributions to economics, the focus of Bateman's sketch is the Keynesian Revolution in macroeconomic policymaking. Here she emphasizes that Keynes's key contribution was his recognition that the state could intervene to bolster aggregate demand when the economy failed to recover on its own as a result of price and wage stickiness. As Bateman notices, the mechanisms are still an issue of live debate, as some of Keynes's heirs prefer to focus on his views on risk and uncertainty as explanations for the failure of economic actors to facilitate a return to equilibrium. While the distinctions among New Keynesians, Neo-Keynesians and Post-Keynesians are desperately important to their practitioners, most mainstream economists are not especially interested in the nuances. The more important disagreements are between Keynes and classical liberals and the monetarists.

In Chapter Eight, Scott Scheall presents Keynes's arch-rival, Friedrich Hayek, who shares with the remaining thinkers considered in this volume the achievement of having been awarded a Nobel Memorial Prize in Economics (1974). Hayek is most closely aligned with the Austrian School of economics and was a leading proponent of classical liberalism. He was motivated by an interest, shared with so many writers in this volume, in the intersection of psychology and economics, from whence he derived his methodological individualism. As with Keynes, Hayek wanted to understand the mechanics of disequilibria in business cycles, and over time became a leading critic of equilibrium theory. Hayek was the first to apprehend the inflationary potential of Keynesian policies and became a staunch opponent of any form of economic planning. His main preoccupation, however, was with understanding the acquisition and coordination of knowledge at a societal level, and with the limitations of economics as a discipline, which he saw as an inadequate guide to policymaking. As Scheall concludes, Hayek's scepticism and his openness to other fields underpin his greatness.

Victoria Bateman returns in Chapter Nine with her sketch of Milton Friedman, who won the Nobel Memorial Prize in 1976 chiefly for his contributions to monetary theory. Friedman is known to laymen for his vigorous defence of free-market capitalism and his bitter opposition to Keynesianism in all its forms. Bateman begins by discussing Friedman's method, which represented an abrupt rupture with previous economists, who regarded economics as a moral science. Friedman wanted to reconstruct economics as a positive science, on a par with physics or chemistry, yet with the appreciation that the complexities of economic phenomena would defeat attempts to reduce the economy to a series of mathematical models. Friedman's economic methodology was governed by a conviction that the occult laws of the market would always prevail, even if they could not be entirely apprehended by economics.

In his empirical work, he used the inevitable 'lags' in macroeconomic policymaking to argue that government intervention to stabilize the economy would be at best useless and at worst inflationary. In the face of high inflation in the 1970s, Friedman's monetarism found itself in the ascendancy. Yet as Bateman acknowledges, Friedman's critique of Keynes was more subtle than those of many subsequent mainstream neoclassical economists. Her subject's commitment to markets as self-equilibrating remained the hallmark of his thought.

Karen Horn has the challenging task of introducing John Forbes Nash Jr in Chapter Ten. Unlike the other thinkers covered in this volume, Nash's contributions to economics (for which he was eventually awarded a Nobel Memorial Prize in 1994) were largely inadvertent, an application of his 'game theory' to a cognate field. Nash's contribution was to theorize non-cooperative, non-zero-sum games of *n* players. The solution, popularized by his thesis supervisor, Alfred Tucker, as the Prisoner's Dilemma, is known as the Nash equilibrium. Despite the limitations noted by Horn, this concept gave economists a revolutionary new tool for describing market failures, or suboptimal outcomes of scenarios in which agents (households and firms) rationally attempted to maximize their own utilities. As she notes, Nash's non-cooperative games also sparked an interest in strategic thinking in economics. Horn's sympathetic account of Nash's illness and his eventual recognition is moving. Most readers will know Nash, if at all, through Russell Crowe's celebrated characterization in *A Beautiful Mind.*

What do we make of the use of models in economics? George Box, a British statistician, is famous for his bon mot that 'all models are wrong, but some are useful.' The reason that the Ptolemaic model of the heavens (with Earth at the centre rather than the sun) survived as long as it did was that it was useful to those tasked with maintaining liturgical calendars for the Roman Church. The Copernican Revolution started with the quest for a better method for calculating dates. Likewise, in mainstream economics, 'realism' is not necessarily the point. Unlike diorama, the standard by which models are judged is their ability to adequately predict economic phenomena, and not the richness of their description of reality. The parsimonious nature of Nash's description of these non-cooperative games is what made them useful to economists. To argue that a model is not 'realistic' is really to argue that it misses something important.

In Chapter Eleven, Michelle Baddeley presents Daniel Kahneman, who won the Nobel Memorial Prize in 2002 for his integration of psychology and economics, and particularly his contributions to understanding human judgement and decision-making under uncertainty, in short for his recognition that economics was missing something important. Baddeley presents a moving account of Kahneman's background as a Lithuanian Jew in Occupied France and then as an adolescent and adult in Israel. Baddeley describes how Kahneman, with his cherished collaborator Amon Tversky, came to establish behavioural economics via their work on cognitive biases and heuristics, which gave rise to Kahneman's Prospect Theory. Baddeley's discussion of Kahneman's later works emphasizes his attempts to theorize different kinds of utilities beyond the expected utility (or for Kahneman 'acquisition utility') at the heart of economic theory. As she notes, 'experienced utility' and 'remembered utility' may differ considerably, which can be used to enrich notions in behavioural economics such as hyperbolic discounting. Baddeley also notes his contributions to experimental economics and his trans-disciplinary legacy.

Jonathan Conlin returns in Chapter Twelve with his sketch of Amartya Sen, who won the Nobel Memorial Prize in 1998 for his contributions to welfare economics. Conlin locates Sen's interest in the economics of welfare provision and famine prevention in his childhood experiences of the Bengali Famine, which claimed the lives of two million rural Bengalis. Sen's formulation of the problem as a 'failure of exchange entitlements' shifted attention from conventional narratives in agricultural economics about the causes of famine to focus on exchange relations. Yet as Conlin observes, Sen's reputation rests on broader foundations, in that his contributions to social choice theory were methodological as well as substantive. Sen's Capability Approach emerges as his most significant achievement, as it focuses attention on human agency and serves to shift the discussion from equality to equity. Sen's economic thinking is, as Conlin concludes, a call to action and a return to the normative economics rejected by Friedman.

Emmanuelle Bénicourt closes the volume with a critical account of Joseph Stiglitz in Chapter Thirteen, whom she introduces by drawing attention to his indefatigable activism and his opposition to the ideological baggage of mainstream economics as conventionally practised. Yet as Bénicourt notes, Stiglitz's scientific reputation, including his Nobel Memorial Prize (2001), rests on his contributions to micro theory, specifically his work with Robert Akerlof and Michael Spence on asymmetric information as a source of market failure. In Bénicourt's account, Stiglitz, for all his iconoclasm, shares with Bateman's Keynes a commitment to reforming and correcting the excesses of capitalism, not to overturning the capitalist order. Stiglitz emerges as a mainstream economist who rejects neoliberalism. While that may not sit well with Bénicourt, who objects that many of the models her subject uses are stylized and 'unrealistic', Stiglitz shares this position with most of the contributors to this volume.

In that sense, Friedman's rejection of 'normative economics' was very much an interlude in the history of economic thought. If, in the wake of the Great Recession (2007–12) and the rising levels of inequality of the early twenty-first century, economics is taking a 'moral turn', then this would have been unsurprising to most of the authors in this volume. From the mercantilist writers mentioned above to Stiglitz himself, most economists were concerned with economic policymaking, that process of making capitalism fit for human life. Hopefully what this volume helps readers understand is how far that kind of stance is possible within the economic mainstream. We will have succeeded twice over if readers also come away with an admiration for the quality and richness of great economic thinking.

ONE

ADAM SMITH

Jonathan Conlin

One morning in January 1778 Adam Smith left his home in Edinburgh's Canongate and walked up the Royal Mile to the Customs House in Exchange Square. It was his first week at work as a Commissioner of Customs. Inside he was confronted with a large board listing all the contraband goods it was now his duty to hunt down and destroy. For centuries men of business struggling in the face of foreign competition had successfully lobbied their rulers to introduce such restrictions on foreign imports. Without such import bans, import tariffs and 'bounties' (state subsidies), they argued, foreign nations' economies would prosper at the expense of the home economy. The Commissioners of Customs not only collected these tariffs, they prosecuted those who attempted to import goods in defiance of such bans.

There is something rather strange about the idea of Smith, renowned father of free-market economics, joining the customs service. Smith opposed protectionist duties and tariffs, as well as guilds and other institutions that restricted the movement of workers from one trade to another. If these barriers were removed, he argued, an 'invisible hand' would lead each to invest their labour and capital in the trade they were best suited for, improving quality, encouraging innovation, lowering prices and raising living standards for all. Not only was the power to direct how humans invested their time, effort and money a despotic infringement of natural liberty, no ruler could be trusted to use that power wisely.

If proof were needed of the futility of trade restrictions, Smith did not have to look very far. Standing in the Customs House that morning, Smith glanced down from the board to inspect his own wardrobe. As he later wrote to the Member of Parliament and Lord of Trade William Eden, Smith found 'that I had scarce a stock, a cravat, a pair of ruffles, or a pocket hankerchief which was not prohibited to be worn or used in Great Britain'. 'I wished to set an example,' he continued, 'and burnt them all,' cheekily advising Eden against examining 'either your own or Mrs. Edens apparel or household furniture, least you be brought into a scrape of the same kind'.[1]

Though intended as a humorous dig, Smith could not help but draw the lesson: trade prohibitions always fail to produce the intended effects, that is to prevent the consumption of foreign articles where those goods were cheaper or better than those produced at home. Prohibited goods still entered the country, albeit as contraband carried by smugglers, on which the Customs collected no dues. Not only that, but Smith's French ruffles ended up costing him more, to compensate the smugglers for the extra costs incurred by their need to keep out of sight.

Prosecuting smugglers must have been a particularly unpleasant duty for the new Commissioner, considering Smith saw smugglers as honest men criminalized by imprudent legislation. One regulation intended to boost English wool production had made the export of wool a crime punishable by death. 'Like the laws of Draco,' Smith thundered, 'these laws may be said to be all written in blood.'[2] Protectionism assumed international trade to be a game of beggar-thy-neighbour. It encouraged European nations to stake exclusive claims to large sections of the globe for exploitation by incompetent, monopolistic trading companies such as the East India Company.

An imperial system founded on protectionist tariffs fostered untold violence, slavery and destruction. It reflected a 'mean rapacity, the monopolizing spirit of merchants and manufacturers, who neither are, nor ought to be the rulers of mankind'.[3] A strong anti-imperialist, Smith saw conflicts like the Seven Years War (1756–63) between Britain and France as yet more 'bounties' given to these greedy men of business. In 1776, just as the American War of Independence began, Smith would even urge British ministers to abandon their North American colonies without a fight. Tellingly, that conflict had been triggered by the introduction of new tariffs on tea, tariffs intended to help the struggling East India Company. This had made life rather unpleasant for Smith's fellow customs officers in Boston, who were tarred and feathered.

In 1776 Smith published *An Inquiry into the Nature and Causes of the Wealth of Nations.* The two-volume work extended over more than a thousand pages. While seventeenth- and early eighteenth-century British writers such as William Petty and John Locke had written the odd pamphlet or essay debating questions of trade policy, taxation, specie and so on, Smith's contemporaries immediately recognized that *The Wealth of Nations* represented a new genre. 'You have formed into a regular and consistent system one of the most intricate and important parts of political science,' the Scottish historian William Robertson wrote, predicting that the work 'will occasion a total change in several important articles both in police [policy] and finance'.[4]

Although the term 'oeconomy' existed in Smith's day, 'economics' or 'economist' did not, and 'oeconomy' was primarily used to refer to the efficient and thrifty management of a household – *oikos* being the Greek word for household. It was also used metaphorically, to refer to the husbandry of the natural world as a whole. The 'oeconomy of nature', that all-encompassing and awe-inspiring disposition of phenomena, revealed the infinite care and wisdom of the Creator to mankind. To identify patterns in the distribution of resources (human labour, coal, wheat) and in the interactions of human beings was to learn something about the Creator's nature and plans for Creation.

In the course of the nineteenth century 'economics' emerged as a discrete academic discipline, with its own professorial chairs, learned societies and distinct jargon. Economics was a science, but one of the social, rather than the natural sciences. It concerned itself with concepts such as rent and utility which did not have an independent existence outside the human mind that conceived them. Its practitioners revered Smith's *The Wealth of Nations* as the foundation of their discipline, even if they rarely read beyond the first few chapters.[5] Twentieth-century economists followed suit, and the Chicago School of Milton Friedman and George Stigler in particular saw Smith as the father of their brand of neoclassical, free-market economics.

Smith had, they claimed, correctly characterized the market as 'a morally free zone' in which all agents sought to maximize their own utility, while his 'invisible hand' supposedly demonstrated the necessity of restricting the state's role to defence and upholding the rule of law.[6] Any step beyond the pale drawn by Smith would hamper economic growth by stymieing the selfish individuals whose interactions revealed a supreme intelligence: no longer that of a Creator God, but of 'the market', an entity whose wisdom nonetheless exacted a similar degree of reverence. It could even seem as if 'the market' was a totally distinct realm, where the rules and conventions governing everyday life could not and should not apply. Those who found the contrast unattractive were held to be squeamishly immature and idealistic. As the anti-hero of Oliver Stone's 1987 film *Wall Street*, Gordon Gekko, put it after ruthlessly despatching a rival, 'business is business': 'If you want a friend, get a dog.'

Starting in the 1990s, however, cracks began to appear in this interpretation of Smith, what Jerry Evensky has referred to as 'Chicago Smith'.[7] This involved reconsidering the relationship between *The Wealth of Nations* and Smith's first book, *The Theory of Moral Sentiments* (1759). The *Theory*'s discussion of human passions and, in particular, the central role it gave to sympathy had seemed difficult to relate to *The Wealth of Nations*' focus on interests and the market. Many agreed with the Chicago economist Jacob Viner, who argued in 1926 that any attempt to resolve this 'Adam Smith Problem' would detract from a full appreciation of either work – while nonetheless concluding that *The Wealth of Nations* was the more 'mature' work.[8] It is this consensus that has been challenged by recent scholarship, which has argued that the *Theory* and *The Wealth of Nations* complement and complete each other, and that Smith's model of human behaviour is built around a web of social instincts and customs, rather than being (as Stigler claimed) 'erected upon the granite of self-interest'.[9]

Kirkcaldy Customs

Philosophers are made, not born. At least according to Smith. A philosopher and 'a common street porter' might display 'the most dissimilar characters', he noted, but the differences in personality, income and talent resulted 'not so much from nature, as from habit, custom, and education'.[10] One boy did not become a philosopher because of his extraordinary brain, nor did the other become a porter because he had been born with extra-strong muscles suitable for carrying things around. In Smith's day, as in ours, the main determinant of a child's future income was its parents' income, not its own intelligence or 'genius'.

This is not something we find easy to admit. Our appetite for utility encourages us to see the philosopher and the porter as truly 'fit' for their respective positions in society. In Smith's case, it does seem as if 'habit, custom and education' played a greater role than 'nature'. Luck played a part as well. Whether it was the shift from feudal pastoralism to intensive farming or that from cottage industry to factory production, the small town on the Firth of Forth in which Smith was born in 1723 had much to teach an observant young man.

Today Kirkcaldy has a population of 46,000, largely supported by linoleum production. The city gained administrative independence in 1644 when Charles I made it a royal burgh, freeing it from the control of the local feudal landlord, the abbey of Dunfermline. Elsewhere in

Scotland, however, the medieval system of feudal land tenure persisted, notably among the Highland clans. Those clans were governed by ties of personal loyalty to the clan chief, not contract. Farmers and shepherds followed their chief into battle – disastrously so in 1745, when the clans rose in support of the Jacobite claimant to the British throne, Bonnie Prince Charlie, only to be mown down by the professional troops of George II at the Battle of Culloden.

Once free from feudal ties, Kirkcaldy developed a mixed economy. Alongside sheep-herding, forestry and agriculture there was proto-industrialization (farmers took in flax to work up into linen in their spare time), industrialization (a nail works, shipyards) and both local and international trade. Smith's father was well placed to observe all this activity. Indeed, it was his duty to do so, as customs officer for Kirkcaldy. The elder Smith was secretary to the third Earl of Loudoun, whose support had doubtless helped him secure a post in the customs. Patronage tied father and son in service to a particular segment of the Scottish landowning aristocracy. These earls and dukes supported the 1707 Union between the Scottish and English monarchies, which had created the United Kingdom of Great Britain. Although England's fashionable elite soon came to romanticize the vanishing world of the Scottish clans with their kilts and bards, Smith recognized that 'the Union was a measure from which infinite Good has been derived to this country.'[11]

Alongside 'habits and customs' like patronage, education was equally important in shaping Smith's development. Kirkcaldy's town council had built a two-room school in 1723. The system of parish schools found across Scotland as well as its fine universities reflected a widespread respect for education, sufficient to lead almost all Scottish parents to make the financial and other sacrifices (including the loss of their child's labour, a valuable commodity in itself) necessary to send their children to school for a few years. In school Smith not only learned reading, writing and arithmetic, but Latin and some Greek.

An eighteenth-century edition of the *Encheiridion* survives with Smith's name on it. Compiled by a pupil of the first-century Greek philosopher Epictetus, the *Encheiridion* or *Handbook* teaches us to rid ourselves of the fantasy that we have power over our bodies, possessions or other external things, when we only have power to control our inner state. We achieve true freedom and tranquillity through self-knowledge, silencing the desires that threaten to enslave us and achieving command over our emotions. The Stoics and other great philosophers of antiquity were lifelong companions for Smith.

In 1737 Smith entered the University of Glasgow. Smith was heavily influenced by his Moral Philosophy professor, an Ulster Presbyterian named Francis Hutcheson. Hutcheson formed part of the so-called 'New Light' movement within Presbyterianism, which sought to soften its harsh, Calvinist view of human nature. Hutcheson's lectures encouraged Smith to view human nature as a worthy focus of study, as something with its own structure, rather than something condemned to sinful disorder. Human nature was a network of 'springs', 'parts' and 'appetites', as well as a 'wonderful natural contagiousness' which led us to share our passions with our fellow humans.

After completing his studies in Oxford Smith returned to Kirkcaldy, delivering a series of well-received lectures on rhetoric in nearby Edinburgh. These lectures were open to paying subscribers. Such intellectual diversions together with the reforms introduced at the University of Glasgow by Hutcheson (who lectured in English, rather than in the usual Latin) catered to a new appetite for philosophizing among the elite and middling rank. Speculation, which had previously seemed dangerously heretical or simply dull, now provided men and even women with food for polite conversation at tea tables and in coffee houses. Appointed to a professorship at Glasgow in 1751, Smith picked up where Hutcheson left off, managing to persuade a number of aristocrats to send their boys to university. University was no longer only for those destined for the law or the Church.

Trading Passions

Smith's *Theory of Moral Sentiments* appeared in 1759. This book seeks to classify the full gamut of human passions, and to identify the mechanism by which humans determine whether this or that action or individual is praise- or blameworthy. Smith finds this mechanism in the behaviour of his fellow man, in instincts established by 'Nature', rather than in a set of divine commandments 'revealed' to certain prophets by God, as the Ten Commandments had been revealed to Moses. Whether this 'Nature' revealed the mind of a Creator God was not, it would seem, an urgent question for Smith. While Smith's close friend, the philosopher David Hume, openly challenged revealed religion, and was persecuted as a result, Smith was more prudent.

Smith's ethics are founded on sympathy, that 'contagiousness' which Hutcheson had noted, but not seen as very significant. Today sympathy is often understood as a passion in itself, as sorrow expressed in response to the suffering of others. For Smith sympathy is not a passion, but rather the means by which we become aware of any and all passions. Sharing passions sympathetically brings pleasure, even where the passion being shared seems unpleasant, as with grief. This longing to share our passions is challenged, however, by the obvious fact that one person can never feel quite the same 'pitch' of this or that passion as another. As a result, Smith explains, each of us learns from a young age to 'flatten' the 'pitch' of our passions to a level that we know others will sympathize or 'go along with'.

This level varies from passion to passion, in a fashion conducive to the good order of society. Passions derived from the body, for example, like lust and hunger, are not easily shared by others. We therefore do not express these passions much, knowing that it is unlikely that anyone else will 'go along with' us. In Smith's account of human society this bidding and offering of passions is constantly being carried on among humans. Such haggling could be described as a kind of marketplace of passions, but Smith prefers a musical metaphor: though actor and spectator could never achieve a 'unison', 'there may be concord, and this is all that is wanted or required.'[12]

Having considered how we judge others, Smith addresses how we judge ourselves. Smith believes that we seek to approve of ourselves, and that the love of 'self-approbation' is the love of virtue.[13] This was a daring claim for him to make. In 1714 the Anglo-Dutch philosopher Bernard Mandeville had published his *Fable of the Bees,* in which he had argued that all acts of charity and benevolence were selfish, and that vanity (rather than virtuous thrift) served the public interest by encouraging expenditure and hence fostering growth. 'Private vice, publick benefits' neatly summed up his argument, which shocked contemporaries as exemplifying the kind of depravity that inevitably resulted when philosophical speculation got out of hand.

The notoriety of Mandeville's *Fable* encouraged Hutcheson and others to insist that humans could be benevolent, without their charity masking some roundabout manner of advancing their own interest. They could act independently of their interest, that is, disinterestedly. In his *Essay on the Nature and Conduct of the Passions and Affections* (1728) Hutcheson proposed that humans had a 'moral sense' by which they perceived '*Virtue*, or *Vice* in our selves, and others'.[14] In his *Theory* Smith suggests that Hutcheson and Mandeville are equally guilty of treating mankind harshly, by demanding that humans only follow purely disinterested motives. 'Benevolence may, perhaps, be the sole principle of action in the Deity . . . who stands in need of nothing external,' Smith notes. But

> so imperfect a creature as man, the support of whose existence requires so many things external to him, must often act from many other motives. The condition of human nature [would be] peculiarly hard, if those affections, which, by the very nature of our being, ought frequently to influence our conduct, could upon no occasion appear virtuous, or deserve esteem and commendation from any body.[15]

Smith argues that Mandeville overlooked an important distinction between the desire for praise and the desire to be praiseworthy, presenting both as vices. Smith acknowledges that individuals often act from a combination, that the two are 'blended together', but argues that it is foolish to follow Mandeville in attributing 'to the love of praise . . . every action which ought to be ascribed to that of praise-worthiness'.[16] 'The desire of doing what is honourable and noble, of rendering ourselves the proper objects of esteem and approbation, cannot with any propriety be called vanity.'[17] We all condemn those who seek praise without being praiseworthy (as we cannot sympathize with them).

Part of us, Smith admits, craves the praise of others and seeks to avoid their censure. This is 'the man without'. Only 'the weak, the vain and frivolous' are fully satisfied with how things appear to this 'man'. This is because all of us learn as children that praise and blame are often given to those who do not deserve it, owing to the natural messiness of the world as it is. Thus we put ourselves before a 'higher tribunal', whose judge looks beyond appearances to consider whether we earned that praise or that blame, whether we are in fact praise- or blameworthy: 'We . . . sett up in our own minds a judge between ourselves and those we live with . . . a person quite candid and equitable . . . who has no particular relation either to ourselves, or to those whose interests are affected by our conduct.'[18] Smith calls this judge 'the man within the breast', or the 'impartial spectator'.

Trading Places

A two-year (1764–6) expedition to France as tutor to the son of the Duke of Buccleuch gave Smith his only experience of foreign travel. Introduced by his friend Hume, then working as secretary to the British ambassador in Paris, Smith circulated among the *salons* of the great *philosophes* of the Enlightenment. Locked together by ties of history, repeated wars and mutual fascination for each other's literature and fashions, the leading minds of Britain and France communicated frequently in this period, and Smith's works were quickly translated into French. 'We have nothing to compare with him,' wrote the famous French *philosophe* Voltaire, 'and I am embarrassed for my dear compatriots.' Although we cannot be sure that Smith met the philosopher Jean-Jacques Rousseau, he certainly engaged with the latter's *Discourse on Inequality* (1755).

Rousseau sees agriculture as the first stage in society, and so imagines how the first property owner threw up a fence around a plot of what had been common land. 'The first man who, having enclosed a piece of ground, bethought himself of saying "This is mine", and found people simple enough to believe him, was the real founder of civil society.'[19]

> So long as [humans] undertook only what a single person could accomplish, and confined themselves to such arts as did not require the joint labour of several hands, they lived free, healthy, honest, and happy lives . . . But from the moment one man needed the help of another; from the moment it appeared advantageous to any one man to have enough provisions for two, equality disappeared, property was introduced, work became indispensable, and vast forests became smiling fields, which man had to water with the sweat of his brow, and where slavery and misery were soon seen to germinate and grow up with the crops.[20]

Smith disagrees. As a species *Homo sapiens* is inconceivable outside society. To describe humans as entering society and 'beginning each to observe the others, and to desire to be observed himself' is for Smith profoundly misleading: without this mutual regard and sympathetic sharing of passions there is no self and no human consciousness. Were it possible for a human being to survive to adulthood in isolation (marooned on the proverbial desert island, for example), that unfortunate individual would be unable to conceive of a self.[21] Smith also recognizes, correctly, that agriculture was not the first phase of society, but the third. The 'Age of Hunters' (what we would call hunter-gathering) and 'Age of Shepherds' (pastoralism) came before that of farmers. Land became property only when previously nomadic tribes settled down, by a process in which tribal leaders granted lands to their leading followers.

Without a pre-social 'state of nature', there is no point reconstructing the thought processes that primordial men and women had gone through on the threshold of society. Smith pulls the rug out from under a raft of political thinkers who sought to understand government and sovereignty in terms of an 'original contract' made at this point in human history between ruler and ruled. Rather than trading certain pre-social rights ('natural rights') for protections given by the ruler (a system of law and order, say) humans had never stood on a threshold separating 'nature' and 'civilisation'. Smith's indifference to a language of natural or inalienable rights as well as a notion of consent in a contract between ruler and ruled continues to isolate him from much of the debate that goes on in politics.

While at the French court in Versailles Smith met François Quesnay, physician to Louis XV. Quesnay had begun writing about the grain trade in the early 1750s, and Smith would have known his entries on 'Farmers' and 'Grain' for the famous encyclopaedia edited by Diderot and D'Alembert. Quesnay understood agriculture to be the only source of a nation's wealth. Whereas agricultural outputs exceeded inputs, in the case of trade and manufacturing you only got out what you put in. Quesnay provided a diagram or 'Economic Table' that supposedly captured the French economy as a whole, showing how capital flowed between the agricultural, manufacturing and trading sectors. This marked the birth of economic modelling. By the time Quesnay met Smith he had refined this table and was preparing to publish a book whose title (*Physiocratie*) would give him and his disciples their more familiar name: the Physiocrats.

Smith's admiration for Quesnay was strong: had the latter lived, Smith would have dedicated *The Wealth of Nations* to him. The work's discussion of the relative productivity of different economic sectors reflects this, in arguing that agriculture was the most productive, and the international carry trade the least. Admiration was tempered by a concern that the Physiocrats might have become overly attached to their tidy models. However well-meaning and philosophical the ends, the means of implementing these new policies (including liberalization of the grain trade) were despotic. As he would note much later, in the 1790 edition of his *Theory*, the 'Man of System . . . seems to imagine that he can arrange the different members of a great society with as much ease as the hand arranges the different pieces upon a chess-board', when the reality was that, 'in the great chess-board of human society, every single piece has a principle of motion of its own.'[22] In a cruel twist that hastened the end of the French monarchy in the 1789 Revolution, experiments with the liberalization of the grain trade were indeed misunderstood by the general populace as a case of their royal 'father' removing his protection in order to swell the profits of a new breed of grain speculators.[23]

The Wealth of Nations

Long walks along the beach at Kirkcaldy and a series of short stays in London in the 1770s allowed Smith further opportunities to test and develop the ideas he would advance in *The Wealth of Nations*. In contrast to the *Theory*, this book is clearly structured as a scientific treatise, with an opening 'Introduction and Plan' as well as extensive footnotes and an appendix. The main text is organized into five books. Smith begins by considering the division of labour in a well-known passage describing pin making:

> To take an example, therefore, from a very trifling manufacture; but one in which the division of labour has been very often taken notice of, the trade of the pin-maker; a workman not educated to this business (which the division of labour has rendered a distinct trade), nor acquainted with the use of the machinery employed in it (to the invention of which the same division of labour has probably given occasion), could scarce, perhaps, with his utmost industry, make one pin in a day, and certainly could not make twenty. But in the way in which this business is now carried on, not only the whole work is a peculiar trade, but it is divided into a number of branches, of which the greater part are likewise peculiar trades. One man draws out the wire, another straights it, a third cuts it, a fourth points it, a fifth grinds it at the top for receiving the head; to make the head requires two or three distinct operations; to put it on, is a peculiar business, to whiten the pins is another; it is even a trade by itself to put them into the paper; and the important business of making a pin is, in this manner, divided into about eighteen distinct operations.

Thanks to this division of labour ten workers could make 'upwards of forty-eight thousand pins in a day'.[24]

In view of the fame of this passage, it is worth noting that Smith does not see this particular observation as novel. This boost to production had, he notes, 'been very often taken notice of'. Its potential is unleashed not by human wisdom but by 'a certain propensity in human nature . . . to truck, barter, and exchange one thing for another'.[25] This trading instinct is unique to humans, and reflects the fact that, unlike other animals, humans cannot survive without each other's help. At the same time, however, every human recognizes that he is more likely to secure this assistance from another person if 'he can interest their self-love in his favour'. 'It is not from the benevolence of the butcher, the brewer, or the baker, that we expect our dinner, but from their regard to their own interest.'[26] It was this passage above all which supporters of 'Chicago Smith' relied on.

The degree of specialization achieved, however, is dependent on the size of the market in which the pins can be sold. In a 'remote country' (that is, one that is geographically isolated, separated from population centres by physical obstacles such as mountains, deserts or seas), Smith notes, every man has to be butcher, brewer and baker to his family, because a small community cannot sustain full-time butchers, brewers or bakers. Specialization is also limited thanks to another problem with a barter economy: the fact that one cannot always be sure of finding someone willing to trade. The butcher has slaughtered a cow and has plenty of surplus meat that the baker would like to have. But the butcher does not need bread right now, and bread is all that the baker has to offer. The butcher will need bread next week, but by then the meat will have gone off, freezers not being available. The two are 'mutually less serviceable to one another'.[27]

Hence the invention of money, and its sole purpose as 'an instrument of commerce', as a store of value. The value of money is what Smith calls 'exchange value', to differentiate it from 'use value'.[28] Value in exchange reflects 'the real price of commodities', a 'natural price' 'equal to the quantity of labour which it enables' the possessor 'to purchase or command. Labour, therefore, is the real measure of the exchangeable value of all commodities.' It is difficult to estimate this price, however, as it is difficult to measure the 'hardship' or 'ingenuity' of different kinds of labour.[29] Whereas in the 'original state of things' the labourer received the 'whole produce' of his labour, ever since 'the appropriation of land and the accumulation of stock' the owners of land and the capital (what Smith calls 'stock') invested in manufactures have deducted something to ensure themselves a profit after allowing for wages as well as the cost of raw materials and overheads.[30]

'The higgling or bargaining of the market' establishes a 'rough' estimate, one which may not match the 'natural price' of labour, but which Smith describes as 'gravitating' towards that price. This gravitation works thanks to the self-adjusting mechanism of 'effectual demand', that is, 'the demand of those who are willing to pay the natural price of the commodity.'[31] If supply of the commodity is below this level then competition among buyers leads the market price to rise. This encourages production of that commodity (including the workers themselves, as 'demand for men . . . necessarily regulates the production of men'),[32] which in turn leads the price to move down towards its 'natural' level. If supply is above this level then labour and capital are withdrawn and production declines, at least until the diminished supply causes the price to rise again.

Prices, wages, profits and rent all have natural (today's economists would say 'real') rates which vary according to whether the nation in is an 'advancing, stationary, or declining condition', as well as according to the laws and institutions in force, as Smith's comparison of China and Holland demonstrates.[33] Smith's theory nonetheless posits what economists would later call a general equilibrium, in which real net national income is maximized by the free exchange of the market. Economists from David Ricardo onwards would criticize Smith's notion of rent and theory of wages as confused and underdeveloped.[34] As James Tobin noted at the bicentenary of Smith's death, there are many problems with Smith's equilibrium. It suggests a market that opens, sets a price, then clears completely. In the real world, markets set so-called 'spot' prices constantly, before markets clear (and markets may never clear completely).[35]

Nor does Smith consider how money and saving affect his equilibrium. Changes to the money supply or to people's appetite for saving will cause nominal prices to drift wide of the real price determined by the amount of labour expended. As John Maynard Keynes famously demonstrated in the 1930s, nominal prices and wages may be 'sticky', and fail to return to those levels.

We should remember that *The Wealth of Nations* was the first attempt to explore these concepts and was founded on observation of an economy that functioned differently to that with which later economists were familiar. It seems harsh, for example, to criticize Smith for failing to allow for economic cycles when it is unclear whether such cycles existed before the nineteenth century.[36] What is clear is that Smith sees the advent of individual land ownership (which Rousseau depicted so tragically) and the accumulation of surplus 'stock' (capital) as prerequisites for the economic growth unleashed by the division of labour.

Book Two of *The Wealth of Nations* considers capital in more detail, distinguishing between what we would call fixed, circulating and human capital. Smith praises paper money as enabling capital mobility by creating 'a waggon-way through the air'. The 'Daedelian wings of paper money' (a reference to the story of Dedalus and Icarus) are 'Daedelian', however, precisely because of the dangers associated with 'excess of banking'.[37] This was a serious danger in Great Britain before the Bank Charter Act of 1844, when private banks were permitted to issue their own banknotes. In his discussion Smith shows himself to be a devotee of the real-bill doctrine, in so far as he perceives a distinction between 'real bills of exchange' (in other words, IOUs issued against goods and services, which circulated widely in the eighteenth-century economy) and the rest, produced by merchants 'drawing and re-drawing' upon each other (issuing each other IOUs in cases where no underlying exchange of goods or services had taken place).[38]

Smith cites the 1772 crash of Douglas, Heron and Company (the Ayr Bank) as a cautionary tale of the harm caused when such banks mistakenly held that their job was 'augmenting the capital of the country' rather than 'rendering a greater part of that capital active and productive than would otherwise be so'. Smith urged state restrictions on banknote issuance, even though he admitted it was 'a manifest violation of natural liberty' for the state to prevent individuals willing to accept banknotes from being able to do so. It was nonetheless justified, as banking was an area in which a 'few individuals' could 'endanger the security of the whole society' by exercising their liberty in a reckless manner.[39]

Smith adopts a more historical approach in Book Three, 'Of the different progress of opulence in different nations'. This progress sees societies pass through successive ages: that of hunters is followed by that of shepherds, then come farmers, then the age of manufactures. Manufacturing, and therefore cities, can only grow when there is a large enough surplus capital gleaned from agriculture to invest in the 'conveniencies' and 'luxuries' that the former provide.[40] But in 'the modern states of Europe', Smith notes, this order had not been followed.

This was because of the perverse incentives that operated under the feudal system that emerged after the collapse of the Roman Empire. Feudal lords oppressed their tenants, robbing them of security and hence discouraging them from improving the land. Restrictions on the movement of grain prevented those who were able to produce a surplus from selling it. Naturally the more enterprising fled to the cities, giving an artificial boost to manufacturing and foreign trade.

The most important result of this inversion occurred when the feudal lords encountered the luxuries produced by the city's manufactories and by foreign trade, something that could not have occurred had the natural order been followed. Such lords lived surrounded by an army of retainers, for lack of anything else on which to spend the rents paid to them by their tenants. Though these retainers were regularly let off their rents when they couldn't pay and enjoyed free food, they lacked security, as this bounty depended entirely on the 'good pleasure' of the lord, who had his retainers' property and lives at his command.[41] When the lord went to war with a neighbouring lord his retainers went too, and did the fighting and dying.

The lords were 'masters of mankind', Smith notes, and hence followed the usual 'vile maxim': 'All for ourselves, and nothing for other people.' But this changed once foreign trade and manufacture provided these masters with luxury goods. Smith is dismissive of the bargain these lords struck: 'For a pair of diamond buckles perhaps, or for something as frivolous and useless . . . for the gratification of the most childish, the meanest and the most sordid of all vanities, they gradually bartered their whole power and authority.'[42] The knock-on effects were profound for the retainers, who were let go. Eager to increase his rental income the lord agreed to give his tenants longer and more secure tenure in return for investment in improvements to the land that would allow them to produce more and pay the lord a higher rent.

Without subservient hangers-on willing to risk their necks for their lords, the lords' ability to undermine 'the regular execution of justice' and engage in pointless yet violent feuding was curtailed. 'A regular government was established in the country as well as in the city, nobody having sufficient power to disturb its operations in the one, any more than in the other.' Though lordly hospitality had been curtailed (no more free meals in the great hall), the masses now enjoyed security and tranquillity, along with a better quality of life. A 'revolution' was thus brought about by two classes of people 'who had not the least intention to serve the publick'.[43]

Book Four sees Smith's assault on the protectionist web of import and export restrictions that rulers introduced in order to maintain a positive balance of trade with their trading partners. In order to prevent gold being exported to pay for, say, porcelain, rulers provided subsidies to domestic porcelain manufacturers while imposing heavy import duties to discourage porcelain imports. Trading companies were given monopolies preventing others from trading with colonies, whose own economic activities were subject to other restrictions. Such restrictions inevitably inspired trading partners to impose their own restrictions. Trade wars escalated into real wars.

This perversion of commerce from its rightful role promoting international peace and understanding into a source of conflict was just one result of rulers' unhealthy obsession with the balance of trade:

> Nothing . . . can be more absurd than this whole doctrine of the balance of trade, upon which, not only these restraints, but almost all the other regulations of commerce are founded. When two places trade with one another, this doctrine supposes that, if the balance be even, neither of them either loses or gains; but if it leans in any degree to one side, that one of them loses, and the other gains . . . Both suppositions are false. A trade which is forced by means of bounties and monopolies, may be, and commonly is disadvantageous to the country in whose favour it is meant to be established . . . But that trade which, without force or constraint, is naturally and regularly carried on between any two places, is always advantageous, though not always equally so, to both.

Such restrictions harmed the very nations they were designed to benefit because they presumed to direct the flow of capital investment rather than let an 'invisible hand' lead that capital to the sector of the economy where it would be most productive.

> As every individual, therefore, endeavours as much as he can both to employ his capital in the support of domestick industry, and so to direct that industry that its produce may be of the greatest value; every individual necessarily labours to render the annual revenue of the society as great as he can. He generally, indeed, neither intends to promote the publick interest, nor knows how much he is promoting it . . . By pursuing his

> own interest he frequently promotes that of the society more effectually than when he really intends to promote it.[44]

The phrase 'invisible hand' appears only once in *The Wealth of Nations* and once in the *Theory*: in both cases it is 'an' invisible hand, not 'the' invisible hand. Adherents of 'Chicago Smith' nonetheless see it as the axle around which Smith's entire thought turns. An intriguing theory advanced by Emma Rothschild suggests that Smith intended the hand to be seen as both 'ironic . . . in its intimation of the existence of an all-ordering providence', and 'unironic, in its intimation that there can be order without design; that a society can be prosperous without being conducted by an all-seeing sovereign'. Seen in this way the hand is a persuasive device, 'a sort of trinket'.[45] Like utility, so the hand is very effective when it comes to fashioning pleasing models of the economy or political systems, but does not draw attention to the real engines and instincts that cause humans to act.

As Rothschild notes, the risk of adopting 'invisible hand explanations' is the risk of missing the irony directed at those who, like the Physiocrats, fell in love with the appearance of utility displayed by their tidy models. If the establishment of property, division of labour and free trade have brought about growth while at the same time releasing individuals from bondage and insecurity, then that is to be credited to the progress of opulence which Smith explains in terms of a web of interlocking instincts and desires that the 'invisible hand' fails to capture. To use an analogy Smith employs himself, it is as if we looked at the moving hands on a clock face and attributed an intention (to tell the right time) to those hands, rather than looking at the interlocking springs and gears which in fact cause the hands to move.[46]

Alongside the 'disposition to truck, barter and exchange' we should also note another 'spring' driving this progress: the desire to 'better our condition' which Smith discusses in his *Theory*. Smith argues that a disposition to admire 'the rich and great' deludes us into forgoing pleasures already within our reach, expending considerable 'toil and anxiety' to achieve a state that will not increase our happiness. This is because happiness comes not from possessions but from 'being beloved'. Yet Smith concludes that 'it is well that nature imposes upon us in this manner' as 'it is this deception which rouses and keeps in continual motion the industry of mankind', transforming 'rude forests' into 'fertile plains'.[47] Smith thus recognizes that commerce creates a consumer society, one in which economic growth is partly based on producing new needs, for ever more 'trinkets of frivolous utility' whose acquisition comes at the cost of new anxieties.

The final, fifth book of *The Wealth of Nations* considers taxation and the role of the state. Here Smith recognizes another unpleasant result of the 'progress of opulence': the repetitive, robotic toil to which the majority of non-agricultural workers are condemned. The idea that the division of labour leads to 'alienation' or 'estrangement' of workers from their work would lie at the heart of Karl Marx's criticism of what he called capitalism. In the *Economic and Philosophic Manuscripts of 1844* Marx argues that because the working man does not own what he produces and is, in fact, 'coerced' into making it, the produce of his labour confronts him as 'something hostile and alien'.[48] Smith writes that 'The man whose whole life is spent in performing a few simple operations . . . has no occasion to exert his understanding.' 'He naturally loses, therefore, the habit of such exertion, and generally becomes as stupid and ignorant as it is possible for a human creature to become.'[49] 'Dexterity' here seems to result in 'deformity'.

Smith's immediate solution to this problem is state-sponsored education. The 'Publick' should set up a schoolhouse in every parish and pay part of the teacher's salary, the remainder coming from fees.[50] To claim that Smith advocates a minimal state, therefore, is incorrect: alongside defence and upholding the rule of law the state has important regulatory (including banking regulation, as we have seen) and educational functions to perform. As a response to the 'alienation of labour' problem, however, education can seem unsatisfactory. Patricia Werhane has argued that Smith's choice of words has obscured an important distinction between the worker's labouring (their 'dexterity') and their productivity. While the former is their inalienable property, with the specialization of labour the latter becomes a commodity that the worker is free to barter on the best terms they can secure. If this commodity is valued more highly in another sector than the one the worker finds themself in, therefore, the worker is free to change job.[51] Smith's dislike of guilds stems from the restrictions they placed on this movement between trades.

Head, Heart and Hand

Smith's final years were dogged by an unspecified intestinal complaint which led him to put aside draft works on law and government and focus on revisions to his *Theory of Moral Sentiments*. The emphasis placed on 'prudence' in the new Part VI of the *Theory* could be seen as a case of Smith trying to lessen the contrast between the *Theory* and *The Wealth of Nations.* Smith defines prudence as 'care of the health, of the fortune, of the rank and reputation of the individual'.[52] The prudent man betters his condition not through speculation, but by first cultivating 'real knowledge and skill' in his chosen profession, and then practising it with 'assiduity and industry'. The virtue of prudence commands only 'a certain cold esteem', however, rather than 'love and admiration'.[53]

Only when we move beyond this prudence can Smith begin to speak of 'the wise and virtuous man', whose virtues address the happiness of others as well as himself. In contrast to the retiring prudent man, the magnanimous man actively seeks the praise of others, and hence craves their attention too. This leads him to seek glory, which receives a warm rather than cold esteem. To win this esteem the individual must restrain both those passions that flare up at rare moments of great tension (fear and anger) as well as those that constantly seek to seduce us (the love of pleasure and praise). He must obey the direction of his impartial spectator.

As we have seen, far from encouraging 'selfishness', it can seem as if Smith denies us a true 'self'. We are a series of performances, which become more persuasive the more adept we become at approximating a range of other individuals' emotional states. This was the basis of Rousseau's complaint against commercial society, that it created a society based on dissimulation (that is, acting).[54] Yet Smith's wise and virtuous man can, it seems, step out of this hall of mirrors and find a place to *be.* He achieves what Smith calls 'superior prudence'.

'Superior prudence' exhibits the same 'wise and judicious conduct' as is found in the prudent man, but 'directed to greater and nobler purposes than the care of the health, the fortune, the rank and reputation of the individual'. It is joined to valour, benevolence and self-command. 'It is the best head joined to the best heart,' Smith writes, 'It is the most perfect wisdom combined with the most perfect virtue.'[55] Whether all humans are capable of acquiring this 'superior prudence' is in a sense beside the point: what is more important is that 'nature' has endowed all humans with a set of instincts that not only lead them to recognize the superiority of this 'prudence' but nudge them towards it.

In his renowned 1784 essay 'What is Enlightenment?' the Prussian philosopher Immanuel Kant defines Enlightenment as 'man's emergence from self-imposed immaturity': self-determination replaces reliance on the guidance of priests, rulers or 'rules and formulas'.

Smith's emphasis on the role of instinct and unintended consequences as well as his scepticism of utility-oriented models seem to disqualify him from consideration as an 'Enlightened' thinker. For him the 'progress of opulence' is one we cannot fully control or master. We often serve the public interest without intending to.

Rather than a source of anxiety or disappointment, however, Smith sees this as evidence of the beneficence of Nature. A concern for mankind led Nature to build fail-safes into the universal order, endowing humanity with a resilience that is more than a match for its imperfections. Just because we fail to fashion a society founded on 'superior prudence' does not mean that we are condemned to chaos. Another, colder, utilitarian prudence stands ready to perform a similar function:

> Man, who can subsist only in society, was fitted by nature to that situation for which he was made. All the members of human society stand in need of each others assistance, and are likewise exposed to mutual injuries. Where the necessary assistance is reciprocally afforded from love, from gratitude, from friendship, and esteem, the society flourishes and is happy. All the different members of it are bound together by the agreeable bands of love and affection, and are, as it were, drawn to one common centre of mutual good offices. But though the necessary assistance should not be afforded from such generous and disinterested motives, though among the different members of the society there should be no mutual love and affection, the society, though less happy and agreeable, will not necessarily be dissolved. Society may subsist among different men, as among different merchants, from a sense of its utility, without any mutual love or affection; and though no man in it should owe any obligation, or be bound in gratitude to any other, it may still be upheld by a mercenary exchange of good offices according to an agreed valuation.[56]

In the two centuries after Smith's death in 1790 it was assumed that his thought sought to encourage this 'mercenary exchange' among merchants concerned only with that system's 'utility'. Thanks to the revival of interest in *Theory of Moral Sentiments* we are coming to recognize that in fact Smith considered this rational world to be second-best. With Smith's hand, head and heart, we can reorient ourselves towards a 'common centre'.

TWO

DAVID RICARDO

Helen Paul

David Ricardo began his writing career as a political economist when economics was in its infancy as a discipline. Ricardo was born to a Jewish family in 1772, just a few years before the publication in 1776 of Adam Smith's *The Wealth of Nations.* It took time before economics emerged from the shadows of its mother disciplines of politics and philosophy. Ricardo was in middle age when his great friend Thomas Robert Malthus was given the first chair in political economy in the United Kingdom – at the East India Company College rather than a university per se.[1] Ricardo himself never held such a post. He had been a successful stockbroker and was able to retire early, enter politics and devote himself to his studies. His magnum opus was *On the Principles of Political Economy and Taxation.*[2] This systematic and comprehensive approach to the economy was a response to *The Wealth of Nations.* The two books were characterized by Denis O'Brien as 'the two great sources for Classical economics' which were then 'blended and developed by later economists, especially J. S. Mill'.[3]

Ricardo also encouraged the dissemination and discussion of economic ideas and was interested in the careers of the next generation of political economists. They went on to take the first chairs in the established universities. Ricardo's successful career in the stock market, his sociability and willingness to engage with others, his parliamentary career and, of course, the *Principles,* all helped to make him the pre-eminent economist of his age. In later years, his name became synonymous with free trade. After the Second World War, free trade was the panacea that could cure all ills. Ricardo became a figurehead linked to the founding of the great international trading blocs. Whether Ricardo himself would have approved is another question.[4]

Undergraduate economists are introduced to Ricardo via the concepts of comparative advantage and Ricardian equivalence. Historians of economic thought might also consider Ricardo's work on the theory of value and his scientific approach. This chapter outlines Ricardo's life and times and provides a brief introduction to these concepts.

Key Concepts

Adam Smith advocated the specialization of labour.[5] The division of labour allows society to produce more output overall. Smith also had faith that self-interested behaviour, within moral limits, would lead to a favourable economic outcome.[6] Excessive government intervention was not needed. Ricardo applied the same conditions to international trade. Instead of butchers and bakers, countries became the units of analysis. Ricardo argued that 'under a system of perfectly free commerce, each country naturally devotes its capital and labour to such employments as are most beneficial to each. This pursuit of individual advantage is admirably connected with the universal good of the whole.'[7] Smith had already argued that if a foreign country could produce a good more cheaply than the British could make it themselves, then Britain should import that good.[8] This is the principle of absolute advantage.

Ricardo illustrated his theory of comparative advantage with a simple example using basic arithmetic.[9] For simplicity, say the world consists only of Portugal and England.[10] The only two goods produced are cloth and wine. The cost of production is denoted in hours of labour. England takes 100 hours to make 1 unit of cloth and 120 hours to make 1 unit of wine. Portugal takes 90 hours to make 1 unit of cloth and 80 hours to make 1 unit of wine. Clearly, the Portuguese are more efficient in their production methods for both cloth and wine. Ricardo's great insight was that trade was still beneficial. The English make 1 unit of cloth in 100 hours but less than 1 unit of wine in the same time period. Portugal takes 80 hours to make 1 unit of wine, but cannot make 1 unit of cloth in the same period. If the English specialize in cloth and the Portuguese in wine, then they can both be better off if they trade. Without trade, the English take 220 hours to make 1 unit of each good. The Portuguese would take 170 hours to do likewise. The total amount produced is 2 units of each good. The English can produce 2.2 units of cloth in 220 hours. The Portuguese can produce just over 2 units of wine in 170 hours. Total production has increased for both goods. Therefore, there is more to go around. Ricardo showed that, under the assumptions of his model, trade was still beneficial even if one country had an absolute advantage. This result is counterintuitive, but powerful.[11] Once heard in the lecture room, few students forget it.

Just as it is not always beneficial to buy domestic products, it may not be a good idea to cut taxes. If the economy is faltering (production is cut back and consumers spend less money), the government may try to give it a boost.[12] One tactic is to cut taxes and hope that consumers start to spend their money on goods and services. Ideally, a virtuous circle of increased consumption and economic growth will result. However, Ricardo spotted that taxpayers might wonder if a tax cut today was simply going to be followed by tax rises tomorrow.[13] They would then save their pennies rather than spend them. The promised economic growth would not appear and the government would have to raise taxes.

Like the theory of comparative advantage, Ricardian equivalence challenges the usual assumptions that the public and policymakers may hold. There are plenty of assumptions in this model that may not hold in practice. Even though it was named after him, Ricardo himself had doubts about the empirical validity of the concept. It was not really put to the empirical test until many years later.[14] Policymakers should nonetheless be aware of the public's capacity to make reasonable predictions about future tax rises.

Another example of Ricardo's ability to find simple, but powerful, economic insights can be found in his 1820 speech to the House of Commons about the Corn Laws.[15] The Corn Laws restricted imports of corn in order to protect domestic producers. Confusingly, the term 'corn' was used in Ricardo's day to refer to the chief cereal crop of a given district: in England this was usually wheat, in Scotland, oats. Ricardo was aware that dependence on foreign corn (a dietary staple) might lead to weakness in time of war. He stated that this argument had 'a degree of plausibility to it'.[16] However, he argued that if a country sold excess grain to Britain then it must be growing the crops specifically to sell to Britain. He stated, 'in the event of war with us, such a country would suffer extreme distress.'[17] He also wondered whether Britain would ever be dependent on one country for grain, rather than on several. Ricardo was again able to move beyond the obvious to consider a more nuanced approach. This is not to say that his arguments always hold, but that they show an ability to think in a systematic way, to think of the economy as a whole system of interactions.

Ricardo also lent his name to the idea of 'Ricardian rent'. Rent here does not refer to the sums paid by tenants, the contractual rents that they had agreed to pay. For Ricardo: 'Rent is that portion of the produce of the earth, which is paid to the landlord for the use of the original and indestructible powers of the soil.'[18] He contrasted two adjoining farms of the same size. One had been improved with drainage, hedges and the like and the other left untouched. A tenant would pay more for the first farm than for the second, but both sets of payments would be commonly termed 'rent'. For Ricardo, only the portion due to the 'original and indestructible powers of the soil' was rent. The premium charged for the improvements was really a payment for the use of capital employed providing those improvements: laying hedges, digging drainage ditches, spreading manure.

Ricardian rent is not much heard of at undergraduate level as the discussion has moved on. Comparative advantage remains Ricardo's key direct contribution to the field of economics. However, his ideas provided food for thought for others and his sociability encouraged economic thinkers to meet and discuss their work.

The Dawn and Early Morning

In 1910 Jacob Hollander summed up the age of Ricardo: 'To the historical economist, it is the fifty years of the industrial revolution; to the political historian, it is the half century of the Napoleonic influence; to the historian of economic thought, it is the dawn and early morning of classical political economy.'[19] In this dawn and early morning Ricardo was able to converse with generalists but few specialists. It was not yet the age of the university economics department with its large faculty and vast cohorts of students.[20] It was still possible for a self-taught man to write a pamphlet on economic subjects and have it published and acclaimed as a key text. However, it is not clear how many people read Ricardo's work and understood it well enough to critique it. With all published works, there are varieties of readings and understandings. Ownership of a book does not imply that it is read; a book may be read in part rather than in whole, and reading does not guarantee understanding. Ricardo's writing style might not have helped.

Ricardo and Smith in that 'early dawn' had the status of great savants. Smith was the holder of a prestigious professorial chair which gave him the necessary *gravitas*. Ricardo's proven ability in the stock market gave credence to his opinions on a range of economic matters. Academic economics was in its infancy and Ricardo had fewer rivals than he would have had today. In Edinburgh, Dugald Stewart's lectures on political economy (with heavy focus on *The Wealth of Nations*) began in 1799. In England, political economy was only taught as a separate subject from 1805 onwards. Malthus was appointed the first 'Professor of General History, Politics, Commerce, and Finance' at the new East India College at Haileybury.[21] The college was set up to provide practical training for East India Company employees, not to debate the finer points of academic economics. Lectures on political economy at the University of Cambridge only began in 1816.[22] Ricardo's masterwork, the *Principles*, was published a year later.

Peach summarized the later academic approaches to Ricardo, and that offshoot of his thought, 'Ricardianism'.[23] Peach showed how later writers, such as Karl Marx and John Maynard Keynes, read wildly different meanings into Ricardo's work. Like many 'isms', there is a difference between the original thinker and the school that coalesced around his thoughts. Peach noted the 'quirks, foibles, and peculiar agendas of [Ricardo's] interpreters and critics, and the undoubted confusion between Ricardo's and Ricardian economics'.[24] Peach attributed some of this confusion to Ricardo's own writing style. As a largely self-taught individual who had spent his professional career as a broker, it is understandable that Ricardo's writing is sometimes unclear. He lacked the classical education of many of his peers. His friend Malthus had received a very good, if slightly unusual, education.[25] Ricardo did not have the same advantages, although he obviously had a vast amount of practical experience of finance. He had also decided to take up the study of mathematics when he was around 25 years old, alongside chemistry and mineralogy.[26] These pursuits may not have helped his literary style.

James Mill (father of John Stuart Mill) advised Ricardo to polish his writing style. Mill senior wrote 'you are already the best *thinker* on political economy, I am resolved you shall also be the best writer.'[27] Mill asked Ricardo to 'perform an exercise – a school exercise' whereby Ricardo would write letters showing step by step how his theories operated. Mill demanded that after each step, Ricardo should ask himself 'what comes next?' It is interesting that Ricardo's explanations of comparative advantage and Ricardian equivalence focus on that one question: what comes next? If taxes are reduced, what comes next? The public may believe that a tax rise is to follow. They then postpone consumption. If one country focuses its attention on producing wine and another on producing cloth, what comes next? If the assumptions of the model hold, an increase in total production results. Unless the people of England wish to drink cloth and the Portuguese wish to make coats out of wine, trade comes next. Ricardo made his comparative advantage argument clearer by using a numerical example, like a simple school exercise. If we accept Ricardo's assumptions in building his model, then the numbers 'prove' that he is right. This approach contrasts strongly with normative theories about how the economy *should* operate.[28]

Whether or not Ricardo's assumptions hold, his reliance on economic models as the bedrock of his theories makes him an economist in the modern sense. It also led Ricardo into what is now known as the 'Ricardian vice'. O'Brien wrote that Ricardo would 'take hypothetical premises, deducing conclusions from these premises, and making no attempt to verify the results. It has remained the method of the pure theorist ever since.'[29] O'Brien also argued that: 'Ricardo's system was, if not entirely the first, certainly the first sweepingly successful example of economic model building. Its essence was the "corn model" of aggregate economic relationships.'[30]

Whether or not the 'corn model' was truly part of Ricardo's system, he was concerned that Britain would starve without corn imports. He argued that Britain's attempt to rely on her own corn would result in economic stagnation. Poorer-quality land would be used for corn production. Capital and labour expended on this marginal land could have been more profitably employed elsewhere.[31]

Supporters of the Corn Laws believed that if they kept out foreign corn then Britain would be better off. At least, the landowning class would have its own corn production protected by a reduction in competition. Insular protectionist arguments were forcing up the price of corn. The poor were particularly affected, but so were urban consumers in the newly industrialized areas of the country. Ricardo and Malthus wrote to each other regularly about the price of corn and how it might affect the rest of the economy.[32] Their disagreements enabled Ricardo to hone his arguments. However, neither allowed their intellectual debates to detract from their friendship.

Keynes thought that Ricardo and Malthus's correspondence was the 'most important literary correspondence in the whole development of Political Economy'.[33] Notably, it was Keynes who had encouraged Sraffa with his Ricardo project and lent 'his active support, particularly in the search for unpublished material'.[34] Sraffa found that Ricardo had four main correspondents with whom he was in constant communication over a period of years. Malthus was obviously amongst them. The other three were James Mill, John Ramsay McCulloch and Hutches Trower. All played a part, directly or indirectly, in encouraging or popularizing Ricardo's ideas. Mill's son, John Stuart Mill, was invited to stay at Ricardo's country estate without his family when he was only fifteen. He and Ricardo talked at length on economic subjects.[35] Mill junior, of course, went on to become a key figure in the next generation of economists. McCulloch reviewed Ricardo's *Principles* in the *Edinburgh Review*. Sraffa argued that this was 'decisive in establishing Ricardo's fame and popularising his doctrines'.[36] After Ricardo's death McCulloch also printed a set of Ricardo's works with a brief biography.[37] McCulloch explained that his motive in publishing was 'the high esteem in which Mr Ricardo's works are held, and their increasing scarcity'.[38] The *Principles* were included, along with some other writings and published speeches. It would be interesting to learn why Ricardo's writings were simultaneously held in high esteem and yet also scarce. That conundrum may never be solved. In any case, Ricardo's *Principles* remained in print.

'Semitic Origins'

Eric Roll characterized Ricardo as 'without doubt the greatest representative of classical political economy'.[39] Roll also highlighted the anti-Semitism that was present in some assessments of Ricardo. An American economist called Carey made reference to Ricardo's 'Jewish subtlety' and labelled him as 'an unliterary Jewish stockbroker'.[40] Alfred Marshall (the subject of Chapter Five of this book) stated that 'the faults and virtues of Ricardo's mind are traceable to his Semitic origin: no English economist has had a mind similar to his.'[41] Of course, Ricardo was English as well as of Jewish origin. His ability to think unconventionally may be due in part to an unconventional upbringing and exposure to different religious traditions.

Ricardo's understanding of economics was rooted in his practical experience of the stock markets, an apprenticeship that many contemporary writers lacked. His knowledge of the international Jewish trading and kinship networks may have given him an internationalism that Marshall's 'English' economists were denied. He was also a clubbable man whose great friend Malthus was a noted political economist as well. Both were concerned with the living standards of the population as a whole, rather than merely with the interests of the landed elite. Their intellectual circle included such luminaries as Jeremy Bentham and the writer Maria Edgeworth, as well as many political economists whose names are now somewhat obscure.[42]

David Ricardo was born in 1772 in the City of London to a Sephardi family. His father, Abraham, had been a stockbroker in Amsterdam.

The Ricardos were originally Portuguese Jews who had emigrated to the Netherlands to escape from persecution. David himself spent two years in Amsterdam in his formative years.[43] In 1773 Abraham Ricardo obtained one of only twelve brokerships allotted to the Jewish community in London. This entitled him to legally act as a broker. He could be found on 'Jewes Walk': the southeast corner of the Royal Exchange. His house was 'part residence, part counting house'.[44] Abraham was also a fiscal agent for the Sephardi community.[45] He moved from trading in commodities to trade in bills of exchange and public securities. In 1792 his business address was at the famous Garraway's coffee house.[46]

David's father was devout and extremely strict. David himself did not receive much in the way of formal education except in religious studies. He began working for his father at the age of fourteen as a clerk and messenger on the London stock exchange. In 1792 the family moved house to Bow in east London. There David met Priscilla Ann Wilkinson, the daughter of a Quaker surgeon. They married, much to the disapproval of both sets of parents. David's mother never spoke to him again and he was disinherited by his father.[47] The family said the memorial prayer of the dead to symbolize that David was effectively dead to them now.[48]

Abraham Gilam has argued that in the Georgian period the 'upper strata of Anglo-Jewry secularized whilst losing their Jewish identity'.[49] He listed a number of prominent individuals including the first archivist of what is now the National Archives, Sir Francis Palgrave (né Francis Cohen). Gilam also added that: 'David Ricardo and the Radical politician Ralph Bernal are another two names that can be added to this list. Jews clearly realized that society would not accept them . . . Advancement in rank, status, and power was conditioned by renunciation of Judaism.'[50]

This may be true for many, but not necessarily for Ricardo. He may have had a sincere conversion experience or converted for love of Priscilla (and these motivations are not mutually exclusive). Quakerism was not useful to social climbers. Like Jews, Quakers (or Friends as they call themselves) were subject to discrimination and to legal restrictions.[51] Quakers were emancipated piecemeal, by three separate Acts of Parliament, passed in 1833, 1837 and 1838.[52] When Ricardo met Priscilla, she was a member of an outsider religious group just as he was.[53] In addition, Ricardo knew he would be disinherited by his father when he married her. As Ricardo stayed in the same line of business as his father, where Jewish kinship networks were important, being disinherited was not an obvious path to advancement. Ricardo could also have Anglicized his name like Cohen did, but chose not to. Gilam's assessment is perhaps too harsh.

When Ricardo took his seat in Parliament in 1819, he had to take an oath on 'the true faith of a Christian'.[54] He had, in William Wilberforce's words, 'ceased to be a Jew'.[55] Or more properly, he had ceased to be an observant Orthodox Jew. His true religious feelings are unknown, but his exposure to different faiths may have forced him to challenge received wisdom. His Jewish upbringing introduced him to the international finance markets.

It also exposed him to anti-Semitism. The connection between finance, finance-phobia and anti-Semitism ran deep. In a parliamentary debate about bullion one MP asked 'what security was there that foreign Jews . . . would not deem it a good speculation to make a run upon the Bank of England?'[56] The enduring Waterloo myth is an anti-Semitic fable of insider trading that attached itself to David Ricardo, as well as the Rothschilds. The myth alleges that a prominent Jewish figure was the first person to know of the outcome of the Battle of Waterloo (18 June 1815) and was able to profit on the stock market from this information. Brian Cathcart noted that the individual is usually identified as Nathan Meyer Rothschild. Cathcart showed how the myth originated and was embellished.[57] For instance, the Rothschilds were supposed to have set up a relay system of riders to carry the news from the field of battle (near Brussels) to the English Channel. In some later versions, the riders were replaced by pigeons. There is no mention in the Rothschild archives of any of this.[58] Cathcart convincingly demonstrated that the Waterloo myth was concocted to smear the Rothschilds. It was then revived by the Nazis and others to attack all Jews.

In the Ricardo variant of the myth, Ricardo's reaction to the good news allegedly was to sell British securities. His actions convinced observers that Waterloo was lost and prices on the London market dropped. Ricardo then bought up shares at bargain prices.[59] If true, then Ricardo's great achievement on the stock market was to profit from insider knowledge about a battle that left thousands dead. To modern observers it is as palatable as Waterloo teeth.[60] However, there is no evidence to show that anything about the Waterloo myth is true. Ricardo's wealth came from another, if related, source. Ricardo had assisted the government as a contractor for part of the National Debt.[61] He was therefore helping the war effort and stood to lose a fortune if Britain lost. The victory at Waterloo brought Ricardo great wealth, but due to his long-standing involvement in government debt. The news of Waterloo was brought to London not by mythical carrier pigeon, but by Major Henry Percy. Percy publicly appeared in a vehicle with captured French eagles poking out of it.[62] Insider trading would have been very difficult to accomplish after that spectacle appeared on the streets.

A New Career

Ricardo's Waterloo wealth did enable him to retire from the stock market. He bought a great estate in Gloucestershire: Gatcombe Park is fit for a princess.[63] He also had a house in London's fashionable Grosvenor Square.[64] Ricardo had become interested in what was then known as political economy. Joseph Schumpeter later explained that 'Ricardo's thought was inspired by *The Wealth of Nations*, which he took up in 1799 when boring himself at a health resort.'[65] Hollander described Ricardo's first publication, *The High Price of Bullion, a Proof of the Depreciation of Bank Notes* (1810), as a 'pamphlet of some forty pages, quickly conceived and hastily written'.[66] Ricardo's most famous work, *Principles of Political Economy and Taxation*, was published in 1817.

Ricardo opened his *Principles* with a discussion of value and then addressed rent, prices, wages, profits, foreign trade and a variety of different taxes. Ricardo viewed the economy as a system that divided 'the produce of the earth' between the proprietor of land, the owner of capital and labourers. 'To determine the laws which regulate this distribution, is the principal problem in Political Economy' wrote Ricardo.[67] In his preface Ricardo acknowledged his debt to Adam Smith and to his friend Malthus.[68] He also thanked his French correspondent, Jean-Baptiste Say, now known for his eponymous law.[69] The *Principles* became a key founding text of classical economics.

Like many of his contemporaries and followers, Ricardo was interested in what made something valuable (which was not necessarily what set its market price). The French Physiocrat, François Quesnay, had created a *Tableau oeconomique* in 1758.[70] This table was 'one of the earliest examples of the rigorous application of scientific method to economic phenomena'.[71] Quesnay began with land and those who worked upon it. Anyone who was not part of agriculture was part of a sterile class. Merchants, artisans and manufacturers were not deemed to be productive. They did not create value, but merely transformed the value created by agriculture into other forms. The source of value has implications for a variety of social questions. If land was the source of true value, the mercantile sector clearly had few claims on society's resources. Adam Smith and Ricardo also grappled with theories of value but with labour, rather than land, as a starting point.[72] The first words in the first chapter of the *Principles* are: 'The value of a commodity, or the quantity of any commodity for which it will exchange, depends on the relative quantity of labour which is necessary for its production, and not on the greater or less compensation which is paid for that labour.'[73]

By Ricardo's time, the industrialization process had reduced the omnipotence of agriculture. Many people were employed in manufacturing and its attendant service sector professions of selling, transporting and financing. Ricardo worked in the financial sector and had been brought up in a city, rather than on a landed estate. It was therefore unlikely that Ricardo would accept Quesnay's land-based view of the economy.

G.S.L. Tucker noted that since the late nineteenth century it has been common to claim that Ricardo influenced Marx's views on a labour theory of value.[74] Ricardo's real influence on Marx is a subject for debate. George Stigler argued that Ricardo did not have a labour theory of value per se. He outlined the various interpretations of Ricardian theories of value that have appeared.[75] There is no clear consensus on what Ricardo intended. Likewise, Friedrich Hayek coined the term the 'Ricardo effect' to describe how rising wages encourage capitalists to substitute capital for labour. Various others, including Nicholas Kaldor and Mark Blaug, have argued that Ricardo had never outlined the effect.[76] Ricardo's legacy is heavily contested.

Substance over Style

In 1823 Thomas Attwood MP was able to claim, in front of Ricardo, that Malthus was 'undoubtedly the greatest authority in this country, or in Europe, in all questions connected with political economy'.[77] Malthus's most famous idea was that population growth would always outstrip a growth in the food supply in the long run. Short-term improvements would simply lead to more births and more mouths to feed. Famine would inevitably result.[78] This is the Malthusian trap. Malthus can easily be imagined as a humourless pessimist, especially when writing passages like this: 'Gigantic inevitable famine stalks in the rear, and with one mighty blow, levels the population.'[79] Thomas Carlyle's famous criticism of economics as 'the dismal science' is often, incorrectly, taken to refer to Malthusianism.[80] However, Malthus was also capable of great humanity and wit. His writing style is entertaining and he was capable of creating memorable and evocative passages, such as: 'The citizen who has retired, and whose ideas, perhaps, scarcely soar above or extend beyond his little garden, puddling all the morning about his borders of box will, perhaps, live as long as the philosopher.'[81]

In Malthus's work, we see the concerns of an intelligent, witty man whose examples come from the world around him: the world of the farm and the village. Malthus called for a variety of obstacles to free labour markets to be removed, noticeably the requirement for poor people to live in their own parish to claim poor relief.[82] Rather than being the forbidding patrician of legend, Malthus could be a radical critic. He castigated the rich for colluding amongst themselves to keep wages low. His discussions of how markets work are not abstract, but are rooted in his compassion for the sufferings of the poor. His great friend Ricardo shared many of his concerns.

Ricardo and Malthus's correspondence takes up nearly a whole volume of Sraffa's eleven-volume set. The deep friendship between the two men is evident. They met frequently and discussed much. In August 1814 Ricardo wrote to Malthus hoping for an opportunity to 'discuss those important points in our shady groves' at Gatcombe.[83] The two men's wives also socialized with each other.[84]

The following year Ricardo lamented in another letter to Malthus that he had so few 'political economists' of his acquaintance that he did not know whether his work was being read.[85] Ricardo also wrote candidly of his shortcomings as a writer: 'It is a matter of mortification to me that my execution has been so faulty.'[86]

Literary tastes change over time. However, Ricardo's sentences do tend to run on. Here is an example:

> Without some weapon, neither the beaver nor the deer could be destroyed, and therefore the value of these animals would be regulated, not solely by the time and labour necessary to their destruction, but also by the time and labour necessary for providing the hunter's capital, the weapon, by aid of which their destruction was effected.[87]

Malthus is the more entertaining writer and hence was probably more widely read by a general audience. Ricardo was the better economist.

Ricardo's Posthumous Reputation

In 1983 a study of the 'Half-Lives of Dead Economists' was published, investigating how often economic thinkers were cited in academic journal articles. Ricardo was ranked at number fourteen for all journals. He stood ninth in rankings for economics journals. Of authors who died before 1900, Ricardo was ranked sixth, Malthus ninth. Unsurprisingly, Adam Smith and Karl Marx stood higher than Ricardo for all rankings.[88] Maybe the debates surrounding Ricardo's real intentions have contributed to the number of citations.

Ricardo remains of interest to historians of economic thought, but his name is also remembered outside those circles. When the Royal Economic Society held a bicentennial exhibition to honour Ricardo, it was attended by the Lord Mayor of London and the Treasurer of the Political Economy Club (founded by Ricardo and Malthus in 1821) as well as by a large audience. One exhibit was a 'massive silver vase' presented to Ricardo by the Stock Exchange List of 1807 to 'commemorate his part in securing the war loan contract for the stock exchange'.[89] Originals of his correspondence with Malthus and others were on display. Apparently 'a large number of persons, particularly from the near-by Stock Exchange', visited the exhibition over the course of ten days.[90] That is perhaps fitting, as Ricardo was one of the first political economists to emerge from a stock exchange background.[91]

Ricardo's posthumous reputation was given a huge boost by the publication of Sraffa's multi-volume critical edition of Ricardo's works and letters.[92] Few unpublished letters slipped through Sraffa's net. One that did was published in its entirety in the *Economic Journal*.[93] It answers an unknown question posed by one Francis Finch of West Bromwich. Such is Ricardo's standing that major academic journals are willing to publish any letter, no matter how dull or obscure, in order to fill a lacuna. For Checkland, the hunt for such manuscripts provided 'the element of the romantic, so singularly lacking in Ricardo's life'.[94]

This analysis of the 'unromantic' Ricardo seems a little harsh. Ricardo's letters to Malthus sparkle with humanity and kindness. Indeed, romance was the reason for Ricardo's final break with his birth family and with his faith (although other factors may have been at work). Ricardo's family life with Priscilla appears to have been a happy one. Their children assimilated into the landed elite. David Ricardo junior was a Justice of the Peace at Tetbury. He sentenced Betty Judge for 'maliciously destroying turnips' in 1828: a crime against the landed order if ever there was one.[95] Ricardo senior had died five years before at the relatively young age of 51. Sadly he did not have much time to enjoy puddling about his borders of box.

The austere model-building approach and its attendant Ricardian vice were associated with a man who was anything but austere in his personal relationships. James Mill advised Ricardo to cut back on his social life, to devote more time to study. Ricardo was admonished to resist 'the most frivolous of social calls'.[96] Ricardo himself claimed that Gatcombe was 'always full of visitors' and on one occasion he and his wife entertained 49 people to a dance and supper.[97] The party continued until four in the morning. On that occasion, Ricardo only had four hours' sleep so perhaps Mill had a point. Yet his sociability also allowed him to converse with the great thinkers of his day as well as the small number of political economists then active. The changes in the price of corn or the effects of protectionism were not abstract puzzles to be solved as an intellectual exercise. Ricardo and Malthus were haunted by the prospect of, as Malthus puts it, famine levelling the population with one mighty blow.

Ricardo may have ended his life as a member of the landed elite, but he started it in an immigrant Jewish family who had suffered persecution. This may have influenced his economic thought, but also his ability to empathize with the marginalized members of his society. His wife's Quaker origins may have had some influence as well. Ricardo's time in the stock markets helped him to understand how economic agents behave in the wider economy. His Waterloo wealth enabled him to retire and take up political economy almost as a hobby. Adam Smith's *The Wealth of Nations* provided the catalyst to this change in career. Ricardo's *Principles* was, like *The Wealth of Nations*, an attempt to describe the whole of economic life. Academics now argue over what Ricardo really meant by his, sometimes lengthy, sentences about corn or value. Undergraduates are still taught his elegantly simple ideas about comparative advantage and Ricardian equivalence. Long after his death, Ricardo became a symbol of the benefits of international trade and his name became synonymous with trading systems intended to be a bulwark against narrow protectionism. Whether or not modern trading blocs are truly Ricardian, they were founded to avert warfare and to promote economic growth through cooperation. Ricardo advocated cooperation and lived up to this principle in his attempts to create a community of scholars. He was also, like all his contemporaries, acutely aware of the human cost when warfare replaced peaceful economic competition.

THREE

JOHN STUART MILL

Joseph Persky

John Stuart Mill was not just a philosopher. As much as Marx, he was an analyst, advocate and prophesier of a sweeping reconstruction of the emerging capitalist economy. He saw the mid-nineteenth century, the present in which he lived, as a transitional period. He built his understanding of the economy on a political economy of progress, put together from a range of classical elements drawing on the work of Smith, Bentham, Ricardo, Malthus and his father, James Mill.[1] For John Stuart Mill, the Industrial Revolution had opened a new and exciting period rich with the potential for progress. Mill anticipated that the rapid capital accumulation ushered in by the Industrial Revolution would lead to a stationary state, not to be feared but to be embraced, a stationary state ultimately characterized by worker cooperatives. The stationary state would do away with the central role of capitalists, replacing them not with nationalization and state planning, but with labour-managed firms. Under this new regime, land rents and inheritance would be taxed for the common good, education would be universal, women would participate as equals, minorities would find opportunity and welfare would be compassionate and generous.

Yet Mill, the economist, is often dismissed as a minor post-Ricardian, the shallow encyclopaedist of laissez-faire and the classical school. Where Smith is identified with the invisible hand, Malthus with the dangers of overpopulation and Ricardo with the promise of comparative advantage, Mill the economist is left without a defining, central contribution to economics. Yes, Mill is the famous champion of liberty and utilitarianism, but all that is viewed by both philosophers and economists as fundamentally philosophy and not economics. The purpose of this short essay is to correct this distortion of Mill's contributions to economics. Whatever his accomplishments as a philosopher, Mill's approach to economics is comprehensive, including a theory of history and a socio-psychology of economic behaviour. While Mill accepted much of the classical interpretation of production, he broke new ground with his insistence that laws of distribution, as opposed to laws of production, are malleable and subject to conscious human intervention. Most importantly, Mill should be identified with his construction of a political economy of progress, a serious radical theory and reform programme that anticipated a transition from capitalism to a cooperative economy.[2]

Biography

John Stuart Mill's childhood was an eclectic and, by his own account, loveless affair. The story has been told numerous times.[3] Yet it bears retelling when we think of Mill not only or even primarily as a philosopher, but rather as a radical economist committed to the reform and reconstruction of society. As the historian Bruce Mazlish put it some forty years ago, 'Mill's economic writings, like his father's, carry with them a psychological message whose significance we can, however haltingly, try to comprehend.'[4] This proposition is particularly true of Mill's radical economics that marks such a strong break with his father's classical liberalism.

Mill was born in 1806, the first of nine children of James and Harriet Burrow Mill. While the size of their family attests to the activity of their marriage bed, Mill's parents shared little else in common. In his *Autobiography*, Mill wonders that his father, a committed Malthusian with quite limited resources, would have undertaken the support of such a large family.[5] More telling, in an unpublished early passage he speculated that his parents' relationship had no foundation 'in the inducements of kindred intellect, tastes, or pursuits'.[6] According to Mill, neither parent evinced a loving manner. In the finished work Mill speculates that his father 'had much more feeling than he habitually shewed, and much greater capacities of feeling than were ever developed. He resembled most Englishmen in being ashamed of the signs of feeling, and, by the absence of demonstration, starving the feelings themselves.'[7] In an earlier draft he goes further and traces this character to his parents' 'ill assorted marriage'.[8] And in his first notes for this passage Mill wrote, 'In an atmosphere of tenderness and affection he [James Mill] would have been tender and affectionate.' Mill expands the indictment:

> That rarity in England, a really warm-hearted mother, would in the first place have made my father a totally different being, and

> in the second would have made the children grow up loving and being loved. But my mother, with the very best of intentions, only knew how to pass her life in drudging for them. Whatever she could do for them she did, and they liked her, because she was kind to them, but to make herself loved, looked up to, or even obeyed, required qualities which she unfortunately did not possess.[9]

It is not surprising that Mill suppressed much of this material from his *Autobiography*. It is surprising that in this remarkable memoir, he effectively suppresses almost all mention of his mother.[10]

If Mill's father lacked warmth, he did not lack intensity of interest and commitment to John Stuart. Famously James Mill set John Stuart an amazingly rigorous course of home schooling starting with Greek. This instruction presumably began at age three, although Mill had no memory of the start of his studies. At eight he took up Latin and two years later went through the first six dialogues of Plato. These exercises were carried out 'in the same room and at the same table at which he [James Mill] was writing'.[11] Greek and Latin were supplemented with arithmetic. Then Mill took up history, including Hume and Gibbon. The elder Mill also pushed John Stuart to write poetry in English. James thought highly of Milton and Burns, but not so well of Shakespeare. He was uninterested in nineteenth-century poetry. This early education was supplemented by readings in chemistry.

Starting at twelve the home curriculum turned to logic which John Stuart, writing in his autobiography, considered the very bedrock of 'whatever capacity of thinking I have attained'. In this he held logic much superior to mathematical studies where the tightness of argument made careful 'ratiocination' unnecessary. Returning to Plato, John Stuart endorses wholeheartedly the Socratic method. Like his father, John felt that no other author had done as much to shape his 'own mental culture'.[12] The course of study then culminated in Mill's fourteenth year with intensive reading of Ricardo and Smith. And this marked the end of Mill's more or less formal education as closely directed by his father.

Mill maintained that his father's educational experimentation with him showed that many children might acquire considerable amounts of higher education in their early youth. He insisted that he was not 'by nature extremely quick of apprehension', nor did he possess 'a very accurate and retentive memory', nor was he 'of a remarkably active and energetic character'. He insisted that 'in all these natural gifts I am rather below than above par' and 'what I could do, could assuredly be done by any boy or girl of average capacity and healthy physical constitution.'[13] Just as important, Mill is sure that his education 'was not an education of cram'. His father had always emphasized not mere rote memory but the process of thinking for oneself. Mill summarizes the meaning of his own education in an adage: 'A pupil from whom nothing is ever demanded which he cannot do, never does all he can.'[14] At the same time he is convinced that the process created a 'state of mind' that was not 'humility, but neither was it arrogance'.[15] Finally, and somewhat wistfully, he notes that his father's educational plan in effect isolated him from children his age and their physical pursuits.

Mill traced to his father not only his interest in logic and reasoning, but also much of his moral understanding. Perhaps most basic was the fact his father 'found it impossible to believe that a world so full of evil was the work of an Author combining infinite power with perfect goodness and righteousness'.[16] This left James Mill something of a classicist accepting of Stoic standards for personal conduct, but advocating Epicurean notions (in the form of utilitarianism) for public purposes. John Stuart also noted a bit of the cynic in his father, who greatly discounted the rewards of pleasure. There is a sense in which this description would apply to the son as well as the father, perhaps with the exception that John Stuart developed a strong romantic streak despite his father's pessimism.

His father also brought to John Stuart two impressive friends who further shaped his thinking: David Ricardo, the brilliant formalizer of economic theory, and Jeremy Bentham, the eclectic and creative mainspring of utilitarian thought. Around this time John Stuart also spent a year in France with Bentham's brother, a year that laid the basis of his lifelong fondness for that country. During his stay he spent time with Jean-Baptiste Say, the French economist famous for Say's Law (that supply creates its own demand), which can be traced to Mill's father. While in Say's home, Mill met briefly with Henri de Saint-Simon (1760–1825), French proponent of a meritocratic organization of society and developer of a progressive theory of history. In the 1830s Saint-Simon's followers strongly influenced Mill's world view.

With this rich education Mill began to explore his career possibilities, still very much controlled by his father. At first he studied law with John Austin, a utilitarian of some note. But in 1823, when John Stuart was just seventeen, James obtained, 'for me appointment from the East

India Company in the office of the Examiner of India Correspondence, immediately under himself'.[17] Mill maintains that this was a fine choice, since it was relatively undemanding work that allowed him considerable time for his own researches. He professes that he did not mind giving up the financial rewards of the law. The only drawback he mentions is that his position in the East India Company left him ineligible to run for political office.

At this point Mill was actively involved in what he labelled 'Youthful Propagandism'. He wrote for the new *Westminster Review* and participated in debating societies of the Radical movement. He even experimented with a bit of direct action, being briefly jailed for distributing birth control literature written by the old radical Francis Place.[18] Mill reflected in his *Autobiography* that by late 1821 he had formulated 'what might truly be called an object in life; to be a reformer of the world. My conception of my own happiness was entirely identified with this object.'[19]

Here, then, is the young Mill at twenty years old. He continued his extraordinary and intense relationship with his father first in his home school and then at work. He considered his father repressed. He was more than disappointed with his mother, whom he described as unloving. He was committed to a somewhat grandiose goal of changing the world. It is not totally surprising that against this background Mill experienced a severe depressive episode. In a famous description Mill writes:

> I was in a dull state of nerves, such as everybody is occasionally liable to: unsusceptible to enjoyment or pleasurable excitement; one of those moods when what is pleasure at other times, becomes insipid or indifferent . . . In this frame of mind it occurred to me to put the question directly to myself. 'Suppose that all your objects in life were realized: that all the changes in institutions and opinions which you are looking forward to, could be completely effected at this very instant: would this be a great joy and happiness to you?' And an irrepressible self-consciousness distinctly answered, 'No!' At this my heart sank within me: the whole foundation on which my life was constructed fell down. All my happiness was to have been found in the continual pursuit of this end. The end had ceased to charm, and how could there ever again be any interest in the means? I seemed to have nothing left to live for.

Of the plan for changing the world nothing was left. He had 'awakened from this as from a dream'.[20]

By his own account Mill did not seek aid from his father with these psychological problems he felt the elder Mill would not have understood. Rather he recovered slowly after a charged emotional response to a passage in Marmontel's *Mémoires* relating to that author's experience of taking on an adult role after the death of his father. It is hard to avoid the conclusion that Mill's depression was bound up with ambivalent feelings about his father and his own difficulty in taking on the adult role of a reformer.[21] His turning to Romantic poets of the nineteenth century, especially Wordsworth, for solace was itself a form of rebellion. But more to the point of the present essay, he identifies his new explorations with his intensive reading of Comte and the Saint-Simonians. He now began to appreciate their 'criticisms on the common doctrines of Liberalism'. And his 'eyes were opened to the very limited and temporary value of the old political economy, which assumes private property and inheritance as indefeasible facts, and freedom of production and exchange as the dernier mot of social improvement'.[22] While Mill never embraced the 'machinery' of the Saint-Simonians, they clearly set him on a new course, one that would not take full shape for another 25 years.

Key to Mill's new thinking was the struggle each of us undertakes to achieve meaningful self-determination.[23] This struggle is central to Mill's philosophy and his understanding of psychology.[24] It is central to his argument in *On Liberty*. And it is just as central to his development of a political economy of progress.

Before leaving the *Autobiography* and the influences that shaped Mill's quest, we must devote some attention to what he describes as the most valuable friendship of his life. Mrs Harriet Taylor was his close friend after 1830 (when Mill was just 24) and his wife after 1851. She is now recognized as a major participant in Mill's writings on progress.[25] For some twenty years Mill and Taylor were more than close friends, but most likely less than lovers. In that period they discussed feminism, poetry and political economy.[26]

There should be no surprise that Mill was influenced by Taylor. Indeed he tells us this explicitly. While he states that Harriet had little impact on the first major work to bring him serious notice, *A System of Logic*, he particularly credits her for his work in economics. In a dedication he added to several presentation copies of *Principles of Political Economy*, Mill calls Taylor 'the most eminently qualified of all persons known to the author either to originate or appreciate speculations on social improvement' and acknowledges that many of the ideas included in the volume 'were first learned from herself'.[27] Mill broadly praises Mrs Taylor for giving a 'tone' to the entirety of the *Principles* that 'never treats the mere arrangements of modern society as final'.[28] This proposition becomes the very radical core of the work which emphasizes the 'distinction between the laws of the Production of Wealth, which are real laws of nature, dependent on the properties of objects, and the modes of its Distribution, which, subject to certain conditions, depend on human will'.[29] Beyond this overarching point, Mill takes great pains to credit Harriet with being the stimulus for his including the chapter on 'the Probable Future of the Labouring Classes'. As we shall see, it is precisely in this chapter that Mill's political economy of progress reaches its fullest conclusion.

More traditional economists, including most notably Friedrich Hayek (1951), have regarded Harriet Taylor and her influence on Mill as a most unfortunate accident. But surely Taylor completed Mill's resolution of his mental crisis as neatly as can be imagined. Mill, racked over the purpose and meaning of reform, took up with Taylor, a beautiful, confirmed radical feminist. She gave encouragement and form to his building a political economy of progress. She helped him shape the dimensions of his rebellion. Mill's concern with self-determination became something more than just a plaintive whine over the coldness of his own childhood home and his father's over-zealous educational methods. Rather, he extended that concern to the entirety of the 'Labouring Classes' as he endorsed their replacement of the harsh discipline of the capitalist manufactory with the rational, self-affirming character of workers' cooperatives.

Mill's *Principles* maintained its message over seven editions. Like his *Logic*, the *Principles* was well received. It almost immediately became the standard text in political economy and was particularly enshrined at Oxford and Cambridge.[30] In part this may reflect the ease with which a reader or professor might concentrate on either the orthodox sections of the work (such as the defence of laissez-faire) or the more radical (such as the advocacy of worker cooperatives).

Mill's two most famous and lasting works were produced relatively late in his life. *On Liberty* (1859) put forward what has become the basic defence of modern civil and personal liberties, while his essay *Utilitarianism* (1861) offered a radical utilitarian understanding of history and justice consistent with his work on the political economy of progress. After Harriet's death and his retirement from the East India Company, Mill finally took a stab at direct political participation as a Member of Parliament for Westminster (1865–8). Here he ran aground on the broad hostility to his advocacy of the vote for women. This reaction was not entirely new to Mill, for his political reformism had continually been ridiculed by press and elements of the public.[31] And, indeed, he continued to push for reform. For example, he took on a range of responsibilities in the land reform movement of the day. In this period he relied heavily on his stepdaughter Helen Taylor who took up her mother's role and was in her own lifetime to move further to the political left.[32]

Competition and Property

Mill wove his rebellion, his radical political economy of progress, out of the very materials provided by classical economics, Smith, Ricardo, Malthus and his own father. Chief in his inheritance from the classical writers was Mill's understanding of the role of competition. Even as he wrote his most radical material on cooperatives, Mill brought to the fore the need for the decentralized system of cooperatives to maintain a commitment to competition. As Mill well recognized this was his most striking disagreement with the ideology of socialists in his day.[33]

Thus Mill wrote,

> I agree, then, with the Socialist writers in their conception of the form which industrial operations tend to assume in the advance of improvement [i.e. cooperatives]; and I entirely share their opinion that the time is ripe for commencing this transformation, and that it should by all just and effectual means be aided and encouraged. But while I agree and sympathize with Socialists in this practical portion of their aims, I utterly dissent from the most conspicuous and vehement part of their teaching, their declamations against competition.[34]

For Mill, as for his classical forebears, the great material progress of the Industrial Revolution emerged from the creative and constructive competition made possible by the liberal relaxation of custom, aristocratic privilege and royal monopolies. Adam Smith's 'obvious and simple system of natural liberty' is the very starting point of Mill's understanding of political economy. Indeed, Mill's major fear and most telling indictment of private property in the modern economy is precisely that it is so often not the product of individual effort in a free competitive economy, but rather, despite the growth of competition, it too often reflects the dead hand of the past, the power of inheritance and outright skulduggery.

Mill muses about what conditions might justify private property in a more perfect world, 'a community unhampered by any previous possessions'. Here a 'body of colonists occupying for the first time an uninhabited country; bringing nothing with them but what belonged to them in common'. If these colonists adopt a system of private property, 'it would be accompanied by none of the initial inequalities and injustices which obstruct the beneficial operation of the principle in old societies.' He imagines an initial egalitarian distribution of the 'instruments of production' and goes so far as to suggest that 'compensation might be made for the injuries of nature, and the balance redressed by assigning to the less robust members of the community advantages in the distribution, sufficient to put them on a par with the rest'.[35] And Mill leaves little doubt that in this ideal system of private property the institution of inheritance would be greatly curtailed, since the principle of private property in no way guarantees to individuals 'the fruits of the labour and abstinence of others, transmitted to them without any merit or exertion of their own'. Such transmissions are 'not of the essence of the institution' which 'in every defence made of it, is supposed to mean, the guarantee to individuals of the fruits of their own labour and abstinence'.[36]

Mill is painfully aware that such an ideal-type is in sharp contrast with the real world of the nineteenth century:

> The social arrangements of modern Europe commenced from a distribution of property which was the result, not of just partition, or acquisition by industry, but of conquest and violence: and notwithstanding what industry has been doing for many centuries to modify the work of force, the system still retains many and large traces of its origin. The laws of property have never yet conformed to the principles on which the justification of private property rests.

In a coda worthy of Marx, Mill asserts that these laws of property 'have made property of things which never ought to be property, and absolute property where only a qualified property ought to exist.

They have not held the balance fairly between human beings, but have heaped impediments upon some, to give advantage to others; they have purposely fostered inequalities, and prevented all from starting fair in the race.'[37]

The ideal system of private property looks quite different from the reality of the day. Still, from a historical perspective, Mill credits the 'increased security' of property as generating 'a great increase both of production and of accumulation. Industry and frugality cannot exist where there is not a preponderant probability that those who labour and spare will be permitted to enjoy.' This increasing security of property along with greater allowance of competition and an explosion of scientific understanding are the foundation of the historical increase in material prosperity that had been realized by 'civilized nations'.[38]

Accumulation

Mill adopted Smith's basic approach to accumulation. Smith introduced the distinction between productive and unproductive labour.[39] Like Smith, Mill basically identifies productive labour with the generation of material wealth amenable to accumulation. This expansion of the nation's stock of material wealth is the heart of production.[40] Each year capitalists advance stocks of food, clothing, materials and tools to their workers. These capital stocks devoted to employing productive labour are capable of expansion. Quite simply, workers produce more than they eat. Mill is explicit on the point:

> The cause of profit is, that labour produces more than is required for its support . . . [I]f a capitalist supplies a party of labourers with these things [food, clothing materials and tools], on condition of receiving all they produce, they will, in addition to reproducing their own necessaries and instruments, have a portion of their time remaining, to work for the capitalist. We thus see that profits arise not from the incident of exchange, but from the productive power of labour.[41]

If the capitalist decides not to consume the entire surplus created in this manner, but rather to invest at least a portion of it, then he feeds the engine of accumulation.

Mill crystalized the classical understanding of the rapid growth of capital in the first half of the nineteenth century. Productivity, enhanced by modern institutions and a new dynamic application of science to production, was driving the capitalist economy. This was the 'progressive state'.

At the same time, Mill, like Ricardo, feared the destructive consequences of Malthusian population growth. If accumulation began to raise wages, Malthus had taught that even small increases in wages would lead to rapid population growth. And population growth inevitably put pressure on natural resources, raising rents and food prices, while lowering profits. Ricardo had seen in this scenario a decline into a 'stationary state'. Ricardo had argued that only free trade, tapping the substantial grain production of Germany and the United States, could put off the denouement for a time.

Mill, of course, was a supporter of free trade. But he found a broader message in the classical growth story. He asked what the labouring classes could do about Ricardo's depressing forecast. How could the labouring classes, in effect, take history into their hands? In phrasing such a question he combined his commitment to fundamental reform and his understanding of classical economics. The result was nothing less than a radical programme for the labouring classes. The two central points were to achieve control over population growth and to replace the system of capitalist manufactories with worker-controlled cooperatives. History created the moment. The progress of the hundred years before 1850 had been based on the accumulation undertaken by the capitalists coupled with a blossoming of scientific insight. Mill was hopeful that the labouring classes could now take effective control of this new economy.

The first step was to consciously slow the growth rate of the labour force, thus short-circuiting the Malthusian mechanism that kept workers near subsistence wages. The issue was critical for the future of the labouring classes. If workers could show restraint, the immediate result in an economy characterized by the rapid accumulation of capital would be rising wages. If the population could be stabilized an ever 'greater capital would be distributed in wages among the same number of labourers'.[42]

The prospect according to Mill was not dim. The growing education and industrial experience of the workforce was producing a disciplined class capable of demonstrating restraint in achieving its goals. Mill was optimistic, if somewhat tentative. The point was clear. 'Only when, in addition to just institutions the increase of mankind shall be under the deliberate guidance of judicious foresight, can the conquests made from the powers of nature by the intellect and energy of scientific discoverers become the common property of the species, and the means of improving and elevating the universal lot.'[43]

It should be noted that controlling population growth, in addition to raising workers' wages, could be expected to have beneficial effects on the situation of women, currently chained to a narrow home life of childcare forced on them by custom and large families. While Mill did not generally favour married women working outside the home, he did look forward to a time when married women would participate actively in the political and social life of the community.[44] Indeed, he had criticized his father, James, a committed Malthusian, for having created a large family and in the process left his mother with little alternative to the drudgery of housework.

Mill hoped if workers could gain control of population growth their wages would rise. But as a serious Ricardian he expected that if wages rose, profits would fall, and this was the key to his second major point for working-class autonomy. Of course, Ricardo had expected profits to fall, but that scenario was to be driven by rising rents. As noted above, if the working classes failed to exert control over their growth, Mill made the same prediction.[45] But if the labouring classes could master their mindless reproduction, Mill anticipated and encouraged a very different outcome. In particular he reasoned that as the profit rate fell, capitalists would be less and less eager to undertake active investment and management. This shift would then set the stage for the expansion of worker cooperatives.

Mill argued 'There is at every time and place some particular rate of profit, which is the lowest that will induce the people of that country and time to accumulate savings and to employ those savings productively.'[46] Nor is this point a distant one. Indeed Mill held

> When a country has long possessed a large production, and a large net income to make savings from, and when, therefore, the means have long existed of making a great annual addition to capital . . . it is one characteristic of such a country that the rate of profit is habitually within, as it were, a hand's breadth of the minimum, and the country therefore on the very verge of the stationary state.[47]

Before looking at this radical prospect in some detail in the next section, it is crucial to note that Mill was very much aware that the fall of profits might be slowed or even checked by 'counteracting circumstances'.[48] This list, somewhat discouraging to the path of reform, testifies to Mill's acuity as a student of capitalist accumulation.

The first counter-tendency is the destruction of capital which inevitably follows periods of 'over-trading' and 'speculation'. Here Mill, drawing on the work of Sismondi, draws a picture of the business crises that anticipates the core of twentieth-century macroeconomics.[49] Much capital in the run-up to the bust had been over-invested in fixed machinery and structures, and hence 'ceased to have any influence on wages or profits . . . Establishments are shut up, or kept working without any profit, hands are discharged and numbers of persons in all ranks, being deprived of their income, and thrown for support on their savings, find themselves, after the crisis has passed away, in a condition of more or less impoverishment.'[50]

Mill argues that cycles of this type slow the fall of profits, but points to the continued growth of capital as evidence that the periodic destruction of capital is not the most important counter-tendency. More significant, according to Mill, are the improvements in production technology. Mill argues that a cheapening of wage goods will allow a rise in real wages even as real profits rise.

Next on Mill's list is 'the acquisition of any new power of obtaining cheap commodities from foreign countries'.[51] Here again Mill argues that the major impact of such foreign trade is to cheapen the necessities for domestic workers.

Finally, and with most prescience, Mill points to the 'emigration of capital'. He argues that such emigration has been 'for many years one of the principal causes by which the decline of profits in England has been arrested'.[52] Mill anticipates that much of this capital will go into agriculture and infrastructure in colonies and trading partners. Hence, the export of capital reduces the growth of wages, even as it may well cheapen imports.

Mill's discussion of counteracting circumstances is something of a tour de force of political economy. Writing in the mid-nineteenth century he sees in the seeds of the then present the future course of capitalism. He pulls together the major realities of the modern economy: the macro business cycle, the continuing growth of productivity, the expansion of trade and the turn to foreign investment. Yet this picture was not his final word. He sincerely felt that the counter-tendencies would be insufficient to the task; that the fall of profits would continue to an effective minimum; and that the economy would move towards a stationary state. Indeed, 'the increase of wealth is not boundless' and at the end of what political economists term 'the progressive state lies the stationary state . . . [A]ll progress in wealth is but a postponement of this, and each step in advance is an approach to it.'[53]

The End of Capitalism

Each of the most prominent classical economists before Mill had anticipated a stationary state. But as Mill points out, each had approached that state with trepidation. For example, Smith had seen the progressive state as the most favourable to the bulk of the population. In effect, the early political economists had identified the stationary state with stagnation, if not outright decay. Mill, however, made a major shift in his reading of his stationary state. Stimulated, perhaps, by his rebellion against his father's pessimism, Mill saw in the stationary state not stagnation, but potential liberation. Encouraged by and in collaboration with Harriet Taylor, in his chapter 'On the Probable Futurity of the Labouring Classes', Mill paints a picture of a new world in which the working classes would have the opportunity to determine their own course.

Mill's criticism of nineteenth-century capitalism was devastating:

> I confess I am not charmed with the ideal of life held out by those who think that the normal state of human beings is that of struggling to get on; that the trampling, crushing, elbowing, and treading on each other's heels, which form the existing type of social life, are the most desirable lot of human kind, or anything but the disagreeable symptoms of one of the phases of industrial progress.[54]

Acknowledging that the progressive state might be 'necessary' and preferable to endless petty warfare, Mill looks forward to a post-capitalist economy.

Central to this vision is the expansion of labour-managed firms and cooperatives. Capitalism is characterized by productive accumulation and the employment relationship. We have seen what Mill expected to happen to the process of accumulation as profits fell to a minimum. Even more radical was his prescription for production itself. Perhaps it is difficult for us to recognize the relative novelty of the capitalist employment relationship as it emerged from the Industrial Revolution.

Before that time workers had been slaves or serfs or servants. There had been peasant farmers and tenant farmers. But what we recognize as the modern employment relation had been relatively rare, the exception rather than the rule. The radical Mill anticipated in his stationary state, not a move back to petty production, but a move forward to cooperative production.

The core of the argument is surprisingly persuasive. Mill and Harriet Taylor were clearly attracted to cooperatives on normative grounds. Mill's brilliance was to assemble a convincing positive analysis that makes cooperatives seem not just attractive but a necessary result of economic evolution and industrial history. The change in the working classes is manifest. The world is changing. 'The working classes have taken their interests into their own hands, and are perpetually showing that they think the interests of their employers not identical with their own, but opposite them.'[55] Where does this change come from?

> That question was decided, when they were taught to read, and allowed access to newspapers and political tracts; when dissenting preachers were suffered to go among them, and appeal to their faculties and feeling in opposition to the creeds professed and countenanced by their superiors; when they were brought together in numbers, to work socially under the same roof; when railway enabled them to shift from place to place, and change their patrons and employers as easily as their coats; when they were encouraged to seek a share in government, by means of the electoral franchise.[56]

Mill goes on to make the conclusion of this economic and social evolution crystal clear: 'In the present stage of human progress, when ideas of equality are daily spreading more widely among the poorer classes . . . it is not to be expected that the division of the human race into two hereditary classes, employers and employed, can be permanently maintained.'[57] Workers must ultimately be owners so that they will be committed to their jobs and capable to grow in their work activity.

How is this change to be effected? Mill recognized that his argument for the expansion of peasant proprietors in Ireland and other less developed economies might suggest that he would more broadly support a return to petty production both in agriculture and industry. But he sees such plans as impractical and destructive. 'A people who have once adopted the large system of production, either in manufactures or in agriculture, are not likely to recede from it.'[58] Moreover, petty production is hopelessly wrapped up with patriarchal domination. Taking a broader view, Mill argues, 'The aim of improvement should be not solely to place human beings in a condition in which they will be able to do without one another, but to enable them to work with or for one another in relations not involving dependence.'[59]

The capacity of the labouring classes to make decisions in a rational manner has been greatly enhanced by education. And this process will not stop. 'There is a spontaneous education going on in the minds of the multitude.'[60] For Mill, these developments point towards a major reform in industrial organization. Given the new intelligence of the working classes Mill cannot believe 'that they will be permanently contented with the condition of laboring for wages as their ultimate state'.[61] Mill anticipates then one of two possible outcomes, either some sort of 'association of labourers with the capitalist' or 'perhaps finally in all, association of labourers among themselves'.[62]

The idea of profit sharing with capitalists already had a history in British political economy. The English mathematician Charles Babbage (1791–1871), famed for his path-breaking work on programmable computing, had early advocated profit sharing.[63] After Mill, in the late nineteenth century, profit sharing was endorsed by such prominent British economists as William Stanley Jevons and Alfred Marshall. It had the appeal of addressing worker discontent, without requiring major structural change.[64]

Mill, however, suspects that workers will want more than a share of the profits. Increasing in intelligence and education, more aware of their capacity, they will push for full-scale cooperatives. As Mill puts it:

> The form of association, however, which if mankind continue to improve, must be expected in the end to predominate, is not that which can exist between a capitalist as chief, and workpeople without a voice in the management, but the association of the labourers themselves on terms of equality, collectively owning the capital with which they carry on their operations, and working under managers elected and removable by themselves.[65]

Mill, never the advocate of expropriation, anticipated that the capital for cooperative ventures might be raised from worker savings in combination with loans. Especially as the economy enters a stationary state, loans should be easily obtained on reasonable terms. After the historic period of rapid capitalist accumulation, as profits fall towards a minimum, many prosperous savers will see little reason to themselves undertake investment in and management of businesses. Under such circumstances they will be eager to transfer their funds to worker-controlled enterprises.

Marx was to anticipate a transition from capitalism to socialism marked by the centralization and concentration of production as capital struggled to maintain profits against the tendency of a falling rate of profit. By contrast, Mill looked forward to a far more peaceful transition as capital recognized the inevitable and more or less graciously accepted its role of minor rentier.[66]

Mill took this optimistic view, in part, because he fully expected worker-managed firms to be more efficient than traditional firms. He traced these potential gains first to a great reduction in the 'class of mere distributors' under cooperative organization. Mill goes so far as to suggest that the growth of this class of middlemen, 'far more than the gains of capitalists', has diverted so much of production from the producers themselves. He thinks that producer cooperatives, following the lead of the Rochdale consumer cooperatives, will have much less interest in this largely useless activity. Even more important, according to Mill, will be the stimulus the cooperative enterprise will give to the involvement of the workers. Currently workers focus on avoiding effort. Under cooperative organization it becomes workers' 'principle and their interest . . . to do the utmost, instead of the least possible'.[67] This greater efficiency raises productivity and gives cooperatives a major advantage in competition with traditional firms. Even more importantly the underlying change in attitude represents a 'moral revolution in society' and a 'transformation of human life'. In the end it brings forth 'the conversion of each human being's daily occupation into a school of the social sympathies and the practical intelligence'.[68]

Eventually Mill expects owners of capital to accept 'terminable annuities'. The result would be a fundamental move towards a more just society:

> In this or some such mode, the existing accumulations of capital might honestly, and by a kind of spontaneous process, become in the end the joint property of all who participate in their productive employment: a transformation which, thus effected, (and assuming of course that both sexes participate equally in the rights and in the government of the association) would be the

> nearest approach to social justice, and the most beneficial ordering of industrial affairs for the universal good, which is possible at present to foresee.[69]

Mill's Place in Economics

Mill contributed much more to economics than just his political economy of progress. He made major improvements in economists' understanding of supply and demand. Indeed, Schumpeter suggested that Marshall's formalization of supply and demand curves, the foundation for modern microeconomics, was just a rigorous restatement of Mill's work.[70] Mill greatly expanded on Ricardo's foreign trade theory by characterizing the nature of international trade equilibria. The early neoclassicist economist F. Y. Edgeworth in the late nineteenth century described Mill's treatment of foreign trade in the *Principles* as 'The Great Chapter', while the modern economist John Chipman called Mill's Law of International Value 'one of the great achievements of the human intellect'.[71] In addition, Mill did important work on money and on financial panics. Thomas Sowell credits him with being the 'first classical economist to explore directly the possibility of a demand for money beyond the transactions demand', while the macroeconomist Brad DeLong sees Mill as putting together the first coherent explanation of financial panics.[72] Mill also developed the economics of race, slavery and tenancy and defence of individual liberty extended to the treatment of African slaves and tenants in the new world.[73] Mill also wrote extensively on public finance.[74]

In this short essay we haven't explored any of these important topics in economics, let alone Mill's contributions to so many other fields. Rather we have concentrated on a close reading only of Book IV of his *Principles,* entitled: 'Influence of the Progress of Society on Production and Distribution'. It is my claim that these writings are the most exciting and significant in Mill's economic oeuvre. Together with his justifications of proposals to expand public education of the poor, to greatly limit inheritance and to tax away increments in land value, his endorsement of cooperative production pointed towards nothing less than a complete revolution in the economic sphere.

It is perhaps understandable that a right-leaning critic of Mill's political economy of progress like Friedrich Hayek would charge Mill with having simply mouthed the utopian socialism of Harriet Taylor without having made serious argument.[75] The position taken here is far different: stimulated by Taylor's views, Mill put together a compelling case for the cooperative economy. That case builds on the classical logic of accumulation, rising wages and falling profits in an exciting new direction. What more convincing, intellectual rebellion against his father's orthodoxy could Mill have constructed?

And what of the critique from the left? Here, too, somewhat ironically, Mill is accused of being too soft and gentle, even naive. But now his softness is identified in his resistance to revolution and nationalization. Capitalists will not give up their power without a fight; cooperatives are notoriously difficult to manage; discipline and guidance, centralization and national planning are needed. Possibly so. But the twentieth-century experience with that other path has hardly proven positive. Against that history, it may still be Mill's political economy of progress that holds the richest promise for all of us.

FOUR

KARL MARX

Paul Prew

The mere mention of the name 'Marx' conjures up images, both endearing and malign. The originator of a diverse and enduring school of thought, who famously asserted, 'I, at least, am not a Marxist', is an imposing intellect who cannot be ignored.[1] There is no questioning the influence Marx's thought has had since he put pen to paper in the nineteenth century, but the meaning and value of his thought remain the subject of great debate. The writing of Karl Marx and Friedrich Engels, his long-time friend and collaborator, consumes fifty volumes of the collected works. Any short introduction to Marx's thought will necessarily omit certain ideas while overemphasizing others, if only to make such a summary possible. This chapter hopefully provides a general overview of Marx's thought while drawing attention to specific insights of interest to those broadly familiar with his ideas.

During Marx's youth the climate in the German states was repressive. People who engaged in small acts of dissidence, such as attending a free speech rally, were subject to arrest and surveillance.[2] Clearly this environment shaped Marx's sympathies. By the time Marx entered the University of Bonn in 1835, he was already predisposed to joining political discussion groups. He was, however, both an exceptional student and quite a rowdy drinker. His reputation forced his father to move him to another university, in Berlin. There Marx became engaged to his future wife, Jenny von Westphalen.[3] Poetry Marx wrote for her survives in various archival collections, although the quality of it suggests his choice of writing political economy was the correct one.

While at the University of Berlin Marx focused on philosophy and became interested in the ideas of G.W.F. Hegel. Although Marx was dismissive of the religious aspects of Hegel's thought, he did adopt Hegel's dialectical approach, but turned it 'right side up again' and applied it to political economy. In Hegel, the dialectic was a philosophical understanding of how thought becomes reality.[4] Hegel, Marx argued, sought to arrive at the concrete through an iterative process of the contemplation of the abstract.[5] For Marx, the dialectic was not merely philosophical, but a means to study society. The scholar must research the object of study in great detail, illuminating the 'inner connection' of the relations to be understood.[6]

In Marx's 'original rough version of *Capital*', known as the *Grundrisse* (German for 'outline'), he sketched out 'The Method of Political Economy', his dialectical method.[7] Marx held that seventeenth-century political economists had mistakenly begun by considering broad abstractions of population, the state, classes and so on.[8] The correct approach was to start with more concrete, simple concepts and then proceed to the more general abstract conceptualization. One could then return to consider the whole, this time as a network of concrete relations instead of mere abstractions.

For Marx, analysis must always understand the abstract in its own historical moment. Concepts like money and labour exist across historical periods, but their concrete, historically specific forms must not be applied to prior societies. In early societies money existed, but its role was limited; it did not 'penetrate all economic relations'.[9] The centrality of capital in society dictates that money assumes a specific role not found in prior societies. Therefore societies must be understood in terms of the type of production that dominates them. While settled agricultural societies subjugate other forms of production, such as industry, to agriculture, the opposite is true of bourgeois society. Agriculture must conform to capital.[10]

After completing his doctoral thesis in 1841, Marx continued his research, but came to realize he would not obtain a professorship at a German university due to the political climate. His colleague Bruno Bauer was dismissed from the University of Bonn for his views.[11] As editor of the newspaper *Rheinische Zeitung* from 1842 to 1843, Marx wrote articles about public rights to collect firewood and the plight of winegrowers.[12] He grew increasingly concerned for the struggles of the working class. This was partly thanks to the articles Engels wrote for the *Rheinische Zeitung* detailing the appalling conditions of the working classes. These would culminate in Engels's 1845 book *The Condition of the Working Class in England*, with its lurid accounts of Manchester slums:

> The streets are generally unpaved, rough, dirty, filled with vegetable and animal refuse, without sewers or gutters, but

> supplied with foul stagnant pools instead. Moreover, ventilation is impeded by the bad, confused method of building of the whole quarter, and since many human beings here live crowded into a small space, the atmosphere that prevails in these working-men's quarters may readily be imagined.[13]

The *Rheinische Zeitung* was banned, and Marx moved to Paris to work on a new newspaper.[14] After the first issue this paper too was banned and arrest warrants were issued for Marx and others involved in its publication.[15] Marx took advantage of the more radical environment in Paris to throw himself more deeply into a study of political economy. Another one of Engels's 1844 articles that inspired him had sketched out the 'Outlines of a Critique of Political Economy'.[16] The pair finally met later that same year.

Marx became intent on demonstrating, with sound scientific and empirical grounding, two fundamentally interconnected realities: (1) people's exploitation under bourgeois commodity production makes them less than fully developed human beings; (2) this condition was limited to only a small portion of human development, and a society is possible where people would be able to realize their free, creative, social selves. Combining his philosophy and political economy research skills, Marx set about contrasting the current bourgeois society with the core essence of humans, their species being.

The concept of species being provides an illustration of how Marx contextualizes an abstract concept historically. In the summer of 1844 in France, Marx drafted a manuscript to organize his thoughts regarding the 'economic structure of bourgeois society'.[17] In the 'Economic and Philosophic Manuscripts of 1844', Marx outlined his ideas regarding alienated labour that would eventually make their way into *Capital* in the section titled 'The Fetishism of Commodities'. In this fashion Marx's concept of species being and the alienation of wage labour demonstrates how he integrated his earlier research and notes into his more polished work intended for publication, calling into question the notions of a 'young' and 'mature' Marx.[18]

In the 1844 manuscripts Marx described species being, the essence of human beings, as 'conscious life activity' in 'work upon the objective world' in a social context.[19] Marx's understanding of species being anticipates his comments on communal systems and his study of anthropological societies, especially those he termed 'primitive communism'.[20] While Marx in the 1844 manuscripts did not systematically outline species being in relation to primitive communism, Engels's discussion of the evolutionary origins of the human species in his unfinished work *Dialectics of Nature* clearly parallels Marx's concept of species being. Engels described the evolutionary development of the human species as an interplay of people's interaction with nature in a social context. Identifying the importance of the co-development of the hand, brain and larynx, Engels mirrors Marx's focus on the centrality of labour, consciousness and social activity in metabolism with nature.[21]

The historically specific origin of species being is thus rooted in the evolutionary trajectory of the early communal systems 'among all civilised nations at the dawn of their history'.[22] Species being results from the evolution of the human species as it used its hands to interact with nature in the creative mental process to meet needs in a social context. The underlying motive of human beings is not rooted in crude biological instincts, 'a fictitious primordial condition', but situated historically and anthropologically in the concrete realm of early hominid societies.[23]

Marx contrasted the concept of species being with the alienation of the labourer in the historically specific context of the private property relations in bourgeois society. According to Marx, alienation consisted of the estrangement of 1. '*the product of labour*' 2. 'the *act of production*' 3. '*species being*' and 4. '*man* from *man*'.[24] Marx begins, as in *Capital*, with the commodity – the object of the worker's labour.

> This fact expresses merely that the object which labour produces – labour's product – confronts it as *something alien*, as a *power independent* of the producer. The product of labour is labour which has been embodied in an object, which has become material: it is the *objectification* of labour. Labour's realisation is its objectification. Under these economic conditions this realisation of labour appears as *loss of realisation* for the workers; objectification as *loss of the object and bondage to it*; appropriation as *estrangement, as alienation*.[25]

The product of a worker's labour embodies the labour put into it by the worker.

When the object of that labour is a commodity and no longer belongs to the worker, it is something that no longer provides direct sustenance but represents the debilitation of the worker for the benefit of another. For the worker, the object of one's labour no longer produces the direct 'means of life' because nature is no longer the object of the worker's labour. Instead, the object of labour becomes the embodiment of the degradation of the worker. 'It produces beauty – but for the worker, deformity . . . It produces intelligence – but for the worker, stupidity, cretinism.'[26]

In *Capital*, Marx describes 'The Fetishism of Commodities and the Secret Thereof' to bring the role of the commodity as the embodiment of labour into sharper focus. A commodity in the marketplace hides the reality of labour, however. What the worker puts into the product, in the form of labour, is viewed as something inherent in the product itself. The qualities of the product do not appear to arise from the labour of the worker, but appear, mysteriously, as properties of the product. The social relations between producer and user are obscured by the commodity form. 'There it is a definite social relation between [people], that assumes, in their eyes, the fantastic form of a relation between things.'[27] With commodities, the process of production is not social production to meet needs, but an exchange relation between objects. The social nature of one's toil and the embodiment of labour in the product is hidden by the 'mystical character of commodities'.[28]

As an example, someone who buys a pen only thinks about the quality of the pen insofar as it can aid the person in writing letters. The person who purchases the pen does not think about the labour of the workers who produced it, how much labour time was put into making it. The consumer is only concerned about the mystical qualities of the pen itself, how well does it write. The consumer does not understand the pen as the embodiment of someone's labour because the exchange is not a social relationship. The consumer is merely exchanging wages for a commodity in the marketplace, an exchange relation between things – money and pen.

Following the alienation of the product, Marx turns to the alienation in the act of production. While the object of labour is the embodiment of labour, under wage labour, the object of labour is the embodiment of alienation. Likewise, the act of labour is an alienated activity. Within the communal labour of species being, labour may be life-affirming, but under wage labour, the activity becomes toil – a coerced, unhappy, ruinous, alien activity. The act of production is no longer the direct activity of satisfying needs, but becomes a secondary means, divorced from the labourer's self-realization. Workers feel like themselves outside of work, engaged in activities also associated with animals, such as 'eating, drinking, procreating'.[29]

Marx continues the discussion of the alienation by outlining the estrangement of species being. For Marx, the centre of human existence is people's interaction with nature. The relationship between people and nature is not merely one of convenience, but of necessity. People must interchange with nature to survive; however, meeting needs through nature is not limited to the most basic of needs, as it is with other animals.

> An animal forms objects only in accordance with the standard and the need of the species to which it belongs, whilst [a person] knows how to produce in accordance with the standard of every species, and knows how to apply everywhere the inherent standard to the object. [A person] therefore also forms objects in accordance with the laws of beauty.[30]

By producing through the interaction with nature, people exhibit their species being. Alienated production in bourgeois society strips people of their species being by stripping from them the conscious, free activity of production and transforming it into simply a means to survival, an alienated activity. No longer do people directly engage nature, further stripping them of their species being.

The final estrangement is that of people from each other. Since the act of production is the alienation of the person from the product, it is also the alienation of the person from the producer. The alienation of others is a necessary result of the alienation of product, production and species being. Since the commodity mystifies the real human toil in the act of production, people are estranged from each other and their species being – their free, conscious, social production. The social relations of free productive activity are replaced with the alienated relations of commodity production. 'Hence within the relationship of estranged labour each [person] views the other in accordance with the standard and the relationship in which [one] finds [oneself] as a worker.'[31] Instead of communal production to meet social needs, people are reduced to labourers, toiling merely for the means to their own existence. As such, people are isolated from each other, their social relations concealed, and they confront each other as alienated workers, not free, creative, social producers.

Marx's ideas regarding alienation are anchored to the analysis of commodity production in bourgeois society, not to be generalized to other societies. As stated above, Marx situates alienation historically.

Marx concludes, 'True, it is as a result of the *movement of private property* that we have obtained the concept of *alienated labour* (*of alienated life*) in political economy.'[32] Alienated labour is a concept tied to the very specific relations in bourgeois society, not to be confused with a general malaise or an endemic drudgery purportedly inherent in all labour. This distinction in Marx allows the ability to comprehend why someone would hate paid labour but find fulfilment in the same activity (sewing or woodworking, for example) in the evening. The former is the denial of one's self while the latter is the affirmation of one's species being.

The 1844 manuscripts became available in published form in the early twentieth century. The concept of alienation thereafter attracted widespread and sustained interest. A number of notable texts focus specifically on the concept.[33] Some books address alienation in contemporary society, like Al Gini's *My Job, My Self* (2000). Gini draws a direct connection between the alienation in the act of production and the mental health of the workers, as well as job satisfaction. The less people are able to exercise their mental capacity in their work, the less happy they are.[34] The historical specificity of the concept of alienation allows for a substantive investigation of the issue and also allows for the concept to be adapted to more contemporary production relations.

Marx concludes the discussion of alienation by asking 'to whom' the alienated product and activity belongs? The answer to his question lies in his analysis of the commodity. 'If the product of labour does not belong to the worker, if it confronts [the worker] as an alien power, then this can only be because it belongs to some *other* [person] *than the worker*.'[35] In the commodity, Marx locates the relationship between the owner and the worker. In the 1844 manuscripts Marx identifies the relationship as active alienation of the product of the worker's labour through appropriation. While workers lose the product of their labour to the owner in the active alienation from their own direct subsistence, workers receive wages as merely a means of subsistence. In *Capital*, Marx focuses more squarely on value. Where the 1844 manuscripts describe the alienation resulting from '*receiving the means of subsistence*', the relationship is further demystified in *Capital* through the discussion of value and the working day.[36]

Capital, published in 1867, was the culmination not only of Marx's life work but also of decades of dedicated study. While the published output of most thinkers is limited to closely edited texts or articles, a large portion of Marx's published work consists of unfinished manuscripts and notes. Marx was a meticulous researcher, and the preparatory work for *Capital*, spanned many years. He incorporated notes produced between 1850 and 1853 in the *Grundrisse*, and in 1857–8 drafted a manuscript merely for 'self clarification'.[37] Despite his copious editing and preparation, Marx included revisions and clarifications in the second edition of *Capital* and suggested further changes that his failing health prevented him from implementing.[38] Marx died on 14 March 1883, before he could complete the revisions for Volume One and see Volumes Two and Three into print, leaving Engels to edit and assemble *Capital*, his friend's seminal work.[39]

Capital

In *Capital* Marx begins with the commodity because it embodies all the important relations in bourgeois society: value, exploitation, exchange, accumulation, world market and so forth. Value, a concept Marx adopted from Smith and Ricardo and sought to clarify, is the starting point of the discussion of the commodity in *Capital*. Marx divides value, as do Smith and Ricardo, into use and exchange value. Use value is the utility of an object to the person who consumes it. Use value is inherent in the properties of the thing itself.[40] Use value meets a need and may be as simple as a stick to scratch in the ground or as complicated as a computer to calculate the trajectory of a satellite. Exchange value, however, is independent of use value except for the necessary reality that an item with no use value has no value.[41] There is hardly any reason to exchange for something that has no use or meets no need.

Before Marx considers exchange value, he endeavours to illuminate the element common to all commodities that allows them to be commensurable (exchangeable in the marketplace).

> Therefore, first: the valid exchange – values of a given commodity express something equal; secondly, exchange-value, generally, is only the mode of expression, the phenomenal form, of something contained in it, yet distinguishable from it . . . there is nothing left but what is common to them all; all are reduced to one and the same sort of labour, human labour in the abstract.[42]

As Marx stated above, labour is embodied in the commodities, and the crystallization of human labour-power is value.[43] Again, returning to the historical specificity of the abstract concept, Marx notes it is incorrect, in a certain respect, to assert there are two types of value, use and exchange. 'A commodity is a use-value or object of utility, and a value.'[44] Only in an exchange relation does a commodity take the form of exchange value. Around this very idea, the core of Marx's analysis pivots. He squarely situates labour at the centre, both in terms of his conceptualization of the free, conscious, productive social being as well as his analysis of the exploitation inherent in bourgeois commodity production. Labour produces value, and it is the value arising from labour that all products have in common that allows them to be commensurable in exchange.

At this point in the text Marx lashes out against the Mercantilists and 'Free-trade bagmen' who annihilate all concept of value except in terms of the relative value between unassociated commodities in the market, their exchange value.[45] 'For them there consequently exists neither value, nor magnitude of value, anywhere except in its expression by means of the exchange-relation of commodities, that is, in the daily list of prices current.'[46] For Marx, their incomprehension of value leaves them with no underlying common measure of value to determine the relative value of commodities on the market. Ricardo specifically confronts the problem by criticizing the use of corn instead of money as the standard measure of value, but concludes, 'Of such a commodity [as a common measure], we have no knowledge, but we may hypothetically argue and speak about it, as if we had.'[47]

Consistent with the dialectical method of political economy, Marx's analysis of the simplest concept, commodity, transitions to a higher level of abstraction, circulation of commodities. Beginning with the commodity, the source of value in labour, and the concealment of these relations, Marx sets about demystifying the source of profit in commodity production. To do so Marx identifies the circulation of commodities in the market. He depicts the first circuit as C–M–C where 'C' is equal to a commodity and 'M' is money. In this circulation, someone exchanges a commodity for money, and then uses the money to exchange for another commodity. The circuit comes to an end when the person consumes the commodity.[48] For example, someone sells a piece of pottery, receives money and purchases bread. The circuit terminates when the person consumes the bread.

The circuit of more interest to Marx is M–C–M, the purchase of a commodity with money, and the sale of the commodity to receive money in return. Initially, this circuit seems to go nowhere; money is exchanged only to return with the same amount of money.[49] Marx amends the circuit slightly to accommodate the goal of bourgeois society: M–C–M', where M' is the equivalent of M with an additional amount of M. The additional amount of M is called 'surplus value'.[50] For the capitalist, the whole purpose is the reinvestment of the surplus to renew the cycle and generate ever more surplus value. The desire for never-ending accumulation is the overriding purpose of the capitalist.

> Accumulate, accumulate! That is Moses and the prophets! . . . Accumulation for accumulation's sake, production for production's sake: by this formula classical economy expressed the historical mission of the bourgeoisie, and did not for a single instant deceive itself over the birth-throes of wealth.[51]

The bourgeois society is characterized by this circuit of accumulation, subjecting every capitalist to its motive. All other considerations must be subjugated to the motive of accumulation. 'Use values must therefore never be looked upon as the real aim of the capitalist.'[52] Therefore, capitalists have no concern for the utility (or disutility) of their products except in their ability to be exchanged for further accumulation.

The next step in the demystification of bourgeois society is the identification of the origin of surplus value that allows accumulation, the transformation of M–C–M'. Returning to his discussion of value and labour, Marx re-centres the analysis on the labour performed by the worker in the process of production. He begins with a critique of those he terms 'vulgar economists'.[53] These economists claimed that the owners make their profit by selling a product for greater than the purchase price of its component parts. According to this view, workers are unable to sell their labour power for greater than its cost (unlike the business owner), and thus workers receive no profit from their labour power.[54] According to Smith, labour produces value in production, but nearly all labourers in bourgeois society work for another who supplies the workers with materials necessary for their work. Profit is the deduction, from wages, of the share of the value taken by the business owner for advancing the workers the materials of production.[55] Profit is, in effect, a fee paid by the worker for the privilege of working for the business owner. In both of these explanations the business owner's actions are responsible for producing profit. Marx felt the explanations were unsatisfactory and set about describing the origin of profit in production.

For Marx, the working day is the key to the origin of profit and the production of surplus value. In order for the system of commodity production to work, there must first exist 'free' labour: free in the sense that the person 1) is not obligated to someone else, for example, as a slave, and 2) cannot survive without wages, meaning they do not own the materials necessary for their own survival such as land, machinery and so forth. Individuals who do not possess the capital necessary for their own livelihood are compelled, if they are to survive, to sell the only commodity they have, the capacity to work, 'labour-power'. The capitalist purchases not a definite amount of labour, but the worker's capacity to work over a given time-frame, a working day. Thus the capitalist does not purchase a specific amount of energy expended by the worker, but, basically, contracts the worker for the day, leaving the specific amount of energy expended, and value produced, to vary.[56]

The total amount of value produced during the working day is divided into two components. The first is the amount of value necessary to keep the worker alive in good health, as well as the worker's family. Like any other commodity, the value of the product is equal to the amount of labour necessary for its production. Thus the value of the labour-power sold by the worker is equal to the amount of labour time necessary for the reproduction of the worker, and family.[57] The portion of the working day consumed to produce the value necessary to meet the subsistence needs of the worker is called 'necessary labour-time'.[58]

Once workers complete the necessary labour-time, they continue to produce more value, but this value is not for themselves; it is for the capitalist. The worker 'creates surplus-value which, for the capitalist, has all the charms of a creation out of nothing'.[59] The workday is divided between the necessary labour and surplus labour. Likewise, the workday is divided between necessary value and surplus value. By identifying the production of surplus-value in the labour process, Marx is able to argue that exploitation is inherent in the system of commodity production. The extraction of value from the labour of workers is not a qualitative question of working conditions, but an empirical question of the origin of value. 'The rate of surplus-value is therefore an exact expression for the degree of exploitation of labour-power by capital, or of the labourer by the capitalist.'[60] Whether workers are thought to be pampered or abused in any number of disparate contexts, they remain alienated from the product of their labour and exploited, since the sale of their labour-power is the source of the capitalist's profits.

The goal of the capitalist is, as mentioned above, to accumulate. The workday is one of the means through which individual business owners attempt to expand their capital. The workday is divided into the necessary and surplus labour, and it is in the capitalist's interest to extract as much surplus labour as possible from the worker.[61] This may be accomplished by 'lengthening the working day and intensifying labour'.[62] It is in the interest of the capitalist to make the working day as long as possible to extend the amount of surplus value that the workers produce above the cost to reproduce themselves.[63]

> But in its blind unrestrainable passion, its were-wolf hunger for surplus labour, capital oversteps not only the moral, but even the merely physical maximum bounds of the working-day. It usurps the time for growth, development, and healthy maintenance of the body. It steals the time required for the consumption of fresh air and sunlight. It higgles over a meal-time, incorporating it where possible with the process of production itself, so that food is given to the labourer as to a mere means of production, as coal is supplied to the boiler, grease and oil to the machinery. It reduces the sound sleep needed for the restoration, reparation, refreshment of the bodily powers to just so many hours of torpor as the revival of an organism, absolutely exhausted, renders essential.[64]

The capitalist, in their individual interest, will attempt to prolong the working day to the greatest length possible, at the expense of the health of the worker. Only through the pervasive struggle of worker against capitalist to settle, in legislation, the proper length of the workday has the workday been reduced from its maximum.[65]

While Marx's examples tend to be rooted in a manufacturing context, a contemporary example of the extension and intensification of the workday can be identified in white-collar employment, in office work. Jill Andresky Fraser documents the role technology plays in further diminishing our social lives by further infringing on our control over our productive activity. Work hours are extended as expectations about the number of hours required for a job increase and technology 'spills' into personal time.[66] Employees are increasingly expected to answer emails and return calls during personal time.[67] Fraser argues that employers intentionally encroach upon workers' lunches to increase their output. The employers, through these mechanisms, are extending the workday with the purpose of extracting more surplus value from the workers. At the same time, white-collar wages have stagnated, and the fear of losing one's job due to downsizing has added to the pressures on workers to be more productive while at work, intensifying productivity.[68] These trends are also linked to the alienation discussed above. Because bosses control workers' time, workers lose valuable interaction with friends and family.[69] The extension and intensification of labour leads to greater alienation from the act of production, from others and from species being.

Towards the *Manifesto*

The combined alienation of the worker and the exploitation inherent in commodity production was not just an academic or philosophical question for Marx. As he noted in the eleventh of his *Theses on Feuerbach*: 'The philosophers have only *interpreted* the world in various ways; the point is to *change* it.'[70] In 1846 Marx began forming, and participating in, various political organizations such as the Communist Correspondence Committee and the Communist League.[71] At the end of the second congress of the Communist League in 1847, Marx and Engels were chosen to write the manifesto outlining its principles.[72] Written before *Capital*, the *Manifesto of the Communist Party* represents a combination of the goals of the Communist League and the distillation of Marx's ideas up to that point in time.

In the *Manifesto* Marx and Engels outline a trajectory in which the bourgeois society undermines its own future. The underlying logic of capital accumulation demands that capitalists must perpetually revolutionize production. 'The need of a constantly expanding market for its products chases the bourgeoisie over the whole surface of the globe.'[73] Accumulation grows, and the sheer amount of capital in the economy expands. Marx refers to the ever-growing expansion of capital in the bourgeois society as the concentration of capital. Accumulation accelerates, but this expansion of capitalist accumulation also leads to the merging of capital into a few hands.[74] 'One capitalist always kills many.'

> Capital grows in one place to a huge mass in a single hand, because it has in another place been lost by many. This is centralisation proper, as distinct from accumulation and concentration.[75]

The destruction of smaller capitalists by larger capitalists, and the consolidation of wealth in few hands is centralization.

Caught between the worsening condition of the working classes relative to the capitalist elite on the one hand, and the ever-increasing centralization of capital on the other, the bourgeois society is pushed to the verge of open class war. In the *Manifesto* Marx and Engels conclude with a ringing cry: 'Let the ruling classes tremble at a Communistic revolution. The proletarians have nothing to lose but their chains. They have a world to win. WORKING MEN OF ALL COUNTRIES, UNITE!'[76] In *Capital* Marx asserts that

> Along with the constantly diminishing number of the magnates of capital, who usurp and monopolise all advantages of this process of transformation, grows the mass of misery, oppression, slavery, degradation, exploitation; but with this too grows the revolt of the working class, a class always increasing in numbers, and disciplined, united, organised by the very mechanism of the process of capitalist production itself . . . Centralisation of the means of production and the socialisation of labour at last reach a point where they become incompatible with their capitalist integument. This integument is burst asunder. The knell of capitalist private property sounds. The expropriators are expropriated.[77]

As with other ideas, so Marx's analysis appears, and reappears throughout his work, more refined and integrated into his broader conceptualization at every iteration.

Although the themes in the *Manifesto of the Communist Party* are both rooted in Marx's earlier work and rehearsed in his later publications, it is a polemical work intended to make a specific political statement at a precise historical moment. Reflecting on its merits, Marx and Engels felt that the *Manifesto* was essentially correct in its theoretical principles, but was less grounded in historical analysis.[78] The *Manifesto* also simplified class relations and the role of the government in revolution.[79] It was intended to rally the exploited classes of Europe into action, and was not, like *Capital*, to be a systematic study of bourgeois society.

The *Manifesto*, published in 1848, was uniquely suited to its historical moment in time. Europe was about to erupt into an open clash between the ruling elite and their opponents. In the ensuing revolts, Marx was expelled from Belgium and made his way to Cologne.[80] There he started a newspaper, the *Neue Rheinische Zeitung*, which reported the revolutionary activity going on across Europe.[81] Pressure began building on the paper from government forces. In the end, Marx was again expelled to France.[82] It was not too long after this that he was forced to leave France for London.[83]

In London Marx would reflect on the recent revolutionary activity in Europe and conduct the research necessary for writing *Capital*. In the *Eighteenth Brumaire of Louis Bonaparte* Marx would analyse the failure of the revolution in France. The text is an application of the historical method to a specific event. Marx begins by outlining the conditional nature of social change and human agency.

> [People] make their own history, but they do not make it just as they please; they do not make it under circumstances chosen by themselves, but under circumstances directly encountered, given and transmitted from the past. The tradition of all the dead generations weighs like a nightmare on the brain of the living.[84]

According to Marx, the events of the French revolution and counter-revolution are rooted in the material class interests of the wealthy who owned land (landed aristocracy) and the wealthy who owned capital (capital bourgeoisie). The ideological differences between the groups are rooted in the class differences.

> Upon the different forms of property, upon the social conditions of existence, rises an entire superstructure of different and distinctly formed sentiments, illusions, modes of thought and views of life. The entire class creates and forms them out of its material foundations and out of the corresponding social relations.[85]

The failure of the French revolution of 1848 resulted from the opposition of the capital bourgeoisie to both the working class and the landed aristocracy. The conflict of the two wealthy classes led to the coalition of Napoleon III with the peasantry, eventually leading to Napoleon's consolidation of power as emperor of France.

Marx's analysis of the French revolution highlighted the historical contingency of worker rebellions and the transition to communism. The latter process is predicated on the working classes gaining political power.[86] As the French revolution of 1848 demonstrated, the process is not a certainty. If the working classes are successful, the aim of the communist society is to eliminate private property and establish a society where labour is no longer isolated alienated labour, but a communal activity. The *Manifesto of the Communist Party* suggests certain measures to begin the process: abolition of private property; progressive income tax; eliminating inheritance; confiscating rebel property; centralizing banking, communication and transportation; improvement of the soil; participation by everyone in the labour of society; eliminating the distinction between town and country by decreasing the concentration of people; and free education. As the working class deepens the reforms and eliminates the domination of one class by another, political power will dissipate.[87]

However, communism is not simply the elimination of private property, but the realization of species being. If private property is eliminated, but the relationships of society change only in that the community is now the possessor of the private property, communism would only be realized in crude form. If workers still work for wages, but are paid by the community, it would replicate the relations of private property.[88] To be fully developed communism, people must be able to achieve their species being.

> In a higher phase of communist society, after the enslaving subordination of the individual to the division of labour, and thereby also the antithesis between mental and physical labour, has vanished; after labour has become not only a means of life but life's prime want; after the productive forces have also increased with the all-round development of the individual, and the springs of common wealth flow more abundantly – only then can the narrow horizon of bourgeois right be crossed in its entirety and society inscribe on its banners: From each according to [one's] abilities, to each according to [one's] needs![89]

Once past the initial stage, communism was the transcendence of alienating labour to allow people to engage in social activity that affirmed people's species being while meeting the needs of the whole. It was, however, not an easy process.

> In order to abolish the *idea* of private property, the *idea* of communism is quite sufficient. It takes *actual* communist action to abolish actual private property. History will lead to it; and this movement, which *in theory* we already know to be a self transcending movement, will constitute in actual fact a very rough and protracted process.[90]

In the years after the revolutionary ferment of 1848 and his subsequent relocation to London Marx focused on his seminal work, *Capital.* While attempting to prepare it for publication, however, Marx experienced severe financial difficulties. He attempted to support himself by publishing newspaper articles and shorter books, but relied heavily on Engels for financial support. Though his income was apparently sufficient to satisfy his basic needs, Marx sought to maintain the trappings of a middle-class lifestyle.[91] Progress on *Capital* was also slowed by health problems plaguing Marx and his family. Marx suffered liver problems, and his wife, Jenny, fell desperately ill from smallpox. She would recover, but Marx relied on Jenny to transcribe his poor handwriting and manage much of his affairs.[92]

While the revenue from newspaper contributions was helpful, Marx held this work in contempt.[93] In 1850 and 1851 he was, however, able to spend considerable time in the British Museum researching economic history.[94] He continued to be distracted by his contrary nature and proclivity to critically digest anything he felt relevant to his study. He also became involved in the Working Men's International Association (The International), which took considerable time away from *Capital.*[95] While Marx did not form the International, he penned its Inaugural Address and Preamble as well as its rules.[96] Marx was able to produce the *Grundrisse* as a rough draft of *Capital* in 1858, but was sidetracked by his study of political economy. The final corrections for the finished first volume of *Capital* were not delivered until August 1867.[97]

Legacy

The legacy of *Capital* is undeniable. The work of Marx has been incorporated into contemporary analyses of the global economy.[98] Samir Amin in his *Capitalism in the Age of Globalization* returns to Marx to assert the primacy of the logic of capital to drive global economic polarization. Reforms on the part of the government and international agencies like the World Bank and International Monetary Fund are, Amin contends, insufficient to address this polarization, because of the underlying goals of capital. As in Marx, the capitalist world economy is not in need of reform, but is fundamentally oriented to favour the interests of the few through the accumulation of the surplus value workers produce.[99]

In contrast, Joseph Stiglitz raises Marx's name only to dismiss the failure of the Soviet economic model. Instead of the underlying logic of capital as the source of global crisis, Stiglitz points to differences in state policy as the source of differences in inequality.[100] For Stiglitz, the imposition of a collection of policies, called the Washington Consensus, directly contributes to the failure of global poverty reduction.[101] Marx as well as Amin would argue that the growing inequality and poverty are the result of the fundamental logic of capital; workers' conditions, be their pay high or low, will tend to deteriorate relative to the accumulation and centralization of capital. Amin argues that the aim of state institutions is to facilitate capitalist accumulation, causing the inequality and poverty mentioned by Stiglitz.

Interestingly, recent scholarship on Marx has expanded into the study of the environment. Marx's analysis of nature is rooted in the necessary premise of human beings' interaction with nature. Labour is 'an eternal nature-imposed necessity, without which there can be no material exchanges between [people] and Nature, and therefore no life'.[102] Returning to the themes of the 1844 manuscripts, interaction with nature is a necessity for one's survival as well as the full development of species being: 'Labor is, in the first place, a process in which both [people] and Nature participate, and in which . . . [a person] starts, regulates, and controls the material re-actions between [oneself] and Nature.'[103] Marx understood this necessary relationship as a 'metabolism' between people and nature.

The accumulation logic of capital led to the exploitation of nature as well as labour: 'Moreover, all progress in capitalist agriculture is a progress in the art, not only of robbing the labourer, but of robbing the soil; all progress in increasing the fertility of the soil for a given time, is a progress towards ruining the lasting sources of that fertility.'[104] As a result of capitalist agriculture, the natural metabolic processes of the environment are interrupted. The concentration of humans in cities, distanced from the fields that produced their food, causes ecological problems. 'In London, for instance, they find no better use for the excretion of four-and-a-half million human beings than to contaminate the Thames with it at heavy expense.'[105] This town–country divide creates a 'rift' in nature's metabolism.[106]

Contemporary authors have incorporated Marx's analysis into their study of the environment. In their text *The Ecological Rift: Capitalism's War on the Earth*, John Bellamy Foster, Brett Clark and Richard York specifically adopt Marx's concept of metabolic rift and apply it to contemporary circumstances.[107] In another application of Marx's work to the environment, Nicholas Georgescu-Roegen relates the entropy law (in doing work, energy tends to become unusable) to economics to come to a grave conclusion about the prospects of future generations. The entropy law states that energy tends to move from usable forms to unusable forms in the process of doing some form of work. The burning of coal will generate steam energy, but it also loses some heat that can no longer be used to do further work. 'The thesis that I have endeavored to develop,' he writes, is 'that the basic nature of the economic process is entropic and that the Entropy Law rules supreme over this process and over its evolution.'[108] Due to the progress of technology, society has shifted from readily available solar energy to earth's mineral resources, which are much less abundant. The result, according to Georgescu-Roegen, is that civilization reaches closer to its end the more technology is applied to consume Earth's material resources.[109] Other authors have since combined entropy and Marx to critically evaluate the effects of capitalism on the environment.[110]

Given Marx's method and the scope of issues that he covered, it is unsurprising that he continues to inspire new authors and approaches. His work has spawned a number of 'schools' of thought: dependency theory, the Frankfurt School, structural Marxism, Leninism and the world-system perspective, to name just a few. His thought has been incorporated into gender and race studies, most notably by W.E.B. DuBois. Recent applications of Marx to environmental issues demonstrate the flexibility of his method and insights. Few economic thinkers can claim such a broad and profound influence as Karl Marx, but Marx, admittedly, had far more he hoped to accomplish. A telling sign of this is the section in the third volume of *Capital* on 'Classes', with which Marx is most closely associated. It barely spans a page. The chapter ends, enigmatically, with the words 'Here the manuscript breaks off.'[111]

FIVE

ALFRED MARSHALL

Katia Caldari

Alfred Marshall was born in London on 26 July 1842, the second son of the five children of William Marshall and Rebecca Oliver. As an adult, he was described as a 'small slight man with bushy moustache and long hair, nervous movements, sensitive and unhealthy pallid complexion and preternaturally keen and apprehending eyes'. Alfred's character was certainly influenced by his father.[1] A clerk in the Bank of England, William Marshall was a typical mid-Victorian paterfamilias, particularly severe and with a strong sense for discipline, softened however by the 'constant gentleness' of Rebecca.[2] At the age of nine Alfred entered the Merchant Taylors, an Anglican school with a strong reputation for classical studies. In 1861 he won a prize life fellowship at Oxford, but turned it down, deciding to go to Cambridge instead, to study mathematics. He took the Tripos examinations in January 1865, including papers on Euclidean geometry, applied mathematics and theoretical physics.

Soon after his graduation Marshall was appointed to a temporary teaching position in mathematics at Clifton College in Bristol, returning to Cambridge in 1868 as Lecturer in Moral Sciences. Along with his interest in mathematics, he had become interested in philosophy, and attended the meetings of the Cambridge Philosophical Society, the Cambridge Reform Club and the Grote Club.[3]

In those years Marshall began what he himself defined as his 'apprenticeship in economics', studying the works of several of the thinkers addressed in this volume (Smith, Ricardo, Mill) as well as German economists such as J. H. von Thünen and W. Röcher. He filled his copies of their works with copious annotations, which often took the form of diagrams or equations, particularly on the concepts of value, money, labour and capital.[4]

Marshall's interest in philosophy transcended mathematics and economics alike, however, to the point that in a letter from 1900 written to James Ward, Professor of Mental Philosophy and Logic at Cambridge, Marshall declared that 'mental science' had been his 'home', at least until 1871, when

> The increasing urgency of economic studies as a means toward human well-being grew upon me. About 1871–2, I told myself the time had come at which I must decide whether to give my life to psychology or economics. I spent one year in doubt: always preferring psychology for the pleasures of the chase; but economics grew more and more in practical urgency, not so much in relation to the growth of wealth as to the quality of life; and I have settled down to it.'[5]

In Victorian Britain poverty, health, housing and labour conditions certainly were urgent problems. They were widely discussed by politicians and intellectuals as well as economists.[6] This discussion gave birth to some forms of moderate socialism that did not advocate the end of capitalism, such as those championed by the Fabians, trade unions, Friendly Societies and cooperatives – institutions with whom Marshall corresponded, collaborated and, sometimes, conflicted.

Marshall started his career as an economist endeavouring to understand and solve the problem of poverty, a central question in all his reflections and writings. As stressed by Marshall himself before the Royal Commission for the Aged Poor (1893): 'I have devoted myself for the last twenty-five years to the problem of poverty and . . . very little of my work has been devoted to an inquiry which does not bear on that.'[7] For him one of the most dangerous aspects of poverty was to be found in the large masses of people with 'poor physique and feeble will, with no enterprise, no courage, no hope and scarcely any self-respect whom misery drives to work for lower wages than the same work gets in the country'.[8] That precious potential hidden inside each individual was thereby neglected and hence wasted: a most grievous loss for the country.

Marshall was very critical of the suggestion that the problem of poverty could be solved through charity or automatic relief. As he explained to Helen Bosanquet, leader of the Charity Organization Society (COS), editor of its review, and member of the Royal Commission on the Poor Laws and Relief and Distress in 1905–9, 'poverty and pain, disease and death are evils of much less importance than they appear, except insofar as they lead to weakness of life and character & that true philanthropy aims at increasing strength more than at diminishing poverty'.[9] For him – in the spirit of J. S. Mill's investigations into 'ethology', or the science of character – the only serious remedy was connected with the improvement of people's character, which required a general betterment of quality of life and labour conditions as well as a widespread diffusion of education. Through education the poor would improve their character (and become all 'gentlemen' and chivalrous) and better their condition both in the workplace and in society.[10] Education would transform unskilled into skilled labour and therefore increase labour's efficiency. Marshall considered the relation 'education–skilled work–higher labour productivity' a crucial element for the economic progress of a country. For this very reason he often emphasized that 'the best investment of the present capital of the country is to educate the next generation.'[11] Anticipating the modern concept of human capital, he insisted that 'we must regard a man as intelligent capital and try to make him productive.'[12]

Other elements were not to be overlooked: most notably a good quality of life in terms of housing and environment (clean and spacious houses, green space, clean air and so forth) and in terms of adequate labour conditions. These, too, were important influences on human character. In a speech given at the Cambridge Reform Club, in 1873, he emphatically remarks: 'Is it not true that when we say a man belongs to the working classes we are thinking of the effect that his work produces on him rather than the effect that he produces on his work?' and notes, 'the rougher the work of the body, the lower the condition of the mind.'[13] According to Marshall, work was not to be considered as 'a punishment for fault' but a precious tool for the formation of character and, more broadly, for progress.[14] He paid close attention to the kinds and the conditions of work: employments that promoted culture, a sense of responsibility and breadth (rather than narrow-mindedness) enabled employees to become 'gentlemen'. Unskilled, repetitive occupations demanding long hours of heavy physical exertion, by contrast, occupations that tired and restricted the mental faculties and took place in unhealthy environments, were prejudicial to the workers' character.

An interest in such topics is undoubtedly related to what Rita Tullberg has called Marshall's 'tendency to socialism', to his involvement with the Co-operative Movement, the Charity Organization Society, Christian Socialists and trade unions.[15] Though the label was still widely shunned by the respectable middle class, Marshall openly called himself a 'a socialist', one who 'endeavours to promote the social amelioration of the people'.[16] In the Preface to *Industry and Trade* (1919) he writes that he 'remained under the conviction that the suggestions, which are associated with the word "socialism" were the most important subject of study, if not in the world, yet at all events for me'.[17]

Alongside his Moral Sciences teaching at St John's College Cambridge, Marshall taught economics to women students of Newnham Hall: here he met Mary Paley, who became his wife in 1877.[18] According to the regulations of the time (changed in 1882), Marshall's marriage obliged him to resign his fellowship at St John's. He had to leave Cambridge. He went first to Bristol as Principal of University College and Professor of Political Economy, and then, in 1883, to Oxford as Fellow of Balliol College and Lecturer in Political Economy. Henry Fawcett's death a year later created a vacancy for the Chair of Political Economy at Cambridge, for which Marshall successfully applied. At that time in Cambridge the teaching of Political Economy was part of the Moral Sciences Tripos. From his inaugural lecture on 'The Present Position of Economics', it was evident that Marshall sought to enhance the status of economics as a discipline by founding an autonomous Tripos in Economics and Political Sciences (duly established in 1903). With this end in mind he carefully framed the meaning, content and methodology of 'economics' – the label 'moral philosophy' was now firmly put to one side.

'Economics' was to be conceived as the science which is 'on the one side a study of wealth; and on the other and more important side, a part of the study of man'.[19] This 'man' was not 'an abstract economic man; but a man of flesh and blood'.[20] Economics is the branch of the social sciences that addresses business activities; it inevitably involves the desire for a material reward expressed in monetary terms. However, in Marshall's view, 'man's conduct in the business part of life' was largely influenced also by 'his personal affections, by his conceptions of duty and his reverence for high ideals'.[21] Moreover, if the quantifiable money motive made economics more exact than any other branch of social sciences, it nonetheless remained far less exact than the physical sciences, in so far as it 'deals with the ever changing and subtle forces of human nature'.[22] By dint of its multifaceted subject-matter, economics was a very complex science. Identifying an adequate methodological approach was a far from trivial question.

A Question of Method

The term 'neoclassical' was coined in 1900 by Thorstein Veblen, who noted a shared hedonistic premise uniting the classical school and the Cambridge School founded by Marshall.[23] The term indicated the continuity between the classical economists such as Smith, Ricardo and J. S. Mill on the one hand and Marshall's thought on the other. It is indeed true that Marshall recognized Mill's influence on his approach. As he noted in its preface, the *Principles* represented 'an attempt to present a modern version of old doctrines with the aid of the new work, and with reference to new problems, of our own age'.[24] But Marshall also underlined the limitations of his classical predecessors, such as Ricardo's 'tendency to indulge in excessively abstract reasonings'.[25] They were guilty of viewing man as 'a constant quantity', and of failing to acknowledge 'how liable to change are the habits and institutions of industry'.[26]

In order to be a science, economics had to be abstract, theoretical and deductive. But this was not sufficient; like the science of navigation, economics had two sides: 'one the analytical which is based in eternal laws of nature; the other realistic, which constantly changes, as man's needs and resources develop'.[27] If economics adopted an exclusively abstract and deductive approach, therefore, it became mere 'elegant toying', useless to understand real problems.[28] Induction as well as deduction was called for; they 'go hand in hand', Marshall wrote, recalling Schmöller and the German Historical School, although he reminds us that 'facts by themselves are silent.'[29]

According to this important premise, economics is not *the* perfect method but it should use *every* method known to the sciences (physics, philosophy, biology and so forth). Thus the mathematical method is only one among the several tools economic science may use: obviously, as Marshall notes (and given his background it could not be otherwise), mathematics plays a necessary role, providing 'a marvellous terse and exact language for expressing clearly some general relations and some short processes of economic reasoning'.[30] However, its utility is limited to the first steps of the analysis, when the matter and relations under consideration are simplified: 'while a mathematical illustration . . . may be complete in itself and strictly accurate within its clearly defined limits, it is otherwise with any attempt to grasp the whole of a complex problem of real life . . . in a series of equations.'[31]

By means of mathematics we can represent 'an edifice of pure crystal' that, however useful in throwing some light on real problems, is limited in its scope. While necessary to acquire some basic familiarity with a complex matter, mathematics should have been put to one side as analysis proceeded. Marshall had served his apprenticeship in economics translating Ricardo's and Mill's reasoning into mathematical forms, but in his main work, *The Principles of Economics* (1890), diagrams and equations are placed in the footnotes or in the appendices. Economics is a complex science that deals with manifold problems and relations; its complexity derives from that of its main focus, human nature. Strictly connected with human nature and human life is another important factor, 'time', considered 'a chief cause of . . . difficulties in economic investigations'.[32] Marshall tried to overcome this problem by developing a static method and introducing the so-called *Ceteris Paribus* pound: accordingly, the economist has

> to go step by step; breaking up a complex question, studying one bit at one time, and at last combining his partial solutions into a more or less complete solution of the whole riddle. In breaking it up, he segregates those disturbing causes, whose wanderings happen to be inconvenient, for the time in *a pound called Ceteris Paribus*. The study of some group of tendencies is isolated by the assumption other things being equal: *the existence of other tendencies is not denied, but their disturbing effect is neglected for a time.*[33]

Clearly the more the issue is circumscribed the more precisely it can be dealt with; but it corresponds less closely to 'real life', where 'other things' are very often *not* equal and constantly change.[34]

The time-period analysis which characterizes the *Principles of Economics* is developed through the distinction between 'short' and 'long' periods, referred to as the equilibrium between demand and supply for a single commodity. Recalling his early writings 'On Value' and 'On Wages', Marshall distinguishes between temporary equilibrium, short-period equilibrium and long-period equilibrium, where the crucial difference between them is the capacity of adjustment that supply has in response to demand: almost inexistent in a very short period (say one day, in which supply cannot be altered), very limited in a short period (say three months, in which small adjustments might be made in quantities offered), large in the long period (say five years, when scale of production and business organization could be modified accordingly).[35] However, Marshall was aware of the simplification implied in this approach: 'for the element of Time . . . is itself absolutely continuous . . . [and] nature knows no absolute partition of time into long periods and short.'[36] He nonetheless felt that it was 'the Principle of Continuity' that constituted the book's 'special character'.[37] This principle – synthetized in the motto 'Natura non facit saltum' (Latin: Nature does not jump) – allows us also to see that there is no caesura 'between normal values and "current" or "market" or "occasional" values'.[38]

This perspective moves Marshall away from the classical tradition and its clear-cut distinction between normal and market values and explains, at least in part, his disavowal of his first book, *Economics of Industry*, written with his wife and published in 1879. This volume, although rather critical of some parts of J. S. Mill's theory (such as the wage doctrine), has a clear Millian structure and a strong classical flavour, with a clear distinction between normal (long-period) and market (short-period) values, emphasized by their treatment in two different sections of the volume.[39] As recalled by another Cambridge economist, J. M. Keynes, Marshall 'grew very unfriendly' to his first book and 'after the publication of the *Principles* he suppressed it and replaced it in 1892, with an almost wholly different book under the same title, which was mainly an abridgement of the *Principles* . . . [*Elements of Economics of Industry*]'.[40]

In the attempt to introduce 'time' to his economic analysis Marshall elaborated the so-called representative firm, which represents 'in miniature the supply curve of the industry'.[41] Just as in a forest one tree may be chosen as representative of all the other trees (each of them at different stages of growth and decay), so in an industry firms may rise and fall, yet the representative firm can be taken as constant in its relative size.[42] The representative firm, therefore, would allow dealing with a long-period equilibrium without forgoing the several individual firms in disequilibrium, which belong to the industry in question.

However, the representative firm becomes problematic because of the so-called 'reconciliation problem', which arises when change – due to passage of time and its irreversibility – is dealt with in an equilibrium framework. If through the representative firm Marshall could 'visualize an industry supply schedule that was distinct from the cost functions of the heterogeneous set of firms comprising in the industry' and develop his equilibrium analysis along the supply schedule–curve, it nonetheless prevents him from the possibility of taking into account time irreversibility.[43] Marshall was deeply aware of the difficulty of introducing this irreversibility into his analytical framework. On this basis he had to recognize that that 'theory is out of touch with real conditions of life'.[44]

Marshall's Project

The *Principles of Economics* was written between 1881 and 1889 and published in 1890. It went through eight editions, the last of them in 1920. During this thirty-year period Marshall kept working on the book, trying to solve its 'more grievous obscurities'.[45] He was never satisfied. According to the original project, *Principles* should have been the first volume of a treatise in two parts, but the second volume never appeared and in the preface to the eighth edition Marshall had to confess:

> It is now thirty years since the first edition of this volume implied a promise that a second volume, completing the treatise, would appear within a reasonable time. But I had laid my plan on too large a scale; and its scope widened, especially on the realistic side, with every pulse of that Industrial Revolution of the present generation, which has far outdone the changes of a century ago, in both rapidity and breadth of movement. So ere long I was compelled to abandon my hope of completing the work in two volumes.[46]

In the following years Marshall began work on an alternative companion work entitled 'National Industries & International Trade', to be published in three volumes. This project also remained unfulfilled: the first volume was published in 1919 with the title *Industry and Trade*; the second in 1923 as *Money, Credit and Commerce*; the third volume remained unpublished, although Marshall never abandoned his project. Notes for this volume on economic progress are preserved at the Marshall Library Archive at Cambridge.

The *Principles of Economics* is considered Marshall's magnum opus. It was a success from the moment it was first published. As underlined by Joseph Schumpeter: 'The book was a great performance. And this performance was presented in a most attractive garb that suited to perfection the humors of the time and the prevailing conditions in the field of economics – indeed it does as much credit to the judgement as it does to the genius of the author.'[47] It remained the most important book on economics until at least the 1920s, particularly in Britain.[48] This does not mean that it did not encounter severe criticism, which finally resulted in an oversimplified understanding of Marshall's contribution to economics, often reduced to a handful of tools that are still found in most economic textbooks (demand and supply curves, elasticity of demand, partial equilibrium, consumer's surplus). Many argued that the 'core' of Book v, devoted to the 'General Relations of Demand, Supply and Value', was undermined by the rest of the book, given over to a kind of incoherent and ambiguous 'trimming'.

As Samuelson put it: 'Marshall was a victim of what the modern Freudians call self-hate. He was a good chess player who was ashamed of playing chess, a good analytical economist who was ashamed of analysis.'[49] However, as we have seen, the *Principles* was designed as an introductory volume, which was to have been followed by others. Marshall himself reminds us that Book v only 'deals with abstractions'. As such (in keeping with Marshall's methodology), we could argue that his critics are attributing too much significance to this part.[50] To comprehend Marshall's true contribution to economics and the subjects on which he concentrated most of his energy it is therefore necessary to go beyond the *Principles of Economics* (and especially Book v) and consider his other writings, most notably *Industry and Trade*, but also the preparatory notes for the volume on progress.

Industry and Trade, 'a study of industrial technique and business organization; and of their influences on the conditions of various classes and nations', is a comparative study of some countries' industrial development, characteristics and leadership. Its motto, 'The many in the one, the one in many', is strictly connected with that of the *Principles* ('Natura non facit saltum'), a connection that Marshall explains as follows:

> the maxim that 'Nature does not willingly make a jump' (*Natura abhorret saltum*) is specially applicable to economic developments. Partly in consequence, economic conditions and tendencies show, even more than most others, the One in the Many, the Many in the One: for those, which prevail at any place and time, reflect the habits of action, thought, feeling and aspiration of the whole people, or at least some large part of them. Each reacts on the character of the population: but the roots of all are deep set in the human characteristics of the place and time: thus the One is seen in the Many. And conversely each tendency embodies in some degree almost every influence, that is prominent then and there: insomuch that a full study of

> it would present incidentally a nearly complete picture of the whole: thus the Many are seen in the One.[51]

Money, Credit and Commerce was published in 1923, one year before Marshall's death: its interest is more limited than the other volumes, especially because it is a sort of 'pastiche', 'pieced together with earlier fragments, some of them written fifty years before'.[52] But the limited scope of the volume is explicitly admitted by Marshall himself, who notes in the preface that the volume accomplishes only 'one-half of the [original] task', which was inherent to 'the study of the influences of the conditions of man's life and work'.[53] He goes on to write that 'a little progress has been made in regard to the second half,' but he never finished. He died in Cambridge a year later, in 1924.

Britain's Declining Competitiveness

In the late 1880s Britain confronted new, rapidly industrializing competitors such as Germany, France and the United States. The concern that British industries were losing ground led to the appointment of an 1886 Royal Commission to which businessmen and experts – including Marshall – gave evidence. Data on exports attest to a relative decline in the volume of British exports, especially for steel, iron and, from the late 1890s, textiles. Whereas Germany and the USA were profiting by the so-called second industrial revolution, Britain stayed true to her trusted methods, failing to move with the times. This explains why her decline in terms of productivity and competitiveness went from bad to worse in the following years. Marshall was one of a number of people who had been expressing concern about the condition of the British economy for more than a decade before the Royal Commission.

This concern frames all Marshall's reflections and explains his careful analysis of industrial organization and detailed study of the organization of labour, firms, industry and trade, and especially international trade. Back in 1875, using a legacy from an uncle, he spent four months in America where he met with several economists, trade unionists and workers and observed American industry up close.[54] He was a regular visitor to factories throughout his life, in Germany as well as Britain. Here he found proof of the influence of the conditions of work on the character and efficiency of the workers and noted how the mechanical work of modern factories tended to make workers an appendage of machinery, with negative effects on their character, physique, mental acuity and, therefore, on the well-being of society as a whole. It was during his 'wanderjahre among factories' that Marshall became persuaded of the dangers of large businesses and developed his preference for small and medium-size firms.[55]

Marshall was the first economist to consider industrial organization as the fourth productive factor, along with the classical trio of 'land, work and capital'. The issue of industrial organization is introduced in Book IV of *Principles* but developed more deeply in *Industry and Trade*. By means of a historical and comparative study, Marshall underlines the tendencies that were then progressively shaping the chief economies (mass production and the ever-larger businesses) and develops a detailed analysis of standardization, technical influences on the size of firms, marketing, organization and scientific management. While noting that large-scale business was a sign of industrial times, Marshall emphasized the importance of small and medium firms: industrial reality is and must be made of small and medium as well as large firms; each type of firm has good reasons for existing and has its own advantages and disadvantages. Marshall does not contrast large firms with small ones, but weak ones – those without initiative and innovation. He recognized that 'size' was important and could make an important difference in terms of productivity and technical efficiency. He remained convinced, however, that small firms could compete with large businesses if clustered in the same district.

An industrial district (such as Lancashire, which Marshall knew well) is characterized by a special 'atmosphere', which makes human relationships easier and fosters an exchange of ideas and information that drives innovation. The presence of that 'atmosphere' is the main difference between an industrial district and a large firm. It takes time to develop the requisite experience, the cumulative growth of knowledge, that enables districts to meet external changes. In a district, each firm specializes in one stage of the productive process, and each stage is not isolated but related to the others. In a district, firms are in competition with one another, but there is also a cooperative spirit born of physical proximity, shared history and the contiguity of their markets. Large size, by contrast, breeds structural rigidity, bureaucracy and routines that prevent businesses from adapting quickly to change. This is why, for Marshall, small and medium firms – 'the best educators of the initiative and versatility' – were to be considered the chief means to avoid economic decline.

Marshall gave the flexibility/rigidity relationship particular attention. In the late 1860s, while still deeply involved in philosophy, he gave four lectures at Cambridge's Grote Club: 'The Law of Parsimony', 'Ferrier's Proposition One', 'Ye Machine' and 'The Duty of the Logician or System-maker to the Metaphysician and to the Practical Man of Science'. In these papers there is a focus on psychology, to the study of the functioning of the human mind, the working of mental activities and the features of human knowledge. In the first two papers Marshall criticizes traditional psychology's mechanistic epistemology, which denied self-consciousness. In 'Ferrier's proposition one', Marshall particularly focuses on self-consciousness, which he sees as one of the two requirements for a 'general theory of psychology . . . capable of being developed into the true one'. In the third paper, 'Ye Machine', Marshall studies the functioning of mind, mixing together Babbage's studies on artificial intelligence and the evolutionary psychology of Bain and Spencer. Finally, in the fourth paper Marshall deals with the debate sparked by the discovery of non-Euclidean geometries.

These early philosophical writings are of great importance in understanding Marshall's reasoning on several topics: from his idea of the growth of knowledge, understood as the product of a mix of routine and innovation, to the rejection of the neoclassical concept of *homo œconomicus* in favour of 'a man of flesh and blood'; from his view of industrial and social organizations to the use of partial equilibrium analysis; from his critical position towards some political and social issues such as socialism, trade unions and bureaucracy to the idea that progress must advance slowly. For all these subjects, the paper 'Ye Machine' is particularly relevant: the mind is considered as a system of subsystems which evolves with experience and which is characterized by a certain set of routines (its 'character'); human actions and mental processes are based on a mixture of standardization and variation as natural selection identifies successful routines for repetition, while variation and foresight explore new paths when routines fail. External changes elicit mental and physical reactions: through the process of trial and error, man tries to face unknown and uncommon events. Successful trials are likely to be repeated and therefore to become 'routines'. Man uses the same routine when he faces a similar or analogous situation. Human actions and mental processes consist of a certain number of routines, but there must also exist a degree of freedom, because new events occur continually and the human mind must be free to start new processes of trial and selection.

The growth of knowledge is 'a never-ending process requiring both creativity and standardization', for which imagination plays a crucial role.[56] It is not by chance that, according to Marshall, imagination is a fundamental faculty for the economist – along with perception and reason – helping 'to put him on the track of those causes of visible events which are remote or lie below the surface, and of those effects of visible causes which are remote or lie below the surface'.[57] The 'machine' is endowed with a proper character, which gives it the power of anticipating the future and which evolves with experience. This is true also for individuals, who therefore cannot be considered simply as 'economic men', driven by short-term satisfactions. The working of a human brain strongly resembles that of a flexible production system (small firms rather than large ones, especially when collected in industrial districts) because both must exhibit the ability to change, evolve and create.[58] This explains Marshall's view of large integrated businesses as overly rigid and insufficiently plastic, as well his suspicion of business organization based on scientific management, on account of its bureaucratic structure, based on a fixed determination of functions and roles.[59]

The study of the human mind is also important in Marshall for the analysis of marketing activities and for explaining evolution, which must unavoidably rely on a certain degree of stability but also on the possibility to change. The necessary coexistence of change and stability, freedom and routine, also helps to better understand Marshall's analytical tool of partial equilibrium. As the machine needs a certain degree of stabilized routines in order to face sudden unexpected events, so, from the analytical point of view, the *Ceteris Paribus* pound allows us to concentrate on certain elements, leaving aside those that are not implicated in the change.[60] The structure and working of 'Ye Machine' finally helps us to understand Marshall's criticism of trade unions, socialism and bureaucracy in so far as they may also become too rigid, hampering change, creativity and freedom of action.

The High Theme of Progress

Economic progress is the underlying topic in almost all Marshall's writings and was the subject of his last, unfinished book: in fact, according to Marshall 'the growth of mankind in numbers, in health and strength, in knowledge, ability, and in richness of character is the end of all our studies.'[61] The concept of progress with its complexity cannot be fully understood by means of equations and quantitative relations, as Marshall carefully warns in Book v of *Principles:*

> The theory of stable equilibrium of normal demand and supply helps indeed *to give definiteness to our ideas*; and in its elementary stages it does not diverge from the actual facts of life . . . But when pushed to its more remote and intricate logical consequences, it slips away from the conditions of real life. In fact we are here verging on the high theme of economic progress; and here therefore it is especially needful to remember that economic problems are imperfectly presented when they are treated as problems of statical equilibrium, and not of organic growth.[62]

These words point to another important feature of Marshall's approach, the role he assigned to biology. Contemporaries such as Walras, Menger and Jevons sought to make economics as 'exact' a science as physics. Marshall felt economics to be closer to biology than to physics or mechanics, the subject-matter of which 'is constant and unchanged in all countries and in all ages', where changes were 'in the quantity and not in the character of the forces at work'.[63] For him, 'the Mecca of the economist lies in economic biology' because 'economics, like biology, deals with a matter, of which the inner nature and constitution, as well as the outer form, are constantly changing.'[64] In *Principles*, especially in Book v, Marshall admittedly employed several mechanical analogies, but this only served to clarify once more the scope of that volume: the simple relations of cause–effect typical of mechanics are suited for a study intended as a 'general introduction'. 'In the latter stages of economics, when we are approaching nearly to the conditions of life,' however, 'biological analogies are to be preferred to mechanical.'[65]

Biology helps economists focus on life, change and evolution, with an understanding of progress as 'organic growth' rather than 'mere increase or decrease'.[66] Evolution proceeds in an incremental fashion, and although over time there may be some crucial steps, the passage from one step to another is not sudden: 'Natura non facit saltum,' recalls Marshall, as progress (like evolution) needs to maintain a certain degree of stability within the change. This is true for each human being whose body, in becoming older, undergoes successive physical changes while preserving a certain stability. It is all the more true for institutions that are in being for a much longer time than individuals.

This is a very important and necessary condition for Marshall: 'though institutions may be changed rapidly; yet if they are to endure they must be appropriate to man: they cannot retain their stability if they change very much faster than he does. Thus progress itself increases the urgency of the warning that in the economic world, Natura non facit saltum. Progress must be slow.'[67] Therefore, even if progress results in an increase of man's command over nature, it demands the development of the higher faculties that allow men to use that power correctly, otherwise 'progress' has to be considered with 'grave suspicion'.[68]

For Marshall, progress has a dynamic dimension that occurs more in qualitative than in quantitative changes, and therefore cannot be characterized exclusively in terms of added increments of 'wealth', because it involves other and more important factors. In fact, 'the production of wealth is but a means to the sustenance of man; to the satisfaction of his wants; and to the development of his activities, physical, mental and moral.'[69] True progress implies an increase in human well-being that is given by a necessary minimum level of material wealth *plus* a number of elements. Marshall gave great attention to the different aspects connected with individuals' quality of life, such as the quality of natural resources (air, water), housing and working conditions as well as urbanization. His idea of progress is very close to the modern concept of sustainable development.[70]

Alongside his support for competition and free markets, Marshall always stressed the important role of government in guaranteeing some fundamental goods and services of public interest. In 1897 Marshall contributed to another Royal Commission, this time on local taxation. In the Commission's report he emphasized that 'the constructive work of government . . . is itself life in one of its highest forms', and taxation, local and central, was to be considered 'but a means' to that end.[71] Ten years later his position had apparently shifted, however; 'intensity of State activity' was only foreseen 'for social ameliorations that are not fully within the range of private effort'.[72] Marshall suggested that right understanding of laissez-faire should be 'Let everyone work with all his might; and most of all let the Government arouse itself to do that work that is vital, and which none but Government can do efficiently.'[73]

Marshall was, on the other hand, rather sceptical and critical of a possible direct active role of the state in economic matters. Not only does the state create 'scarcely anything', but even if 'its vast resources enable it to buy the most up-to-date plant,' its bureaucratic structure and rigidity would prevent it from keeping pace with change.[74] State intervention is, therefore, only justified for control and not for management activities. For Marshall there were two important exceptions for which state management was not only accepted but even suggested: the postal service and, at least in part, railways.

The role of the state is particularly depicted in the notes left for his last unfinished book where he writes: 'it is reasonable to suppose that the chief aim of the Government of a Western country is to promote the well-being of the people.'[75] Among the services Marshall's state provides its citizens are streets, parks, telegraphs, telephones, water, gas, electricity supply, agricultural drainage and irrigation, universities, museums, hospitals and even 'the supply of meat, fruit, and other things which the consumer cannot test for himself'.[76] The state must also guarantee adequate houses for everyone, to allow them to grow 'healthy in mind and body'. It must ensure reasonable incomes, large enough to enable the citizen to support a family.[77] Not only does the state have a duty to guarantee appropriate conditions of life to its citizens, it may and on occasion must intervene in the economic sphere, limiting the free play of the market.

The state may also restrict freedom of action in the case of citizens of 'a lower order than the average man' such as 'madmen, idiots, and perhaps habitual drunkards', whose actions are deemed injurious to the public weal. The same is true in the case of those greedy individuals who neglect higher ends in order to increase individual material gain.[78] The most important function Marshall attributed to the state, however, is education: the state must guarantee a proper education to every class of the population, especially the poor, as education stimulates latent human resources and so represents a form of investment in man, the subtlest instrument of production, and the most productive. Moreover, education assists distributive justice by raising the wages of unskilled workers via an improvement in their capabilities.

In order to perform all these various tasks, the state needs funds, largely raised by taxation. Although it was a crucial topic in Marshall's reflections, as Peter Groenewegen notes 'he never wrote a general treatise on taxation and failed to complete the segment on tax foreshadowed for Book x of Volume 2 of the Principles.'[79] However, there are several 'interesting fragments on taxation', along with the two works he published on this topic: *The Memorandum on the Classification and Incidence of Imperial and Local Taxation* (1897) and *National Taxation after the War* (1917).[80] Marshall favoured progressive income taxes, although he also devotes attention to other taxes, on houses and land, on motor-cars, on saving, on income and wages, and on natural resources.[81] They are all evaluated in terms of equity, efficacy and consequences for well-being.

In the essay entitled 'National Taxation after the War', which appeared in an edited volume published in 1917, Marshall focuses mainly on the problem of the equity of the burden of national taxation. Once the necessaries of life are assured to everyone, taxation should proceed by shares 'graduated very steeply'.[82] However, according to Marshall, very high taxes were to be avoided not only because they could encourage evasion but also because they tended to create important distortions: if levied on capital they 'tend to check its growth and to accelerate its emigration'; if levied on large incomes they 'may check energy and enterprise'.[83] In any case direct taxation was to be preferred to indirect taxation, being more 'economical in operation' and easier to 'graduate'.[84] As he wrote in a letter to the Swedish economist Eli Filip Heckscher: 'I am a great admirer of direct taxation: and I should be glad to see any increased taxation which it may be necessary to impose on English working classes, levied directly.'[85] Particularly relevant was the so-called 'fresh air rate' suggested by Marshall in the *Memorandum for the Local Taxation* (1897). It was a tax on land with 'special site value', as distinguished from the rural land subjected to a rather low taxation. The tax had to be spent 'by local authority under full central control' on 'breaking out small green spots in the midst of dense industrial districts, and on the preservation of large green areas between different towns and between different suburbs which are tending to coalesce'.[86]

Legacy

At Marshall's death, the Cambridge School of Economics dominated the British academic scene. The achievements of its many students demonstrate the success of the school Marshall founded, promoted and developed 'as his child'. As Groenewegen notes, this success would probably 'have astonished him had he lived to see it'.[87]

The Cambridge School of Economics was particularly admired for its business education and industrial economics, distinguished by the emphasis given to economic history, statistics and questions of welfare. Among Marshall's pupils two names deserve a special mention: Arthur Cecil Pigou and John Maynard Keynes. Starting from Marshall's insights and reflections, both of these men developed an original approach: Pigou founded the so-called 'welfare economics' and Keynes became the father of modern macroeconomics. Their theories, for different reasons and mostly unintentionally, came to overshadow Marshall's own contribution, even in its most original and rich aspects.

Only recently has new research drawing on Marshall's correspondence, notes and unpublished works (notably the psychological essays) allowed a rediscovery of the father of economics, and a reassessment of his whole contribution.

SIX

JOSEPH SCHUMPETER

Mário Graça Moura

The Austrian-American economist Joseph Schumpeter is invariably considered one of the major names in twentieth-century economic thought, on a par with his contemporary John Maynard Keynes. In particular, he is credited with having placed innovation and entrepreneurship at the centre of the analysis of capitalism. Schumpeter himself often emphasizes the contrast between his vision and that of standard economics. He acknowledges the strong influence of the father of general equilibrium theory, Léon Walras, but dissents from the Walrasian view that economic life is passive and merely adaptive. He rejects the conception that economic change is an impersonal adaptation to external disturbances. 'In the Smith-Mill-Marshall theory,' Schumpeter protests, 'the economy grows like a tree . . . each situation grows out of the preceding one in a uniquely determined way.' Yet 'this is not so . . . response to objective opportunity is not uniquely determined and cannot be predicted'.[1]

Schumpeter's aim is precisely to explain how the economy *evolves* due to the endogenous emergence of novelty. Rather like Karl Marx, he has 'a vision of economic evolution as a distinct process generated by the economic system itself'.[2] In this vision, individuals are capable of a creative response, a response that 'creates situations from which there is no bridge to those situations that might have emerged in its absence'.[3] In the economic sphere, creative response means innovation, which is the function of entrepreneurs.

Entrepreneurial action is a creative *response*, however. It is contingent on the entrepreneur's subjectivity as well as on the context, including the specific institutional set-up. In the capitalist case, this institutional set-up encompasses private banks with the power to create means of payment: capitalism's characteristic way of financing innovation is through credit creation. In turn, the clustering of innovations so financed, as well as the process of absorption and adjustment that ensues, mean that business cycles – the recurrence of prosperity and recession – are a constitutive feature of the capitalist process.

But this is not all. Schumpeter is interested in the sociology as well as the economics of capitalism. The competitive process whereby innovative firms and industries come to replace conservative ones – the process of *creative destruction*, in Schumpeter's famous phrase – is also a process in which individuals and their families rise and fall in the social scale. Successful entrepreneurs acquire capitalist positions, whereas members of the capitalist class who fail to adjust to the new tend to lose their status. Through this rise and fall, the capitalist class renews itself whilst capitalism is reproduced in time.

Simultaneously, though, the capitalist process also tends to transform its own institutional framework. Capitalism, Schumpeter conjectures,

> creates, by rationalising the human mind, a mentality and a style of life incompatible with its own fundamental conditions, motives and social institutions, and will be changed, although not by economic necessity and probably even at some sacrifice of economic welfare, into an order of things which it will be merely [a] matter of taste and terminology to call Socialism or not.[4]

The Man and His Work

The man who formed and worked out this vision was born in a small Moravian town in 1883.[5] Now in the Czech Republic, Moravia was then part of the Austro-Hungarian empire. Schumpeter's widowed mother married an Austrian aristocrat, a retired high-ranking army officer. Because of this, Schumpeter was educated in an elite school in Vienna, where he also attended university. He completed his law degree in 1906, taking courses in economics, history, mathematics and philosophy. Friedrich von Wieser and Eugen von Böhm-Bawerk, distinguished economists of the Austrian School, were among his teachers.

Schumpeter soon left Vienna for Berlin and London, where he attended lectures, and worked for a while as a lawyer in Cairo. He then submitted his first book, a methodological defence of equilibrium economics, for his *Habilitation* (similar to a PhD degree) at the University of Vienna.[6] He subsequently (1909) secured a position as an 'extraordinary' (as in supernumerary) professor of economics at the University of Czernowitz, now Chernivtsi, in Ukraine. It was there that he wrote his second book, which presents his theory of economic evolution.[7] He went on to become a professor of economics in Graz, Austria, in 1911, visiting New York's Columbia University as an exchange professor in 1913/14. In 1914 he published his first history of economics, which was commissioned by Max Weber, one of the fathers of sociology.[8]

The First World War led to Schumpeter's involvement in politics. He wrote secret memoranda, which circulated in aristocratic circles, outlining a conservative, anti-German programme for Habsburg Austria–Hungary. In 1919, however, he participated in the 'Socialization Commission' created by the German government to study the takeover of the coal industry. Shorty afterwards, he was appointed Austrian Minister of Finance in a ruling coalition of socialists and conservatives, serving as an independent. He lasted just seven months. He went on to serve as president of a bank from 1921 to 1924: another unhappy experience, as the bank had to be restructured and Schumpeter was left with large debts, later repaid in full. He returned to academia only in 1925, becoming a professor in Bonn, Germany.

During this turbulent period, as well as in his Bonn years, Schumpeter was co-editor of the *Archiv für Sozialwissenschaft und Sozialpolitik*, the leading German journal in the social sciences. He produced long essays on money, on the viability of the capitalist state after the war, on imperialism, on the possibilities of socialism, and on social classes, as well as a methodological appraisal of Gustav von Schmoller, the leader of the German historical school, and the revised edition of his second book, later translated into English as *The Theory of Economic Development*.[9]

While a professor in Bonn, Schumpeter spent a few terms at Harvard University as a visiting professor (in 1927/28 and 1930), and he also lectured in Japan (in 1931), where he was much admired. His *Wanderjahre* finally ended in 1932, when he was appointed professor at Harvard. He remained there until his death in 1950, taking U.S. citizenship in 1939. In this phase of his career, he produced three books: the flawed, gigantic *Business Cycles*, which expands the argument of the *Theory* in the light of history; *Capitalism, Socialism and Democracy*, which discusses the tendency of capitalism to evolve into socialism and how socialism might work; and the unfinished, posthumously edited *History of Economic Analysis*.[10]

Schumpeter was president of the American Economic Association in 1948. Earlier he had been president of the Econometric Society, of which he was one of the founders. At the time of his death, he was slated to be the first president of the International Economic Association. Still, he must have felt somewhat isolated in his last years. In the 1940s academic economists had largely surrendered to Keynes, whose economics Schumpeter rejected. Moreover, the formalization of economics – a trend that he had encouraged – progressively distanced theory from history.

Indeed, Schumpeter's influence on contemporary economics is hardly commensurate with his reputation as one of the great economists of the century. His historical and evolutionary viewpoint does not fit well with the mathematical-formalist approach now dominant. While he is always cited in discussing innovation or entrepreneurship, topics that have risen to prominence since the 1980s, his invocation is often tokenistic.

Much of this also applies to other major figures in the history of economic thought, of course. Unlike many such figures, however, Schumpeter never envisaged the foundation of a school. He left his stamp on many of his students and colleagues but had no real intellectual successors. Evolutionary economists have certainly built on his legacy since the 1970s.[11] His writings on 'Schumpeterian competition' and on 'long waves' have inspired many. Taken as a whole, however, his work remains underexplored. In many respects, it seems ahead of its time, which explains tensions and inconsistencies caused by a mismatch between his evolutionary inclinations and the equilibrium paradigm to which he remained committed.

Only a fraction of Schumpeter's huge bibliography is considered in the following sections, which discuss his theory of economic evolution and his conception of the capitalist process, his theory of business cycles, his theory of social classes, his reflections on late capitalism and its self-destruction, and his unique achievement as a historian of economics.

Economic Evolution and the Capitalist Process

The *Methodenstreit* – the dispute on the role of 'exact' theory in the social sciences initiated in the 1880s by Carl Menger, the leader of the Austrian School, and the aforementioned Gustav von Schmoller – did not produce a victor or a consensus. Appearing in a context still marked by severe methodological controversy over theory and history, Schumpeter's first (1908) book is typically provocative. Schumpeter attempts to convince his audience of the merits of 'pure' or 'exact' theory – of equilibrium economics – whilst contending that the *Methodenstreit* was pointless. There is, he submits, no contradiction between the 'historical' and the 'abstract' approach. Each simply addresses different problems, hence it makes no sense for either to claim universal validity.[12]

His conception of pure theory differs from his Austrian teachers', though. Influenced by instrumentalist philosophy of science, Schumpeter announces, more or less anticipating Milton Friedman, that the assumptions of pure theory are just convenient hypotheses and, in particular, have no psychological significance.[13] Pure theory, Schumpeter writes, is interested not in 'acting men' but only in the quantities of goods in their possession, describing the changes of these quantities 'as if they were carried out automatically'.[14]

Schumpeter's second book underwent considerable modifications, which we will not trace, between its first (1912) and second (1926) editions. The latter was translated into English in 1934 as *The Theory of Economic Development*. The book presents his theory of economic 'evolution' – a term that Schumpeter came to prefer to 'development'.[15] Its opening chapter, on the 'circular flow of economic life', may perhaps surprise the reader. In a nutshell, it describes how a competitive economy adapts to changes in data and displays a tendency to general equilibrium. The influence of Walras is clear. Interestingly, though, the adaptive process that Schumpeter describes is hardly mechanical or automatic, contrary to what the proclamation above might lead us to expect.[16]

First, the circular flow rests on routine and does not suppose optimization. Schumpeter observes that 'the assumption that conduct is prompt and rational is in all cases a fiction.' He goes on to argue that this fiction 'proves to be sufficiently near to reality, if things have time to hammer logic into men', but he also concedes that adaptative responses always take time and meet 'many obstacles in unpreparedness, the lack of means, and so on'.[17] Second, the circular flow supposes rules of conduct that facilitate, yet cannot be confused with, actual behaviour. Individuals may rely on rules, but they always have to think and to decide.

It is hard to see how the entrepreneur or innovator, the agent in which Schumpeter is most interested, could be endogenous to a mechanical equilibrium system. Indeed, 'he has no function of a special kind there, he simply does not exist.'[18] If our interpretation of the circular flow is not mechanical, however, adaptation and innovation begin to appear in a different light. Because 'even current decisions contain elements that have not been contained in inherited routine,' there is no sharp division between adaptive and innovative responses, no 'sharp line between what is and what is not "enterprise."'[19]

In the *Theory*, however, Schumpeter prefers to emphasize this dividing line whilst insisting that the entrepreneur comes from 'within the system'. The circular flow deals with adaptative processes, caused by changes in data, which embody a tendency to equilibrium. As for development (or evolution), it is spontaneous change 'arising from within the system which so displaces its equilibrium point that the new one cannot be reached from the old one by infinitesimal steps. Add successively as many mail coaches as you please, you will never get a railway thereby.'[20] In other words, evolution is defined by the carrying out of innovations, a concept that encompasses the introduction of new goods and new production methods, the opening of new markets or new sources of inputs, and the implementation of new forms of industrial organization.

According to Schumpeter, carrying out these innovations supposes aptitudes that, like other aptitudes, are unequally distributed. However, 'nobody ever is an entrepreneur all the time, and nobody can ever be only an entrepreneur.'[21] It is preferable to speak of the entrepreneurial function, therefore, rather than of the entrepreneur as a person. This function consists essentially in getting things done, a task that must not be confused with invention. Indeed, the production of ideas is, in itself, economically irrelevant: 'the fact that Leibnitz suggested the idea of the Suez Canal exerted no influence whatever on economic history for two hundred years.'[22]

The entrepreneur's task is a distinct one because 'carrying out a new plan and acting according to a customary one are things as different as making a road and walking along it.' Beyond the circular flow, the individual is 'without those data for his decisions and those rules of conduct which are usually very accurately known to him', and must therefore be much more consciously rational than in ordinary pursuits. Moreover, individuals are usually psychologically reluctant to step outside routine. The environment's resistance to innovation must also be surmounted. 'Where the boundaries of routine stop,' Schumpeter writes, 'many people can go no further, and the rest can only do so in a highly variable manner.'[23] This is why entrepreneurship is a particular instance of the phenomenon of *leadership*.

How, though, is the entrepreneur supposed to operate? Innovation requires command over means of production which, under Schumpeter's full employment assumption, have to be withdrawn from their current uses. This in turn requires money. Yet in the circular flow as Schumpeter conceives it there are no significant savings such as might be invested in new ventures. As will be apparent, savings are primarily a result of evolution. Under these conditions, the financing of innovation requires credit, which banks have the power to create ad hoc; and this method of financing innovation is the distinctively capitalist one.[24] Thus, the banker, producer of as well as middleman in purchasing power, has the fundamental role of selecting entrepreneurial projects. Schumpeter remarks that most 'catastrophes' in the history of capitalist evolution can be accounted for by 'the failure of the banking community to function in the way required by the structure of the capitalist machine'.[25]

Once entrepreneurial ventures are financed by credit creation, by an increase in the existing means of payment, the capitalist process 'begins', so to speak, with its characteristic features. Clearly it is impossible to understand it 'abstracting' from money. In Schumpeter's conception of this process, capital is the purchasing power available for entrepreneurs: 'not a factor of production but a distinct agent which stands between the entrepreneur and the factors. It can be created by banks because balances can.'[26] With capital, the successful entrepreneur makes a profit. Profit has a monopoly element, but eventually it vanishes in the process of competition that it stimulates. The origin of the largest part of savings lies in entrepreneurial profits, the essential source of industrial fortunes. The entrepreneur must, however, pay interest. There is now a premium on present over future sums, because the former can be used to yield bigger future sums. Innovation, then, is the cause (or at least a sufficient cause) for the emergence of interest in the business sphere.

A counterpart of his theory of capital, Schumpeter's theory of interest as a monetary phenomenon – interest is, as he puts it, 'a payment for balances with which to acquire commodities and services, not for the commodities and services themselves that may be bought with those balances'[27] – was quickly attacked by his teacher Böhm-Bawerk. It remains questionable for many. Also controversial is Schumpeter's theory of business cycles, to which we now turn. Though it is presented in the *Theory*, its most elaborate version appears in *Business Cycles* in 1939.

As is apparent in his 1926 essay on Schmoller, Schumpeter modified his original position on the relation between theory and history, and *Business Cycles* reflects the view that historical experience is a prerequisite to understanding cycles, and that theory and history must cooperate. His increasingly conspicuous historical proclivities do not, however, alter his initial commitment to equilibrium economics. 'We do not attack traditional theory, Walrasian or Marshallian, on its own ground,' Schumpeter submits, 'the logical schema of that theory is . . . right "in principle"', although it 'works tolerably well only within the precincts of tried experience and familiar motive.'[28] His theory of business cycles is part of the theory of the capitalist process that we have been presenting.

Business Cycles

From the outset Schumpeter acknowledges that economic fluctuations have multiple causes, including natural and political ones. He adds that purely economic cycles are absent from the world of the circular flow, even if it should encompass growth (of population, for instance), for mere growth gives rise only to adaptive processes. If there be a purely economic cycle, then, it must be due to 'the way in which new things are, in the institutional conditions of capitalist society, inserted into the economic process and absorbed by it'.[29] Schumpeter claims that indeed there is such a cycle: innovation, financed by credit creation, is sufficient to produce alternating phases of prosperity and recession. How is this proposition established?

In line with the theory of evolution that we have been presenting, Schumpeter starts from a competitive equilibrium, and brings in the entrepreneur: a 'new man' who, with capital created by a bank, founds a new firm. Innovations, Schumpeter writes, 'are, as a rule, embodied, as it were, in new firms which generally do not arise out of the old ones but start producing beside them . . . in general it is not the owner of stage-coaches who builds railways.'[30]

But there will be many entrepreneurs, of course, not just one. It is critical for Schumpeter's cycle theory that, instead of being evenly distributed in time, entrepreneurs appear in groups or swarms: for a while, other entrepreneurs, in increasing numbers, follow in the path of innovation.

This clustering of entrepreneurial activity occurs because innovation becomes easier, particularly in the same or related fields. The path of innovation 'becomes progressively smoothed for successors by accumulating experience and vanishing obstacles'. Still, Schumpeter remarks, there will always be definite limits on advance in any particular direction. Moreover, the appearance of entrepreneurs en masse radically upsets the initial equilibrium, which means that calculation and the planning of new things, always uncertain, become increasingly precarious. 'In order to carry out additional innovations, it is . . . necessary to wait until things settle down.'[31]

With a swarm-like appearance of entrepreneurs, and the subsequent slackening and stoppage of entrepreneurial activity, it is easy to glimpse the emergence of prosperity and recession. The creation of new purchasing power gives rise to new expenditure, but it will be a while before innovative projects yield their results. Additional producers' spending will quickly be followed by additional consumers' spending. As there are no unemployed resources, prices of factors of production will rise, as will money incomes and the prices of consumer goods. Costs will therefore rise, but so will the receipts of established firms. However, the new products will gradually flow into the market, competing with the old ones, and then the picture begins to change. Whilst competition intensifies, expenditure will be reduced. Entrepreneurs start repaying bank loans and new entrepreneurial borrowing will eventually stop altogether. Many established firms will have to undergo a painful process of modernization and some will not survive. In sum, there will be

> adaptation to the new things created, including the elimination of what is incapable of adaptation, resorption of the results of innovation into the system, reorganization of economic life so as to make it conform to the data as altered by enterprise, remodeling of the system of values, liquidation of indebtedness . . . as soon as the entrepreneurial impulse ceases to act which propelled it away from its previous neighborhood [of equilibrium], the system embarks upon a struggle toward a new one.[32]

In this new neighbourhood of equilibrium, output will have changed, absolute prices will be lower and the price system will be different, and 'what at first appears as entrepreneurial profit finally increases the permanent real incomes of other classes.'[33] From this neighbourhood of equilibrium, enterprise will resume.

It is worth remembering that Schumpeter's basic model of business cycles is not intended to reproduce actual business cycles. Many features of cycles and of the capitalist process are absent. Some are contemplated in his so-called second and third approximations.

The second approximation brings in a secondary wave of prosperity – ignited by, but quantitatively much more important than, the primary wave – which amounts, in part, to a cluster of errors. In Schumpeter's basic model, error is irrelevant since there would be 'ups and downs and . . . also losses without any errors'.[34] Now error becomes essential. Innovation gives rise to new expenditure, and many established firms react to the new situation assuming that better business will continue indefinitely.

> Speculation in the narrower sense of the word will take the hint and . . . stage a boom even before prosperity in business has had time to develop. New borrowing will then no longer be confined to entrepreneurs, and 'deposits' will be created to finance general expansion, each loan tending to induce another loan, each rise in prices another rise.[35]

In short, 'present earnings which are ephemeral and future earnings which are imaginary, are capitalized.'[36] Reckless and fraudulent enterprise will also appear.

The turn of the primary wave breaks this secondary wave of prosperity. A painful process of readjustment and the elimination of obsolete firms would always be inevitable, but now there is much more to adjust and to eliminate. Recession will tend to develop into depression, which feeds upon itself. The economy will experience 'a downward revision of values and a shrinkage of operations that reduce them, often quite erratically, below their equilibrium amounts'.[37] Firms which could have survived will now die.

A fourth phase of the cycle, recovery or revival, will eventually bring the system back to a new neighbourhood of equilibrium, which will, however, differ from that which would have been attained in the absence of depression. Though normally averse to making policy recommendations, Schumpeter intimates that the case for government action in depression is, 'independently of humanitarian considerations, incomparably stronger than it is in recession'.[38]

Closer to reality as the second approximation is, Schumpeter recognizes that much is still missing. For example, savings and imperfect competition ought to be taken into account. His third approximation does something else, though. He observes that there is no reason why innovation should give rise to just one wave-like movement. Taking the historical record of capitalism into account, he distinguishes three simultaneous cycles, named after the researchers who suggested them – Kondratieff cycles of just under sixty years (long waves); each containing six Juglar cycles of just under ten years; each containing three Kitchin cycles (possibly not caused by innovation) of just under forty months.

Schumpeter's edifice cannot quite stand the weight of this third approximation, though. Clearly, shorter cycles must now rise from situations disturbed by longer cycles. So the basic proposition that the process of innovation starts only from neighbourhoods of equilibrium must be given up.[39]

Despite this fragility, Schumpeter's theory highlights important features of cycles that other theories miss. It portrays the cycle as a constitutive feature of the capitalist process, with a role: the cycle is neither an accident nor is it necessarily pathological. Relatedly, it rejects the conception that cycles are purely monetary phenomena, originating in the sphere of money and credit. The sufficient cause of the cycle is 'in its nature independent of the machinery of money and credit', even though it 'could not without it produce the particular kind of effects it does'.[40] Finally, Schumpeter's theory is a forceful warning against thinking in terms of macroeconomic aggregates, which obscures what really matters: the process of innovation.

The Theory of Social Classes

Schumpeter repeatedly associates entrepreneurial success with a rise in the social scale. He also intimates that his vision of evolution is applicable beyond the economic sphere. Indeed, he occasionally compares entrepreneurs and other leaders. His 1927 essay on social classes illuminates all these observations. It is not just an example of the ease with which Schumpeter slides from economics into sociology. It is arguably the piece where he articulates a general theory of social order and social change, of which his other writings are, in a sense, applications.[41]

In this essay, Schumpeter scrutinizes two problems. First, he wants to understand the rise and fall of families within a class structure. This problem is split in two: the rise and fall of families within a given social class; and the movement of families across class lines. Second, he proposes to explain the rise and fall of whole classes. The factors that account for this rise and fall also explain why class structure exists.

With regard to the first problem, Schumpeter notes that the relative position of families within a class is always shifting; and that class barriers are, again without exception, surmounted. Both these processes are argued to reflect 'the different degree to which families are qualified to solve the problems with which their social environment confronts them'. That is, they reflect differences in aptitude, with respect to certain functions and 'to leadership, along lines that are in keeping with those functions'.[42] Individuals are said to differ in their leadership aptitudes as they differ in their ability to sing, although a tradition of leadership helps its attainment and practice.

As to the second problem, Schumpeter argues that the rise and fall of social classes depends, on the one hand, on the success with which their members fulfil their characteristic function; and, on the other, on the relative social significance of that function (or of other functions which class members take on). The relative social significance of a function is always 'determined by the degree of social leadership which its fulfillment implies or creates'.[43] Whilst the functions of the peasant and the warrior in the Middle Ages are both socially necessary, they do not have the same relation to social leadership. The individual warrior is less replaceable than the peasant. Social leadership means 'to decide, to command, to prevail, to advance' and would not exist if life 'always ran its course in the same way and by the same routine'.[44]

Schumpeter adds that class structure is actually 'more a matter of social value, once achieved, becoming firmly established'.[45] This 'entrenchment' process and its perpetuation must always be specifically explained. Nevertheless, the relative position of social classes is ultimately conditioned by differences in aptitude.

In the context of this theory of social classes, Schumpeter's theory of the capitalist process outlined in the previous sections of this chapter appears in a somewhat different light. The capitalist process can be interpreted as the process in which a class structure and the corresponding institutions are reproduced across time. In particular, it is the process in which the capitalist class is reproduced *and* renewed. Entrepreneurial success – rendered possible by capital, which banks have the power to create – leads to capitalist positions, which will not last indefinitely in the absence of further entrepreneurial success.

Schumpeter actually resorts to the capitalist case in presenting his theory of classes. In so doing, he also takes the opportunity to contrast his viewpoint with that of Marx. Contemplating the rise and fall of families within a class, he writes:

> A first reason for shifting family position is offered by the automatism of accumulation, asserted by Marx. The 'capitalist' who is bigger . . . outstrips the poorer one in the competitive field and forces him to the wall. This view is a typical example of how bias in favor of a theory blinds the theorist . . . Manifestly, the captured surplus value *does not invest itself* but must *be invested* . . . the social logic or objective situation does not unequivocally determine *how much* profit shall be invested, and *how* it shall be invested, *unless individual disposition is taken into account.*[46]

What is required to enhance family position within the capitalist class is precisely departure from routine, which depends on leadership aptitudes. Similarly, most families have risen from the working or craftsman class into the capitalist class 'because one of their members has *done something novel*, typically the founding of a new enterprise'. This method of social ascent – doing something novel – has been crucial in all societies, 'but never so much as in the world of capitalism'.[47] For 'in the institutional pattern of capitalism there is machinery, the presence of which forms an essential characteristic of it, which makes it possible for people to function as entrepreneurs without having previously acquired the necessary means. It is leadership rather than ownership that matters.'[48]

But Schumpeter's theory of social classes is also a theory of how a class structure passes away. Implicitly, it contains a theory of the demise of capitalism. The entrepreneur's importance must eventually diminish, Schumpeter often intimates, 'just as the importance of the military commander has already diminished'.[49] We shall meet this theory in the next section.

Late Capitalism

From the outset, Schumpeter's presentation of his theory of evolution is punctuated by reminders that the 'competitive' capitalism to which he is referring, where entrepreneurs are 'new men' who found 'new firms', has a tendency to evolve into 'trustified' capitalism. In the latter, innovation is 'not any more embodied *typically* in new firms, but goes on, within the big units now existing, largely independently of individual persons'.[50] Once the owner–manager of a firm, the entrepreneur may be difficult to identify in this new setting: 'aptitudes that no single individual combines can . . . be built into a corporate personality', whereas chairmen 'may be mere co-ordinators or even figure-heads'.[51] Indeed, innovation 'becomes "automatised," increasingly impersonal and decreasingly a matter of leadership and individual initiative'.[52]

As we have seen, Schumpeter's theory of business cycles does not incorporate the persistence of imperfect competition. It is never reformulated so as to integrate trustified capitalism. Schumpeter just offers occasional observations connecting these topics, noting for instance that, in a world of large firms with direct access to financial markets, credit creation will be comparatively less important and economic fluctuations milder.

However, he does provide a rhetorically powerful, albeit fragmentary, account of innovation in trustified capitalism. It appears in *Capitalism, Socialism and Democracy* (1942) and has been discussed ever since. The contrast between Schumpeter's descriptions of innovation under competitive and trustified conditions has been embodied in two models, often encountered in evolutionary economics and beyond, and somewhat infelicitously known as Schumpeter Mark I and Schumpeter Mark II. In the former model, invention is exogenous and innovators 'outsiders'; in the latter, 'insiders' engage in research and development activity to reproduce their market power positions.

In essence, Schumpeter's argument in *Capitalism* comprises three points. First, he retrieves his conception that capitalism is 'by nature a form or method of economic change and not only never is but never can be stationary'. Its essential feature is a process of *creative destruction* that 'incessantly revolutionizes the economic structure *from within*'.[53]

Second, he points out that received theory excludes evolution. It relies on a *ceteris paribus* proviso and fails to capture the nature of capitalist competition. Indeed, it is rather 'like *Hamlet* without the Danish prince':[54]

> It is . . . competition within a rigid pattern of invariant conditions, methods of production and forms of industrial organization in particular, that practically monopolizes attention. But in capitalist reality as distinguished from its textbook picture, it is not that kind of competition which counts but the competition from the new commodity, the new technology, the new source of supply, the new type of organization . . . This kind of competition is as much more effective than the other as a bombardment is in comparison with forcing a door, and so much more important that it becomes a matter of comparative indifference whether

> competition in the ordinary sense functions more or less promptly . . . competition of the kind we now have in mind acts . . . also when it is merely an ever-present threat. It disciplines before it attacks. The businessman feels . . . in a competitive situation even if he is alone in his field or if, though not alone, he holds a position such that investigating government experts fail to see any effective competition.[55]

Obviously, this passage yields an indictment of the theories of imperfect competition or of monopoly. Schumpeter's third point is precisely that 'monopolistic practices' are hardly peripheral but 'acquire a new significance in the perennial gale of creative destruction'.[56] Investing in this uncertain setting, he writes, is like shooting at an indistinct target that is moving jerkily. Protective devices, such as patents, will be secured. But these devices, which economists usually approve of, are merely particular instances of a larger category of practices often indispensable in the process of creative destruction.

The recognition that these practices have a function, Schumpeter clarifies, merely establishes 'that there is no general case for indiscriminate "trust-busting" or for the prosecution of everything that qualifies as a restraint of trade'. Markets dominated by a firm or a few large firms are not necessarily innovative. However, a monopoly position in industry 'is in general no cushion to sleep on. As it can be gained, so it can be retained only by alertness and energy.'[57]

In fact, it is not just that 'monopolistic practices' are often unavoidable in the process of creative destruction. Schumpeter contends that 'big business' has become the most powerful engine of progress. Though 'mere size is neither necessary nor sufficient', big businesses, with their research departments, have been responsible for an increase in living standards which could not possibly have been achieved under the perfectly competitive conditions that economists often favour.[58]

But this achievement has momentous consequences for the future of capitalism. In the bureaucratized corporation, innovation becomes the business of trained specialists. It becomes routinized, depersonalized office work. The social position of the entrepreneur, and hence of the capitalist class, is thereby undermined, as the knight's once was. Warfare never ceased in the course of human history, of course, yet it became increasingly mechanized and independent of leadership attributes; which affected the social position of the nobility. Similarly,

> since capitalist enterprise . . . tends to automatize progress, we conclude that it tends to make itself superfluous . . . The perfectly bureaucratized giant industrial unit not only ousts the small or medium-sized firm and 'expropriates' its owners, but in the end it also ousts the entrepreneur and expropriates the bourgeoisie as a class which in the process stands to lose not only its income but . . . its function.[59]

This thesis of the obsolescence of the entrepreneurial function, which recovers Schumpeter's theory of social classes, is a central element of his theory that capitalism tends to self-destruct – not because of its failure, as in Marx, but, in a typically Schumpeterian paradox, because of its success. Though its precise meaning is not quite unequivocal, the obsolescence of the entrepreneurial function can be seen as a particular manifestation of a process of 'rationalization' with some Weberian overtones.[60]

Schumpeter argues that, though rationality is not a capitalist creation, capitalism develops and generalizes it. The capitalist cost–profit calculus, a product of economic rationality, 'propels the logic of enterprise'; and the rational attitude spreads from the economic sphere to the other spheres of life. It changes man's tools, philosophies, medical practices, 'his picture of the cosmos, his outlook on life, everything in fact including his concepts of beauty and justice and his spiritual ambitions'.[61] In other words, the capitalist process 'reshapes not only our methods of attaining our ends but also these ultimate ends themselves'.[62] It destroys metaphysical belief, as well as mystic and romantic ideas. It produces not just the modern corporation, with its technology and organization, but 'the mental attitude of modern science, the attitude that consists in asking certain questions and in going about answering them in a certain way', or indeed 'utilitarian ideas about the betterment of mankind which . . . seem to withstand rationalist criticism better than, say, the fear of God does'.[63]

The capitalist process, then, tends to destroy pre-capitalist institutions, many of which actually sheltered it. Eventually, it also tends to undermine its own institutional framework. The rise of the modern corporation means 'substituting a mere parcel of shares for the walls of and the machines in a factory', which affects capitalist motivation – as does the rationalization of private life and the 'disintegration of the bourgeois family'.[64] Moreover, capitalism's rationalist, critical frame of mind 'does not stop at the credentials of kings and popes but goes on to attack private property and the whole scheme of bourgeois values'.[65] In short, capitalism produces anti-capitalist policies (high taxation and regulation, for example) or, more generally, a hostile legislative, administrative and judicial practice: capitalism becomes 'fettered' capitalism.

Schumpeter conjectures that the tendency towards self-destruction inherent in capitalism also creates the conditions for the emergence of socialism. Socialism, which he dislikes, is 'an institutional pattern in which control over means of production and over production itself is vested with a central authority'. Can it work? 'Of course it can,' Schumpeter confidently replies.[66] But the reasoning that supports this assertion now looks old-fashioned. Like most economists in the 1940s, Schumpeter failed to understand the Mises–Hayek arguments against socialism (or on the nature of the market). Instead, he thought that the soundness of socialism, or at least of its 'pure logic', had been established by a set of equations.[67] His unwavering commitment to Walrasian equilibrium theory is hardly innocuous and leads him hopelessly astray.

Of course, Schumpeter cannot avoid writing with his usual verve and he offers penetrating observations here and there, especially in sociological digressions. His discussion of the economics of socialism is, however, beyond repair.

The History of Economics

An astonishing accomplishment remains to be mentioned. Schumpeter counts as a first-rank historian of economics as much as a great economist. He wrote abundantly and brilliantly on the topic throughout his life, but his most important achievement is the posthumously edited, incomplete *History of Economic Analysis* (1954).

The scope of this history is unique and its erudition unsurpassable. Despite its sometimes fragmentary nature, it is nearly 1,200 pages long. It starts in ancient Greece and moves through the medieval Scholastics and the philosophers of natural law right up to the 1940s, addressing a much wider range of subjects and authors than one might expect. For example, Part III, on the period from 1790 to 1870, includes a chapter on 'the intellectual scenery' which discusses, among other topics, the zeitgeist of the period and its philosophy, romanticism and historiography, evolutionism, psychology and logic.

Apart from its range and depth, *History* is also graced by Schumpeter's idiosyncratic style:

> Nations remained amorphous agglomerations of individuals. Social classes were not living and fighting entities but were mere labels affixed to economic functions (or functional categories). Nor were the individuals themselves living and fighting beings: they continued to be mere clotheslines on which to hang propositions of economic logic . . . Critics sneered. They saw that all this was poor sociology and even poorer psychology . . . they failed to see that, for a limited range of problems, this was at the same time sound methodology.[68]

The best-known section of *History* is Part I, on scope and method. It is here that Schumpeter presents the techniques of economic analysis (economic history, statistics and theory, to which economic sociology is later added) and that we find the statement that economic history is 'by far the most important', even if it needs the help of 'theory': 'I wish to state right now that if, starting my work in economics afresh, I were told that I could study only one of the three but could have my choice, it would be economic history that I should choose.'[69] 'Theory' is defined, in an instrumentalist fashion, as a set of 'mere instruments or tools framed for the purpose of *establishing* interesting results'.[70]

It is in this first part as well that Schumpeter discusses the relationship of science and ideology, which is also the topic of his presidential address to the American Economic Association.[71] The problem of ideology arises from the recognition that scientific evolution is not a purely intellectual process. On the contrary, the scientist's choice of problems and approaches is socially conditioned and, in this sense, ideological: in Marxian language, it is part of the superstructure. The scientific thought of an epoch reflects the location of scientists in a given social environment, which conditions them 'to see certain things rather than others, and to see them in a certain light', perhaps even endowing them 'with a subconscious craving to see things in a certain light'.[72]

Schumpeter notes that 'systems of political economy', expositions of comprehensive sets of economic policies founded on principles like liberalism or socialism, are ideologically conditioned. So is the ensemble of 'opinions and desires' on economic subjects that 'float in the public mind', which he calls 'economic thought'.[73] But what about economic analysis, the 'scientific' aspect of economic thought?

Schumpeter argues that analytic effort, or at least truly innovative analytic effort, must be preceded by a cognitive act that provides a preliminary 'picture of things as we see them': by a 'vision'. This vision, which is both fundamental to seeing things in a new light and ideological by nature, is then treated according to certain rules of procedure. Factual and theoretical work, interacting with one another, 'eventually produce *scientific models*, the provisional joint products of their interaction with the surviving elements of the original vision'. Those rules of procedure, or so Schumpeter claims, 'are almost as much exempt from ideological influence as vision is subject to it'. They often stem from fields 'that are little or not at all affected by ideology' and 'they tend to crush out ideologically conditioned error from the visions.' At least they produce a considerable 'narrowing [of] the sphere of ideologically vitiated propositions'.[74]

Another frequently discussed feature of *History* is its appraisal of Walras as 'so far as pure theory is concerned . . . the greatest of all economists'; and of his equilibrium system as 'the only work by an economist that will stand comparison with the achievements of theoretical physics'.[75] The reasons for this assessment coincide with those conveyed in Schumpeter's first book.[76] The most fundamental scientific question, Schumpeter writes, is whether analysis of the interdependence between economic phenomena yields the (if possible, unique) determination of 'all the prices and quantities of products and productive services that constitute the economic "system"'.[77] This is essential for '*any* exact science'; otherwise 'a field of phenomena is really a chaos that is not under analytic control.'[78] Accordingly, the Walrasian system of equations 'is the Magna Carta of economic theory – the technical imperfections of that monument of constitutional law being an essential part of the analogy'.[79]

Schumpeter's concept of the 'Ricardian Vice' is also well known. This refers to David Ricardo's interest in 'the clear-cut result of direct, practical significance'. To obtain it, he took as many things as possible as 'given' and piled up simplifying assumptions, so that 'the desired results emerged almost as tautologies.' He had 'the habit of establishing simple relations between aggregates that then acquire a spurious halo of causal importance', whilst the important things are 'bundled away in or behind these aggregates'.[80] Keynes is accused of proceeding similarly.

In a nutshell, *History* may be argued to describe the complex process whereby a 'classical situation', which summarizes and consolidates previous analytical achievement, eventually emerges out of struggles and debates, to be superseded by new breaks with tradition or revolutions.[81] No doubt a book with this purpose is somewhat intimidating for beginners. Its main flaw as a history lies, however, elsewhere. Connoisseurs of Schumpeter's writings will recognize his own theories behind his opinions. But there are very few explicit, and just a few implicit, references to himself. The reader may not realize that the book's author is one of the major figures in the history of economics.

But why exactly is he a major figure? For some, the reasons for Schumpeter's status may appear difficult to pinpoint. This is because his legacy is neither a school nor a neatly worked out theoretical system, much less a set of clear-cut policy recommendations. Essentially, it is an imposing vision, of which some elements (such as innovation, entrepreneurship and capitalism) are elaborated in detail: a vision of how the economy evolves as a result of creative and adaptive responses, which also transform the institutional sphere.

Put differently, Schumpeter proposes and contributes to an evolutionary programme. His work eloquently reminds us of questions that are fundamental and remain somewhat opaque. It reminds us, moreover, that economic theory is unable to answer these questions on its own. History, in particular, is indispensable.

SEVEN

JOHN MAYNARD KEYNES

Victoria Bateman

John Maynard Keynes was a product of the time in which he lived, an era that spanned two world wars, the 1929 global Great Depression and a retreat from globalization in the face of rising nationalism. Rather than being fatalistic, Keynes was an idealist who imagined a brighter future, and, more importantly, who believed that intellectuals like himself had the ability and the moral obligation to actively engineer it.

Keynes was not afraid to challenge the status quo, both inside economics and in his life outside the discipline, which was one of intense artistic and philosophical engagement. According to Russell Leffingwell, a U.S. Treasury official who worked with Keynes at the Paris Peace Conference (1919), Keynes was 'always perverse, Puckish . . . a bright boy, shocking his admiring elders by questioning the existence of God, and the Ten Commandments!'[1] His major achievement, crystallized in his 1936 book *The General Theory of Employment, Interest and Money*, was to confront economists with the fact that capitalist economies can fall into situations of deficient demand, which could ultimately threaten the fabric of democracy and the freedoms of a liberal society. Rather than blaming workers themselves for unemployment, Keynes shifted the blame towards the market system, ultimately encouraging a more cooperative relationship between the state and the workforce. Through his work in government during the world wars, Keynes also helped give birth to a new system of national accounts, giving the state the measurement tools needed to properly monitor and ultimately manage the economy. By the end of his life in 1946, the globalization into which Keynes was born was back on a new track. He helped to arm the global economy with an entirely new set of international institutions, ones that not only supported economic goals such as monetary stability and the lowering of trade barriers, but that also went on to underpin an international human rights agenda and decolonization.

Whilst Keynes is often characterized as being anti-capitalist, he was capitalism's ultimate protector, often said to have saved capitalism from the capitalists. According to Henry Simons (1936), the *General Theory* had the potential to become the 'economic bible of a fascist movement'.[2] However, were it not for his ability to engender hope amongst the general public in the ability of economists to fruitfully mix the market and state – in a way that could take the best of both worlds – it is likely that fascism and communism would have advanced much further than they were able to do in the middle of the twentieth century. Keynes offered a third way. The consequence was that he was not much liked either by the free market economic mainstream or by socialists.

Beatrice Webb, the Fabian, wrote that 'Keynes is not serious about economic problems; he plays a game of chess with [economics] in his leisure hours. The only serious cult with him is aesthetics.'[3] Perhaps the only thing that united socialists and free marketeers was not taking Keynes seriously. At least not in the beginning. For the economic mainstream of the day, lumped together by Keynes as the Classical School, he was little more than a rebellious pseudo-intellectual. The Chicago economist Frank Knight thought of Keynes as an 'anti-intellectual' who was 'taking the side of the man-in-the-street' and 'passing the keys of the citadel out of the window to the Philistines hammering at the gates'.[4] By supporting increased government spending and the creation of extra money by the Central Bank, Keynes enraged the economic mainstream and seemed to be pandering to populist sentiment. Ironically, though, he did so in a style of writing that was difficult to read, arguably turgid and certainly esoteric, which probably won him more rather than fewer followers in the academic sphere.[5] The economist Paul Samuelson wrote that the *General Theory* swept across the profession much like 'the unexpected virulence of a disease first attacking and decimating an isolated tribe of South Seas islanders'.[6]

Whilst Keynes did not impress everyone, for the younger generation of economists he offered a new hope. In the 1920s and 1930s capitalism faced the double-headed beast of communism and fascism, both of which involved the heavy hand of the state. What Keynes offered was an alternative: a reformed version of capitalism that could deliver full employment and prosperity without the need for the 'prison camps, executions and bestial interrogations' that all too often accompany alternatives to capitalism, despite the good intentions of socialists.[7] One student from 1930s Cambridge noted that 'Keynes's reformed capitalism had everything and more the Fabian generation had looked for in socialism: it was morally speaking egalitarian, it was fully employed, it was generous and gay.'[8]

By 1965, having astutely manoeuvred a life of not only academic theorizing but also policymaking, Keynes had posthumously made it to the front cover of *Time* magazine, which wrote that Keynes was 'a prime influence on the world's free economies'. His particular blend of state and market had by then won over policymakers and academic economists alike, reportedly leading Richard Nixon to declare in 1971 that 'we are all Keynesians now.'

In what follows, we will look at the life and times of Keynes, noting the powerful effect on his work of his experience of globalization followed by war and depression. We will go on to outline Keynes's economic thinking and how this thinking challenged free-market economists' faith in the capitalist system. As we will see, central to Keynes's work was a belief that the future is completely unpredictable. This unpredictability makes investment, and with it the economy, inherently unstable.

However, Keynes was not alone in his belief in the unknowable future. It was a feeling he shared with the Austrian School, which nevertheless arrived at rather different results in terms of the role of government in the economy. Whilst Keynes saw a greater role for government in terms of inspiring confidence in the future and underpinning investment to stabilize the economy, Austrian economists do not. The great challenge to Keynes's work therefore comes not in the form of standard free-market thinking, which in many ways simply assumes away the problems that Keynes addressed, but, instead, in the form of the Austrian School.

Where Keynes is most vulnerable to challenge is not in his critique of the market, which, as we will see, can be defended against the most ardent of free-market thinkers, but, instead, in the faith he placed in policymakers and the state. Since we cannot be expected to predict the future, how can we possibly expect the government to do so? If they cannot, anything other than short-term or relatively limited interventions risks taking the economy in the wrong direction.

Globalization, War, Depression and Back Again

Keynes was born into an age in which the market was triumphant: an age of globalization. The British Industrial Revolution had moved Britain from being nothing more than a backwater to being the world's leading economy.[9] By the latter half of the nineteenth century, not only did Britain 'rule the waves', British financiers were facilitating the construction of international transportation networks across the globe, allowing the movement of everything from corn to clothing across thousands of miles. With their origins in the Industrial Revolution, new steam and iron technologies brought railways and steam shipping, making possible a dramatic lowering of transport costs. The world was metaphorically smaller and flatter. Not only were goods markets experiencing rapid integration, so were labour markets and capital markets. Around 30 million people emigrated from Europe to the USA in the century after 1820, whilst British capital-exports funded the building of infrastructure and opened up large tracts of land to produce for international markets.[10] Writing in 1982 one economic historian noted that never before or since had one economy invested so much across the world.[11] By 1914 the world was so interconnected that few could have imagined that countries would soon be replacing amicable trading relationships with unmatchable military operations. The First World War brought destruction where there had previously been harmony. It also brought personal disarray to Keynes's own intellectual life and left a lasting legacy on his political views.

Unlike his pacifist friends from the Bloomsbury Group, a group known for their bohemian and liberal values, Keynes joined the war effort, making his first move into policymaking circles. He left behind academic life in Cambridge to join the Treasury, where he advised the British government on how best to fund the war. By 1919, and with the war over, Keynes was involved in peace negotiations, including those concerning war 'reparations': how much the losing countries should be expected to compensate the victorious. Whilst many politicians took a hard line, Keynes was of the view that a lasting peace would require a more economically forgiving settlement: that crucifying Germany would neither be good for Germany nor good for the rest of Europe in the longer term. In his 1919 essay 'Proposals for the Reconstruction of Europe', Keynes warned that 'If we aim deliberately at the impoverishment of Central Europe, vengeance, I dare predict, will not limp.'[12] His 'Economic Consequences of the Peace', published in 1919, argued for a kinder, more cooperative outcome to the peace negotiations. Ultimately, Keynes did not get his own way and his predictions of the consequences of a vindictive peace settlement proved remarkably accurate.

By the 1920s Germany was struggling to pay the reparations due, and all of Europe was struggling to rebuild. When it came time to repay short-term war debts, many European governments found themselves unable to cope. Unconvinced of governments' ability to repay, in part due to continued debates about reparation payments, bond holders insisted on having their money back. By 1922, with too few people willing to buy government bonds, and an inability to get higher taxes through parliament, continental countries were turning to the printing press to pay their bills. The result was hyperinflation, which rocked Germany, France and Belgium. In Britain, by contrast, where Keynes's Treasury had been much more successful in putting in place means to fund the war through taxation and long-term (as opposed to short-term) debt, the opposite problem had appeared: deflation. Whilst the victory of the war brought an immediate post-war boom, very soon the optimism turned to pessimism and a deep depression set in. By 1921 the British unemployment rate had risen to over 10 per cent and exports were collapsing.[13] Whether one looked to the continent or within Britain itself, economies were in turmoil. The war had cast a long shadow.

For Keynes, these economic ravages of war represented a major threat to the kind of free and open society cherished by himself and his Bloomsbury Group friends. Writing in the *Manchester Guardian* in 1922 Keynes argued that:

> The real struggle today, just as in the second quarter of the nineteenth century, is between a view of the world termed liberalism or radicalism, for which the primary object of government and of foreign policy is peace, freedom of trade and intercourse, and economic wealth and that other view, militarist or rather diplomatic, which thinks in terms of power, prestige, national or personal glory, the imposition of a culture and hereditary or racial prejudice. To the good English radical, the latter is so unreal, so crazy in its combination of futility and evil, that he is often in danger of forgetting or disbelieving its actual existence.[14]

Only by facing up to the flaws of capitalism, and then giving economists the responsibility to correct them, could liberalism be saved. For many of Keynes's contemporaries, however, economic problems were not a result of too much capitalism but of too little; the consequence of interventions in the market driven by wrong-headed left-leaning policies that sought to help workers, but which in fact did the opposite. High unemployment was, for example, blamed on everything from rising trade unionism to a reduced willingness to work, arguably the result of an expansion in welfare payments that had begun before the war under Prime Minister David Lloyd George.

Whilst the majority of contemporary economists effectively blamed workers themselves for their own predicament, Keynes argued that the suffering was instead the fault of the market. This vein of thinking, which could not have been more of a challenge to the economic status quo, began with a work titled 'The Economic Consequences of Mr Churchill'. In this pamphlet Keynes argued that the high unemployment faced by Britain at the time was a result of an excessively high exchange rate that had hurt demand for British exports and resulted in interest rates that had been set too high, out of a desire to support an overvalued exchange rate. In 1925 Winston Churchill, then Chancellor of the Exchequer, had taken the decision to return Britain to the Gold Standard – an international system of fixed exchange rates – at the pre-war parity of $4.86 to the pound. According to Keynes, and given that the British economy had been much weakened by the war, this old parity was far too high. He estimated that the exchange rate would have needed to have been at least 10 per cent lower for Britain's competitiveness to be maintained on a par with that before the war. Rather than blaming workers for the unemployment they faced, Keynes blamed government policy.

Keynes's thinking ran against the grain of economic thinking. Whilst seemingly attractive, many economists remained unconvinced by Keynes's ideas. As far as economists were concerned, if the exchange rate was too high, prices should fall, serving to make British goods more attractive once again. The only reason they wouldn't fall would be if workers presented an obstacle: refusing to take cuts in their wage alongside lower prices, which would mean that firms' costs would be too high and that job losses would therefore be inevitable. Workers, not the free market, were squarely to blame.

By 1929 depression and unemployment was not only a British phenomenon, but was spreading across the world. The stakes were now even larger than before, and so, to properly challenge contemporary economic thinking, Keynes needed a full-blown theory of his own. He needed to show that an economy could end up in a position in which – through no fault of either workers or firms – spending ('demand') would be insufficient to keep everyone in work.

In his *A Treatise on Money*, published in 1930, followed by *The General Theory of Employment, Interest and Money*, published in 1936, Keynes made his case, which went on to revolutionize economics.

Contrary to the economic mainstream, which assumed that when left to its own devices the market would ensure that everyone who wanted a job could find a job, Keynes argued that only by coincidence would the economy tend to a situation of full employment. Rather than taking a back-seat role – one of laissez-faire – Keynes argued that governments had a duty to actively manage the level of spending in the economy to ensure that there was sufficient demand to mop up all the goods that the economy was capable of producing. This brought fiscal policy to the fore: rather than balancing their books on an annual basis, Keynes argued that governments should spend during periods of recession and save during booms, only equilibrating taxes and government spending plans across the business cycle.

By the start of the Second World War, the problem turned into one of too much demand rather than too little. The state was spending like never before. Cognizant of the hyperinflation in recent memory, the British government was keen to draw on Keynes's economics to help it manage demand, but in a downward as opposed to upward direction. The problem was twofold: first, on the demand side, the war made dual-income families the norm as both men and women were conscripted either on to the battlefield or into munitions factories; second, as the government took command of production, directing factories to switch their resources to producing tanks and guns, the number of consumer goods on sale shrunk. In combination, these two factors – extra demand combined with a contraction in supply – risked pushing up prices to unmanageable levels. Keynes was brought on board to both measure demand in the economy and to examine by how much and through what means it could be restricted so as to avoid excessive price increases. By the conclusion of the war, Keynes's influence on economic policymaking was beginning to take root. His work in government, alongside that of Richard Stone and James Meade, had given birth to modern national income accounting.

However, despite believing that governments may need to intervene to manage their economies, Keynes was no communist. Rather than throwing the baby out with the bathwater by disposing of markets altogether, Keynes believed that with a little bit of well-timed intervention, markets could be made to function reasonably well, including ensuring that everyone who wanted a job could find one. Keynes was attempting to save the market from itself, to make sure that society could enjoy its many advantages, including the individual freedom to choose, whilst disposing of its darker side in the form of boom and bust.

Keynes was a defender of liberal values and looked outwards rather than inwards. Indeed, not only did he influence domestic economic policy, he also helped to build a new international economic order for the post-Second World War age.

Keynes's new international order was one that recognized the benefits of globalization. He was well aware of what could happen when countries turned their backs on one another. Having achieved new heights of development in the latter half of the nineteenth century, international markets disintegrated at a surprisingly fast rate in the period between the world wars. Tariffs rose in response to the Great Depression of the 1930s, and revolutions and fascism increased the number of countries pursuing autarky. Economic growth was contracting and with it so was world trade, with each feeding on the other in a vicious downward spiral. Global trade unravelled and restrictions on labour markets (including immigration policies) increased: the world economy deglobalized. Following this interwar experience, policymakers arrived at two conclusions that greatly influenced policy after the Second World War.[15]

The first was that a complete reliance on markets internally could not always guarantee full employment: Keynesian (interventionist) economic policies and the welfare state were born. Internally, therefore, a 'mixed' as opposed to fully free-market economic strategy was pursued. Second, when it came to international markets, tariff policies were shown to have been self-defeating, having resulted in a contraction of international demand that hurt not just the rest of the world but also the domestic economy. International goods markets were, therefore, to be freed. Through the joint work of Keynes and the American economist Harry Dexter White, the Bretton Woods system – named after the location where the United Nations Monetary and Financial Conference took place – was born.

This system was a step on from the fixed exchange rate system of the previous era, one that Keynes had held responsible for the severe recessionary tendencies in Britain in the 1920s. To begin with, there was greater flexibility for countries to devalue, allowing overvalued currencies to be adjusted downwards. In addition, capital flows between countries were restricted, limiting the likelihood of speculative attack and reducing the exposure of national governments to the whims of international capital. This in turn gave national governments a greater degree of control over their domestic economic policy. In sum, the new system relied on free flows of goods but not free flow of capital.

Tariff barriers were to be removed, but not barriers to capital flows. In practice, this meant that there were limits to the amount of currency that an individual could take into and out of an economy.

Under the watchful eye of this new international economic order, the world economy entered the golden age of the 1950s and 1960s. Nowhere experienced this more than Europe: unemployment was low, as was inflation, and trade and investment were booming. By the late 1960s, however, the fixed exchange rate system was coming under pressure and so a wholesale shift to flexible exchange rates occurred in the 1970s. At the same time, capital markets were deregulated. International markets were now free to reach levels of integration not seen since the first big globalization of the late nineteenth century. However, lacking the anchor of a fixed exchange rate, one which limited central banks' ability to recklessly print money, inflation soon got out of hand. Before long, European countries were seeking to return to fixed exchange rates, albeit this time with free movement of capital. The end result was the euro.

For Keynes, the eventual failure of the Bretton Woods system and the modern-day trials and tribulations of the euro would have been entirely predictable. Bretton Woods was a compromise: a compromise between what Keynes wanted and what Dexter White wanted for the Americans. There remained one wish that Keynes was never granted: a system of 'surplus recycling' in which stronger economies helped out weaker economies in a mutually cooperative manner. For the Americans after the Second World War, such a system sounded too much like subsidizing war-torn Europe. In the modern day context of the euro, such a system sounds too much like a handout from export-strong Germany to southern Europe. However, as far as Keynes was concerned, only if stronger economies stood by to help weaker ones would a system of fixed exchange rates – one in which individual economies lacked the ability to alter their exchange rate or interest rate – survive. Stability was not free, it came at a price. Where stronger countries do not play by the cooperative rules, instability becomes the order of the day. Whilst Bretton Woods was certainly an improvement on the interwar Gold Standard, which not only had Keynes blamed for Britain's interwar woes but which Barry Eichengreen has held responsible for the global Great Depression, it only went so far.[16]

Economic Theory: Keynes versus the Classics

Keynes's economic thinking was not only a response to the economic conditions that surrounded him, conditions which took him from the height of globalization in the late nineteenth century to war and depression in the interwar years, and then, after the Second World War, to a rebuilding of the global economy. Keynes's *General Theory* also represented a direct assault on his contemporaries within the economics profession.[17]

According to classical economics, free markets provided a stabilizing force. Periods in which people could not find jobs but were desperate to work should not occur. If markets can function freely, prices and wages should naturally adjust to the level at which everyone who wants a job has a job, and every firm is able to produce the number of goods it desires. Situations in which businesses are suffering from a lack of spending by consumers, leading them to make employees redundant, should never occur. As far as this pre-Keynesian thinking was concerned, the economy's output and income were determined 'on the supply side', by the economy's ability to produce. This supply-side determined level of production is sealed by the economy's innate capabilities: by its level of technology, the amount of machinery and the number of people who wish to work.

The diagram below shows why the labour market should always reach a point at which the number of people who want to work is exactly equal to the number of jobs on offer, meaning that periods of high unemployment should not occur.

Figure 1: The labour market

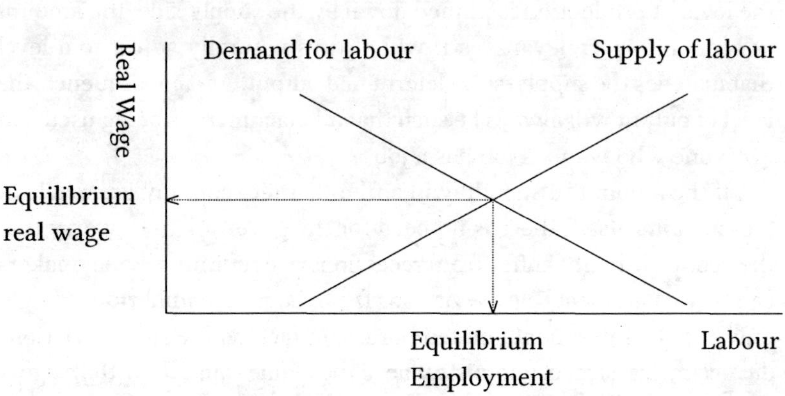

The 'supply of labour' line shows the number of workers who want to work at each possible wage rate; it slopes upwards because as the wage increases, more and more workers choose to work. The 'demand for labour' line shows the number of workers that firms want to employ at each possible wage; it slopes downwards because as the wage falls, employing workers becomes 'cheaper'. So long as wages are flexible, they will naturally adjust to the point at which the two lines cross. At this magical point, what workers want to do (the amount of labour they want to supply) and what firms want to do (the amount of labour they want to demand) are precisely equal. Here we are at what is called the 'market-clearing wage'. To see why the economy will naturally reach this point, suppose for a moment that wages rise above this market-clearing level. At such a point, the demand for labour is less than the supply of labour: the higher wage makes it too expensive for firms to employ the same number of people as before, meaning that some workers who would like to work are now out of jobs – they simply cannot find firms who are willing to employ them. Faced with a lack of jobs, workers will accept wage cuts until the point is reached at which everyone is once again in work and the wage is back at the market clearing level. Hence, so long as there are no interferences in the market – such as trade unions and minimum wage laws – everyone who wants a job should be able to find one, and all firms should be able to find the labour they need to produce the number of goods they wish to produce.

The demand side of the economy was, as far as classical economics was concerned, able to look after itself. So long as markets are free and flexible, and people are fully informed, the amount of spending in the economy should naturally adjust to the level required to mop up all of the goods the economy is capable of producing. In other words, the level of production is pinned down by the supply side; the amount of spending is irrelevant, as it will always naturally adjust to a level that matches the supply-side-determined output. As a consequence, the level of output will always be such that all machinery is being used and everyone who wants a job has a job.

If the amount of spending in a free-market economy is capable of looking after itself, there is no need for the government to worry that the economy might suffer from recessionary conditions. Policymakers can take a back-seat role. Deviations from the neat 'equilibrium' should only ever be infrequent and temporary. In fact, where such deviations did occur, Classical economists placed the blame squarely with the government or with workers themselves for interfering with free-market forces. As far as they were concerned, the best thing that the state can do for the economy is to make the market as free as possible, enabling wages and prices to adjust quickly enough to naturally equilibrate the economy in the case of an adverse shock.

Working from the context of this classical economic mindset, economists in the 1920s and 1930s blamed the high unemployment that surrounded them on either of two sets of forces. First, interferences in the economy, which prevented wages and prices from adjusting. These interferences were said to include trade unions, which had been strengthened during the First World War, and unemployment benefits, which were increased and expanded in scope after the war. Here, the ultimate people to blame were the workers – whether for joining trade unions or for electing a government that is too interventionist. The second potential source of unemployment was thought to have resulted from the effect of the war on the 'supply side' of the economy – on its ability to produce goods using technology and machinery in combination with workers. If the economy is less productive, firms will not be able to pay the same wage as before. The argument is that in response to the lower wage, some workers find that work simply does not pay and, as a result, actively choose to withdraw from work. The result is 'voluntary unemployment'. However, whichever of the two sources one identifies, it is the unemployed who are blamed and not the market economy itself.

Keynes was far from satisfied with this contemporary explanation of unemployment. The poverty and unhappiness of the unemployed made him convinced that unemployment could result from a failure of the market itself, rather than any deficiency of workers: that insufficient demand was possible and that it could leave companies with too little demand for labour. Whilst in practical terms his point seems rather straightforward, trying to convince economists proved much more difficult. As far as classical economics was concerned, there should always be sufficient demand to enable all the goods being produced in the economy to be purchased, leaving no business – or worker – wanting for more. The key to understanding why is as follows: The value of every good being produced in the economy, such as a TV costing £1,000, results in an equivalent amount being paid out as wages or income. This might consist of, say, £500 worth of wages and £500 worth of profits for the owners of the firm. Whatever is not paid out to workers must inevitably end up in the pockets of the owners of the firms as profits. Hence, whatever an economy produces, people (whether workers or owners of firms) will have the means to buy, so long as everything that is earned is actually spent.

Classical economic theory then tells us that this *potential* for people to purchase all of the goods that are being produced in an economy will always translate into *actual* spending. Whilst the amount that people wish to spend out of their wages and profits may fall below the amount that an economy is producing (because some naturally wish to save), so long as firms borrow (to invest) the same amount that consumers choose to save, it will pump the spending power back into the economy. As far as classical economists argue, interest rates will always adjust to make sure that investment equals saving, and, with it, total spending in the economy is equal to the value of what is being produced: if people save more than firms wish to invest, the banks are awash with savings and so will offer loans at lower interest rates. In response, firms will borrow more, mopping up the excess savings. Equally, if there is too much demand for loans from firms wanting to invest relative to the amount that people want to save, then the interest rate will be pushed upwards, as a result of which fewer firms will want to borrow. In this way, the amount of investment in the economy will always be exactly equal to the amount that people wish to save. Since any savings will always be borrowed and spent, total spending will always be exactly equal to the amount required to make sure that all of the goods the economy is capable of producing are being purchased, keeping everyone in jobs. The conclusion is, therefore, that a free-market economy will not produce periods of escalating unemployment as everything that is being produced in the economy is always being bought.

For Keynes, such hopeful thinking represented only one of many possible outcomes for the economy. It was a special rather than a normal case. In the first chapter of the *General Theory*, which, being one page in length, is perhaps the shortest first chapter of any book, he was at pains to point out that:

> I have called this book the *General Theory of Employment, Interest and Money*, placing the emphasis on the prefix *general*. The object of such a title is to contrast the character of myarguments and conclusions with those of the *classical* theory of the subject, upon which I was brought up and which dominates the economic thought, both practical and theoretical, of the governing and academic classes of this generation . . . I shall argue that the postulates of the classical theory are applicable to a special case

> only and not to the general case, the situation which it assumes being a limiting point of the possible positions of equilibrium. Moreover, the characteristics of the special case assumed by the classical theory happen not to be those of the economic society in which we actually live, with the result that its teaching is misleading and disastrous if we attempt to apply it to the facts of experience.[18]

Central to understanding Keynes's idea is to first of all recognize that the future is completely unknowable. Keynes was not only an academic economist, he was also a regular follower of the stock market, and an able mathematician. Each morning, he would sit reading the financial press, trying to work out patterns that he could exploit as a canny investor – not just for himself, but for King's College whose investment portfolio he was entrusted to manage. His investment strategy seemed to be working until, unexpectedly, one day in 1929 the markets began to fall, and fall further, and further still. This personal experience made Keynes stop and think. It made him realize that no matter how much one tries to predict it, the future is beyond prediction.

If the future is unknowable, it makes investing very difficult. In Chapter Twelve of the *General Theory* Keynes writes that:

> Our knowledge of the factors which will govern the yield of an investment some years hence is usually very slight and often negligible. If we speak frankly, we have to admit that our basis of knowledge for estimating the yield ten years hence of a railway, a copper mine, a textile factory, the goodwill of a patent medicine, an Atlantic liner, a building in the City of London amounts to little and sometimes to nothing; or even five years hence. In fact, those who seriously attempt to make any such estimate are often so much in the minority that their behaviour does not govern the market . . . Most, probably, of our decisions to do something positive, the full consequences of which will be drawn out over many days to come, can only be taken as the result of animal spirits – of a spontaneous urge to action rather than inaction, and not as the outcome of a weighted average of quantitative benefits multiplied by quantitative probabilities. Enterprise only pretends to itself to be mainly actuated by the statements in its own prospectus, however candid and sincere.[19]

When making investment decisions – whether it be a company deciding whether to expand, an individual deciding whether to invest in a buy-to-let property or each of us deciding what to do with our pension pot – it is necessary for us to attempt to make predictions about the future. When it comes to the stock market, if we cannot predict the future, we cannot calculate the true value of a stock (or of the stock market in general). As a result, the stock market has no anchor – instead, stock prices will 'blow with the wind' like an unanchored ship, reflecting whatever people in aggregate have come to believe will happen in the future. Investors therefore jump on bandwagons, fearful of missing out on something, overconfident one moment and then overcome by panic the next. If a feeling of exuberance takes hold, stock prices will go up and up until something rings the metaphorical alarm bell, at which point they will tumble back to, and perhaps beyond, reality. These waves of optimism and pessimism translate into severe fluctuations in investment activity and stock market boom and bust, destabilizing the economy.

Keynes offered a very different theory of investment to that of his predecessors. The Classical theory of investment relies on investment in the economy responding to the interest rate; if there is too much in savings and so too little spending in the economy to keep everyone in work, interest rates are assumed to naturally fall (after all, the banks are awash with people's savings). It then becomes cheaper to borrow and invest and so investment rises. The extra investment spending then offsets the lack of spending by consumers, preventing anyone losing their jobs. But, for Keynes, it was not clear that the interest rate would naturally fall in the face of an initial excess of savings over investment.

Money plays a central role in Keynes's thinking: it offers a degree of security when faced with an unknowable future. Hence, if savers start to become particularly worried about the future, they are likely to hoard their savings in the form of money (under the bed or otherwise) rather than to properly invest those savings, whether directly in the stock market, providing a source of funding for businesses, or indirectly through the banking system, which in turn makes loans to businesses. This ability to hoard savings in the form of money means that savings do not automatically feed through to investment; the result is that the economy can end up in a position in which there is too little spending. The Classical view that the spending power that is lost when people save would automatically be pumped back into the economy through investment (as savings get recycled into the hands of investors) was, Keynes argued, false.

Even if the interest rate did fall in response to too little spending in the economy (in the form of people saving too much), Keynes was not convinced that it would bring forth the amount of investment needed to get the economy going again. Rather than the interest rate being the key driver of investment, Keynes argued that investors' 'state of confidence' in the future was much more important, along with the all-important 'animal spirits'. Since the future is, for Keynes, unknowable, the degree of optimism or pessimism about the future can have a great influence on how much firms want to invest. If firms feel they have reason to be concerned about the future, even very low interest rates may not be enough to induce them to borrow all of the available savings in the economy to invest – after all, why borrow money to invest in expanding your capacity if consumers are not spending much, even if it is cheap to do so? The result is that investment may not be enough to mop up the economy's savings and so total spending in the economy can fall below the level required to make sure all available goods on the shelves of shops are sold. As unsold goods build up in the stock rooms and factories across the country, firms make people redundant. This leads to a further reduction in spending as the newly unemployed workers reduce their spending, leading to ever greater stockpiles of unsold goods, more redundancies and so on in a vicious circle. Pessimistic beliefs about the future become self-fulfilling. This left government with the role of inspiring confidence in the future by promising to step in to boost demand should it ever be needed. Of course, where consumers and businesses had faith that government would behave in this way, a recession would be avoided as optimistic feelings about the future would also be self-fulfilling.

The Theoretical Red Herring: Price and Wage Stickiness

Whilst for Keynes the economy could become trapped in recession as a result of deficient demand, Classical economists felt that the market would always offer a way out. They argued that the free-market economy will automatically recover from the tendency to recession through the natural adjustment of prices and wages. In recessions, all policy-makers therefore had to do was to sit back and wait for prices and wages to fall. The kinds of heavy-handed intervention suggested by Keynes would not be necessary.

With lower prices, people would feel richer – any savings (or 'wealth') they have accumulated will allow them to buy more than ever before, in response to which they will naturally start to spend more. Furthermore, with lower prices, the economy will become more competitive and therefore, so long as it is open to world markets, it will be able to 'export' its way out of recession. Prices will keep falling until they reach the point at which total demand is back at its old level and all unsold goods are once again being bought. The only (temporary) problem is that with prices falling, the 'real' cost of employing a worker increases: if the firm is still paying the same wage as before (in pounds), but the value of what the worker is producing is less (given the lower prices at which goods are sold), workers effectively become more expensive. In an effort to avoid being made redundant, however, workers will supposedly rationally choose to accept a cut in their wages that is in line with the lower prices, leaving them as well-off as before in terms of the number of goods they can afford. Workers are just as happy as before the shock, and, with costs back in line with prices, so are firms. The economy is back in balance again.

The implication is that reductions in demand – in spending in the economy – should not create a problem so long as prices and wages are free to adjust. Only a lack of awareness of the demand shock or interferences in the free market that prevent wage and price adjustment from taking place will stop the natural adjustment process kicking in, leading to a prolonged recession.

After Keynes's death, economists therefore reached a compromise between Keynesian and classical thinking: Keynes's demand deficiency problem was accepted as a possibility only in the short run, when prices and wages may be 'sticky', whilst in the long run classical economics was thought to prevail. Keynesian and classical economics were synthesized. In order to make the economy resilient to demand shocks, it was therefore argued that prices and wages should be as flexible as possible. Hence, from the 1970s onwards, free-market governments attempted to reduce the power of trade unions, making wages more flexible, whilst simultaneously breaking up and privatizing some of the big monopolies (such as utility companies) in an attempt to prevent price fixing, making prices more flexible.

However, not all followers of Keynes were happy with this compromise, or with the return to free-market thinking that it seemed to offer. For staunch Keynesians, falling prices brought more problems than they solved. In fact, they had the potential to make matters worse rather than better. To begin with, relying on falling domestic prices to make your goods more internationally competitive, allowing an economy to export its way out of recession, may not be feasible if other economies are also in recession or if globalization is under attack, making growth through exports tricky. Even relying on falling prices to stimulate domestic as opposed to export demand may not be sufficient. Whilst people with wealth may feel richer following a reduction in prices and so may be happy to spend a bit more, there are also plenty of people in the economy with debt, for whom falling prices only serve to increase their debt's 'real' value. For example, for a worker who has debt as a result of taking on a mortgage, falling prices and wages may make paying the mortgage much more difficult than they had anticipated, increasing the chance of default. Similarly, a firm that has debt as a result of previously borrowing, say, $100,000 will now (with prices falling) have to sell many more goods than it was initially expecting in order to repay this debt. The difficulty that firms and individuals subsequently face repaying their debts would, according to Irving Fisher, risk undermining the stability of the banking system.[20] Hence, if the economy is quite indebted, falling prices may actually lead to lower rather than higher spending and even a full-blown banking crisis, only serving to make matters worse and not better.

Rather than falling prices encouraging spending, as mainstream economists tend to argue, they can in fact do the opposite, getting the economy into a vicious circle. The implication is that economies are not always self-correcting; governments who sit around and wait for the economy to naturally recover – blindly maintaining their faith in the free-market adjustment process – may very well find themselves waiting forever, whilst presiding over an ever greater economic problem and ever growing social unrest. That sitting around, according to Keynesians, explains why the 1929 recession eventually turned into a depression, something that a little bit of early stimulus could have helped to avoid. Only the forced government spending of the Second World War and associated rearmament provided an eventual escape from the misery.

However, as far as modern-day Post-Keynesians are concerned, at the centre of Keynes's argument was not price and wage stickiness, as the economic textbooks came to suggest, and still suggest today; it was the fact that the future was inherently unknowable. No amount of price and wage flexibility would compensate for the possibility that the economy can fall into a trap of pessimism. And, as far as Keynes was concerned, modern-day financial markets made it all the more likely, something on which the economist Hyman Minsky has built.[21]

According to Keynes, the ease with which the stock market allows shares to be bought and sold with negligible transaction costs exacerbates the tendency to short-termism. It is this short-termism that makes the stock market more volatile than it otherwise would be, and which therefore makes it difficult for firms to raise the funds they need for long-term investment. We cannot be sure that financial markets will fund firms and sectors that deserve investment (as opposed to those who don't) when they are driven less by 'fundamentals' and more by excessive short-term speculation. Given the vital role that investment plays in long-term growth and also in ensuring that there is no demand deficiency (that there is sufficient investment to mop up savings), the instability of investment was, for Keynes, the central concern. Stabilizing investment should, he thought, be a central priority.

Keynes's Real Nemesis: Hayek and the Austrian School

Whilst in practice Keynes's thinking came to be challenged by a rebirth of Classical thinking in the course of the 1970s and 1980s, his real nemesis is the Austrian School. Unlike other free-market schools of thought, the Austrians share Keynes's belief in the natural instability of the market economy, and in the unknowable future. They do not, however, have the same faith as Keynes when it comes to the policymakers' ability to know and do better than the private sector.

Once we identify the unknowable future as being central to Keynes's thinking, rather than sticky prices and wages, it is not mainstream free-market economics that provides the most compelling attack on Keynesian thinking but, instead, the Austrian School of thought. Austrian thinking has much more in common with Keynes than does classical thinking or its neoclassical and new classical variants.

Like Keynes, Austrian economists do not assume that the capitalist economy is naturally stable. However, they see recessions as the product of over-investment in boom times, rather than a result of underinvestment. For Austrians, having run out of other productive opportunities during boom times, investors end up backing speculative investments that are not always worthwhile. Policies to stimulate investment of a Keynesian kind will only serve to make matters worse rather than better. The economy is in periodic need of a recession to shake out the unproductive investments such that it can get back on its feet.

Furthermore, whilst Austrian economists in many ways agree with Keynes that the future is unknowable, they argue that it is just as unknowable to the policymaker as it is to the private sector. Trusting in government to guide investment in the economy could therefore very easily take us in the wrong direction. What is instead needed is the variety that capitalism provides: businesses and investors who each have different ideas about the future and who each do their own thing, one of which will turn out to be right. Assuming that a single person – the state – will always back the right horse would be wrong-headed. The policymaker cannot tell what the future holds and so may end up ploughing taxpayers' money into a series of white elephant projects. Whilst economists working in the standard free-market tradition questioned the motives of policymakers and politicians, with public choice theory showing that they cannot be assumed to be benevolent, it is policymakers' inability to predict the future that presents just as much of an obstacle to the practical application of Keynesian thinking, according to the Austrian School. Even if the state is trustworthy and uncorrupt, it cannot be expected to know what the future holds. Whilst Keynes presented a believable attack on the market, he did not accompany it with a convincing enough case that governments can do much better.

Whilst Austrians may be right to suggest that there is a limit to what governments can do to stabilize the economy, this was not a message that proved appealing at the time of the Great Depression. It is a pity, then, that the most notable Austrian economist, Friedrich Hayek, never published a review of the *General Theory*.[22] In the absence of a direct confrontation between Keynesian and Austrian thinking, Keynesianism did not receive the kind of challenge it might otherwise have received from what would have been, and what still is, its best-equipped opponent. Without the challenge, and in the words of John Hicks, the economist who famously went on to formalize Keynes's thinking in the form of the IS-LM model, Hayek 'slipped through our fingers'.[23]

There is, however, one natural check on the activities of the state that can be identified within Keynes's own thinking, but which can only be understood in the wider context of his work. Keynes was not only an economist, he was a man of the world, a liberal who believed in a free and open society and in countries that look outward rather than inwards. Whilst he is often associated with anti-globalization thinking, Keynes was aware of the powerful benefits that international integration could bring, particularly in the form of the free movement of goods, services and people. Born into an era of globalization in the second half of the nineteenth century, and having seen it collapse after the First World War, Keynes helped to put in place the international institutions – such as Bretton Woods – needed for a return to globalization after the Second World War. Globalization not only creates a buoyant demand-side environment, helping to avoid recession, it also serves to keep governments in check by preventing them from abusing the power they are granted by the electorate to manage the economy in a Keynesian manner. Where they get it wrong, international comparisons make it abundantly clear for all to see, meaning voters can hold their governments to account. Market-based competition between states can be as powerful a disciplining force as competition between firms. It is, therefore, in a global, outward-looking world that Keynes's brand of mixing markets and the state can prove most beneficial. It is in times of retreat from the rest of the world that we have to worry about his particular brand of state interventionism turning into something else entirely; into, ironically, the communism and fascism that Keynes's thinking fought to avoid.

EIGHT

FRIEDRICH HAYEK

Scott Scheall

Friedrich August Hayek was born in Vienna on 8 May 1899, to parents of solid *Bildungsbürgertum* (educated bourgeois-liberal) stock and he was surrounded by scientific discussions from a young age. His father was a physician and a botanist, who taught part-time at the University of Vienna and who instilled in his eldest son a deep respect for the career of university professor. Hayek's mother was the daughter of a well-known statistician, and a distant cousin of the famous philosopher Ludwig Wittgenstein.

The fact that Hayek was born in Vienna at the turn of the twentieth century is significant for his development as a social scientist. The cultural splendours of *fin de siècle* Vienna are well known. Among the city's denizens during Hayek's youth were world-renowned composers (Mahler, Schönberg), artists (Klimt and the Vienna Secessionists), writers (Zweig, Musil, Kraus, Schnitzler), philosophers (Brentano, Meinong), architects (Loos, Wagner), natural scientists (Mach, Boltzmann, Schrödinger), psychologists (Freud) and, of course, economists. The Austrian School of economics founded by Carl Menger, and carried on by Eugen Böhm von Bawerk, Friedrich von Wieser and, later, Joseph Schumpeter and Ludwig von Mises, was at the international apex of the profession in the first decades of the century.

To be born at that time and in that place was to experience a series of previously unseen social cataclysms, which the keenest minds were unable to predict, let alone prevent. It meant participation in the First World War, with all its horrors. It meant witnessing the post-war dismemberment of the Austro-Hungarian Empire and the abdication of the Habsburg monarchy, who had ruled large swathes of Central Europe since the eleventh century. It also meant suffering the notoriously pestilential conditions of post-war Vienna. Of special significance to Hayek's later career, a disastrous hyperinflation rampaged across much of Europe, hitting Germany and the former Austro-Hungarian Empire especially hard.[1] This episode followed from political decisions taken by the erstwhile Central Powers to finance expenditures during the war years and beyond by printing more and more money. As a result, the *Bildungsbürgertum* saw their savings and prospects evaporate.

Erwin Dekker has recently argued that the economists of the Austrian School are best interpreted as 'students of civilization', who sought to understand how the disasters of the world wars emerged from the same Central European milieu that gave rise to the School itself, with its prized liberal values of individualism, toleration, pacifism and internationalism.[2] According to Dekker, these scholars came to understand that civilization is possible only at the high cost of restraining many of our deepest instinctual drives, such as the instinct to enforce uniformity on those different from ourselves, and to shun our practical responsibilities and ethical duties. Preserving Vienna's comparatively liberal culture required that members of the Empire's many distinct nationalities and religious groups treat each other civilly, and with mutual respect; it meant keeping contractual commitments, protecting the bodies and property of others and peaceful participation in civil society and the democratic process. Unfortunately, just at this moment, appeals to the people were heard from both extreme ends of the political spectrum, promising a rationally reconstructed and improved society, if only these primitive instincts were indulged rather than restrained. Both socialism and National Socialism promised utopia by way of the deliberate expropriation and, if necessary, extermination of some faceless 'other': for socialists, the bourgeoisie; for fascists, non-Aryans. Both political philosophies gave licence to some of our worst inclinations to envy, insularity, tribalism and violence.

Hayek developed many of these themes over a long career that spanned seven decades of a century marred throughout by vicious totalitarian politics. However, beyond arguments of this sort, he confronted those who aspired to control and plan society with an insurmountable epistemic difficulty. Regardless of the alleged moral splendour and excellence of any ethical principles that might appear to justify the endeavour, anyone who wishes to control society faces a knowledge problem. Put simply, they do not know how to do it and, more to the point, they *cannot* know how to do it. Society, in all its ugliness and beauty, is determined more by unintended consequences than by the intentional realization of political designs.

The Vienna Years: Methodology, Monetary Theory and Mises

Hayek enrolled at the University of Vienna in late 1918 upon his return from service in the Imperial Army. During his first years at the university, Hayek was especially attracted to the study of psychology. In 1920 he wrote his first surviving academic essay, an extension and criticism of the psychological theory of the influential Viennese physicist Ernst Mach. On Hayek's view, consciousness is an emergent property of the relations between networks of neurons in the brain. Hayek's teachers encouraged him to develop his theory further, but he set the project aside to focus on other coursework and did not return to it for nearly thirty years.[3]

Hayek chose economics over psychology for its superior job prospects, a reasonable explanation, if rather banal for a future Nobel Laureate.[4] Ironically, Hayek was first introduced to the Austrian School of economics by Othmar Spann, an economics professor at the University of Vienna, who was neither a member of the School nor otherwise an inspiration to Hayek. Spann gave Hayek his first copy of Menger's *Grundsätze der Volkswirtschaftslehre* (*Principles of Economics*), the founding charter of the Austrian School.[5] However, Spann's own 'intuitive universalism', according to which social-scientific reasoning proceeds from ingrained knowledge of holistic social entities, such as the aggregates of modern macroeconomics, was anathema to the economists of the Austrian School, who have long denied the methodological value of holistic approaches to economics.[6]

The methodology of the Austrian School is individualistic. According to Menger and his followers, any adequate explanation of social phenomena must start with the actions of individuals. From an Austrian perspective, to analyse social phenomena using aggregative concepts, such as Gross Domestic Product (GDP), which simply adds up everything produced in the economy without distinguishing apples from oranges or screwdrivers from computers, is to neglect much of what is interesting about economic phenomena. The methods of the Austrian School are also theoretical. Indeed, Austrian economists were early adopters of the now widely accepted view that sensory experience is theory-dependent, meaning that, without the aid of a theory to distinguish the individual objects of perception from each other, without criteria to differentiate, say, a visual experience of a dog from one of a cat, you would not see these *things*, but just an undifferentiated mass of visual stimuli.[7] Finally, the methods of the Austrian School are thoroughly subjectivist. Given that the actions of any individual are a consequence of their subjective perspective, social analysis must proceed as far as possible from what is known about these subjective perceptions. It is this unique methodological blend that has always distinguished the Austrian School from other schools of economic thought.[8]

After completing his first doctorate, Hayek needed a job. He turned for advice to Friedrich von Wieser, with whom he would soon complete a second doctorate.[9] Wieser wrote a letter of introduction and told Hayek to visit Ludwig von Mises, who was then managing the temporary *Abrechnungsamt* (Office of Accounts) organized to settle international debt claims associated with the war. For reasons related to his religion (Jewish), his politics (arch-liberal) and his attitude (difficult), Mises was never given the professorship at the University of Vienna that he was due. Mises's haughty response to Hayek's arrival in the *Abrechnungsamt* has become the stuff of legend. Wieser's letter referred to Hayek as a talented young economist; 'If this is so,' Mises asked, 'why haven't I seen you at my lectures?' Hayek had in fact attended a few of Mises's talks, but was turned off by his fervent commitment to classical liberalism. At the time, Hayek's politics inclined towards the soft, non-Marxian, Fabian socialism favoured by Wieser. This proved little hindrance to a working relationship with Mises, however, and Hayek was hired on the spot.[10]

Mises soon disabused Hayek of his youthful attachment to socialism. First in an influential paper published in 1920 and later in the book *Socialism* (1922), Mises argued that the administrators of a socialist commonwealth isolated from market activity could never possess the knowledge necessary to purposefully bring the supply of goods in line with demand. In a society in which all private property had been confiscated by the state there would be no market, and hence no prices.[11] Without prices, the socialist administrators could not calculate the profits and losses of their operations. How would they therefore keep supply in line with demand?[12] Hayek later wrote of the profound impact of Mises's book. 'It gradually but fundamentally altered the outlook of many of the young idealists returning to their university studies after the World War. I know, for I was one of them.'[13]

Hayek worked in the *Abrechnungsamt* until early 1923, when he left on a research trip to the United States. There he conducted statistical research on economic fluctuations and the monetary policies of the recently established U.S. Federal Reserve. Upon his return to Vienna in 1927 he and Mises created the *Österreichisches Institut für Konjunkturforschung* (Austrian Institute for Business Cycle Research). Hayek served as the Institute's first director.[14]

His first book-length foray into business-cycle theory proper arrived in 1929 (at the same time, tragically, so did the Wall Street Crash and the onset of the Great Depression). In *Monetary Theory and the Trade Cycle*, Hayek considered the methodology of business-cycle theorizing. The main problem was one that Hayek had addressed in earlier work and would return to repeatedly throughout his career: the main theoretical apparatus of economics, the theory of equilibrium ('the theory of supply and demand'), is fundamentally unsuited to an explanation of economic *disequilibria* – recessions (and their opposite, 'inflationary episodes', when the economy is overheated). By assuming that individuals possess complete knowledge, that all technological change is given, and that all economic magnitudes (such as savings and investment) are in perfect balance, equilibrium theory assumes away the possibility of the fluctuations that characterize the business cycle. Economists were confronted with a choice between modifying equilibrium theory to make it a better tool for business-cycle analysis or reinventing the most fundamental theory in all of economics.[15] Hayek adopted the first approach in 1929, arguing that the standard equilibrium framework could explain economic fluctuations if supplemented with various assumptions concerning the use of money and the role of bankers in the economy. He eventually came to believe that more drastic measures were required.

The London Years: Friends and Friendly Rivals

Hayek's work soon came to the attention of Lionel Robbins, the young chair of the London School of Economics (LSE). Unlike many British economists, especially those associated with Cambridge, whose reputation for ignorance of foreign schools of economic thought was well earned, Robbins had visited Vienna several times and was sympathetic to the Austrians' unique approach. Robbins invited Hayek to present a series of lectures at the LSE early in 1931 that would be published later that year as *Prices and Production*, Hayek's business-cycle masterwork.[16]

The world was deep in the throes of the Depression when Hayek arrived in London. The need for an explanation of why and how the world economy had collapsed over the prior two years, and of what, if anything, could be done about it, was profound. Hayek extended the analysis first offered in *Monetary Theory and the Trade Cycle.* In this earlier book, he had rejected Mises's conclusion that only deliberate manipulation of the money supply could set industrial fluctuations in motion. Hayek argued instead that, regardless of the decisions of bankers, oscillations in economic activity were a permanent feature of any economy with an elastic currency, that is, where the money supply can shift independently of the decisions of consumers and producers.[17] Hayek agreed with Mises to the extent that deliberate monetary policy could set the cycle in motion and, as a historical matter, might be the cause of most cyclical episodes in the real world; however, Hayek made the point that, regardless of the motives of bankers, the practical problem of maintaining the economy in equilibrium is ultimately an epistemic one: bankers do not know how to ensure that their lending activities are neutral with respect to real economic activity.[18] The only 'solution' was to eliminate bank credit altogether, but this would mean forgoing its considerable benefits, including the possibility of more rapid economic growth.[19] Thus, Hayek concluded, there was no simple practicable solution to the problem of the Depression. Only time could correct the distortions wrought by the elasticity of the money supply.

Though the policy implications were gloomy, the lectures were nonetheless well received, and Robbins immediately offered Hayek a position at the LSE.[20] For a brief moment virtually everyone in the British economics community became a Hayekian. It would not last.

Robbins saw in Hayek's work a potential counterweight to Cambridge and, especially, the growing influence of John Maynard Keynes. Robbins soon gave Hayek a formal assignment: attack Keynes and Cambridge. The published debate that followed between Hayek and Keynes, for all its renown, was quite brief and, ultimately, a bit underwhelming.[21]

Like many people from the countries defeated in the First World War, Hayek idolized Keynes. A generation older, Keynes first achieved worldwide recognition as the British economic representative to the 1919 Versailles peace conference. Keynes had broken with the British contingent and left the conference over the question of the reparations bill to be put to the vanquished nations. Keynes argued in *The Economic Consequences of the Peace* (1919) that the crippling reparations bill agreed upon by the victors would have disastrous economic and moral consequences for the defeated countries. This stance made Keynes a hero in the German-speaking world, even among the economists of the Austrian School, who would oppose his later economic theories and their policy implications.[22]

Keynes had spent the last half of the 1920s developing what he hoped would prove his magnum opus. Published in 1930, *The Treatise on Money* attributed economic fluctuations to discrepancies between savings and investment.[23] Hayek's main objections to the book were methodological: Keynes failed to ground his analysis upon an elaborated theory of capital, a foundation that Hayek argued was necessary to any substantive discussion of the relationship between savings and investment. Moreover, Keynes's argument ran in terms of the effects of discrepancies between savings and investment upon the (aggregative) general level of prices, rather than upon relative prices between different classes of goods, a methodological approach that Hayek rejected as irrelevant to the cycle. In his response to Hayek's criticisms, Keynes argued that, though it might be nice to build an analysis of economic fluctuations on an adequate theory of capital, it probably was not necessary and, in any case, was impossible, given that, in Keynes's own view, no capital theory adequate to his purposes was then available. Hayek argued in return that Keynes misunderstood the significance of the Austrian theory of capital, which, when added to Keynes's theoretical framework, resulted in a business-cycle theory that looked like Hayek's own. From there, the debate descended into the details of capital theory and the question of the adequacy of Hayek's approach and, very soon thereafter, petered out as the two principals exhausted each other's patience.

From a Hayekian perspective, it is probably apt to adopt the metaphor of winning the battle, but losing the war, at least, the war for public opinion. Most readers in the early 1930s accepted the criticisms that Hayek (and many others – the *Treatise* was widely reviewed in the journals of the day) levelled against Keynes. However, the latter had expressed his own dissatisfaction with the book, so it was perhaps not too shocking when it received withering criticism from others. Keynes retrenched and, a few years later, produced his real masterpiece, *The General Theory of Employment, Interest and Money* (1936). Unfortunately, for reasons that have never been satisfactorily explained, Hayek chose not to review the new book. He offered various explanations for this over the subsequent decades, but ultimately came to agree with the rest of the world that he should have treated the *General Theory* to the same critical analysis he had given the *Treatise*. As he put it in 1963, with some regret, 'I have to the present day not quite got over the feeling that I . . . shirked what should have been a plain duty.'[24]

In 1935 Hayek edited a collection of papers on the socialist-calculation debate, many of which had never appeared in English before. Hayek provided his readers with a historical overview and criticized several proposals that had recently appeared for solving the calculation problem raised by Mises.[25] Mises had assumed a fully collectivized socialist economy completely isolated from all market institutions, most importantly, from all market-determined prices. Hayek showed that even if this assumption were relaxed – if, say, elements of competition were allowed in an otherwise centrally planned economy – it remained highly implausible that conscious political control could outperform the price system as a market-clearing mechanism.[26] Indeed, Hayek argued that any attempt to manage the economy so as to mirror the equilibrating effects of prices would fail to match what unmanaged markets achieve.[27] The problem, again, is an epistemic one: policymakers cannot know what markets *would* do where markets don't in fact exist.

Hayek adopted a different tack against central planning in his most famous book, *The Road to Serfdom* (1944).[28] Talk of the alleged benefits of a planned economy had been on many lips in Britain throughout the Second World War. Hayek argued that those who longed for central planning, including many of his British friends, sorely misconceived socialism if they thought it anything other than a strain of the same disease then infecting Nazi Germany. Both socialism and Nazism were systems of centrally administered economic planning. The only difference between them concerned who would benefit (and, conversely, suffer) from such planning. Socialists proposed to expropriate the bourgeoisie and plan the economy for the benefit of the working classes; Nazis proposed to take from non-Aryans and give to Aryans. Otherwise, Hayek argued, there was little of economic significance to distinguish the two political programmes.[29]

Hayek's argument in *The Road to Serfdom* is often characterized as an instance of the slippery-slope fallacy, that even the slightest movement in the direction of central planning will lead inexorably to totalitarian slavery. His point is more sophisticated than this caricature suggests. At each stage in the central-planning process – from the (presumably, democratic) agreement to adopt planning, through deliberation of which plan to adopt, to the implementation of the chosen plan – resistance will be encountered.[30] There will be those who resist all central planning; those who want planning, but who reject the selected plan; and those who like the chosen plan, but dislike what is required for its implementation and enforcement. The key question is: what are the planning authorities to do about this opposition?

If the plan is to be carried through (it is always possible to give up on central planning and revert to the market), the state planners will have to find some, perhaps unsavoury, way of overcoming this political resistance. Thus, Hayek's argument is not that a single step towards socialism inevitably leads to totalitarianism – the road to serfdom has off-ramps and roundabouts – rather, Hayek's point is that, in the face of inevitable resistance, the relentless pursuit of a central plan will require the infringement of political liberties and various enforcement mechanisms abhorred by those very same well-intentioned socialists who desire planning. Put another way, central planning is an ineffective means to the ends of socialism (social justice, economic equality and so forth).

The Road to Serfdom made Hayek very famous in the English-speaking world, especially after a condensed version appeared in *Reader's Digest*. He toured the United States lecture circuit. The popular magazine *Look* published a cartoon version of the book. Even Winston Churchill referred to the book's argument, if not its title or author, in a speech on the eve of the first post-war election in May 1945 (which his Conservatives lost in a landslide to Clement Attlee's Labour Party). The book was widely reviewed, receiving extravagant praise and vehement denunciation, but little in between.[31]

Despite this publicity (or perhaps in part because of it), by the time Hayek left England in 1950 for the United States and the University of Chicago (where, significantly, he was hired not to the famous economics department but to the unaffiliated Committee on Social Thought), it was generally agreed that, whatever battles Hayek may have won along the way, he (and, by extension, the Austrian School he represented) had been roundly – and finally – defeated in both wars with Keynesians and socialists. Keynes's followers were ascendant throughout the economics discipline, while the British welfare state was mostly in place, without totalitarian consequences. So, Hayek entered an extended wilderness period during which he continued to write and publish, albeit for an audience much smaller than had received *The Road to Serfdom*.

The Chicago and Freiburg Years: The Core Hayek Emerges

It is one of the ironies of Hayek's career that he only truly came into his own as a social theorist when he entered the wilderness. Over the remainder of his career, Hayek developed an approach to social phenomena that synthesized elements from several disciplines: not just economics and methodology, but psychology, biology, philosophy, history and law. The foundation for this transformation was laid in a series of groundbreaking papers published between 1936 and 1948.

In the first of these papers, 'Economics and Knowledge', Hayek developed the scepticism he had earlier expressed concerning the significance of equilibrium theory for certain economic problems.[32] He noted that the concept of equilibrium has a clear meaning in the context of a single economic actor: to say that some person is 'in equilibrium' is to say that they hold an internally consistent plan of action, that they can act without contradiction, as would arise if their plan required the same person to be in two places at one time. But, Hayek asked, what does it mean to say that society, or the whole economy, where no one person knows everything and each of us holds different beliefs, is in equilibrium? What does it mean to say that action at the social level can proceed without contradiction?

It cannot mean merely that everyone is in individual equilibrium in the sense above: even if each of our plans is internally consistent, they might be mutually inconsistent. My plan to, say, buy your car for £1,000 may require that you act in a way that is not part of your plan. If your plan is to not sell your car for less than £1,500, then we cannot both implement our plans successfully. We are not in economic equilibrium. One or both of us must revise our plans if we are to coordinate our actions. Nor is it sufficient for each person's plan to be both internally consistent and mutually consistent with respect to the plans of others: plans might be internally and mutually consistent, yet be contradicted by considerations not accurately reflected in relevant plans. For example, we might each settle on a plan that I will buy your car for £1,250; but, if your car is stolen and sold for parts on the black market before we can consummate the deal, then, again, we cannot both implement our plans successfully, and we are out of equilibrium. Thus, Hayek concluded in 'Economics and Knowledge', equilibrium describes a state in which each person's plan is internally consistent, mutually consistent and correct with respect to facts relevant to the plan's execution. If and only if these conditions are satisfied will each person in society be able to effectively implement their respective plans.

If a state of equilibrium were ever to be realized, it would mean that we could all act without either bumping up against each other or being disappointed by what happens in the world. Obviously no one (not even a mainstream economist) is deluded enough to think that such a state could ever exist in the real world. Rather, economic theories typically assume that, under normal conditions, there is a *tendency* towards equilibrium which, in the real world, where circumstances are ever changing, can never be fully realized. Hayek argued that there is good evidence that the assumption of a tendency towards equilibrium is generally true of the real world.[33] If this condition did not obtain, it would be common to observe, say, two petrol stations a block apart selling the same gallon of gasoline at wildly different prices. That this is rarely, if ever, observed is evidence for the operation of a tendency towards economic equilibrium under normal conditions.

If this is what is meant by equilibrium, then the fundamental problem of economics concerns the various mechanisms that might either help or hinder the tendency for the beliefs of different individuals to become both better coordinated across persons and more accurate with respect to pertinent facts. This is the problem that Hayek took up in 'The Use of Knowledge in Society', regularly cited as one of the most important papers in twentieth-century economics.[34] Under market competition, each individual plans their own economic activity and must adapt their plans to those of other individuals. Under socialism, all economic activity is planned and directed from the centre. Which system of economic planning, Hayek asked, best encourages (or least hinders) the operation of the tendency towards economic equilibrium?[35]

If all the knowledge in society were scientific knowledge, capable of expression in the form of general rules or laws, there would be no question of socialism's superiority to competition. If this were the case, presumably, all the knowledge in society could be gathered up and placed at the disposal of a central-planning politburo. However, Hayek noted that there is a very important kind of knowledge that can never be collected and conveyed to government planners: the knowledge that each of us possesses with respect to our own unique economic situation, or, as Hayek called it, knowledge 'of particular circumstances of time and place'. It is with respect to this kind of knowledge that decentralized planning has a decided advantage over socialism.[36]

Hayek's 'tin example', a description of the role that freely adjusting prices play in coordinating the plans of far-flung individuals, is one of the most famous passages of twentieth-century economics:

> Assume that somewhere in the world a new opportunity for the use of some raw material, say, tin, has arisen, or that one of the sources of supply of tin has been eliminated. It does not matter for our purpose – and it is significant that it does not matter – which of these two causes has made tin more scarce. All that the users of tin need to know is that some of the tin they used to consume is now more profitably employed elsewhere, and that, in consequence, they must economize tin. There is no need for the great majority of them even to know where the most urgent need has arisen, or in favour of what other needs they ought to husband the supply. If only some of them know directly of the new demand, and switch resources over to it, and if the people who are aware of the new gap thus created in turn fill it from still other sources, the effect will rapidly spread throughout the whole economic system and influence not only all the uses of tin but also those of its substitutes and the substitutes of these substitutes, the supply of all things made of tin, and their substitutes, and so on; and all this without the great majority of those instrumental in bringing about these substitutions knowing anything at all about the original cause of these changes. The whole acts as one market, not because any of its members survey the whole field, but because their limited individual fields of vision sufficiently overlap so that through many intermediaries the relevant information is communicated to all. The mere fact that there is one price for any commodity . . . brings about the solution which (it is just conceptually possible) might have been arrived at by one single mind possessing all the information which is in fact dispersed among all the people involved in the process.[37]

The price system accomplishes what could otherwise be managed only by an omniscient and omnipotent dictator. Prices provide to each of us in summary form knowledge that we need to adapt our plans to those of others and to ever-changing circumstances. An important corollary of this is that prices serve this function less well the more they are controlled and manipulated. Related to this, prices are of limited value to the planning authorities, who do not possess the necessary complement of knowledge of relevant circumstances of time and place required to make knowledge of prices effective. Competition allows this knowledge to be used where and when it is needed. The adjustment of a central plan to changing prices will always be too slow relative to what competition can achieve.

In 'The Meaning of Competition', Hayek considered the question of how to evaluate the performance of an economic system. He argued that it is a mistake to appraise real-world markets according to the standard set by the theory of perfect competition. That markets in the real world never perform to the standard of perfection is not an indication of 'market failure'. The relevant question – answered in 'The Use of Knowledge in Society' – is not whether markets are perfect, but whether we can better accomplish our goals with or without market-determined prices.[38] Hayek later extended this argument to show that, much like science, market competition is a discovery procedure, a mechanism for acquiring knowledge that cannot be acquired without it.[39] Thus, the task confronting the central planner is not merely the difficult one of acquiring the relevant data, it is the impossible one of acquiring knowledge that simply does not exist without markets.

What Hayek accomplished in this series of papers was to conceive of an economics that was fundamentally concerned not with goods and services per se, but with the epistemic processes whereby knowledge concerning goods and services is acquired and communicated. Hayek soon came to realize that this innovative vision of social science as concerned primarily with the coordination of knowledge carried implications far beyond society.

Order (née equilibrium) in any domain, social or natural, is a condition of the well-coordinated activities of its elements. Order might be either constructed (as in deliberately designed, implemented and enforced) or spontaneous (unintended, as it were, emerging from the activities of elements that do not aim at the formation of order). The order observed in a (well-run) military organization is an example of a constructed social order, while the order of a free market is an instance of spontaneous social order. In the latter, no one aims to construct a market as such, like military generals design an army; rather, a market emerges unintentionally from the combined pursuit of each person of the goals encompassed in their respective plans. Hayek thought that it was this emergence of well-ordered markets out of the pursuit of individual plans of action that Adam Smith had in mind when he wrote of the 'invisible hand' that guides self-interest to public benefit.

Hayek was a bit embarrassed by the attention he received from *The Road to Serfdom*, given that the book was more normative and 'political' than the sort of serious scientific work upon which he always wanted to build his reputation. In the late 1940s, determined to rededicate himself to rigorous scientific study, Hayek returned to one of his first interests, psychology, and dug out the old paper on consciousness that he had written as a student in 1920. The substance of his theory of mental phenomena had not changed, but after three decades in academia, he was far better equipped to express it. The result was *The Sensory Order* (1952), an important work in Hayek's canon, for it is where he first explicitly recognized the ubiquity of spontaneous order in a context outside of the social sciences. Hayek's cognitive psychology is a forerunner of modern 'connectionist' accounts of cognition, according to which mental phenomena emerge from the links between networks of neuronal firings. In Hayek's language, the sensory (or mental) order is a spontaneous one, an undesigned and unintended consequence of the activities of neurons.[40]

Once Hayek recognized the existence of spontaneous orders, he found them everywhere in both society and nature. Other examples of spontaneous social orders include natural languages, the rules of which are not preordained but emerge from practical use, and the institution of money, which was not designed beforehand, but evolved unconsciously out of primitive barter practices.[41]

Hayek was enormously productive in developing this new approach to social phenomena over the quarter-century between 1950 and 1975.[42] Turning away from an older Austrian conception of the social sciences as methodologically distinct from the natural sciences, Hayek argued that the methods of the social and natural sciences are ultimately the same. However, he noted an important distinction in our ability to predict and explain different degrees of orderly phenomena. Orders can be distinguished as either simple, if they result from the activities of relatively few known (or knowable) elements, or complex, if the elements and relations between them are so numerous as to exceed the limits of human knowledge.[43] The social disciplines are sciences of complex phenomena: we are limited in these fields to explanations of the principle that regulates the activities of the elements, and to predictions of patterns to be found in complex events. We can never fully explain or precisely predict events in the sciences of complex phenomena.[44]

Hayek associated the spectrum between simple and complex phenomena with a range in the cognitive tractability or 'rationality' of the phenomena.[45] Simple orders are rational in a constructivist sense, that is, we possess the knowledge necessary to fully reconstruct them. More complex orders are rational in another sense, which later Hayekians have called 'ecological': such orders could be fully reconstructed, if only we possessed all of the causally relevant knowledge (which we do not in fact possess).[46] Hayek associated this distinction in cognitive tractability of orders of different degrees of complexity with a bifurcation in the attitudes that might be adopted with respect to orderly phenomena. Constructivist rationalists treat all orders, regardless of their complexity, as cognitively tractable – as simple. On the other hand, ecological rationalists recognize the possibility of orders whose complexity outstrips our cognitive abilities.

Constructivist rationalists often support central planning or interventionist economic policies. Ecological rationalists, however, tend to see the epistemic difficulties involved in such policies as, to some extent, beyond our cognitive capacities. Hayek recognized that most social phenomena result from a combination of constructivist and ecological rationality. Few social orders are either completely planned or entirely spontaneous, but Hayek argued that economists had mostly lost sight of even the possibility of spontaneously ordered social phenomena. Having somehow lost their original foundation in the deeply ecological rationalism of Adam Smith, most economists, Hayek thought, had come to embrace constructivism.

After decades of neglect from the mainstream economics community, Hayek was shocked and delighted to be awarded the 1974 Nobel Prize in Economic Science. The prize came at a fortuitous time for Hayek, as the world was then suffering the very inflationary consequences of Keynesianism, of which he and his fellow Austrians had long warned. Hayek's Nobel Prize lecture (reproachfully titled 'The Pretence of Knowledge') excoriated the economics profession for taking the Keynesian turn. He also summarized his vision of an economic science fundamentally concerned with complex phenomena that had been warped by the hubristic constructivist rationalism of Keynesians and socialists:

> If man is not to do more harm than good in his efforts to improve the social order, he will have to learn that in this, as in all other fields where essential complexity . . . prevails, he cannot acquire the full knowledge which would make mastery of the events possible. He will therefore have to use what knowledge he can

> achieve, not to shape the results as the craftsman shapes his handiwork, but rather to cultivate a growth by providing the appropriate environment, in the manner in which the gardener does this for his plants . . . The recognition of the insuperable limits to his knowledge ought indeed to teach the student of society a lesson of humility which should guard him against becoming an accomplice in men's fatal striving to control society – a striving which makes him not only a tyrant over his fellows, but which may well make him the destroyer of a civilization which no brain has designed but which has grown from the free efforts of millions of individuals.[47]

Hayek's reputation rebounded considerably after the Nobel Prize. By the time of his death in March 1992, the notion that he lost both debates with Keynesians and socialists had been rejected by many. The fall of the Berlin Wall and Iron Curtain were potent symbols of the failure of central planning. In seeking to explain these events, many turned to the arguments offered by Hayek and Mises earlier in the century.[48] Though it would be a mistake to identify their eventual policies with Hayek, both Ronald Reagan and Margaret Thatcher came to power mouthing Hayekian arguments in defence of their campaign promises. Keynesianism had been usurped in most economics departments. Though the neoclassical approach that took its place cannot be described as Hayekian or Austrian in any meaningful sense, by 1992 Hayek was once again what he had been for a brief moment in the early 1930s: the most famous economist alive.

Hayekian Economics and the Mainstream

Hayek began his career as 'a very pure and narrow economic theorist.'[49] Over several decades his thinking evolved in such a way that his later economics bore little resemblance to the mainstream. Indeed, Hayek's economics became so saturated with ideas from other disciplines that it has long been commonplace to assert that, at some point in his career, Hayek left economics behind. The secondary literature on Hayek is littered with arguments for this or that purportedly fundamental break in his thinking.[50]

Hayek changed over the course of his long scholarly career, but so did economics. In particular, the discipline became more formalized, idealized and mathematized, all changes for the worse from Hayek's point of view, further instances of the constructivist tendency to treat the modern economy (or any other fundamentally complex order) as simple. Viewed from the perspective of the changes that roiled economics in the interwar and, especially, post-war eras, the question to ask is not whether and, if so, when Hayek left economics, but when did economics leave Hayek?

Like several among those featured in this volume, Hayek was a great economic thinker in large part because he was more than a mere economist. Indeed, one of his most famous quotations expresses a willingness to go beyond economics as a practical prerequisite of a great economic thinker: 'The physicist who is only a physicist can still be a first-class physicist and a most valuable member of society. But nobody can be a great economist who is only an economist – and I am even tempted to add that the economist who is only an economist is likely to become a nuisance if not a positive danger.'[51] Hayek lived this advice. He contributed to fields closely related to economics (methodology, history of economic thought), to fields only peripherally related to economics (intellectual history, the philosophies of science, law, politics) and to fields seemingly far removed from economics (cognitive science, philosophy of mind, epistemology). But, of course, possessing varied interests and even publishing across disciplines cannot suffice to qualify an economist as a great economic thinker. Hayek was a true polymath in the sense that he brought these assorted interests to bear on his work in economics.

The Hayekian research programme is best understood as an elaboration of the thesis that the tools of economics (and of the social sciences more generally) are inadequate to many of the tasks – especially political tasks – to which they are applied. If there is one lesson to take away from Hayek, it is this: economics and the social sciences do not provide knowledge sufficient to realize many of the ambitions of policymakers. This is an important lesson to keep ever in mind, regardless of your political perspective, and a prophylactic against the silliest forms of political hubris. Nor should Hayek's devout classical liberalism hinder an appreciation of his social theory. Yes, Hayek thought classical liberalism less hubristic than other political philosophies, but the Hayekian lesson is relevant across the entire political spectrum. No one party has a monopoly on the pretence of knowledge.

NINE

MILTON FRIEDMAN

Victoria Bateman

Two centuries after the publication of Adam Smith's *An Inquiry into the Nature and Causes of the Wealth of Nations* in 1776, a book commonly seen as the bible of laissez-faire, Milton Friedman (1912–2006) was awarded the Nobel Prize in Economics. Whilst often considered a central figure of the economic 'mainstream', Friedman was, however, a radical. He graduated into an America in the midst of the Great Depression, the fourth child of poor Jewish immigrants from Eastern Europe. Unlike many of his contemporaries, who drew the lesson from the 1930s that the invisible hand had its limits, Friedman became one of the free market's chief advocates. He spoke up for capitalism at a time when its future was in no way guaranteed, when communism was taking root in Eastern Europe and beyond and state intervention in the West was on the rise. This included in the USA, where F. D. Roosevelt's New Deal had created an alphabet soup of government agencies and where Lyndon Johnson's 'War on Poverty' had expanded the benefit system in pursuit of a 'Great Society'. Friedman challenged the economic direction of the day.

In the words of one of his great rivals, Paul Samuelson, 'no 20th-century economist had his importance in moving the American economic profession rightward from 1940 to the present.'[1] According to Friedman, capitalism was not only a means to an end – that of greater economic prosperity – but an end in itself: a guarantor of individual freedom. Socialism itself was not the threat, the concentration of power was. State control simply replaced multiple competing businesses with a single monopoly, run by the state. Whether it was a state monopoly or a private sector monopoly was beside the point for Friedman: either way, a lack of competition would limit the ability of individuals to find alternatives. When the state is in charge of whether and where we work, and what we can or cannot buy, individual freedom is threatened. For Friedman, free markets were not only necessary for economic liberty, they also provided the foundation for political liberty.

Friedman's personal experiences and those of his family framed the way he thought about capitalism. Friedman attributed his parents' survival to the American free enterprise system.[2] They had arrived in New York as unaccompanied teenagers, and, like so many other Eastern European immigrants, alone in the world and with nothing to offer but their bare hands, were faced with making a new life for themselves. Friedman's mother found work as a seamstress and his father as a petty trader.[3] After his father's death, Friedman found casual work to fund his studies and help his family.[4] Whilst his youth was not easy, Friedman certainly did not take the freedoms offered in America for granted and was well aware of the realities of alternative economic systems. It was this background and not the membership of an economic elite that made Friedman sceptical of state intervention and a champion of the free market.

Whilst Friedman's work formed an essential pillar of the Chicago School, one that rivalled Samuelson's Keynesian Harvard, it was not until the 1980s that his influence reached serious public policy circles. After an economic golden age following the Second World War, one in which the state had been expanding and the general public had come to take for granted low inflation, low unemployment and stable growth, the West plunged into a serious economic crisis. This was 1970s 'stagflation': unemployment and inflation escalated alongside one another, economic growth slowed and government deficits rocketed. It was an economic crisis that Friedman had himself predicted, and one for which his brand of laissez-faire combined with monetary restraint – keeping control of the money supply – seemed to offer a solution. Through the presidency of Ronald Reagan and prime ministership of Margaret Thatcher, Friedman's influence brought about a radical overhaul of economic policy; Friedman sat on Reagan's Economic Policy Advisory Board, a volunteer group of twelve economists. However, by his own admission, public opinion is shaped 'by experience, not by theory or philosophy', and 'only a crisis – actual or perceived – produces real change'.[5] It was the public, as much as Friedman's thinking, that was responsible for the neoliberal turn – a turn against the state and in favour of the market.

In what follows, this chapter will outline three of Friedman's key contributions to economics. First, his methodological thinking made famous by his *Essays in Positive Economics* (Chicago, 1953), which led Friedman to champion economics as a science and cast aside normative debates. Second, Friedman's monetary economics, from his theoretical resurrection of the Quantity Theory of Money to his empirical *A Monetary History of the United States* (Princeton, 1963) co-authored by Anna Schwartz. And, third, Friedman's broader political economy, particularly his focus on the virtues of the market. His books *Capitalism and Freedom* (Chicago, 1962) and *Free to Choose* (New York, 1980, co-authored by Rose Friedman) were bestsellers – the former has never gone out of print whilst the latter was accompanied by a ten-part PBS television series.

As we will see, Friedman's monetary economics and political economy were far from novel. Rather than being remembered for original ideas, he should instead be remembered for capturing the moment; for reviving already existing ideas at a time when policymakers and the public were looking for something new. Friedman presented a clear, consistent and comprehensive package, and one that tapped into the rhetoric of freedom, appealing to already deep-seated beliefs amongst the American public. As economic historian Joel Mokyr argues, influential thinkers from Francis Bacon to Karl Marx often swim in a pre-existing channel, becoming known for their ability to reach for the zeitgeist in a way that their colleagues or contemporaries, despite similar thinking, are unable to do.[6] Whether he knew it or not, and to borrow a term from Deirdre McCloskey, Friedman was an expert in rhetoric.[7] It was the combination of his monetary agenda with the other aspects of his work that made him an attractive 'one-stop-shop': thanks both to his promise that economics could be 'positive' (that it could rise above normative matters), seemingly placing all that Friedman had to say on a scientific footing; and to his political economy, which was particularly appealing at the time of the cold war. Never mind trawling through the views of numerous other economists, Friedman had an answer for everything. It was this breadth of thinking, rather than his depth, that helps account for Friedman's success.

Once one looks for depth, Friedman's work soon starts to crumble. Our consideration of each of the three key areas of his work will show that criticisms abound, small and large. The problem was that whilst Friedman eschewed the neoclassical tradition with which free-market economics is much more usually associated, he did not venture far enough. He was a man with one foot in one room and one foot in another, who never made the logical leap – perhaps because to do so would have undermined the appealing simplicity of his underlying message: that the free market can always be trusted. Friedman traded depth for breadth.[8] Where he was most convincing, he drew upon the

Austrian School and other such influences that surrounded him, including the thinking of Hayek; where he faltered, it was often a result of having swum too close to the very neoclassical stream he claimed to have abandoned. As a result, and as we will see, Friedman never quite managed to escape his implicit assumptions that the free-market economy is stable, that it is independent of society and culture and that an economist can remove him- or herself from bias. This was his ultimate undoing, and the undoing of economics more generally by the time we reached the Global Financial Crisis of 2008.

Economic Methodology

Before Friedman, economics was a mixture of art and science. Normative economics was at the forefront of the discipline. In their engagement with policymaking, it was impossible for economists to escape the question of what drives human happiness and what is the meaning of life. Economics was, as a result, filled with debate. It was a subject that drew upon politics, philosophy and religion, unsurprisingly known as 'political economy'. Friedman offered economists a complete reversal: one that made normative considerations subservient to positive economics. For Friedman, fact came before values. Science came before the arts.

In his landmark essay 'The Methodology of Positive Economics', Friedman suggested that by following a certain method, one of empirical corroboration of theoretical predictions, economics could achieve the same degree of objectivity as the natural sciences.[9] Friedman argued that economics could escape the kinds of ethical and value-based judgements that had occupied economists in the past. Positive economics could plough ahead regardless of normative considerations; hard truths would be impossible to contest, something which could help resolve differences of opinion as to the types of outcomes policymakers should be aiming to achieve. Friedman was hopeful that his schema could bring about consensus within the economics discipline: aspects on which all economists could agree, whatever their political or other persuasion, making policymaking significantly easier.

Friedman's idea proved popular.[10] With it, economists increasingly came to think of themselves as scientists, uncovering 'the truth' and arriving at firm answers, rather than endlessly debating issues over which there could never be a 'right' or easy answer.[11] Whilst to some, Friedman was the saviour of economics, adding rigour and setting the discipline free, for others he was the man who led economics down a dark alley. Friedman's methodological paper has, unsurprisingly, been called 'the most cited, influential, and controversial pieces of methodological writing in twentieth-century economics'.[12]

Friedman's notion that economics could somehow be purged of subjectivity is particularly debatable.[13] In the words of Deirdre McCloskey, 'Any economist believes more than his evidence of a suitably modernist and objective sort implies,' leading to conclusions that are more far-reaching than are truly deserved, and often as a result of taking something for granted that is in fact open to debate. An economist's experiences and conditioning will, after all, influence the types of questions they choose to ask, the methods they adopt, the kinds of phenomena they go on to measure and the way in which they interpret their results. According to the Nobel Prize-winning economist of the School of Institutionalism, Gunnar Myrdal:

> Biases in social science cannot be erased simply by 'keeping to the facts' and refining the methods of dealing with statistical data. Indeed, data and the handling of data are often more susceptible to tendencies towards bias than is 'pure thought'. The chaos of possible data for research does not organise itself into systematic knowledge by mere observation . . . If, in their attempts to be factual, scientists do not make their viewpoint explicit, they leave room for biases.[14]

Indeed, as Beatrice Cherrier argues, Friedman's past 'created lenses through which he interpreted new evidence, which he therefore saw as supporting his beliefs', generating a self-reinforcing cycle which, with the 'protective and united' Chicago backdrop and surrounded by people with similar backgrounds, meant that Friedman was 'remarkably immunized' from contrasting influences, including the Institutionalism of Wisconsin. She concludes that: 'Not only were Friedman's theoretical hypotheses informed by a priori beliefs about the stability of the economic system and the harmful effects of government intervention, but the very process whereby he confronted these hypotheses with facts – the collection of data, the choice of discriminating historical events, the modelling, and the interpretation of tests – also appeared undetermined and inconclusive enough to allow Friedman's values to enter the inquiry.'[15]

By contrast with Friedman, the Institutionalism with which Myrdal was associated considered the way in which tastes, technology and economic behaviour are shaped by 'institutions', including habits of thought, something which raises issues of social control: of what, in John. R. Commons's words, individuals 'can, must, or may do or not do'.[16] From a feminist perspective, one can also argue that Friedman's methodological appeal is testament to a socially conditioned taste for machismo, one that has brought an academic bias that places the sciences ahead of the arts, and which sees the sciences as being the most 'rigorous' area of study.[17]

Not only was Friedman mistaken to think that economists could be entirely objective, he seemed to neglect the fact that many of the thinkers with whom neoclassical and laissez-faire economics is associated thought much more carefully and deeply about the normative – ethical – dimension of economics. According to Avner Offer, 'Modern versions of the invisible hand in rational choice theory and neo-liberalism are . . . radical departures from the ethical legacy of Enlightenment and utilitarian economics, and are not consistent with Adam Smith's own position.'[18] And, as Valeria Mosini points out, even the mathematical economic genius that was Léon Walras thought about values as well as facts: his 'proof' of market efficiency came with a caveat that economists needed to think about ethics.[19] For Walras, laissez-faire worked but it was conditional: it needed to operate within an appropriate setting, and one in which economists could not escape normative considerations. For Hayek, economics needed to move beyond simple laissez-faire, to ensure an appropriate institutional setting within which markets would work best.[20] Whilst he did not agree with all of its recommendations, Hayek praised Henry Simons for the publication of his *A Positive Programme for Laissez Faire* in 1949.[21] For many similarly minded economists, the disagreement did not surround whether to embed laissez-faire within the right kind of institutional setting (on which there was a great deal of agreement), but precisely what that institutional setting should entail, concerning which the Mont Pelerin Society was designed to encourage debate. This type of agenda has much in common with the modern-day notion of 'predistribution' and the call to 'reform capitalism'. It was, however, an agenda that came to be banished from liberal thinking once Friedman's methodological thinking caught on, casting normative discussions to one side and raising economics to the level of a science. This ultimately opened the door for the Left to monopolize an agenda of ethics and values, one which would have previously been equally familiar to those sympathetic to laissez-faire.

Aside from his 'positive economics', there are, however, two aspects of Friedman's methodological thinking that receive far less attention and which have relatively more to offer us today.

First, Friedman believed that the experiences of Main Street – and not the writings of academics – determined policy moves and economic outcomes, as summed up in his statement that public opinion is shaped 'by experience, not by theory or philosophy'.[22] Keynes, by contrast, placed greater weight on the power of economists to influence public opinion, writing that 'practical men who believe themselves to be quite exempt from any intellectual influence, are usually the slaves of some defunct economist'.[23] In favour of Friedman, policy and electoral decisions certainly can and do go against the advice of economists, including in the case of Britain's 2016 referendum on its membership of the European Union. And, where economic policy has turned direction, it has often been in response to public opinion rather than economic texts. It was not economic thinking that brought down the Berlin Wall, but the experiences of everyday people: their frustration with the status quo. Neither was it simply the work of David Ricardo and Richard Cobden that brought an end to the British Corn Laws in 1846, ushering in the Free Trade movement: it was the workers and industrialists of the Industrial Revolution campaigning against the tariff protection that was pushing up the cost of living. Rather than being the leaders, economic thinkers with a supportive message often only come to the fore once the charge has begun, riding the popular wave.[24]

Second, Friedman believed that there were real limits to economists' ability to guide or direct the economy. Here, he once again fundamentally disagreed with the methodology of Keynesianism. Whilst Keynes himself did not envisage his magnum opus, the *General Theory*, as a system of equations, many of his followers certainly did. The economist was, as a result, placed in the driving seat of an economy where he or she was in command: able to press buttons to bring about a desired and predictable result. Keynes himself imagined a time in which being an economist would be rather dull and mechanical, much like being a dentist.

Even where economists have departed from Keynesian thinking, they have continued in the mathematical vein. That includes those following in the laissez-faire tradition: the New Classical school. Interestingly, however, and rather unlike Keynesianism, the solution to their equations suggests that it's just not worth the state trying to intervene. Friedman arrived at that same conclusion, although not through complicated maths. As far as he was concerned, this mathematical approach to economics was – if taken to extremes – fundamentally flawed: it led us to 'formal models of imaginary worlds, not generalisations about the real world'.[25] For Friedman, economists needed to accept that their knowledge of the economy is very limited and, by not doing so, they have led the public 'to expect standards of performance that as economists we do not know how to achieve'.[26] It is ironic, therefore, that by encouraging economics to become more 'scientific', Friedman also, perhaps inevitably, led it to become increasingly mathematical.

Monetarism in Theory

Perhaps the most deceptively simple but also fundamental result of Friedman's monetary economics is the point that for money to maintain its value, its supply needs to be carefully controlled. Given that money has existed for millennia, it is, however, no surprise that Friedman was far from being the first economist to think about the impact of money on the economy. He was a man who stood on the shoulders of giants and, as we will see, just so happened to be in the right place at the right time when it came to being remembered for an idea over which he certainly did not have sole ownership.

The impact of money on the economy had long been debated and, in particular, whether it could have 'real' (output) effects as well as 'nominal' (price level) effects. The Mercantilists of the seventeenth century were aware that an excessive inflow of precious metals could inflate prices, though they did suggest that it could also act to the wider benefit of the economy by stimulating trade and production. Irving Fisher and Knut Wicksell set the precedent for modern-day monetary thinking in the nineteenth century, with Friedman following in the tradition of the former, in contrast to the Austrian, Keynesian and Stockholm schools of thought, who followed in the footsteps of the latter. Friedman also benefited from his teacher, Henry Simons, who in the first half of the twentieth century had emphasized the importance of controlling the money supply and the advantages of rules-based monetary policymaking, pointing to the dangers of giving monetary authorities too much discretion. James Angell had, furthermore, recommended a policy of constant money growth to help stabilize the economy, something with which Friedman later became associated.[27]

However, despite having an historical precedent, and far from being the only economist working in the monetary sphere, Friedman's work is commonly seen as having presented the key challenge to the relatively more 'dominant' Keynesian school of the 1950s and 1960s. According to Keynes, economic instability was a natural part of any free-market economy and originated in the volatility of investment. By contrast, Friedman argued that instability was a result of unstable money growth.[28] Whilst Keynesians had de-emphasized the importance of monetary policy, turning to fiscal policy (taxation and government spending) instead, Friedman argued that monetary policy was extremely powerful – a power that accounted for its ability to destabilize the economy.

It was, therefore, against this backdrop that 'monetarism' sought to bring money back into economics and to argue for its prime importance in determining incomes, output and prices. Friedman played a pivotal role in his restatement of the Quantity Theory of Money: an identity that states that $M\bar{V}=P\bar{Y}$, where M represents the money supply, P the price-level, V the velocity of circulation (the frequency with which money change hands) and Y is the level of real output. Assuming that V is stable and that Y is determined exogenously, Friedman argued that this identity gives a clear and tight relationship between the money supply and the price level in an economy.[29]

Whilst reviving the Quantity Theory of Money, Friedman also offered his own flourish, making it a theory of equilibrium between money supply and money demand. Friedman suggested that the demand for money was stable, which ultimately meant that the supply of money played the crucial role in the determination of the price level and the rate of inflation.

In line with his favoured empirical approach to economics, Friedman turned to historical evidence as a means to demonstrate the effect of money not only on prices in the longer run but also, temporarily at least, on output and incomes. Adopting the National Bureau method of investigation of business cycles (following in the footsteps of Arthur Burns and Wesley Mitchell's pioneering work on business cycles), Friedman and Anna Schwartz collected data on the monetary and financial history of the United States, culminating in their gigantic *A Monetary History of the United States.*[30]

Friedman and Schwartz argued that money had historically been the key driver of the ups and downs experienced by the American economy, including the traumatic Great Depression.[31] In other words, it was necessary to control the money supply not only to keep inflation under wraps, but also to help stabilize the economy, eliminating boom and bust. Returning to the equation $M\bar{V}=P\bar{Y}$, Friedman suggested that in the short run, changes in M could powerfully feed through to affect Y (real output) rather than P. Over time, however, Y would return to some exogenously determined level, leaving M to have its effects purely on P (that is, on the nominal rather than the real side of the economy). The Classical Dichotomy – which famously suggested that the real economy was neutral to all things nominal, including money – held in the long run but could, it seemed, be blown off course in the short run. Friedman's conclusion was clear:

> The urgent need, I believe, is to keep monetary changes from being a destabilizing force . . . In my view, this can best be done by assigning the monetary authorities the task of keeping the stock of money growing at a regular and steady state, month in and month out . . . The elimination of monetary uncertainty would promote healthy economic growth by providing a stable environment for both individual planning and social action.[32]

Since the level of output was seemingly immune from money in the long run, Friedman argued that there was no loss from keeping the money supply under tight control – only gain in terms of price and output stability. This was a claim that contrasted with Keynesian theory, which had been supplemented with a Phillips Curve relationship that suggested that higher levels of output and lower levels of unemployment could be achieved at the price of a higher level of inflation: that there was a permanent trade-off between the monetary sphere and the real economy. In his presidential address to the American Economic Association, published as *The Role of Monetary Policy* in 1968, Friedman argued that such a trade-off could only ever be temporary – the result of workers being 'fooled' – and that by attempting to exploit the supposed trade-off, policymakers were in fact destabilizing the economy and pushing up inflation.[33]

Friedman accompanied his demolition of the Phillips Curve relationship with the notion that the economy possessed a 'natural rate' of unemployment. In effect, Friedman argued that, in the long run, the Phillips Curve would be vertical at this natural rate, meaning that it could be consistent with any level of inflation: no trade-off existed in the longer run between inflation and unemployment.

This contrast between the effects of money in the short run and the long run suggested that politicians might be tempted to behave in a way that temporarily boosted the economy, such as before an election, causing a destabilizing boom followed by a bust. Friedman concluded that the best way to stabilize the economy was, therefore, to keep a close watch on the money supply and to ensure that politicians were not tempted to take short-term measures to boost the economy. In other words, policymakers' actions should be restricted. This, together with Friedman's empirical assertion that the money demand relationship was stable, led him to recommend a simple constant money supply growth rule.[34] Even in cases where the economy was subject to adverse shocks, and where one might suppose there was more purpose to giving policymakers discretion, Friedman argued that there would be little benefit to an active policy response – whether fiscal or monetary – as the lags in policymaking and transmission through the economy would mean that any boost would come too late, serving to increase rather than reduce the instability.[35]

Rather than using demand-side measures (including monetary and fiscal stimulus) to try to stimulate the economy, Friedman recommended 'supply-side measures', such as increasing competitive pressures in labour and product markets, including by tackling trade unions, the welfare state, price-fixing and excessive regulation. It was supply and not demand that Friedman argued was key to permanently lowering the 'natural rate' of unemployment and increasing the level of real output in the economy, an argument that neatly fitted the context of the economic growth theory being developed at the time by economists such as Robert Solow.

Monetarism in Practice

Friedman's opportunity to influence policymakers came in the 1970s, a decade commonly seen as having discredited the 'dominant' Keynesian-influenced economic model. Across the world, economies entered recession, unemployment soared and yet, alongside, and seemingly contrary to the Phillips Curve, inflation reached new heights. In the words of Robert Lucas and Thomas Sargent,

> These events did not arise from a reactionary reversion to outmoded, 'classical' principles of tight money and balanced budgets [of the kind Keynes detested]. On the contrary, they were accompanied by massive governmental budget deficits and high rates of monetary expansion: policies which, although

> bearing an admitted risk of inflation, promised according to modern Keynesian doctrine rapid real growth and low rates of unemployment'.[36]

Dissatisfaction with Keynesianism grew.

The backdrop to the economic malaise was a switch from fixed to floating exchange rates: the breakdown of the Bretton Woods system. The fixed exchange rate system had long been policymakers' solution to the potential inflationary risks of paper money. By backing their currencies with gold and then fixing against each other, policymakers were constrained in their ability to print money. With the shift to flexible exchange rates, the cat was potentially out of the bag. Friedman was certainly not a fan of fixed exchange rates, which had been favoured by Keynes, a founding father of Bretton Woods, but was nevertheless aware of the risks, recognizing that flexible exchange rates might require policymakers to look for alternative means to control inflation. Monetary restraint was now needed to bring inflation back under control. At the same time, and having been seemingly neglected throughout the Keynesian era, the supply side of the economy needed to be paid some attention, something which Friedman argued would serve to lower unemployment. Whilst a solution to the problem of high inflation and high unemployment certainly could be found in the Keynesian literature, it was buried deep and so was difficult to find.[37] Friedman, by contrast, offered a clear way forward.

Friedman's policy package, adopted by Reagan in the USA and Thatcher in the UK, involved rolling back the state and unleashing free-market forces. That included privatizing state-owned industries, reducing the power of trade unions and deregulating the economy, including finance. Inflation was to be tamed through the adoption of Friedman's monetary recommendations: a fixed money supply growth rule. The consequence of monetary (and fiscal) restraint was a serious recession in both countries, known as the Volcker Shock in the United States.[38] Over in the UK, the public were told that 'if it isn't hurting, it isn't working.' However, despite policymakers' best attempts, and a deep recession, inflation remained high. The attempt to control inflation by controlling the money supply ultimately failed. As it turned out, the money demand curve was not as stable as Friedman had come to believe, meaning that attempting to control prices by controlling the money supply proved insufficient. Whilst Friedman's final goal – that of keeping prices stable – was, at that point, not in doubt, his means to achieve it certainly was. Other means were therefore pursued. They included a return to fixed exchange rates in Europe, culminating in the Eurozone.

Whilst Friedman's monetary economics proved to be extremely influential, it was not without serious criticism. Empirically speaking, there was a question mark over the direction of causation between output and money. Whilst Friedman and Schwartz had uncovered a correlation between the two, it was not clear that money was in the driving seat.[39] Indeed, Hyman Minsky argued that money is created by profit-seeking financial institutions, who expand the 'money supply' as the economy gains strength and in response to customer demands, and contract credit as the economy turns downward, a response that exacerbates the business cycle. In other words, loans are (too) easy to get when times are good and (too) difficult to come by when the economy is in the doldrums. For Minsky, private sector financial institutions – and not the Central Bank – are the key players and their natural profit-seeking behaviour continually undermines the Central Bank's ability to restrict money supply growth. Rather than being determined by the quantity of reserves, bank lending is affected by the desire of customers to borrow and of commercial banks to lend to them: on the demand side, in other words. As far as Minsky was concerned, it would be extremely difficult for the authorities to maintain a constant growth rule – private sector innovations would inevitably work against it, and in new and unpredictable ways, sometimes resulting in lender of last resort interventions and bailouts that ultimately endorsed the kinds of risks taken by the private sector. Hence, for Minsky, 'the only universal rule for Federal Reserve policy is that it cannot be dictated by any universal rule.'[40]

Friedman's work was not only criticized by the 'Left' but also by a new brand of free marketeers. New Classical Economics replaced Friedman's 'adaptive expectations' model of inflation expectation formation with one of 'rational expectations'.[41] The result was that money was predicted to have not only no 'real' impact in the long run, but also much more limited effects in the short than Friedman had himself suggested. In contrast to Friedman's monetary explanation of boom and bust, New Classical economists therefore proposed an alternative model: a supply-side model, that of the Real Business Cycle. For them, the supply side was the driver not only of long-run growth but also of short-run movements. Demand now had no place whatsoever. To these economists, Friedman had not gone far enough in his critique of Keynesian thinking.

Whilst Friedman's work is commonly pitted against Keynes, there was less division than is commonly believed. To begin with, the very equation that Friedman used to dispose of the Phillips Curve, one which famously incorporated inflation expectations, was in fact provided by Phillips himself, and, if anything, Phillips worried more about the effects of inflation than did Friedman.[42] Phillips was also well aware that his curve depended on a given level of inflation expectation, something for which Friedman was later given credit. It is also untrue to suggest that Keynes had underplayed the importance of money. Much of Keynes's early work was, in fact, dedicated to monetary matters, and in 1930 he penned *A Treatise on Money*.[43]

The real disagreement between Keynes and Friedman is to be found elsewhere: in relation to Keynes's view that economic instability was an inherent part of the free-market economy, rather than simply being the product of monetary mismanagement. Central to this natural instability was Keynes's belief in Knightian uncertainty: the idea that we cannot know the future, which makes investment inherently speculative.[44] Since we cannot know the future, there is little to anchor investment decisions, meaning that they will blow with the wind, and so too will the economy. This extreme uncertainty led Keynes to place much greater weight than did Friedman on the notion that money is not only something we use to make transactions, it is also a store of value: something over which we have a 'liquidity preference'.[45] The extent to which we choose to use money in this way was, according to Keynes, dependent upon the degree of optimism or pessimism in the economy. Whilst Friedman believed in the self-equilibrating properties of the market economy, Keynes did not. Using his theory of liquidity preference, he argued that in a downturn, liquidity preference increases as people increase their demand for money (as a relatively safe asset), selling out of stocks and shares and moving into cash. This extra demand for money prevents downward pressure on the interest rate. Even an increase in the money supply would not help given the rise in money demand.[46] As a result, Keynes disagreed with the view that the interest rate would naturally adjust in a recession in such a way that it would return the economy to something close to full employment. However, by ruling out the type of extreme uncertainty about the future that concerned Keynes, and, with it, Keynes's theory of liquidity preference, Friedman turned a blind eye to natural economic instability and placed too much faith in the self-correcting tendencies of the market.[47]

Virtues of the Market

For an economist schooled in textbook neoclassical economics, Friedman's faith in the market might at first appear naive. After all, in their mathematical formalization of Adam Smith's invisible hand, neoclassical economists had uncovered the multiple stringent assumptions that are needed for markets to guarantee an 'efficient' outcome, including perfect competition, the absence of externalities and perfect information. However, whilst Friedman accepted the stringency of these conditions, he questioned their relevance in the longer run, together with the extent to which the state could really be trusted to improve upon the market outcome, however un-ideal that outcome might be.

Beginning with the assumption of perfect competition, Friedman argued that whilst monopolies existed, they 'are generally unstable and of brief duration unless they call government to their assistance'.[48] Echoing the Austrian School, he acknowledged that it is the ability of firms to make profits that drives entrepreneurs to develop new and better goods to satisfy our many wants. And, where monopoly profits are ultimately attained, it acts as a signal enticing other firms to enter the market who ultimately undermine the monopoly power. Rather than being in a position to resolve the 'problem' of monopoly, Friedman argued that the state is often the root cause, granting licences and enacting regulations that block entry.[49]

In regard to the problem of externalities, Friedman and his followers identified the solution as being more, not less, of the market: the creation of property rights where they do not exist such that people have to, for example, pay to pollute, which then acts as a market deterrent to such activity.

Turning to cases of information asymmetry, Friedman famously argued that, ultimately, it is in a firm's interest not to sell consumers harmful or shoddy goods as it would eventually hit their bottom line as consumers start to search for alternative products. Replacing market production with state production would mean that consumers would have no alternative and so would be more at the behest of a single producer: the state. More recently, and following the Classical Liberal position, Mark Pennington has argued that markets are much better placed than is the state to develop means of overcoming informational asymmetries.[50] This can include, for example, the black box that car insurers can place in your car to track your driving, revealing whether or not you are a good driver and charging you a premium accordingly, and various means of tracking expenditure to judge our health 'type'. Furthermore, whilst the state can attempt to regulate in an effort to make sure that consumers are not taken advantage of by firms who are more 'in the know' than we are, they cannot always be relied upon to know enough themselves to enact the right kinds of regulations – and are at risk of being suckered in by private lobbies.

Even where a case can be made for state intervention – such as with regard to education and healthcare – Friedman pointed out that the provision of funds by the state does not have to equate with the state actually providing schools and hospitals. He proposed a system of vouchers, issued by the government and paid for by the taxpayer, that would allow parents to purchase education for their children on the marketplace. Placing purchasing power in the hands of parents would, Friedman argued, allow them to vote with their feet, leading to the natural expansion of better schools, and the contraction of inferior ones, thereby improving educational quality.

When it comes to the issue of equity as opposed to efficiency, Classical Liberals argue that there is a limit to how much the state should intervene: that charity can often do a better job than can government as it is under pressure from donors to direct funds to schemes that bring about the best results, and, by operating at the grass roots, has better information than does the state on what will and will not work. When provided with charity, it is supposed that individuals strive to improve their lot. However, when provided with welfare as a right, the argument is that individuals can behave very differently, losing their natural drive to take control of their lives and push for self-improvement in an economic sense. It is on these grounds that President Ronald Reagan attacked Johnson's vision of extensive government welfare and a 'Great Society', arguing that good intentions had created the opposite: a nation of, to use the words of Ayn Rand, 'leechers' and 'moochers'. Friedman's favoured system of welfare provision was therefore one of a negative income tax, which made welfare payment dependent upon productive activity.[51]

In sum, Friedman's support for the market does not emanate from a neoclassical mathematical proof of the market's efficiency properties but from the Classical Liberal tradition. It also has a distinctly Austrian – especially Hayekian – flavour. What matters is not whether the market fulfils a long list of neoclassical textbook assumptions (perfect competition, perfect information, absence of externalities and so on) but whether the state has the incentive to work in our best interests compared with firms who are forcibly motivated to do so by the possibility of profit, and whether the state has the information needed to better meet our needs than does the market.

For Friedman, even if the state could be assumed to be benevolent, this would still not solve the problems endemic in state control. State control removes choice and sidesteps the forces of competition, which can prove seriously harmful for consumers. Human beings are not a homogeneous group; we each have our own different tastes and desires. We are each an individual. As such, it would be impossible for the state to acquire the information needed to supply us all with the products and services that our tastes and needs demand. In the market, by contrast, the consumer is king. Businesses have an incentive to produce goods and services that appeal to our various tastes, and competition between firms leads to lower prices and the introduction of new products, incorporating more advanced technology, in the longer run.

With the market, we can each make our own choices and our own decisions and yet somehow, as if by magic, we end up not in chaos but with a reasonable degree of order. We can find numerous types of food on the supermarket shelves, we can choose from hundreds of brands and styles of clothing and we can entertain ourselves with numerous genres of music, literature and art. Without a market, the state would instead have to develop a plan to meet our needs. This involves both calculating the economy's ability to produce and predicting what people want to consume, and then directing production accordingly. Not only is getting the plan 'right' an unlikely task, but so is getting people to act for the common good (to actually stick to the plan); the self-interested response is to 'free-ride' on the efforts of others – after all, under the communist system of sharing everything equally, you will still be fed in the evening. But, of course, if everyone reasons the same way, the result is that everyone goes hungry. Hence, only in small groups where people can monitor each other and build up both a moral obligation and a communal spirit does 'communism' tend to succeed. Outside of small groups, planning will often result in some form of coercion and compulsion as, without it, the plan starts to fall apart and people are at risk of going hungry. According to Hayek, state control, even without intention, places us 'on the road to serfdom'.

Friedman argued not only that the market is a means to an end – the best system yet discovered for delivering economic progress – but that it is also an end in itself. It acts to guarantee individual freedom. In his own words: 'A society which is socialist cannot also be democratic . . . I know of no example in time or place of a society that has been marked by a large measure of political freedom, and that has not also used something comparable to a free market to organise the bulk of economic activity.'[52] Even more emotively, he expresses serious concern that 'sooner or later . . . an even bigger government would destroy both the prosperity that we owe to the free market and the human freedom proclaimed so eloquently in the Declaration of Independence.'[53]

Whilst Friedman deserves credit for highlighting the advantages of the market at a time when it was under attack, there are a number of grounds for being less optimistic, including the following.[54]

First, we have the evidence from economic history. The history of market development suggests that markets are far from sufficient for economic growth, and that the state has, historically speaking, helped as well as hindered economic growth.[55] Furthermore, there is more to the state than the question of size. Recent literature has highlighted the importance of 'state capacity', or what development economists call 'state capability'.[56]

Second, the assumption that competition is always beneficial and will ensure that the 'best' technologies succeed is something that has been questioned by Robert Frank, Brian Arthur and Paul David.[57]

Third, behavioural economics suggests that we do not always have the mental capacity and discipline needed to make the most of the market. Whilst Friedman argues that markets are perfectly placed to produce goods and services that satisfy our desires, George Akerlof and Robert Shiller have shown they can also feed our addictions, exploit our myopia and manipulate and deceive us.[58] According to Avner Offer, one of the most significant behavioural biases we possess is myopia. Since economic prosperity depends on making sacrifices – trading bread today for jam tomorrow – this can be a major stumbling block. Offer argues that numerous twentieth-century government interventions, from compulsory schooling to public pensions and infrastructure projects, helped to overcome this myopia, improving economic outcomes.[59]

Fourth, we have the challenge to Friedman's conception of freedom, which includes Amartya Sen's 'Capabilities' Approach. In the words of economist J. Bradford Delong, 'people in absolute poverty are deprived of both the opportunities and the means to change their status. They lack what the philosopher Isaiah Berlin called "positive liberty" – empowerment for self-actualization – as well as "negative liberty," or freedom from obstacles in one's path of action.'[60] According to Offer, freedom from death or pain is the only type of freedom on which we can all agree and, on this basis, the United States in fact performs rather poorly.[61]

Finally, we have the critique offered by feminist economists, who question the two-part economic division that lies at the heart of Friedman's work: the state and the market.[62] As Offer and Marilyn Waring have made clear, there is a whole other world in which significant economic activity takes place, but which has traditionally fallen outside of the male domain, and which has therefore been neglected by economists. Only by acknowledging and thinking about this third domain can we think holistically about the economy.[63]

This feminist critique naturally has a bearing on welfare provision. As a subject that has been largely built upon the male experience of the world, the 'economic agents' who populate economic models are generally thought to have the means to work and to support themselves independently. The domestic sphere is neglected and the phrase 'dependency' carries with it some rather negative connotations. According to Offer, dependency is not an aberration; it is a fact of life that economists should not ignore.[64] We each transition through several stages of dependency throughout our lives: childhood, periods of study, pregnancy, periods of poor health and old age. In 'traditional' societies, this dependency is dealt with through the family, which takes a heavy toll on women's personal freedom.

As economies develop, family ties start to weaken. As women find opportunities outside of the home, their ability to earn allows them to take charge of their own lives and, in particular, to determine for themselves whether, whom and when to marry. Whilst individual freedom benefits, a gap needs to be filled in terms of dealing with dependency. It is for this reason that historians argue that the welfare state first began to develop in societies that were relatively more gender equal, such as England and the Netherlands, and that this early development of welfare systems enhanced the market participation of women.[65] This is an example of the way in which the state can help to support both market activity and individual freedom.[66]

Conclusion

For his time, coming of age amidst the Great Depression, Friedman was a radical.[67] He was one of only a handful of economists who fought to defend the market against the onslaught of communism and growing tide of state intervention. His brilliance cannot be found in terms of any particular form of originality – after all Friedman drew upon many other great economic thinkers – but in the complete package of ideas that he presented to the public. However, by offering a straightforward policy package that was seemingly consistent and easy to digest, Friedman traded depth for breadth, making his economic thinking wholly inadequate for dealing with the major economic problems we face: poverty, inequality and boom and bust.

Friedman's faith in the ability of economists to rise above normative questions, presenting economics in a 'scientific' way free of personal values, was arrogant and even dangerous, adding to the 'imperialistic' tendencies of the economic discipline and its neglect of the wider social sciences. It also left ethics and values under the command of the Left, making laissez-faire thinking appear disconnected from human needs and real-life considerations alike. Friedman's monetary economics was blind to the non-monetary causes of boom and bust, neglecting the inherent economic instability that is naturally built into any capitalist economy. Furthermore, his defence of the market was overly optimistic, whilst his critique of the state assumed only the worst.

Despite these criticisms, Friedman still has something important to offer today: in terms of economic methodology, the belief that the economy is extremely complicated and cannot be captured by a set of mathematical equations;[68] in terms of monetary economics, his emphasis on the use of historical data;[69] and, finally, his emphasis on the power of freedom, which, when applied to the modern agenda of empowering women across the world, and when put alongside the work of Sen, is just as important today as it was during the cold war.

By the end of his life, at the age of 94 in 2006, his 'monetarism' had been largely discredited but the capitalist system Friedman spent so much of his public life defending was much more firmly rooted. The Soviet system had collapsed from the inside and China was opening its doors to the international marketplace. Not only did longer-term economic growth appear to be secure, economic ups and downs seemed to be a thing of the past. One of Friedman's own students, Robert Lucas, who had himself become a Nobel Prize-winner, had announced that the 'central problem of depression-prevention had been solved'. In other words, the Great Depression would never happen again. Friedman must have died a happy man. It is perhaps fortunate, then, that Friedman did not live to see the tremors of 2008.

Where future thinking will now take us in light of the Global Financial Crisis is still to be determined. However, just as economists' interpretations of the causes of the Great Depression defined the evolution of economic thought from Keynes through to Friedman, our interpretation of the causes of the Global Financial Crisis will largely define the direction we travel in over the next fifty years. As was the case in 1929, critiques of capitalism and calls for greater state intervention are in the ascendant.[70] However, following in the footsteps of Friedman, one can also identify a counter-insurgency: some have pointed to the lax monetary policy that preceded 2008, together with the pressure that was placed on financial institutions by the state authorities to lend to 'sub-prime' areas, increasing the riskiness of the banking system.[71] One could, in particular, envisage a return to a Friedman-style emphasis on keeping money under control, albeit through means other than those proposed by Friedman himself.[72]

Even if history is to repeat itself in the coming years, bringing a return of the state interventionist policy that followed the Great Depression, Friedman's free-market thinking won't be gone for long. As the pendulum swings from the market to the state and back again, and as one crisis follows another, one thing is for sure: like the miniskirt and the beard, Friedman will forever be going in and out of fashion.

TEN

JOHN FORBES NASH JR

Karen Horn

John Forbes Nash Jr was different. He differed from most people in many ways, but two specificities were particularly striking: first, his mysterious mind, which soared to new heights of insight and plunged into the darkest abysses of delusion, and, second, his tremendous impact in an academic field that wasn't his own.

Nash was brilliant. But this brilliance, unlike that of other eminent scholars, was of an extreme, tormented kind that nearly annihilated him. Even before he was awarded the Nobel Memorial Prize in Economic Sciences in 1994, alongside Reinhard Selten and John Harsanyi, it was standard practice in academia to praise Nash as a 'genius'. This recognition had come early. To some extent, his being gifted with such a brilliant, relentlessly working brain seemed to explain and perhaps to justify his odd character, his behavioural idiosyncrasies and his emotional aloofness. Yet the price to pay was higher still: when he was 31 years old Nash slid into paranoid schizophrenia, a long, terrible, disabling mental illness that evicted him from academia.

With this illness, full recovery is improbable. But against all odds, Nash's schizophrenia went into remission in his sixties, allowing him to emerge from his delusions. He was at last well and stable enough to resume some of his scholarly activities. He made public appearances again, displaying a much gentler, more self-conscious persona than he had in his turbulent younger years. After receiving the Nobel Prize, the dramatic and stirring story of his life made it all the way to Hollywood, where Ron Howard turned Sylvia Nasar's excellent and carefully researched – though never officially authorized – biography *A Beautiful Mind* into a much-praised, award-winning movie starring Russell Crowe.[1] The resulting public notoriety for Nash, unwanted and disturbing though it may have been, could be one of the reasons why his name persistently figures at the top of the list of the 'most popular Laureates in Economic Sciences' on the Nobel Foundation's website.[2]

His highly formal, complex and taxing work certainly isn't accessible to a wider audience.

In the academic field of economics, however, Nash has become a familiar name, one that inevitably crops up in modern textbooks. His work has had an important and lasting impact on the discipline, and many scholars have followed in his footsteps. It is evident that the same can be said of a number of great minds. What makes this case particularly remarkable, however, is that Nash was a complete outsider. He wasn't an economist at all. He was a pure mathematician and very much liked to think of himself that way. His training in economics had consisted of a single course on international economics taken back in college. His connection to economics came from game theory, which was a branch of mathematics.

The enthusiastic reception of his work in the field of economics influenced Nash's later development, providing him with a second intellectual home and prompting him to make other ventures into economics. He never came up with an economic theory proper, however, and remained the odd man out. Economic questions sometimes caught his attention and triggered his thinking, yet he looked at them through the glass of game theoretic models rather than economic theory. The puzzle that attracted Nash time and again was the interaction of people with diverging interests: was it possible to model this interaction in a mathematically solvable fashion; and what would the mathematical properties of such a solution be? If so, what would come of the interaction, and why? In this vein, one could find Nash in the later years of his life pondering 'ideal money', for example – a means of payment designed in such a way as to take all the relevant conflicting interests of its users into account. In Nash's intuition, a new sort of Gold Standard based on a basket of material commodities might best be suited to do this.[3] But he was more interested in the logical possibility of such a currency than in its practical realization.

Nash's important contributions were all essentially mathematical. Although less widely known than his contributions to game theory, Nash also helped the pure mathematics community gain new ground in differential geometry and in the study of partial differential equations. He considered the game theoretical papers for which he received the Nobel Prize 'trivial' compared to this 'proper' purely mathematical work.[4] In this chapter, we will nevertheless concentrate on his major contribution to game theory, which he transformed into a fertile field for all the social sciences, not only economics. Today's essential toolkit of economic analysis would be incomplete without the 'Nash equilibrium', as his concept came to be called.

The name 'game theory' is slightly misleading. There is nothing playful about it. Game theory has nothing to say about games of chance such as throwing the dice. It's all about strategy. The field had admittedly emerged from a 1928 paper by the Hungarian-born mathematician John von Neumann on the analysis of familiar strategic games such as merels or chess, as well as card games.[5] Neumann was himself fond of poker. But he was well aware that the scope of his theory could – and should – be extended to embrace all forms of strategic interaction: 'And in the end, any event, with given external circumstances and given agents (supposing the absolute free will of the latter), can be viewed as a game if one takes the repercussions on the interacting agents into account.'[6] In board or card games, just like in real life, people have to think ahead. When the outcome of one's action depends on somebody else's action to a relevant degree, one must try to anticipate what the other will do, adapt to that and try to pre-empt a loss. In game theoretic terms: all players need to devise the best possible strategy for themselves based on the expected countermoves of the other player(s).

Game theory is thus a field dedicated to the analysis of strategic decision-making. Over the decades it has developed a specific vocabulary and an abundantly stocked conceptual toolkit of its own. It has been applied to problems as diverse as the escalation or de-escalation of military conflict, including nuclear deterrence; the bargaining process concerning international climate policy; or the price-setting behaviour in oligopolistic markets. Game theory is also a useful tool for economists when they analyse why countries find it so difficult to strike an agreement on trade policy; when they try to explain the results of wage negotiations between trade unions and employers' associations; when they help to devise a technique for government as it comes up with a set of regulations for a specific market. Game theory has both explanatory and predictive power, which makes it useful for policy advice.

Picking up on another work by von Neumann, the seminal book *Theory of Games and Economic Behavior*, written together with his Austrian colleague Oskar Morgenstern,[7] John Nash showed in his doctoral thesis that optimal individual strategies can indeed be determined. Roughly speaking, Nash did essentially two things in the paper on 'non-cooperative games' that ultimately brought him the Nobel Prize in 1978: he showed that there exists a mathematical solution for any such interaction, with strategies from which no agent would have a sensible reason to deviate, and he worked out the properties of this equilibrium. And by the same token, he firmly established the notion of such a situation as a useful, and universal, analytical concept.[8] It became known as the 'Nash equilibrium' – a concept praised by Roger Myerson, another game theorist and Nobel laureate, in 2007 as 'probably the most important solution concept in game theory', with 'a fundamental and pervasive impact in economics and the social sciences which is comparable to that of the discovery of the DNA double helix in the biological sciences'.[9]

On the Way Up

Though he was no prodigy, and was not exposed to abstract mathematics at home, Nash's talent was evident at an early age. He was born on 13 June 1928 in the small and bustling town of Bluefield, West Virginia, in a middle-class, upward-striving family. On his father's side, the family's roots go back to Texan plantation owners, school founders and teachers; Nash's grandfather, however, a teacher's son, was an unstable character and abandoned his wife and children. From his mother's side, Nash's ancestors came from North Carolina, well-educated and affluent.

John F. Nash Sr was an electrical engineer with a degree from Texas A&M, where he also taught for a while. Dedicated to earning his family greater social respectability, he ended up working for the Appalachian Electric Power Company in Bluefield for 38 years. His wife, Margaret Virginia, had studied languages at Martha Washington College and University of West Virginia, where she qualified as a teacher. Her interests were mainly literary. She taught for ten years before she met her husband and was obliged to resign from her post, married women not being permitted to teach at her school. She concentrated on the education of her own children, John and Martha, born in 1930, instead.

In the family house on Bluefield's Highland Street, John Nash Jr could always be found reading. Sloppy, unfocused and lonely, he earned a reputation for being odd. 'Johnny was always different,' his sister recalls.[10] His grades weren't always good. Of all things, he encountered problems in mathematics, although he liked the subject and Eric T. Bell's book *Men of Mathematics* fascinated him.[11] His problems mostly had to do with the formalism that, as an impatient boy, he found tedious to adopt, especially when his intuition was running at high speed – a recurring source of conflict in his life.

When Nash turned thirteen his parents enrolled him at the local community college for additional advanced mathematics courses. Nash's appetite for complicated mathematical problems had been growing. After graduating, shortly after the end of the Second World War, aged seventeen, Nash left Bluefield and moved to Pittsburgh, Pennsylvania, in the hope of one day becoming an engineer like his father. He was able to attend the Carnegie Institute of Technology on a full scholarship.

Nash didn't last long in his originally chosen field. It was during his very first year that the precocious talent decided to switch from chemical engineering (via chemistry) to mathematics, encouraged by his teachers. After completing the course in less than three years, he applied successfully to all four top graduate mathematics programmes in the country: Harvard, Princeton, Chicago and Michigan. With a recommendation from his Carnegie advisor, Richard Duffin, in his briefcase Nash finally went off to Princeton. Duffin's letter simply stated: 'This man is a genius.'

John Nash had chosen well. At this time Princeton was regarded as the mathematical centre of the universe. Stars such as Albert Einstein, Kurt Gödel and John von Neumann, all émigrés, worked at Princeton's Institute for Advanced Study, a renowned private institution for pure research, located not far from the university. Now that the Second World War was over, the overall atmosphere must have been intellectually rich, dense and inspiring, even though the McCarthy era had already begun and political repression was on the rise in the United States. Nash lived on the campus, where life was 'masculine, monastic, and scholarly', 'mathematical gossip' abounding and game theory becoming a staple of conversation.[12] At Fine Hall, Princeton's mathematics department, Nash avoided reading and skipped classes. He spent most of his time quizzing the professors or his fellow graduate students and working out complicated mathematical problems in his mind while pacing the hallways whistling Bach.

Nash's eccentricity did not make him popular, and his arrogance was legendary. But everybody in the department seemed to appreciate a board game he invented; the students playing it in the common room called it 'Nash'. It is the same as the game known as 'Hex', which was invented independently, a little earlier, by the Danish mathematician Piet Hein. It is an entertaining and demanding strategy game for two players played on a hexagonal grid, where both players aim to link the opposite sides of the board in an unbroken chain by alternately placing stones on unoccupied spaces. The game was mathematically exciting because Nash could prove its two essential properties: the first player always wins unless he adopts a suboptimal strategy or makes a mistake; and there can't be two unbroken chains at the same time.[13]

During his second term at Princeton, Nash also wrote his first sole-authored academic paper, 'The Bargaining Problem'.[14] It wasn't his first publication: at just seventeen, he had published (with his father) a joint paper in electrical engineering.[15] The paper he now had in mind had been inspired by the one elective economics course he had taken back at Carnegie. He had kept wondering how the gains from international trade, or any gains from cooperation, are divided between the parties involved. Economic theory had nothing to say about how exactly this would take place, according to which logic, amounting to which result, generating which respective levels of utility. This was a blind spot. The modern game theoretic approach that Nash got himself immersed in at Princeton now provided him with a perspective from which to tackle this question in mathematical terms. His short paper, essentially a formalization of the interaction in a two-person non-zero-sum game and its solution given a few assumptions, is still relatively accessible, written in a clear, lean and easy style, illustrated by examples and graphs.

Ultimately, Nash set out to write his dissertation, and he chose Albert W. Tucker as his supervisor. His endeavour was ambitious: he wanted to go beyond Neumann's 1928 so-called 'minimax solution' for a two-person zero-sum cooperation game, where each rational player tries to maximize his gain in the outcome which is most disadvantageous to him – a solution that always exists, as Neumann showed formally, if so-called mixed strategies are allowed for. A mixed strategy is a probability distribution of a player's available strategies. Nash also wanted to generalize the approach that Neumann and Morgenstern had laid out in their seminal book.[16] The extension he sought was threefold: (1) He wanted to derive solutions not exclusively for the specific case of games where the players can negotiate in order to strike a bargain, but also for instances where each agent acts independently, non-cooperatively, so that bargaining and binding commitments cannot take place; (2) he wanted the games to be possibly non-zero-sum, which was very important for the application of game theory in economics, because all market interaction, providing opportunity for cooperation, is by definition potentially positive-sum; (3) he wanted the setting to be open and applicable to an arbitrary number, *n*, of players instead of only two. He would later come back to the analysis of cooperative games and derive a method of bargaining ('Nash bargaining').[17]

For the time being, the challenge was again to formalize the overall setting, to derive the optimal strategies for each participant as well as the result of the interaction, and to define and prove the existence of an equilibrium solution. Nash solved the mathematically extremely intricate problem in two different technical ways, at first with the help of Luitzen Brouwer's fixed point theorem and subsequently on the basis of Shizuo Kakutani's more modern variant of it.[18] While the doctoral thesis that Nash submitted, a mere 27 pages, double-spaced and full of handwritten equations, remained unpublished,[19] the second, more elegant version was published as a paper in a mathematical journal in 1950.[20] For the ordinary economist neither makes easy bedside reading.

The Nash Equilibrium

Nash was awarded his doctorate on his 22nd birthday. His thesis did not represent a breakthrough in purely technical terms. It applied tools that were already around, but in a creative, smart and novel way. More importantly, Nash's work brought a conceptual innovation – and one that dramatically increased the applicability of game theory in the social sciences. This innovation was less to do with the fashion in which Nash calculated his way through to the solution of the interaction problem, but rather with a structural distinction that he introduced: he had recognized that it makes a crucial difference, mathematically, whether one looks at cooperative or non-cooperative games. The lack of such a distinction explained why Neumann and Morgenstern were technically unable to provide a proof of equilibrium for *n*-person games. The problem was in the 'packaging'.

Cooperative games, on the one hand, are strategic settings in which the interacting agents can observe what each other does, where coalitions can be formed and binding commitments can be made so that everybody will keep their promises. The analysis of non-cooperative games, on the other hand, can address situations of conflict in which nobody is able to directly observe the behaviour of the other player(s) but needs to determine his own optimal strategy nonetheless. Each player 'acts independently, without collaboration or communication with any of the others'.[21] In a sense, non-cooperative games are the more general form of human interaction, comprising cooperative games as a mere subset; Nash advocated that one should model them identically (dubbed the 'Nash programme'). And in modern, abstract societies, where market interaction no longer necessarily requires face-to-face contact, the non-cooperative setting can definitely claim more relevance: we have to make a host of decisions not knowing exactly what others will do, even though their actions will necessarily have repercussions on our well-being and utility.

In his dissertation (and its twin publication in the *Annals of Mathematics*), Nash proved that in all finite non-cooperative game settings there exists at least one equilibrium point, that is one set of optimal strategies each of which fulfils the condition of being the best strategy whatever the other agents do, so that no player should rationally depart from it. In other words, he had 'formally defined an equilibrium of a non-cooperative game to be a profile of strategies, one for each player in the game, such that each player's strategy maximizes his expected utility payoff against the given strategies of the other players'.[22] This proof was important for economics, in particular with regard to the predictive power of models. To an important extent, the field of economics – specifically microeconomics – is concerned with the study of human reactions to incentives, monetary or not; but incentives may not work as intended when the interactive setting, given the strategies of everybody involved, brings about contradictory optimal strategies.

An example may be helpful at this stage. To keep things simple, let's look at an old classic, the Prisoner's Dilemma, the quintessential static, non-cooperative game with complete information, formalized in a compelling way in 1950 by Nash's thesis advisor, Albert W. Tucker, for teaching purposes.[23] In his short note, Tucker writes:

> Two men, charged with a joint violation of law, are held separately by the police. Each is told that (1) if one confesses and the other does not, the former will be given a reward of one unit and the latter will be fined two units, (2) if both confess, each will be fined one unit. At the same time each has good reason to believe that (3) if neither confesses, both will go clear. This situation gives rise to a simple symmetric two-person game (not zero-sum) with the following table of payoffs, in which each ordered pair represents the payoffs to I and II, in that order:

		II	
		confess	not confess
I	confess	(-1, -1)	(1, -2)
	not confess	(-2, 1)	(0, 0)

> Clearly, for each man the pure strategy 'confess' dominates the pure strategy 'not confess'. Hence, there is a unique equilibrium point given by the two pure strategies 'confess'. In contrast with this non-cooperative solution one sees that both men would profit if they could form a coalition binding each other to 'not confess'.

This is what is also called a 'one-shot' or single-stage game, that is, a setting in which there is only one window for action; one agent is not able to adapt to the other's action, and commitments cannot be enforced. Communication cannot take place. There is perfect information in the sense that both know the possible outcomes, or pay-offs of all available strategies. If both prisoners act rationally, there is an equilibrium solution with strategies that neither of them would have a reason to turn away from. The 'Nash equilibrium', as it became known, consists in both prisoners confessing. For both prisoners, this is of course a suboptimal outcome – they would rather be free.

The suboptimality makes this example disappointing, on the one hand. The demonstration that interdependent rational individual action doesn't necessarily yield the common good for those directly involved is what made it famous. From here, it seemed easy to jump to the conclusion that interdependent rational individual action in the marketplace would just as well generate suboptimal results. On the other hand, one has to bear in mind that in the prisoners' case, their common good is not really what matters. The general public, interested in seeing the law enforced, is of course the ultimate winner here, thanks to the lawmaker having arranged the schedule of fines with a healthy dose of cunning. One would hope for the same when it comes to the government creating new rules and regulations. The banking industry, for example, has seen a host of regulations in the past that were designed without a sound appreciation of the efforts that would be undertaken rationally to circumvent them. The Nash equilibrium was not an optimum for the banks, and it wasn't an optimum for society at large either.

The distinction between cooperative games and non-cooperative games was of course not the end of the game theory story. Nash's concept had drawbacks. For example, there are situations that produce more than one equilibrium; and his theory could not explain which one would prevail. Also, some real-life settings are so complicated that no imperfect human mind could possibly process all the information required, and the rationality assumption, pervasive in economics, might be overblown. And just how realistic is the assumption regarding the irrelevance of mere chance? Nevertheless, Nash's work provided one of the first in a series of logical distinctions that have helped to make Neumann and Morgenstern's approach more and more fruitful over the years. It 'opened the floodgates for refinements' of Nash's universal equilibrium concept.[24]

One further important distinction came with the productive acknowledgement of the difference between 'one-shot' and 'repeated' games; this was done by R. Duncan Luce and Howard Raiffa.[25] While the distinction between static or dynamic settings, or 'normal' and 'extensive forms', was already in Neumann and Morgenstern's book, Harold W. Kuhn introduced extensive games with imperfect information, that is, where the preceding moves of the other players are unknown.[26] The German game theorist Reinhard Selten, who later received the Nobel Prize together with John Nash and John Harsanyi, went on to refine the concept by adapting it to dynamic strategic interaction, where one must also distinguish the different stages of the game and the information that is available at each of these stages (called 'sub-game'). The Nash equilibrium at each individual stage is what Selten called the 'subgame perfect equilibrium'.[27] He also introduced 'trembling-hand' perfectness for Bayesian games – a concept that allows for small strategical mistakes without causing the equilibrium to break down.[28] In his later years, Selten questioned the rationality assumption in game theory and embarked on experimental research, considering himself an undogmatic 'methodological dualist'. As for John Harsanyi, he tackled the pervasive problem of incomplete information in settings of strategic interaction, for which he developed the concept of a 'Bayesian Nash equilibrium'.[29]

But why was all this so important for economics? Broadly speaking, it changed its outlook. At a time when macroeconomics had already received an enormous boost from Keynesian theory, where people were primarily concerned with broad statistical aggregates such as GDP, consumption, investment, public deficit and trade surplus, it rescued the microeconomic perspective from oblivion. This doesn't mean that it was apolitical – quite to the contrary. Instead, game theory has re-centred the focus of economics on individual decision-making and the rules framework in which this takes place. It has made it possible to analyse whether, in a given interactive setting, with people being what they are, the existing rules tend to generate positive results or, in other words, whether the incentives are set in a way that promotes common welfare. With the addition of game theory to the economist's toolkit real-world phenomena such as imperfect competition could be better understood. In an important way, game theory improved the realism in economics.

At the same time, however, the rise of game theory seemed to corroborate the reputation of economics as 'the dismal science', as Thomas Carlyle famously dubbed it. It strengthened the legend according to which classical economics, beginning with Adam Smith and his famous *The Wealth of Nations*, had been incredibly naive, postulating a God-given natural harmony between private interest and the common good.[30] After all, game theory owes its very existence to the fact that things are not that simple, and that, on the contrary, the real world is full of Prisoner's Dilemma situations, situations in which rational individual action leads to suboptimal outcomes. This is similar to the diagnosis of 'market failure' in neoclassical welfare theory. 'Market failure' can in fact be observed everywhere: why else would we worry about public goods not being provided, just because non-excludability causes people not to want to pay for them, although everybody values them? While such objections may seem understandable, they are based on a deep misperception of the question that classical economics, and Adam Smith in particular, sought to answer. The question was not: does the pursuit of individual interest automatically lead to the common good? The question was: for economic wealth to come into being, what can we prudently rely on? There is nothing naive in a question of this sort, nor in the research programme and the theories built around it.

In a similar vein, the rise of game theory fuelled the old criticism that economists use or even advocate an impoverished and therefore *not* very realistic image of man, since they depict agents as hyper-rational, super-informed, coolly calculating, strategically astute and distastefully opportunistic zombies who know no other goal in life than their own immediate self-interest. What a horrible populace in the model world of economics! This is again a misperception. Economics is not really concerned with personal motivation or morality. Economics doesn't argue with man but takes him for what he or she is. Economics is about human behaviour as it is conditioned by the phenomenon of scarcity, by competition and by the rule framework. In order to work out clearly the influence of the rule framework on the decisions that people make and the actions that they take, it is necessary to abstract from everything that is not directly triggered by those rules. It is thus strictly for the purpose of inquiry that one needs to hypothesize that people react to given rules and their modification. Neither the standard neoclassical assumptions of perfect rationality and information nor the game-theoretic focus on strategic interaction claim to offer an image of man. It is important to remember this.

Before the rise of game theory, and Nash's equilibrium in particular, strategic thinking and incentives had little or no place in economics – with the exception of Antoine-Augustin Cournot's and Heinrich von Stackelberg's work on duopoly. The predominant paradigm included the assumption of perfect competition, which means that with a large number of market participants, no single one of them can influence equilibrium prices. All participants are 'price takers'. However, the real world is full of markets where there are only a few suppliers (or, on the other side, clients). Even if there is a multitude, it is possible that evolved custom and fashion restrain behaviour to averages; a possibility that Nash already hints at in his thesis. But when individual or mass action does have an impact, then the reaction of the others becomes relevant. Purposeful economic action requires a strategy. For a duopolist, for example, it makes little sense to hike up the price of the good he produces and sells if his competitor will not do the same. The clients would just switch suppliers, and he would be worse off than ever before. So he needs to come to a good guess of what his rival will do. He may either use abstract probabilities or rely on practical experience. How this plays out is not only important for the two agents directly involved, it also matters for regulation. It is important to recognize dilemma situations and to try and avoid them, if possible (and desirable). And in this sense, as Myerson put it, 'the theory of non-cooperative games that Nash founded has developed into a practical calculus of incentives that can help us to better understand the problems of conflict and cooperation in virtually any social, political or economic institution.'[31]

Downfall, Remission and Honours

Nash's academic career lasted no more than ten years. During these ten years, however, he was very productive. Including his dissertation, he published five important papers in game theory and ten papers on other mathematical issues. After his doctoral thesis he turned to the mathematical problem of manifolds, a topic that had already fascinated him back at Carnegie. He was now striving to improve his status as a pure mathematician and needed to distance himself a little from game theory.[32] He was hoping for a position at the Princeton mathematical department.

At the same time, he got a foot in the door of the RAND Corporation in Santa Monica, California, a mathematically oriented research institution with a clear political purpose. RAND (which is still around today) had been created in 1946 by the United States Army Air Forces as Project RAND ('Research and Development'), under contract to the Douglas Aircraft Company. In 1946, they released the preliminary design of an experimental world-circling spaceship. In 1948, Project RAND was separated from Douglas and became an independent non-profit organization, sponsored initially by the Ford Foundation, to 'further and promote scientific, educational, and charitable purposes, all for the public welfare and security of the United States of America'.[33]

Nash spent the summers of 1950, 1952 and 1954 as a consultant for RAND. In his days, people at RAND were very much concerned with Cold War issues, and the general paranoia about Russians gaining access to American military secrets was growing. As Sylvia Nasar writes, RAND 'was the original think tank, a strange hybrid of which the unique mission was to apply rational analysis and the latest quantitative methods to the problem of how to use the terrifying new nuclear weaponry to forestall war with Russia – or to win a war if deterrence failed'.[34] As Kenneth Arrow, another Nobel laureate (1972) who passed through RAND (in 1948), recalled, 'they were aware that we didn't know what new wars are going to be like, with the atomic bomb, and so they wanted some free thinking.'[35] And they allowed for colourful, quirky people, provided they could obtain security clearance. Addressed to various units of the U.S. Department of Defense, including the Navy and the Air Force, Nash produced classified work on military strategy – using game theory, of course. While the topic sat well with his research concentrating on non-cooperative strategic interaction, Nash wasn't so much interested in current politics. He wanted to be left alone to do his work.

When his hopes for a post at Princeton didn't materialize (his uninspiring teaching and uncollegial nature were still remembered there) Nash ended up as a faculty member at the Massachusetts Institute of Technology (MIT) Department of Mathematics in 1952. His teaching load was moderate, and he concentrated on his manifolds, producing several important papers on the subject.[36] He was now deep into pure mathematics. Politically, this was a tense time, with McCarthy's long arms reaching right into the heart of MIT, targeting, among others, the chairman, deputy chairman and a full professor of the mathematics department. While it is futile to hypothesize about the determining impact of the general political climate on Nash's state of mind and sanity, it does seem safe to say that his environment became precarious, and he must have felt it. The turmoil in his love life certainly didn't help his stability: Nash meandered between male and female lovers. He had various infatuations and affairs with male colleagues before sharing his days with a nurse, Eleanor Stier. Their relationship, however, turned sour and Nash abandoned his partner and their child, John David Stier. He lost his security clearance and his job at RAND in 1954 after being charged for 'indecent exposure', having been arrested by the police in a round-up of homosexuals. Finally he met Alicia Lardé, a gifted MIT physics graduate born to an upper-class family of émigrés from San Salvador. They wed in 1957.

The young couple only had two years of happiness and calm before the storm broke. In 1959 Nash began hearing voices and acting more strangely than ever. Shortly before their son John Charles Nash was born, Alicia felt compelled to have her husband taken to a hospital by force for the first (but not last) time. He was diagnosed as paranoid schizophrenic. The 1960s was a horrible decade for him and his entire family, and Sylvia Nasar's account of it makes for a painful, gripping read. Nash, now victim to the worst, most fantastic delusions, imprudently threw away his secure position at MIT and ran away to Europe, zig-zagging around, trying unsuccessfully to shed his U.S. citizenship, until he was at last repatriated. He heard voices from outer space, felt surrounded by evil powers and thought of himself as a divine messenger who had a special mission. It was too much for his wife, who obtained a divorce.

Nash was in a miserable condition. He underwent various involuntary clinical internments and medical treatments. His former colleagues supported him as much as they possibly could, eventually arranging for appointments at the Institute for Advanced Study in Princeton and steering him towards a position at Brandeis University in Boston. It didn't work. After another breakdown, Nash ultimately moved back in with his widowed mother, then living in Roanoke, Virginia. Yet even during these excruciating times, he always tried to pursue some kind of research.

After some unavailing attempts to begin a new life, Alicia took her former husband back after his mother's death, at first as a mere 'boarder'. Still living in a small, modest house in Princeton, she looked after him, working to support the whole family, while Nash, no longer part of faculty, nonetheless haunted the university's mathematics building for years on end. Students and former colleagues referred to him as 'the Phantom of Fine Hall'. He was considered crazy, but inoffensive. At home, his family situation was complicated by the fact that John Charles, his son with Alicia, was closely following in his footsteps – not only as a mathematician, but also in developing mental illness. He too would be diagnosed with paranoid schizophrenia.

For Nash himself, it was only in the 1990s that the horizon began to brighten, when he was already in his early sixties. In his own view, his unusual remission was due to a strong will: 'Gradually I began to intellectually reject some of the delusionally influenced lines of thinking which had been characteristic of my orientation. This began, most recognizably, with the rejection of politically oriented thinking as essentially a hopeless waste of intellectual effort.'[37] Interestingly, he said this with a small regret. While his visions had showered him with painful and destructive delusions, they had also guided him in mathematics, he believed, providing intuitions that allowed him to see the solution of a problem before knowing how to get there. These visions had been the origin both of his life's worst tragedy and his greatest scholarly successes.

The improvement in Nash's health came just in time. Members of the economics community, having benefited so much from his research, remembered Nash and sought to finally pay him tribute. His name had been suggested for membership in the Econometric Society and for the Nobel Prize before, but nothing had come of it due to his illness. All these honours entail public appearances; talks must be given, conferences attended, active participation in the community is expected. Quite understandably, people were worried that Nash might not be up to the task. As the rumour of his remission spread, however, more and more doors opened up for him. In 1990, he was voted into the Econometric Society. Then, very early one morning in October 1994, his phone rang with news of his Nobel Prize.

At the Royal Swedish Academy of Sciences, however, which has to vote on proposals submitted by the Nobel committee for the economics prize, it had been an unusually close call. While the economics prize is not really part of the Nobel Prize family, it undergoes the same procedures as the other prizes, and tradition has it that decisions should be taken not only by majority, but ideally by unanimous consent. The economics prize, properly called the 'Sveriges Riksbank Prize in Economic Sciences in Memory of Alfred Nobel', was instituted by the Swedish central bank as late as in 1968. The funding comes from seignorage, the net revenue derived from the central bank's issuing currency – which is essentially taxpayer money. There has always been a lot of controversy about the economics prize, given that the father of the Nobel Prize, Alfred Nobel (1833–1896), the Swedish chemist and businessman who had become a millionaire thanks to his invention of dynamite, was critical of economics.

The procedure for the prize is as follows. Each September, the committee sends invitations to thousands of scientists, members of academies and university professors around the world, asking them for nominations for the following year. The committee reviews the nominations, votes on a proposal and then submits its choice to the Academy. In an effort to avoid any leaks, the Academy votes right before the announcement.[38] This time round, the committee had decided to focus on game theory and specifically to honour the advances in the theory of non-cooperative games – fifty years after the publication of Neumann and Morgenstern's seminal book.[39] In hindsight, keeping Nash out would have been unjustifiable, and yet the idea was intensely controversial. Wouldn't he be an embarrassment? Records of the sessions are kept secret for fifty years, but it was reported that in what was considered a major scandal, one member of the committee, Ingemar Stahl, tried to persuade the members of the Academy to vote against the proposition. He almost succeeded.[40]

At the prize ceremony, everything went well with Nash. The money – the three laureates shared the sum of 10 million Swedish crowns – helped to pay back some of his debt, and the honour gave him a boost. Slowly, but surely, he reappeared in the public sphere. He held speeches and gave interviews. When the Lindau Nobel Laureate Meeting in Economic Sciences came into being in 2004, a biannual encounter between the laureates and a select group of students from around the world, Nash became a regular guest. While he hadn't liked teaching in his younger years, and wasn't good at it, he now seemed to enjoy talking to the students, who were obviously fascinated by him and described him as kind, patient and most inspiring. Loyal as ever, Alicia always accompanied him. Her mere presence, he said, gave him stability and peace of mind.[41] They had remarried in 2001.

John and Alicia Nash were together until their very last breaths. Both died in a car accident on 23 May 2015, in a taxi that took them home from the airport. They were just coming back from Norway, where Nash had received the Abel Prize, together with Louis Nirenberg. The Abel Prize is an important mathematics award worth 6 million Norwegian crowns, modelled after the Nobel. It had been instituted by the Norwegian government in 2002. At last, John F. Nash Jr had been honoured for the work he was passionate about and profoundly proud of: 'for striking and seminal contributions to the theory of non-linear partial differential equations and its applications to geometric analysis'.[42] It was late justice, and, in a way, a consummation.

ELEVEN

DANIEL KAHNEMAN

Michelle Baddeley

Daniel Kahneman was born in Tel Aviv in 1934, whilst his mother was there visiting relatives. He was from a Lithuanian Jewish family and his parents had settled in Paris in the 1920s. They became successful and well-to-do. His father worked as a research chemist for a large chemical factory owned by L'Oréal, ironically one of the major financial backers of the French fascist and anti-Semitic movements. As Jews in Nazi-occupied France, the family's existence was inevitably insecure and unstable, and they experienced significant suffering through the Nazi Occupation of France. At one stage, Kahneman's father was arrested by the Nazis and sent to the French internment camp at Drancy, an assembly camp for Jews being deported to the Nazi extermination camps. He was later released thanks to an intervention by his employer, and thereafter the family was forced to move many times.

They fled from Paris to the South of France – until the Germans arrived again. They moved around the centre of France, avoiding the Nazi authorities, at one stage living in a converted chicken coop. As a result Kahneman's early education was varied, and must have been chaotic at times. From his own accounts, he seems to have been somewhat of a loner – not particularly inspired by any one teacher, though his family heritage had a great deal to do with forming his approach to science and research. He developed his academic ambitions early and has said that he grew up thinking he would be a professor.[1]

The family's wartime hardships exerted their toll. Close to the end of the war, in 1944, and just six weeks before D-Day, his father died from a stroke triggered by untreated diabetes. The rest of the family remained in France waiting for permits to enter Palestine, and Kahneman finished his primary education at his French *lycée* in 1946. Then he, his mother and his sister left for Palestine, to join the rest of their extended family.

Though Kahneman is stoical about his childhood, it seems to have had a strong influence on his thinking. In an interview with *The*

Guardian, he emphasized that his wartime tribulations were minor in comparison with what many others had suffered: 'It's nothing compared with other Jewish stories. I was never really hungry. I never saw real violence. There was a lot of resilience.' Nonetheless, this upbringing must have had a profound impact. As a boy, the horrors of Nazism engendered deep fears in Kahneman: a feeling of being hunted and an existence dominated by the primitive need just to live from one day to the next. In the same interview, he remembers: 'I knew that God was extremely busy, so I wasn't going to demand too much. But I was asking for one day at a time. That's what it felt like. It felt like being hunted. We had the mentality of rabbits.'[2]

There are other surprising aspects of his wartime childhood. He began noticing that human behaviour is complex, especially during war. This complexity fascinated Kahneman and it did not lead him to condemn all anti-Semites as evil. He shared these biographical themes with a number of other influential psychologists of his generation. Social psychologists Solomon Asch, Stanley Milgram and Henri Tajfel all came from Jewish backgrounds. All sought to understand the roots of racism and prejudice – though Tajfel and Kahneman were the only ones of this cohort to have direct experience of hardship. The Jewish psychologists of this generation are impressive in their humanity because they aspired not for revenge, but to learn from their experiences by developing a much deeper understanding of human nature, at its best and worst. In different ways, they understood wartime atrocities as human weaknesses, not inherent evil. They understood extreme prejudice and discrimination as the product of human fear and ignorance – hothoused during troubled times and in degrading living conditions.

Even in extreme conditions, people's vicious actions can be tempered by kindly actions, reflecting vestiges of humanity. The young Kahneman experienced instances of this and found it confusing, though it gave him some early insights into the complexities of human nature. One example was the protection his father was given by his otherwise anti-Semitic employer, in securing his release from Drancy, as noted above. The young Kahneman learned from this that human motivations are rarely straightforward.[3] There were other episodes too. In his Nobel Prize autobiographical essay, Kahneman recounts from his childhood a seminal moment that did not turn out as he had feared:

> Jews were required to wear the Star of David and to obey a 6 p.m. curfew. I had gone to play with a Christian friend and had stayed

> too late. I turned my brown sweater inside out to walk the few blocks home. As I was walking down an empty street, I saw a German soldier approaching. He was wearing the black uniform that I had been told to fear more than others – the one worn by specially recruited SS soldiers . . . he beckoned me over, picked me up, and hugged me. I was terrified that he would notice the star inside my sweater. He was speaking to me with great emotion, in German. When he put me down, he opened his wallet, showed me a picture of a boy, and gave me some money. I went home more certain than ever that my mother was right: people were endlessly complicated and interesting.

Once in Palestine, Kahneman completed his high school education. His Nobel Prize autobiography gives the impression that his adolescence was much happier than his childhood; he had many more friends and a much more rounded existence. He lost some of the intellectual obsessions that had dominated his schooling in France. Following the Arab–Israeli War of 1948, the new state of Israel was created and this was to remain Kahneman's home for three decades. A prescient careers advisor suggested either psychology or economics as potential career options, uncanny given that Kahneman settled on the first as his true vocation, and won a Nobel Prize for developing connections between both disciplines. He was able to defer his Israeli military service until after completing his first degree at the Hebrew University of Jerusalem – a Bachelor of Science, majoring in psychology with a minor in mathematics. He spent his summers in officer training school, and during his military service worked on improving experts' judgements for personnel assessments. This marked the beginning of the scientific research into judgement, reasoning and decision-making that would powerfully influence his future career.

Kahneman's new life in Israel coincided with times of great political change. Again, as in France, the circumstances and coincidences of his life must have had a profound influence. In Israel the career benefits from being part of a new nation were significant, particularly for someone with Kahneman's talent and intellectual curiosity. It was a time of change and inexperience for the young nation of Israel. It was also a time for great, new opportunities. Kahneman and his country were growing up at the same time.

He acknowledges that joining a nation-state made it easier for him to make his mark. In his Nobel Prize autobiographical essay he observes that, to modern eyes, it might seem anomalous that his research was so influential in the Israeli army.

> And if it appears odd that a twenty-one-year-old lieutenant would be asked to set up an interviewing system for an army, one should remember that the state of Israel and its institutions were only seven years old . . . that improvisation was the norm, and that professionalism did not exist. My immediate supervisor was a man with brilliant analytical skills, who had trained in chemistry, but was entirely self-taught in statistics and psychology. And with a B.A. in the appropriate field, I was the best-trained professional psychologist in the military.[4]

Kahneman left the army in 1956 and spent some time reading around psychology and philosophy on his own initiative, whilst waiting to travel to the U.S. Then, in 1958, he travelled with his first wife, Irah, to the University of California, Berkeley. Here, he started to develop his eclectic research interests in everything from visual perception through to personality testing and the philosophy of science. Then he went to graduate school at the Austen Riggs clinic in Massachusetts, on a PhD fellowship sponsored by the Hebrew University. For his PhD, Kahneman studied with David Rapaport, a psychoanalytic theorist and a man for whom he had great respect. Rapaport introduced him to the in-depth study of Freud, especially insights around memory and thought. Rapaport focused his understanding of Freud around *The Interpretation of Dreams*, and particularly the concept of cathexis (mental energy). From his time with Rapaport, Kahneman developed early interests in attention and memory. This would inform his contributions, including his early research on attention and effort, through to his insights about utility, specifically remembered utility.

After graduating with his PhD, Kahneman then spent twenty productive years at the Hebrew University – years which included the major parts of his collaborations with his colleague and great friend Amos Tversky. He recalls meeting Tversky: 'My first memory of Amos goes back to 1957, when someone pointed out to me a thin and handsome lieutentant, wearing the red beret of the paratroopers, who had just taken the competitive entrance exam to the undergraduate program in Psychology at Hebrew University.'[5]

Their famous, path-breaking collaborations did not start then but a few years later, when Kahneman invited Tversky to present his research at a Hebrew University seminar. From then onwards, his collaborations with Amos Tversky formed the basis for his most influential contributions to economic psychology and behavioural economics. In many ways Kahneman and Tversky operated as if from one mind – neither one more dominant than the other. Even when determining the author order of their papers there was no dispute, because it was determined at random, via the toss of a coin. The span of their collaborations is marked by two seminal publications. At the start, the well-respected psychology journal the *Psychological Bulletin* published their first joint work, exploring fallacies observed when people are using small numbers.[6] At the end, their last dual-authored paper was their 1996 *Psychological Review* paper on cognitive illusions.[7]

Kahneman continued to collaborate with Tversky for many years, though their joint outputs slowed when they each moved to different parts of the U.S. In 1978 Kahneman moved to North America with his second wife, British psychologist Anne Treisman, first to a professorship at the University of British Columbia and then to professorships in the U.S. at the University of California, Berkeley, and then Princeton University. Tversky's death from a malignant melanoma in June 1996 put a sad and premature end to their collaboration. Their last co-authored paper was with behavioural economists – exploring myopia and loss aversion.

Kahneman and Tversky's deep friendship and intellectual affinity continues to influence Kahneman and his work, in myriad ways difficult to overstate. Kahneman has noted himself that their collaborative endeavours were more productive than their sole ones. Citing an analysis by David Laibson and Richard Zechkahuser, he observed in his Nobel Prize autobiographical essay: 'Amos and I shared the wonder of together owning a goose that could lay golden eggs – a joint mind that was better than our separate minds. The statistical record confirms that our joint work was superior, or at least more influential, than the work we did individually.'[8]

More generally, and beyond his partnership with Tversky, Kahneman was inspired as much by his colleagues as by any mentors or senior figures from his childhood. Alongside the influence of his early experiences of war and then of reaching maturity in a new nation, a theme that defines Kahneman and his intellectual style is his interest in, and capacity for, collaborative work and thinking. From the start of his career he has worked productively with others – from his early collaborations with Jackson Beatty as well as Tversky. He has also collaborated with many other psychologists. Mid-career he collaborated with many of the leading lights from the growing field of behavioural economics, including Jack Knetsch, Shane Frederick and Richard Thaler.

Contributions

What Kahneman and Tversky contributed was an analytical alternative to economists' theories of risk and utility, structured within the mathematical language that economists of the time tended to prefer. This formed the foundation for the growth of behavioural economics, which has multiplied rapidly in output and influence in the decades since the start of Kahneman and Tversky's partnership. Kahneman and Tversky sowed the seeds for this transformation of our understanding of economic and financial decision-making.

More generally, Daniel Kahneman's key contributions, to psychology as well as economics, are on the broad theme of cognition, judgement and decision-making. In assessing his contributions, it is important to understand that Kahneman is an economic psychologist, not a behavioural economist. Behavioural economists' primary discipline is economics but they have an interest in how specific aspects of psychology can explain behaviour and be incorporated into economic theory and analysis. Kahneman was not trained as an economist, but he did have many fruitful collaborations with behavioural economists. Instead, Kahneman is a psychologist adding innovative insights from economics to psychology.

For economists, his most influential work started with his collaborations with Amos Tversky on intuitive reasoning. As noted above, Kahneman spent his early working life with the Israeli military. There he had had opportunities to test his theories and interests in the limits of intuitive reasoning, an interest he has sustained throughout his career. He was also interested, from early on, in the more quantitative aspects of psychology, including statistical analysis. This connected well with the modern economist's reliance on mathematical technique. In this sense, there is significant continuity between his early work and his later work on human misperceptions of risk.

Around 1955, whilst still in the army, one of Kahneman's tasks was to assess candidates for officer training, specifically focusing on the role of personality in the workplace. Are some personality dimensions more important to some combat jobs than others? Kahneman devised methods for screening and allocating soldiers to combat tasks. This sparked his curiosity about the accuracy of experts' evaluations, an interest he developed later in his career, and one he shared with Tversky. For military personnel, he investigated the accuracy of experts' ratings of potential candidates. He noticed that intuition and statistical information are not necessarily connected: 'I was so impressed by the complete lack of connection between the statistical information and the compelling experience of insight that I coined a term for it – "the illusion of validity".'[9]

Interviews and psychometric tests were conducted by what Kahneman later described as small 'cadres' of interviewers.[10] Kahneman identified a range of common mistakes in the judgements of the army's clinical experts when they were assessing personnel. One problem was that the interviewers' ratings did not correlate with the other assessment criteria. As a solution to some of the inaccuracies associated with clinical prediction, Kahneman devised personality profiles which he included in proposed structured interview templates.

Some of the interviewers took umbrage at this interference from a relative novice, and the implication that they should be 'reduced to unthinking robots'. Diplomatically, the young Kahneman backtracked somewhat and a combination of the structured and more actuarial approach that Kahneman had developed, together with the interviewers' expert intuition, proved a most effective compromise. Kahneman suspected that the interviewers' efforts to be reliable, prompted by the structured interview methodology he had developed, increased the statistical validity of their judgements. He also found that, when the clinicians also completed the more 'objective' personality tests he had designed, then these enabled the interviewers to exercise their intuitive judgements far more effectively. As he later observed, 'trying to be reliable made them valid.'[10] Combining intuitive judgement with objective testing was the most powerful combination possible. It was also early evidence that additional objective insights can help people to overcome the biases in their intuitive judgements. This work with the Israeli military formed a foundation for his later work and for his very early research. With one of his graduate school teachers, Edwin Ghiselli, Kahneman wrote a paper about the statistical techniques that Kahneman had developed whilst in the army, for use with data characterized by multiple attributes, published in *Personnel Psychology*, his first academic research publication.[11]

This early research on intuitive reasoning started Kahneman on the track that led to his much more well-known contributions to judgement and decision-making, including the seminal contributions to new approaches to economic decision-making. These earned him his Nobel Prize in Economics in 2002, held jointly with the experimental economist Vernon L. Smith. His most cited works, according to Google Scholar, are his work with Amos Tversky on prospect theory (Kahneman and Tversky, 1979) and their *Science* paper on heuristics and bias. His most influential books include his 2011 book (aimed at a general audience) *Thinking, Fast and Slow* and his *Attention and Effort* (1973), both cited extensively in the academic literature. In addition, Kahneman's collaborations with behavioural economists represent highly significant contributions because they bring together economic psychology and behavioural economics, for example the collaborations with Amos Tversky, Richard Thaler and Alan Schwartz. These works paralleled the evolution of four main interrelated threads in Kahneman's contributions: attention and effort; heuristics and bias; prospect theory (their most significant contribution to behavioural economics); and models of dual systems and selves.

After leaving the army for academia, Kahneman's early research explored associations between pupil dilation and cognitive effort, a collaboration with cognitive psychologist Jackson Beatty. They brought experimental participants into the lab and asked them to listen to series of digits and then recite them back. They found that the participants' pupils dilated as they listened, and then contracted as they recited the numbers back. Making the tasks more difficult increased the participants' pupil dilation. Kahneman and Beatty interpreted this as evidence that pupil dilation correlates with mental effort.[12] This links to significant developments in eye-tracking over the past few decades, with eye-tracking now widely used in behavioural economics and finance experiments. Whilst less generally famous, at least amongst economists, than his later work with Amos Tversky and the behavioural economists, this work has had significant impact in psychology. His 1973 book *Attention and Effort* is one of his most cited research contributions to psychology, but his main contributions to economics were to come in his later work, starting with his collaborations with Tversky.

Heuristics and Bias

For behavioural economists, the most influential phase of Kahneman's career began with his collaborations around heuristics and bias with Tversky. As noted above, this was a famous and impressively fruitful partnership. It combined their early independent work on limits to intuitive reasoning, judgement and decision-making with Kahneman's work on expert judgement and intuitive prediction, which he conducted whilst with the Israeli army. Kahneman and Tversky had first become aware of each other whilst they were serving in the army, but their academic collaboration began in spring 1969 when Kahneman invited Tversky to present his work at one of Kahneman's research seminars. Tversky presented some experimental findings from his collaboration with Ward Edwards, a former mentor.

For these experiments, participants were asked to sample white and red poker chips from a bag and decide whether the chips had come from a bag with seventy white and thirty red poker chips or from a bag containing thirty white and seventy red poker chips. The participant's guesses were broadly in the correct direction but did not factor all information to the extent predicted by laws of probability, specifically Bayes's Rule. Bayes's Rule captures our updating of probabilities. We start with a probability, the 'prior probability', and we adjust this as new information comes along to reach a 'posterior' probability. Bayesian reasoning models are widely used in psychology, and increasingly in economics and econometrics. So Tversky and his mentor had concluded that people are 'conservative Bayesians' and this was the conclusion with which Kahneman and his seminar group took issue. Kahneman later observed:

> The idea that people were conservative Bayesians did not seem to fit with the everyday observation of people commonly jumping to conclusions. It also appeared unlikely that the results obtained . . . would extend to the situation, arguably more typical, in which sample evidence is delivered all at once. Finally, the label of 'conservative Bayesian' suggested the implausible image of a process that gets the correct answer, then adulterates it with a bias.[13]

After the seminar, Kahneman and Tversky met for a coffee to discuss some of the limits to Tversky's interpretation of his results.

Whilst collaborative work is not at all unusual in academia, and is becoming more common with the increasing trend towards multidisciplinary research, the collaboration between Kahneman and Tverksy seemed to take place on a different plane to ordinary collaborations. They were quite different characters with different body clocks (Kahneman was a morning person and Tversky was a night owl). Their personalities were in some senses opposite – Kahneman was a pessimist, Tversky was an optimist. But the alchemy of their partnership was magical. Kahneman has observed that:

> All our ideas were jointly owned. Our interactions were so frequent and so intense that there was never much point in distinguishing between the discussion that primed an idea, the act of uttering it, and the subsequent elaboration of it . . . Some of the greatest joys of our collaboration . . . came from our ability to elaborate each other's nascent thoughts: if I expressed a half-formed idea, I knew that Amos would be there to understand it, probably more clearly than I did . . . The mutual trust and the complete lack of defensiveness that we achieved were particularly remarkable because both of us . . . were known to be severe critics. Our magic only worked when we were by ourselves. We soon learned that joint collaboration with any third party should be avoided, because we became competitive in a threesome.[14]

Their early conversations and experiments led to the publication in 1971 of their first joint paper, 'Belief in the Law of Small Numbers', published in the influential journal *Psychological Bulletin*.[15] This research explored the ways in which experts have false intuitions about probability – falsely inferring that small samples are representative, alongside other common errors in judgements about probabilities. It was a profound paper that identified some common, important limitations to intuitive judgement and consolidated their earlier independent research into the limitations on experts' judgements. Developing these ideas led to the publication of their 1974 article in the journal *Science* which outlined their understanding of heuristics – quick decision-making rules of thumb.[16]

Heuristics are the simple rules we use to decide quickly, when time and information are scarce and/or cognitive loads are high. Kahneman and Tversky were not the pioneers in defining heuristics – that honour belongs to another Nobel Prize-winner, the psychologist and computer scientist Herbert Simon – but they did not make much of a connection with Simon's insights. What they did contribute was an understanding of how these heuristics operate when real people are faced with risky choices. They were also pioneers in the way in which they developed a structured taxonomy of heuristics, and in the way they illustrated the concepts with examples and experimental evidence.

They identified three main types of heuristic: availability, representativeness and anchoring/adjustment. These heuristics are often but (and it is very important to note this) *not always* associated with behavioural bias – a systematic mistake of some sort. When we use the availability heuristic we rely on the information that is most quickly and easily available to us, for example related information that we can quickly remember. Relying on our emotions is a type of availability heuristic because emotions are often very accessible and easy to recall. The representativeness heuristic is about the ways in which we judge different events according to the similarities between them, sometimes drawing misleading analogies – another source of behavioural bias. Anchoring and adjustment is about the ways in which we judge events from a specific reference point. If we are selling something we anchor our expectations of what others will pay to buy it from us according to what we paid ourselves. This gives us a reference point, providing an anchor for our willingness to accept offers from others.

A much wider range of heuristics and related biases has been identified since the publication of Kahneman and Tversky's pioneering works. Kahneman and Tversky also spawned an enormous literature in behavioural economics on heuristics and biases, some of which is collected in their two edited volumes.[17] Thereafter their research moved them increasingly towards a critique of economics, and specifically the rational choice paradigm and related expected utility theory that was then dominating economics. This led Kahneman into his second set of path-breaking contributions to behavioural economic theory – prospect theory.

Prospect Theory and Behavioural Economics

Kahneman's collaboration with Tversky on heuristics and bias provided the seeds for prospect theory – an alternative to theories of risk embedded within standard economic models. Kahneman has remarked that prospect theory was in some senses a random name. He and Tversky had not known what to call it and so settled on something that sounded distinctive. The seminal article on prospect theory was published in the highly regarded quantitative economics and econometrics journal *Econometrica* in 1979.[18] For economists, this is possibly their most influential work, because it represented a direct challenge to expected utility theory, then the standard economic theory of risky decision-making.

Expected utility theory is founded on strong assumptions about rationality and choice, but Kahneman and Tversky argued that expected utility theory could not explain a number of behavioural paradoxes and inconsistencies. Prospect theory could explain them because it has key features that distinguish it from expected utility theory, verified by Kahneman and Tversky in the series of experiments reported in their 1979 article. Prospect theory also incorporated some of their early insights about the fact that people are not good at dealing consistently with very small and very large numbers, partly foreshadowed in their 1971 paper about people's mistakes in believing that small samples are representative.[19] People will have a distorted preference towards certain outcomes or very unlikely outcomes.

Prospect theory also allows that people base their decisions around reference points, rather than starting from zero every time. This connects with the anchoring and adjustment heuristic described above. Prospect theory allows that people's choices are not smooth and symmetric. Losses will have a much stronger impact than gains, linking to the concept of loss aversion – currently very influential in behavioural public policy design and developed further in their later writings.[20] With loss aversion, people will care much more about losing $10 than they will care about gaining $10. People also have asymmetric responses to risk-taking and they will take additional risks to avoid losses; Kahneman and Tversky described this as the 'reflection effect'.

Their work on heuristics and biases, as well as prospect theory, led Kahneman and Tversky into extensive collaborations with behavioural economists, including Richard Thaler and others, on themes consistent with prospect theory, including framing, loss aversion and mental accounting. Thaler in turn inspired a generation of behavioural economists, particularly on themes connecting with behavioural finance, as collected in his edited volumes.[21] For Kahneman and Tversky, this work also marked the end of their fruitful and mutually inspiring collaboration: their paper with Richard Thaler and Alan Schwartz on myopia and loss aversion was their last publication together.[22]

Thinking, Fast and Slow: Dual Systems and Selves

Kahneman's later work has focused on extending his insights about the limits to standard economic models of utility – capturing the idea that our decision-making often reflects interacting forces. His contributions to this approach are simply presented and easy to explore in his 2011 book *Thinking, Fast and Slow*. Here, he develops the idea that our thinking is not simple and uniform in the way described by economists. Instead, it reflects interacting systems: System 1 is emotional and intuitive, System 2 is logical and deliberative. System 2 is slow and lazy because it requires effort, so it has less of an influence on our choices than System 1. Much of our decision-making is propelled by quick instincts and intuitions. So economists focusing on the logical, deliberative System 2 styles of thinking capture just a small sub-set of our decision-making.

The ideas around System 1 and System 2 thinking also connect with his later insights about utility, which complement his and Tversky's work on prospect theory. As explored above, prospect theory is a critique of the treatment of *risk* in expected utility theory. Kahneman's work on dual systems essentially forms the basis of a complementary critique of the treatment of *utility* in expected utility theory. It also links to some of Kahneman's early insights about attention and memory. The connection with thinking systems comes via Kahneman's idea that we have dual selves: an experiencing self and a remembering self. Each of these selves experiences utility in different ways. Kahneman argues that whereas economists conventionally have concentrated on just acquisition utility, it would be more useful to include distinctions between sorts of utility, namely experienced versus remembered utility. In developing some of these ideas, he also connects with new research insights around well-being. With differences between experienced and remembered utility, the implications for well-being are quite different than those consistent with the acquisition utility that is the focus of most economic analysis.

Public Reception and Legacy

Kahneman writes well and clearly but some of his more academic work is esoteric and technical. The articles on prospect theory, for example, are not immediately easy to read. This reflects the fact that the register of Kahneman's writing varies, depending on the audience for whom he is writing. His writing for lay audiences is powerful, engaging and elegant. *Thinking, Fast and Slow* was a non-fiction bestseller and is an important contribution because it covers many of Kahneman's key insights from throughout his career. It brought ideas that were presented in esoteric academic journals elsewhere to a general audience – it was important, given the inherently trans-disciplinary nature of his work, that the ideas be communicated clearly to a wide range of readers. For academic audiences, his work is profound but deeply intellectual, and in parts quite dry and technical for a lay audience, but perhaps less dry and technical than the work of the average economist.

Inevitably, Kahneman's work with Tversky was controversial – just as much of the pioneering work in behavioural economics was. Their ideas have only recently gained respectability across the economics discipline. Expected utility remains the dominant paradigm and economists had been embracing rational choice theory for decades. Many economists had built substantial research reputations around these economic doctrines. Shifting this would have been hard for anyone. Kahneman, with Tversky, responded to some of the critiques, for example via their refinement of basic prospect theory into cumulative prospect theory.[23]

Some of Kahneman and Tversky's experimental evidence was challenged – for example by economists who criticized their experimental designs and protocols, arguing that their experimental findings were not properly documented and reflected the experimental participants' confusion about what they were being asked to do, rather than their behavioural biases. In addition, there were significant definitional disputes, and associated misunderstandings, even with other economic psychologists and behavioural economists. One example was the tension with Gerd Gigerenzer's ideas about the rationality of heuristics.[24] Gigerenzer argues that heuristics are rational decision-making devices. Kahneman argues that heuristics are not always rational. Whoever is correct, it is unarguable that Kahneman and Tversky's research caused many economists to reconsider the nature of risky choice, utility and well-being.

Kahneman was careful to emphasize that their intent was not to overturn the idea of rational decision-making in its entirety. He recognizes that people can and do operate according to rational principles. In his Nobel autobiographical essay, Kahneman emphasized that his work with Tversky is less a broad attack on human rationality and more a critique of economists' rational agent models. But, in contrast to the emphasis adopted by economists, this rational capacity is not defined in the strong form usually embraced by economists. Rather, rationality takes the weaker form, as outlined for example by Herbert Simon, as 'bounded rationality'.[25] People can and do act rationally (depending on how rationality is defined), just not all the time.

Kahneman has observed that he prefers dialogue to undiluted criticism. He is sensitive to criticism, a very human trait that many of us share. So it is not surprising that Kahneman's contributions demonstrate the power of collaboration. He has collaborated with many others across his career, including transdisciplinary collaborations – even before they were fashionable. Kahneman was and is always eager to collaborate – he has remarked that 'collaboration is not only more creative, it is more fun.'[26] The issue of dispute in academic research forms the basis for another of Kahneman's contributions, this time a methodological contribution for scientific research as a whole, focusing on the importance of building constructive dialogue and debate.

In the academic publishing tradition, misunderstandings and unfounded criticisms are sometimes allowed to fester and multiply, without opportunities for debate and dialogue. In behavioural economics, and in economics more generally, this tension has revealed itself, for example, in confusions about what different people mean by the terms 'rational', 'irrational', 'heuristics' and 'bias'. Dialogue is not yet institutionalized within academic publishing, most of which still relies on double-blind peer review. Kahneman has championed solutions to these problems. This focus on constructive dialogue led him to experiment with 'adversarial collaborations' – when intellectual disputes are resolved by the opponents working together on joint authored papers, in which they explore their disagreements and attempt to reach a consensus.[27] His more unexpected collaborations include his long-time adversarial collaboration with Gary Klein around their disagreements about intuitive expertise, and early adversarial collaborations with psychologists Tom Gilovich, Ralph Hertwig and Victoria Medvec, and with economists Ian Bateman, Chris Starmer and Robert Sugden.[28] Outside the adversarial-collaboration format, he has also collaborated in resolving disagreements via his joint writing projects with Dan Ariely and George Loewenstein.

Given that Kahneman is a psychologist it might seem strange to the uninitiated that he won a Nobel Prize in Economics. What he contributed to economics was a new understanding of rationality and its limits, from the perspective of economic psychology. From the 1970s onwards economists were preoccupied with strong assumptions about rationality: rational choice theory was the dominant paradigm. This paradigm centred on the hypothesis that we apply our best rational faculties to all our decision-making and that we reach our choices after logically balancing the benefits against the costs, so as to maximize our own self-interest. In this world, individuals know best what is best for themselves. So most economists assume that we are acting as if we are very clever and well informed.

These rationality assumptions make economic analysis easier. If everyone is behaving in a mathematically rational way then building economic models is relatively simple. From the 1970s onwards, however, this dependence on rationality was challenged, first by economists associated with a Keynesian tradition, and later by mainstream economists too, especially in the aftermath of the 2007/8 financial crises. Keynesians had always had reservations about the strong rationality assumptions of mainstream economic theory, and there were plenty of post-Keynesians predicting financial crises many years before those of 2007/8, for example. This sort of assertion reminds us that Kahneman is not an economist, and so could not be aware of all the different approaches to economics and economists' internecine conflicts. Ironically, in the history of economic thought, John Maynard Keynes was not only overwhelmingly influential and prescient, he also drew strongly on ideas with which Daniel Kahneman might have a lot of sympathy.

A key feature of Kahneman's legacy lies in his contributions to transdisciplinary research. His seminal works cross disciplinary boundaries and the Nobel Prize in Economics was awarded to him 'for having integrated insights from psychologistical research into economic science'.[29] With typical modesty, Kahneman acknowledges that the prize recognized the efforts of Tversky and a new generation of behavioural economists (led by Richard Thaler) as well as his own:

> Although I do not wish to renounce any credit for my contribution, I should say that in my view the work of integration was actually done mostly by Thaler and the group of young economists that quickly began to form around him, starting with Colin Camerer and George Loewenstein, and followed by the likes of Matthew Rabin, David Laibson, Terry Odean, and Sendhil Mullainathan . . . the founding text of behavioural economics was the first article in which Thaler (1980)[30] presented a series of vignettes that challenged fundamental tenets of consumer theory.[31]

Kahneman sought to influence economics from the edges, consolidated by strong partnerships with economists. In a 2012 interview with *The Guardian* he expressed suspicion of economics as a discipline: 'Economists have a mystique among social scientists because they know mathematics. They are quite good at explaining what has happened after it has happened, but rarely before. I don't think of myself as an economist at all.'[32]

While Kahneman was not an economist himself, and in fact was somewhat disapproving of economics and its focus on rational choice – a concern shared by a number of heterodox (non-mainstream) economists – his challenge to economics is more measured than either his critics or champions might claim. Kahneman demonstrated the limits of rationality, he did not seek to refute economics nor to prove that judgement and decision-making are about irrationality. Kahneman's key works, with Tversky, were about encouraging economists to re-think their narrow, restrictive set of assumptions. This is an enduring contribution which is increasing in prominence as today's academic and policymaking communities embrace key insights from behavioural economics.

TWELVE

AMARTYA SEN

Jonathan Conlin

Amartya Sen was ten years old when, in 1943, a famine struck the British-administered province of Bengal. The son of a Bengali chemistry professor, Sen had been born near Dhaka, in what is now Bangladesh. Though the famine largely spared city-dwellers, at least two million Bengalis died from starvation and associated malnourishment and disease. The British authorities appeared unwilling to act, claiming that there was sufficient food. They did not restrict movement of the staple food, rice, out of the region, nor did they take action to import rice from other parts of India or from other countries. A 1945 inquiry accused these officials of ignoring evidence of rice shortages, accusations which contributed to Indian nationalists' demands for an end to British rule.

In 1976 Sen published a paper in *Economic and Political Weekly* entitled 'Famines as Failures of Exchange Entitlements', which was in turn expanded into a 1981 book, *Poverty and Famines: An Essay on Entitlement and Deprivation*. In the years since 1943 Sen had studied economics at Presidency College, Kolkata, completed a doctorate in economics at Cambridge University and been appointed head of the economics department at Kolkata's new Jadavpur University. These were the first stations of an ongoing progress which has seen Sen holding positions at leading universities in the United States, India and the United Kingdom, and garnering a succession of prestigious prizes, including the 1998 Nobel Prize in Economic Sciences.

Sen's revisionist account of the 1943 Bengal famine concluded that the Raj administration had been 'fairly right in its estimation of overall availability, but disastrously wrong in its theory of famines'. Rather than the famine being caused by a lack of food, or Food Availability Decline, supply in 1943 had been 13 per cent higher than in 1941, when no famine was observed.[1] The authorities at the time had been largely correct when they stated that recent adverse weather had not caused a rice shortage. But starvation was not, Sen wrote, merely a matter of what food exists, but how it is distributed among the population. It is a question of who can or cannot 'command' the food. There are a number of 'entitlement relations' which determine an individual's 'title' (or claim) to a share of the available food. Those who own agricultural land, for example, have a claim on the rice grown on that land. An agricultural labourer may not own the land, yet may still have a claim on the rice by virtue of having tilled that land, under a set of 'entitlement relations' known as sharecropping.

In Bengal in 1943 there were many whose 'entitlement relations' were based on exchange. They did not grow their own rice, but traded services (such as haircuts or river transport) or goods other than rice (such as milk or fish) for rice. These goods or services formed their 'exchange entitlement'. What the authorities in 1943 as well as the 1945 inquiry had failed to observe was that the rate of exchange between these goods and rice shifted dramatically against the barbers, agricultural labourers, fishermen and many other groups. These groups could no longer command enough rice to feed themselves and their dependants, and hence they starved. The shift was caused not by adverse weather and crop failure, but by inflation caused by heavy public expenditure – itself related to the fact that the British were busy fighting a war with Japan for control of nearby Burma. Wages for many city-dwellers kept pace with inflation in 1943, but the exchange rate between agricultural labour and rice declined to levels as low as 24 (where the rate in December 1941 = 100).[2] Faced with an increase in the price of rice from 13 rupees per *maund* (82.3 lb) to over 30, many Bengalis put off haircuts and travel, and stopped eating luxuries like fish. Declining demand for haircuts and fish further reduced barbers and fishermen's 'exchange entitlements'.

Poverty and Famines also considered the 1974 famine in Bangladesh as well as famines in Ethiopia and the Sahel, where Sen found similar patterns. In Ethiopia from 1972 to 1974 food prices did not increase by much, even in the hardest-hit Wollo region. In Bangladesh in 1974 the three worst-affected districts actually saw a rise in foodgrains measured by head of population. There was, in short, enough food available on the market, at prices that were only slightly elevated. As in Bengal in 1943, those who starved were the landless, day labourers, pastoralists and transport workers. All of them were far more exposed to the steep decline in the exchange rate between labour and foodgrains than sharecroppers or landowners. In desperation Ethiopia's nomadic cowherders sold all their cows, glutting the market and causing a collapse in the price they received for each cow.[3]

In several of these famines the shift in exchange entitlements had begun long before famine took hold. In Bangladesh in 1974, for example, the amount of rice an agricultural worker could command with a day's labour was in decline long before the floods on which many Bengalis blamed the famine. Had the authorities been looking at the right data, they could have intervened to prevent the famine, by instituting public work schemes which would allow those at the bottom to exchange their labour for rice directly. Instead the government and outside observers were congratulating the country on a decline in poverty, measured as the proportion of population below the poverty line. This data itself failed to observe the fact that while this 'headcount' figure for poverty was improving, the distribution of wealth *among* the poor was shifting. The proportion in 'extreme poverty' was rising sharply in the late 1960s and early 1970s, even as the aforementioned indicators were showing less poverty overall.

Sen's entitlement approach drew attention to the shortcomings of several means of identifying what characteristics make up poverty. The headcount figures pioneered by Charles Booth's 1880s investigations of 'pauperism' in London's East End depended on a poverty line. Nutritional models set their line by working out the number of calories required to sustain life. Each method had its shortcomings; even the calorie model fails to allow for the presence of intestinal parasites, which cause the individual to require more than the minimum to survive. In Bengal in 1943 an approach focused on food supply and the market prevented the authorities from foreseeing famine. As Sen noted, 'shocking disasters can lie deeply hidden in comforting aggregate magnitudes.'[4]

For an academic, of course, picking holes in mainstream theories can be a way of life, or at very least the road to promotion and distinction within one's field. As we shall see, Sen himself contributed many important papers to the raft of equation-heavy papers surrounding matters of relatively esoteric interest within social choice theory, the study of how individual preferences or welfares are combined so as to reach a collective decision. Many twentieth-century economists have built successful careers on the back of a single well-received paper in a high-impact journal, pointing to an intellectually satisfying conundrum or paradox.

Sen's claim to be a great economic thinker rests, however, on a recognition of a responsibility to push beyond this kind of tinkering, and on a claim to have found a new way of measuring the welfare of society. This involved challenging the 'welfarist' school of Abram Bergson and Paul Samuelson developed in the 1940s. Welfarists begin by imagining every possible social state that could exist, given certain restrictions (no slavery allowed, say). They then use a so-called social welfare function to assign values to each state, allowing them to be ranked according to their degree of success in maximizing welfare. The findings can then be used to frame policy recommendations for governments. As we have seen, Sen questioned the manner in which welfarists measured the welfare of a given society, and went on to point out ways in which the restrictions could stymie each other.

Welfarists had already been challenged by James Buchanan and other contractarian and libertarian thinkers who doubted governments' ability and authority to act in the name of maximizing welfare. For them the task of maximizing welfare rightly belonged to the individual, whose choices should not be constrained by restrictions of the kind welfarists imposed. Those restrictions were normative, and embodied welfarists' belief that 'social good' (the welfare of society) can be defined and established. For contractarians the role of government is not to maximize this social good, but simply to maintain a rule-based framework within which individuals remain as free as possible to pursue whatever they see as worth pursuing. Sen subjected welfarism to sustained critique without jettisoning the idea of social good.

As Sen asked in *Poverty and Famine*, what happens when we have challenged all procedures by which poverty has been defined and measured? Do we give up trying to understand the phenomenon, or do we try to see what we can 'salvage'? 'What do we do *then*?'[5] The first section of this chapter considers Sen's answer to this question. Discussion of what Sen managed to salvage from utilitarian approaches and 'welfarism' is a more forward-looking and optimistic endeavour than the term 'salvage' might suggest. Indeed, in another context Sen has described it as embracing 'an embarrassment of riches', of combining different approaches rather than setting them on each other's necks in some Darwinistic attempt to identify the fittest. The second section introduces Sen's most important contribution to economic thought, the 'capability approach', which understands development in terms of the opportunities available to the individual in a given society. Since the 1990s Sen's work has come to emphasize the contributory role that these 'functionings' have to play in furthering a just and tolerant society. Among other things this helped Sen to explain another curious finding about famines – the fact that no democratic state has ever experienced one. The third section considers that work, while the last considers Sen's theory of justice.

Methodological Mongrelism

In his Nobel Lecture entitled 'The Possibility of Social Choice' Sen identified three contributions he had made to economics, which he characterized as 'informational broadening', the use of partial orderings and a weakening of 'consistency conditions'. All relate to the kind of calculations economists make when attempting to evaluate the welfare of a society. What data belongs in such calculations, and what data should be ignored as irrelevant 'noise'? What kind of demands can we make of these calculations, or rather, how much precision or completeness or consistency can we attribute to them? How far can or should we combine different sets of results? Economists had long distinguished between 'ordinal' data, which allows rankings to be made, and 'cardinal' data measuring levels or size. Finally there is the question of what we use the results for. Aggregating calculations that work well as voting systems (to reach decisions) may not work very well when we are after evaluations of welfare.[6]

'Formal economics has not been very interested in the plurality of focus in judging a person's states and interests,' Sen noted. In the eighteenth century Jeremy Bentham may have defined welfare (or 'utility', in Bentham's parlance; the terms became more or less interchangeable) as 'the greatest happiness of the greatest number', but Bentham's self-described heirs simply equated welfare with per capita GDP, with 'whatever the person maximizes (or can be seen as maximizing)'. The appeal of per capita GDP lay in its conduciveness to 'real-valued (i.e. numerical) representation', not in any robustness that we might attribute to the inbuilt assumption that greater income makes us happier or that individuals will always act to maximize their income. 'Mathematical exactness of formulation has proceeded hand in hand with remarkable inexactness of content.'[7]

Sen lays much of the blame on Lionel Robbins, a leading light of the London School of Economics who died in 1984. Indeed, Sen's career to date could be seen as an attempt to heal the violence done to the discipline and to its vision of humanity by Robbins's contention that 'economics deals with ascertainable facts; ethics with valuation and obligations.' In going on to argue that interpersonal comparisons of welfare were impossible as 'every mind is inscrutable to every other mind' (itself a quotation from W. S. Jevons) Robbins had added another stone to this wall, and given further licence to those who understood welfare in terms of the sum welfare enjoyed by the whole society, without considering how that income was distributed among the members of that society.[8] In the following decade the popularity of Pareto comparisons further simplified matters. Named after the Italian Vilfredo Pareto, Pareto efficiency refers to a supposedly optimal allocation of resources in which no individual's welfare can be improved without harming someone else's welfare.

Simplification may have aided the arithmetic of welfare economics, Sen argued, but at the cost of producing results that were illiberal, paradoxical or simply absurd. In 1951 the American Kenneth Arrow's book *Social Choice and Individual Values* presented what became known as Arrow's Impossibility Theorem. The theorem posited that, given three options to rank in order of preference, there was no system of ranked order voting (as opposed to, say, the more familiar 'first past the post system') which could produce an overall ranking while also meeting a set of four criteria. Pareto efficiency was one of the criteria, as was non-dictatorship (that is, the overall ranking must not be the same as that of any one voter, regardless of the others' rankings) and 'binary independence' (a voter's preference of A over B should not change if a third option X is added). Such was the impact of the theorem that it seemed as if Arrow had finished off the very field of social choice theory that he himself had fathered, and for which he would receive the Nobel Prize in 1972.

Sen argued that, though intriguing, the theorem was an artefact of its own informational poverty, itself a result of a Robbins-esque rejection of interpersonal comparisons as well as its imposition of a degree of consistency that might be intuitive, but simply did not accord with how humans behaved in the real world. A similar consistency had been imposed by the American Paul Samuelson, another founding father of social choice theory. Samuelson and his followers built their models around a Weak Axiom of Revealed Preference (WARP), which, rather like the binary independence of Arrow's Impossibility Theorem, held that a preference of A over B could not change if a third option X was added. According to Samuelson's Revealed Preference Theory, the choices made by consumers simply mirror their preferences, and both are oriented on a desire to maximize one's welfare.

There are a number of factors that can make consumers 'disobey' or contradict these rules or assumptions, and that make their choices (not their preferences) vary according to the 'menu' of options they are presented with. Sen gives the example of a guest at a party who is hungry for one apple and finds himself standing by the fruit bowl. It would appear intuitive and rational for her to take one apple regardless of how many other apples there are in the bowl. Her preference, after all, is for one apple. Yet her choice might be 'menu dependent' in so far as she might choose not to take an apple if there was only one apple left, owing to a desire not to appear to deny other guests the opportunity.[9]

In this case demands for consistency may have made Samuelson's models look tidy, but the approach that explained behaviour solely in terms of preferences, 'which are in turn defined only by behaviour' (that is, Revealed Preference), was one that remained 'remarkably mute about human joys and sufferings'.[10] Or as Robert Sugden has put it, 'Utility, when understood in the revealed preference sense, is not a measure of any particular quality (such as pleasure) which might plausibly be judged to be good. It is simply a representation of an individual's choices.'[11]

Sen's way out of the Impossibility Theorem was to loosen the conditions considered as minimal rational requirements, jettisoning Pareto efficiency, for example. Though championed as a totem of individual liberty, when faced with more than two alternatives it revealed a darker side. Given a total set of 100 divided among three individuals, for example, a distribution of 98:1:1 is as Pareto efficient as the much more equitable division of 33:33:34. In 'The Impossibility of a Paretian Liberal' (1970) Sen produced his own Impossibility Theorem, confronting economists with the choice between the Paretian shibboleth and their liberal values.[12]

Attentiveness to Pareto efficiency led welfare economists to overlook inequalities that were otherwise glaring because they considered only the society's total welfare, not how it was distributed, and judged actions or policies only according to their consequences for that sum. No value was attributed to differences in levels among individuals (interpersonal comparison being taboo), only the sum, by which a complete rank of countries' wealth could be produced. A country with three individuals with utilities of 33, 33 and 33 was therefore 'poorer' than one where the three citizens held 98, 1 and 1, even though the latter was obviously a highly unequal society. Yet according to sum ranking, the country's welfare would be increased regardless of whether one gave the additional utility to the citizen who had 98 or one of the citizens with 1. Of course, marginal utility would suggest that the additional unit of utility would be far more beneficial to either of the citizens with 1 than that with 98, but the prohibition on interpersonal comparison renders that point moot.

When it came to evaluating how successfully any given social state had maximized welfare, therefore, welfarists like Bergson and Samuelson's social welfare function were simply looking at the sum total of individual incomes. In 1973 Sen proposed his own function, whereby the per capita income is multiplied by the Gini coefficient, a measure of inequality developed in 1912 by the statistician Corrado Gini. Sen did not make the same demands of his function as Samuelson and others did of theirs. He did not, for example, demand that it produce a 'complete-ordering representation', only a less ambitious 'quasi-ordering' that allowed partial rather than complete rankings. 'The very notion of inequality seems to have this quasi-ordering framework,' he noted, 'The concept is not geared to making fine distinctions, and comes into its own with sharper contrasts.'[13]

Rather than presenting it as the ideal social welfare function, Sen was candid about its limitations: it was helpful for asking some questions, but not others. It was one tool to be used in 'intersection' with others which had their own, different set of limitations.[14] The lesson Sen drew from the Impossibility Theorem was the need to avoid the 'All-or-none approach of traditional theory', whereby robustness, completeness, precision and other statistical or mathematical qualities were acquired at the price of arbitrariness or incarceration inside impossibility.[15] 'Mongrelism', in short, was preferable to 'purity', at least when it came to method. For a discipline wedded to tidy models and graphs, this was highly unsettling and suspect.

The Capability Approach

In their eagerness to understand welfare in their own mathematical terms welfare economists had, it seemed, left out the 'being': well-being had become a matter of well-having. In *A Theory of Justice* (1971) the American philosopher John Rawls had sought to address some of the problems with utilitarian approaches to measuring welfare, defining a set of 'primary goods' necessary to an individual's welfare. Such a set included natural primary goods, such as health and intelligence, and social goods, such as rights, income and 'the social bases of self-respect'. An individual's endowment of such goods could be compared with another person's endowment, and Rawls explored several hypothetical scenarios under which the welfare of those found to be worst-off (measured by 'primary goods') was to be privileged, in obedience to a so-called 'difference principle'.

For Sen, however, this was a case of confusing means with ends. Humanity was too diverse to posit a universal set of 'primary goods'. Even basic nutritional needs (the number of calories necessary to maintain health) varied with climate, longevity and levels of health-care provision.[16] Rawls and others were too focused on the values of things and rights, and neglected the relationship between them and associated 'functionings'.[17] Various 'conversion factors' determined the set of 'capabilities' enjoyed by the individual endowed with those goods.

The gift, or 'endowment', of a bicycle, for example, may be evaluated simply, in terms of the amount of money it could be sold for or in terms of the amount saved in bus or rickshaw fares. For a small trader, the bicycle serves to enlarge the market in which they can buy and sell, and allows more transactions to be squeezed into the same amount of time. In Sen's terms, the bicycle increases the individual's capability set, that range of actions and outcomes that it is possible to perform or achieve. Though it is impossible to realize all these actions or outcomes, welfare is not lost by this failure. On the contrary, welfare itself is best evaluated by focusing on enhancing these 'capabilities', on broadening the range of 'functionings' that are available, whether or not they are realized.

The process by which 'capabilities' become 'functionings' may seem straightforward, so much so that one might wonder whether we need distinct terms. One needs some training to ride a bicycle, but it does not take very long, and there is usually someone around to provide such training at little or no cost. Thereafter, it seems, new 'functionings' beckon: new markets for your goods or services, a broader circle of friends, the life-enhancing delight of feeling the wind in your face or simply imagining where one might go next. The conversion of 'new bicycle' into 'new freedom of movement' is not, however, as straightforward as may appear. A range of 'conversion factors' play their part in determining whether and how far this freedom is enjoyed. These are externalities in the sense that they are unrelated to the bicycle, but they determine whether the endowment of a bicycle does in fact contribute to the recipient's capability set, or just sits around getting rusty. They are the functions that relate goods (the bicycle, in this case) to certain activities and states of being, the well-having to the well-being.

Sen identifies personal, social and environmental conversion factors. Physical handicaps, parasites and disease are personal factors that might restrict the individual's ability to ride the bicycle. Potholed roads, heavy traffic and associated pollution may pose further constraints. Compared to these environmental factors the social ones are far less evident, but arguably play the greatest role in determining whether the bicycle does enhance its owner's capabilities. In many parts of the world (as in Britain in the Victorian period) it is socially unacceptable for a woman to ride a bicycle. It may be hard to distinguish these factors neatly from each other (if high levels of pollution lead to higher levels of asthma, should we label this an environmental or a personal factor?), but that does not lessen their impact.

The capability approach turns our attention to a far broader range of issues than that which simply considers an individual's income or goods relative to the income or goods enjoyed by others in the same society. Social norms, public health and infrastructure are all implicated. If we were advising a government on how to improve low conversion rates in the above example, we might find ourselves discussing everything from deworming to road congestion charges. Such initiatives would, of course, have many effects on many people who did not possess bicycles. Whether the functioning of bicycling is a realized one or not, however, is not the point. The society is the richer and the individual better off, Sen would argue, simply by dint of having this capability added to their set. Though in one sense externalities, the raft of measures that might be taken to address this specific bicycle problem could have beneficial effects on matters central to classical economists' interests: they increase the size of markets, enable greater specialization of labour and so on.

In 1990 the UN Development Programme launched a new benchmark, the Human Development Index. Its chief designer, the Pakistani economist Mahbub ul Haq, sought Sen's advice and endeavoured to incorporate his capability approach. The name itself indicated a shift in focus in how 'development' is understood. Rather than understanding welfare in terms of national income or the openness of markets, the HDI put the 'human' first. Rather than just measuring per capita Gross National Income, the HDI displays a suitably Senian 'informational richness' in combining three benchmarks in one: basic education (measured as mean years of schooling), longevity (life expectancy at birth) and income (Gross National Income or GNI at purchasing power parity per capita).

Sen made the historical case for attentiveness to education and longevity (as an indication of public health provision) in a 1995 book co-written with Jean Drèze, *India: Economic Development and Social Opportunity.* This study drew on the findings of studies devoted to three Indian states with very different ethnic, religious and political orientations (Kerala, West Bengal and Uttar Pradesh), crunching data on life expectancy, infant mortality, literacy and female/male ratio (FMR) alongside the familiar benchmarks based on per capita GNI. As well as comparing different parts of India with each other the authors were particularly interested in comparisons with China.

In the 1990s both China and India could look back on fifty years of development from roughly the same level of per capita GNP. Among the Indian elite, China's one-child policy and its liberalizing markets were often credited with bringing about an 'Asian Miracle', one which Indians felt had passed them by. In addition to justifying aggressive state-sponsored anti-fertility campaigns (including coerced surgical sterilization), China's growth was perceived as teaching the importance of market liberalizing initiatives. To catch up with China's enviable growth, many concluded, bureaucratic red tape known as the 'Licence Raj' needed to be dismantled as a matter of urgency.

In the preface to *Economic Development and Social Opportunity* Sen and Drèze expressed astonishment at the priority given to 'debates on such question as the details of tax concessions to be given to multinationals, or whether Indians should drink Coca-Cola, or whether the private sector should be allowed to operate city buses'. Meanwhile 'the abysmal situation of basic education and elementary health care' and other issues with 'a crucial bearing on the well-being and freedom of the population' were overlooked.[18]

Life expectancy in India was around ten years less than in China. Indian literacy rates were not only lower but showed a greater gender disparity: 39 per cent (female) and 64 per cent (male) versus 68 per cent and 87 per cent in China. Literacy was almost universal among the younger Chinese population, which was far from the case in India. Though the Indian government promised universal primary education to age fourteen, it simply did not allocate the resources to bring it about. Meanwhile the health clinics it provided were fixated on a 'population problem', prioritizing sterilization over inexpensive yet effective measures to combat disease. The data suggested that population growth had little effect on per capita GDP: India's population crisis simply did not exist.[19]

Taken as a whole this historical data demonstrated that, far from public healthcare and universal education being the rewards of economic growth, in China's case the economy grew after the state had already taken big strides in improving literacy and life expectancy. The growth was the reward for the state's intervention. Public health and education were not luxuries that a developing country could only 'afford' once economic growth had reached a certain level. Nor, as many self-proclaimed devotees of Adam Smith and neoclassical economics held, did state intervention in health and education represent so many brakes on economic growth. It was not a question of 'more or less government' but of 'types of governance'.[20] In focusing on the 'Licence Raj' and Coca-Cola, rather than immunization and teachers, India was running the risk of learning the wrong lessons from China.

Agency and Process

Since the early 1990s Sen's thinking around the capability approach has developed, placing increasing emphasis on the 'agent-oriented view', on the 'who' who acts.[21] On a basic level, attentiveness to agency simply recognizes that it matters to us who brings about a change in our welfare, and how. To return to the bicycle example, we don't just appropriate it as if it 'dropped from the sky'; our attitude towards it and to ourselves is different if it is presented to us as a gift, a reward for virtuous behaviour, a right, a lottery prize, a privilege of social rank or a charitable boon. On a more sophisticated level, agency can be constitutive or constructive, shaping the 'who' and the capacity in which they act.

By constituting an educated, well-informed and participatory public (an 'us'), the processes involved in realizing an individual's capabilities can move entire societies in a liberal and democratic direction, holding governments to account and changing the social norms that deny women and certain ethnic or religious groups a full capability set. We learn to value such outcomes not only because of the contribution they make to our capability sets (instrumentally, in other words), but derive benefits such as self-respect from the way in which we secured those outcomes – through coordinated action in concert with others. Freedom is about process, about *exercising* as much as it is about *possessing* certain opportunities or rights as part of some Rawlsian bundle of 'primary goods'.

Having started out by drawing attention to the relationship between goods and states of being, Sen has become interested in how different 'functionings' intersect and can mutually reinforce each other in order to 'expand real freedoms'. Inevitably this has involved thinking about how we should direct such change, leading in turn to consideration of ideas of justice and equity, ideas that have seemed deeply alien to economic thought, if not downright antagonistic to it. In this respect Sen's thought can be seen as a return to the moral philosophy of Adam Smith's day, before economics emerged as a discrete discipline. Despite Smith's reputation as the father of economics, few economists bothered to read Smith thoroughly, let alone bother with other philosophers.

Sen was unusual in having a thorough grounding in this tradition, gained during his Prize Fellowship at Trinity College, Cambridge, a Fellowship that gave its holder complete freedom to study whatever he or she wished. Personal relationships also played their part: Sen's first wife was the niece of an Italian economist, Albert Hirschman, whose *The Passions and the Interests* (1977) addressed Smith and contemporaries such as Montesquieu and Dugald Stewart. Hirschman argued that the development of economic thought from Smith onwards had ignored or actively sought to repress the passions by privileging a supposedly more rational focus on interests and the tidy patterns of behaviour they seemed to create.[22] The lesson Sen drew from both Smith and Hirschman was that humans were not isolated, rational egoists, but a 'complex of psychological and cultural processes'.[23]

In *Development as Freedom* (1999) Sen described his own 'capability perspective' as 'a return to an integrated approach to economic and social development championed particularly by Adam Smith'.[24] Smith understood freedom of exchange as much more than a means of securing economic growth, Sen noted: 'Freedom of exchange and transaction is itself part and parcel of the basic liberties that people have reason to value.' As a result of the way development experts were writing about the role of markets at the time, however, this was not as clear as it ought to be. It had become common to see the market as something that needed defending or justifying in terms of some 'favourable but distant effects', even as a necessary evil, when in fact 'the freedom to participate in economic interchange has a basic role in social living.'[25]

Just as there were those who urged the Indian government to leave literacy campaigns aside until economic growth had rendered them 'affordable', so there have been advocates of the thesis that civil freedoms and political liberties are 'luxuries' which certain states must do without if they wish to enjoy economic growth. This view is often referred to as the 'Lee Thesis', named after the Singaporean prime minister Lee Kuan Yew: Singapore's economic growth is thus held to be a kind of reward for denying Singapore's citizens the freedom to deliberate and discuss how their city-state is run. Sometimes, as at the 1993 Vienna Conference on Human Rights, leaders of authoritarian Asian regimes have argued that political rights are not universal. Rights such as freedom of speech are said to be in tension with so-called 'Asian values' of discipline and obedience to the state. Demanding the expansion of such freedoms, therefore, is supposedly tantamount to cultural imperialism.

Sen sees freedom of exchange and other, non-economic freedoms of speech, assembly and so on as interrelated and mutually reinforcing, rather than negatively correlated (as in the Lee Thesis). Sen posits five types of freedom: political freedoms, economic facilities, social opportunities, transparency guarantees and protective security. For him these are both the ends and means of development, properly understood. They are also universal. As Sen wryly notes, the argument that Asians are culturally indifferent to political rights such as freedom of expression could only be verified by putting the question to a vote in a free election – the very thing authoritarian regimes will never permit.[26]

The most important examples of Sen's 'agent-oriented' approach relate to the unfreedom of women. An influential 1992 article in the *British Medical Journal* noted a tendency for the FMR (female/male ratio) in many Asian countries, including India, to depart from the biologically determined norm. Left to itself this ratio should produce a cohort in which there are slightly more women than men. In areas where dowries are expected and brides cut ties with their parents upon marriage, however, parents are disincentivized to expend care and money on daughters. As the Telugu proverb runs, 'Bringing up a daughter is like watering a plant in another's courtyard.'

As a result of these disincentives the FMR is skewed in many Indian provinces (resulting in 880 women for 1,000 men in Uttar Pradesh, for example), owing to the practice whereby pregnant mothers have the sex of their foetus determined by ultrasound and then choose (or are coerced) to abort the foetus if it is female.[27] Similar effects in FMR occur even among those unable to afford an ultrasound, presumably the result of male infants and children receiving a level of care, food and medical treatment denied to their sisters. The result is an estimated shortfall, or 100 million 'missing women', to quote the title of Sen's 1992 paper.[28]

Rather than view women as 'patients' waiting for state or other agencies to intervene on their behalf, however, Sen argued that fostering women's agency was not only a highly effective means of improving those women's welfare as well as that of their children (of both sexes), but encouraged broader economic growth and the expansion of Sen's four other freedoms. Improving female literacy, for example, turns out to be a more effective means of reducing child mortality than improving male literacy or even measures to reduce general poverty overall. When the female literacy rate rose from 22 to 75 per cent, mortality in under-fives dropped from 156 to 110 per thousand (keeping all other variables constant). When the male literacy rate rose from 22 per cent to 75 per cent, mortality also dropped but by less: from 169 to 141.[29]

The state of being able to read does not strengthen a woman's immune system or inoculate her against disease. To a welfare economist female literacy might seem a 'luxury'; allocating scarce resources to teaching women to read might appear to be a 'waste' of funds which could be spent on more nurses, dispensaries or vaccinations. In India, as in many other parts of the world, women spend the vast majority of their time in the home producing work that is rarely if ever captured by GNP or other measures of output. Even if one were to focus on literacy, therefore, it might seem to make sense to focus on men, who appear to be more economically active. But Sen's observation indicates that, even if the state of being able to read does not grant disease resistance, it does enable 'functionings' by women that are associated with impressive reductions in mortality (we should be careful, however, not to attribute direct causality here, as the use of the verb 'reduced' in the previous paragraph does). Literacy is also associated with greater participation in the formal economy (that is, outside the home) that in turn fosters greater political engagement by women. Literate mothers, for example, are in a position to petition the authorities when their village teacher fails to show up for work.[30]

Some of these effects are unintended. As a devotee of Adam Smith, one might have assumed Sen would point to the echoes of the famous passage from *The Wealth of Nations*, which describes every individual as being 'led by an invisible hand to promote an end which was no part of his intention'.[31] Friedrich Hayek and others interpreted this as a profound insight and a challenge to anyone presuming to tinker with the inscrutable workings of the economy. Sen, however, firmly opposed what he saw as Hayek's conflation of 'unintended' with 'unpredictable'. 'Economic and social reasoning can take note of consequences that may not be intended, but which nevertheless result from institutional arrangements.'[32] If a female literacy programme led to an unintended decline in mortality of under-fives in, say, the Indian province of Kerala, it was not presumptive or irrational to advocate introduction of a similar programme in other provinces or other countries in the expectation of a similar decline. Unintended consequences inform deliberative action, rather than ruling it out entirely.

Sen and Drèze noted another, less happy unintended consequence of economic growth and the social emulation and mobility that it fosters. The FMR could decline, rather than return to balance, as growth led lower 'scheduled' castes to emulate higher 'martial' castes' more patriarchal attitudes. For Sen this was 'a useful reminder of the fact that economic progress on its own does not necessarily do very much to reduce gender inequalities'. In this case the social 'institutional arrangements' of dowry, caste and so on needed to be addressed through 'a process of active social change which has no obvious link with economic growth'.[33] Such change does, however, have clear links to population growth, leading to voluntary reduction in fertility far in excess of anything achieved by state-sponsored sterilization campaigns or other neo-Malthusian interventions.

Sen is certainly aware of the related challenges of counting women in evaluations of welfare, of making women count. In his 1998 Nobel lecture Sen recalled one of the curious findings from his early work on the 1943 famine: the widows surveyed reported hardly any cases of 'indifferent health', while the widowers 'complained massively about just that'. In such a male-dominated society one could reasonably assume that if anything women's healthcare needs would be worse served than those of the men, resulting in women reporting worse health.

The widows' expectations were clearly profoundly different from the widowers', whose gender was associated with a far greater sense of entitlement. 'In a society in which asymmetric norms are quietly dominant' the same level of ill-health can be perceived very differently.[34] The survey had in one sense given the women a voice, in inviting them to comment on their own welfare, but the 'institutional arrangements' were such that their ill-health or misery did not 'count' to the women themselves. In this example interpersonal comparison of mental states, such as might seem the ideal means of evaluating welfare, breaks down.

Danish economist Ester Boserup's 1970 book *Women's Role in Economic Development* was the first study to consider how work was divided up among agriculturalists in developing countries, and to consider the role women might play in development. It was Evelyn Waring's *If Women Counted: The New Feminist Economics* (1988), however, which marked the advent of a feminist economics, one which tackled the failure of accounting measures to include unpaid work by women. Sen's capability approach has been used extensively by Waring's followers. Although Sen has not sought to identify himself as a feminist economist explicitly, he clearly acknowledges a moral duty to enfranchise women (in the fullest sense of the term) and has pointed to many ways in which expanding the capabilities of women also serves to expand those of their children and others in the community, regardless of their gender. 'Nothing, arguably, is as important today in the political economy of social development', Sen writes, 'as an adequate recognition of political, economic and social participation and leadership of women.'[35]

From Equality to Equity

In his work on inequality Sen had noted that in discussing it we tend naturally to adopt a comparative approach. We want to know if society A has more or less inequality than society B. Hence we don't need to subject the observations we collect about either society to the cruel and unusual punishments described in the first section of this chapter: making them comply with a series of demands whose excessive rigour causes them to break down and produce Impossibility Theorems and other results that may as well be nonsense for all the good they are as guides to policy. Comparisons are by their very nature incomplete rankings, but they were good enough to serve.

In his *The Idea of Justice* (2009) Sen identifies a 'comparative tradition' in political philosophy beginning with Smith and Condorcet and continuing with Bentham, Marx and Arrow. Sen uses it to shift from discussions of equality to ones of equity, that is, justice. These discussions have seen Sen engage even more deeply with Rawls and other political philosophers, to an extent which may seem more philosophical than economic. *The Idea of Justice* expands on Sen's previous work on inequality, social choice theory and capability, and on that basis alone is worth addressing here.

Equality and equity might be seen as synonymous. Discussion of Gini coefficients, for example, seems to presume that the best society would be one with a coefficient of 0, in which everybody's income was exactly the same. We might presume that Sen is aiming for a society in which everyone's capability sets are the same. Equality of capability is not, however, justice for Sen, and not only because it would be very difficult to pin down what such equality might look like, given the infinite diversity of human situations, handicaps, abilities and so on. Sen starts from Rawls's contention in *A Theory of Justice* that 'justice is fairness', in which fairness comes before any principles of justice.

Rawls attempted to work out what a perfectly just society would look like by making use of an 'original position' located behind his famous 'veil of ignorance'. Rawls imagines the members of a community retreating behind this veil to deliberate on the kind of society they wish to inhabit. Crucially, none of them knows which particular position they will end up taking in the resulting society. This ignorance combined with their own sense of fairness (and a certain amount of self-interest) will, so the theory goes, prevent them from creating a society in which some are treated unjustly, out of a fear that they might find themselves holding the losing ticket in this social lottery. Once they've thrashed out what this just society looks like, they all step back into the world and get on with living in it.

Sen, by contrast, does not posit a hypothetical ideal or original society and then derive a set of principles or ideal 'institutional arrangements' from it. Sen's critique of Rawls extends to a long tradition of political thought based on the idea of social contract, the original contract humans are presumed to have made among themselves before they left a 'state of nature' (presumed to be asocial) and entered society. As Sen notes, this 'contractarian approach has been the dominant influence in contemporary political philosophy'.[36] Yet for Sen all this is an unhelpful and uninformative distraction. One does not need to agree on what a perfectly just system would look like, he notes, to agree that it is a good idea to abolish slavery. Even if we could know what that ideal system looked like, it would not help us decide which of two alternatives (the status quo and a proposed alternative, say) came 'closer' to it.

'Descriptive closeness is not necessarily a guide to valuational proximity.' Someone who likes red wine will choose white wine over a mixture of red and white, even though the mixture is in one sense 'closer' to their ideal.[37] Sen's comparative approach does not work 'backwards' from a hypothetical ideal, nor does it promise to guide us 'forwards' to such a utopia. 'A systematic theory of comparative justice does not need, nor does it necessarily yield, an answer to the question "What is a just society?"'[38] Sen's idea of justice can seem somewhat modest in its aspirations and the degree of authority Sen claims for it.

Just as he did methodologically in his discussion of Arrow and social choice theory, so here Sen turns a perceived incompleteness or inconsistency into 'an embarrassment of riches', into a plurality that

Sen celebrates as faithful to human diversity. Just as Sen fought against evaluations of poverty built on a proposed universal level of subsistence (defined in terms of calories per day, for example), so he finds the disembodied inmates of Rawls's model intellectually impoverishing. Sen prefers to reach judgements of comparative justice from the position of Smith's impartial spectator, who has the advantage of considering those outside the community, avoiding the 'parochialism' of Rawls's model. Smith's impartiality is 'open' in this sense, while Rawls's is 'closed'; Smith's impartial spectator is more suited to 'global justice', which is not the same thing as 'international justice'.[39]

'The world is certainly divisive,' Sen writes, 'but it is diversely divisive.'[40] An individual may fall into several categories at once, according to their longevity, employment status, nationality, gender, race, age and physical abilities and disabilities. Those who appear favoured by one measure may not be favoured when measured by other criteria: a rich disabled person, for example, is subject to restraints a poor yet able-bodied person is not. Per capita GDP is much higher in the United States than in India, yet African Americans (women as well as men) suffer from mortality rates higher than those of women and men in much poorer countries such as India and China.

Favoured by their far larger income, these Americans are nonetheless denied a 'basic capability to live to a mature age'.[41] Inter-*national* comparisons, however, will not capture this. This is one example where the distinction between global and international justice is obvious. As with the FMRs discussed above, here a relatively unused 'space' for welfare comparisons (gender, rather than income) points to broader inequalities in capability sets. To perceive this denial of a basic 'functioning' or 'freedom' and to deem it to be unjust, one does not need first to work out how long the perfect, most satisfying life would last.

Sen's contribution to economic thought is profound and ongoing. His plea for 'informational enrichment' rescued social choice theory from the early grave to which it seemed to have been consigned by Arrow's 'Impossibility Theorem'. His study of the 1943 Bengal Famine revealed the relationship between entitlement systems and scarcity, noting how much more exposed certain groups were to starvation than others. The critique of welfarist evaluations of a society's welfare led to Sen's most important contribution, the capability approach to welfare, which has changed how national governments as well as international organizations like the UN perceive poverty, illiteracy and ill-health.

Neither revealed preference welfarists like Samuelson nor the contractarians lifted the veil of choice to enquire after the values or mental states that lay behind the choices individuals make. Sen did, advancing what Robert Sugden has described as 'a conception of an individual's good which does not *automatically* assert that whatever the individual chooses is good for him'.[42] It follows that there must be a truly good life out there, to provide us with a way of evaluating such choices. Such a claim to objectivity makes many of Sen's fellow economists uncomfortable. The range of capabilities Sen cites as constituting a life an individual has 'reason to value' could be seen as reassuringly open-ended.[43] Yet for Sugden the question remains of what weighting each functioning is to be assigned. 'How can Sen endorse any particular set of weights as being *objectively* correct?'[44]

Though helpful when confronted with the kind of 'basic functionings' evident in 'desperate poverty', Sen's capabilities approach will, Sugden suggests, get bogged down when other, less easily observed functionings eventually come to be considered.[45] As Dan Usher has put it, 'compared with a set of a commodities in a utility function, a set of functionings in a valuation function is unlimited, overlapping, and frequently unmeasurable . . . there is no analog to the role of income in terminating the list of commodities.'[46] This takes us back to where we started, to the question of how much precision and congruence we should demand. One might counter such a criticism by questioning whether Sen in fact wishes his 'set of functionings' to provide a perfect replacement for welfare-as-GNI.

As the Nobel Committee noted, Sen's thought has served to restore 'an ethical dimension to economics and related disciplines'.[47] In addition to producing improved welfare outcomes, Sen's model has placed increasing emphasis on the process and exercise of capabilities, whose association with apparently non-economic 'freedoms' was made explicit in *Development as Freedom*, where development is defined as 'an integrated process of expansion of substantive freedoms that connect with one another'.[48] The freedom to exchange and to participate in the economy is one of these freedoms. Sen has challenged those who see inescapable trade-offs between economic growth on the one hand and civil liberties, population growth and state-funded education and health-care provision on the other. Although Sen's 'comparative' approach to justice is one he himself attributes to Smith, Sen's thought on equity has proceeded beyond Smith, and represents another important contribution. In Smith's case a sceptical approach to economic modelling and the demands made by equity can appear an invitation to 'sitting still and doing nothing' rather than acting.[49] Though Sen's vision of political economy shares much with Smith, Sen is less willing to 'sit still'. Instead his career could be summed up as a series of answers to the same urgent question: 'What do we do *then*?'

THIRTEEN

JOSEPH STIGLITZ

Emmanuelle Bénicourt

Among all Nobel economics laureates, Joseph Stiglitz stands out by his remarkable activism. He tirelessly addresses conferences around the world, giving speeches lambasting governments and international organizations for implementing policies that favour the rich and powerful at the expense of the poor. Shortly after receiving the prize he published *Globalization and Its Discontents*, a work that attracted considerable attention for attacking the International Monetary Fund (IMF) and its president, Michel Camdessus, whom Stiglitz reproached for his allegedly haughty tone and lack of sensitivity to the sufferings of the poor. Stiglitz also criticized his former colleagues from the Clinton administration: Secretary of the U.S. Treasury Robert Rubin, who is – according to Stiglitz – a champion of bank deregulation, and IMF vice-president Stanley Fisher. Rubin had previously worked for Goldman Sachs, and went back to another Wall Street bank upon leaving office. Although Fisher had worked in the public sector up until his appointment to the IMF, upon resigning the vice-presidency he, too, went to work in the private sector for a very high salary ($2 million). These examples of the turnstile between public and private sectors led Stiglitz to ask, 'was Fischer being richly rewarded for having faithfully executed what he was told to do?'.[1]

The question drew an indignant response from Stiglitz's fellow economists, and marked the beginning of his celebrity. Up until then he had only published one book aimed at a public of insiders and academics, *Whither Socialism?*, which was adapted from his Wicksell Lectures at the Stockholm School of Economics in 1990. Since his Nobel Prize, Stiglitz has become prolific, and publishes books for a general audience at the rate of almost one a year, on themes closely linked to contemporary issues, as one can observe from the titles: *New Ideas about Old Age Security* (2001), *Rethinking the East Asia Miracle* (2001), *Making Globalization Work* (2006), *Fair Trade for All: How Trade Can Promote*

Development (2006), *Time for a Visible Hand: Lessons from the 2008 World Financial Crisis* (2010), *The Great Divide: Unequal Societies and What We Can Do about Them* (2015). Each has been accompanied by numerous articles and interviews carried in journals and newspapers across the world.

The tone Stiglitz employs is often far from being cautious or reserved, contrary to that generally employed by scientists. It is true that economists (whose membership of this category is not beyond challenge) are more inclined to intervene in the media and in public debate than Nobel Prize-winners in physics or in medicine. But no one has matched the activity and activism of Stiglitz, except perhaps Paul Krugman. The latter is, however, more cautious in his commitments, and less willing to stray outside academia.

One might think that Stiglitz, an iconoclast in the eyes of the general public, had produced a body of original work whose scientific contribution broke with convention, and standard representations. But that would be wrong. The articles and publications that have established Stiglitz's reputation pertain to pure theory and remain in the framework of mainstream economic theory, that is 'neoclassical' economic theory. Stiglitz was awarded the Nobel Prize (shared with Robert Akerlof and Michael Spence) for having proposed a series of theoretical models that show how the phenomenon of 'information asymmetry' (in which one party possesses information others do not share) can be the source of inefficient allocations. This is something that corporate leaders, insurers, bankers and so on have always known. Stiglitz, Akerlof and Spence have been rewarded for having proved this 'result' along neoclassical lines, in keeping with rational-choice equilibrium.

According to the Economic Sciences Prize Committee of the Royal Academy of Sweden, 'Stiglitz is . . . one of the founders of modern development economics', the model proposed in the article (co-authored with Robert Shapiro) 'Equilibrium Unemployment as a Worker Discipline Device' being 'an important ingredient in modern labor and macroeconomics', while papers co-authored with Andrew Weiss 'have had a substantial impact in the fields of corporate finance, monetary theory and macroeconomics' and Stiglitz's work with Sanford Grossman 'has exerted considerable influence in financial economics'. Stiglitz is also credited with making 'significant contributions to public economics . . . industrial organization and the economics of natural resources'.[2] This made Stiglitz 'probably the most cited researcher within the information economics literature – perhaps also within a wider domain of microeconomics'.[3]

Stiglitz's work in labour economics, in development economics and in finance has thus been praised by the gatekeepers of 'official science'. Indeed, the Nobel Prize Committee has, with the possible exceptions of Gunnar Myrdal and some econometricians, never awarded the prize to an author standing outside the neoclassical framework. Stiglitz's papers have become reference points of the very same institutions he criticized after he had obtained the prize. The perspectives developed in these papers contributed to his appointment to important positions within these institutions (such as chief economist of the World Bank, and chairman of the U.S. President's Council of Economic Advisers).

One cannot reproach Stiglitz with being inconsistent, with changing his mind, or even with shifting away from the mainstream paradigm after obtaining the Nobel Prize. Indeed, he has never questioned capitalism as a system, although he has thoroughly criticized its biases. He has always evinced great confidence in market economies, provided they are 'competitive', that is, free from the pressures and distortions caused by the actions of monopolies or lobby groups of any sort. Whilst pertaining to mainstream economics, which insists on the benefits of markets and competition, Stiglitz's research highlights that which impedes them from functioning fully and achieving their various advantages. Stiglitz thus belongs to a tradition of neoclassical economists, who are far from all being ultra-liberals. He does however depart from most economists in his incredible capacity for work, which has enabled him to deal with almost all areas of the theory, applying the same neoclassical reading grid to them all.

Stiglitz's personal background, the fact that he grew up in a city where social problems (unemployment and racial segregation) were very present, explains both his conformist and his passionate behaviour. Whilst building his scholarly and academic career within the confines of orthodoxy, he has always been sensitive to the inequalities and injustices of this world, and therefore displayed an early and sustained interest in politics.

Early Interest in Politics

Joseph Stiglitz was born in Gary, Indiana, a declining industrial city not far from Chicago with a significant African American population. This has enabled Stiglitz to experience directly problems of unemployment and racial discrimination. As he says in his Nobel biography, in Gary, 'certainly, the poverty, the discrimination, the episodic unemployment could not but strike an inquiring youngster: why did these exist, and what could we do about them.'[4]

Stiglitz was also shaped by his family, one

> in which political issues were often discussed, and debated intensely. My mother's family were New Deal Democrats – they worshipped FDR [President Roosevelt]; and though my uncle was a highly successful lawyer and real estate entrepreneur, he was staunchly pro-labor. My father, on the other hand, a small businessman, he repeatedly spoke of the virtues of self-reliance. He worried about big business, and valued our competition laws. By the mid seventies, he had become a strong advocate of civil rights. He had a deep sense of civic and moral responsibility.[5]

A brilliant student, Stiglitz began his higher education at Amherst, a renowned liberal arts college much esteemed by the liberal elite of the time, where professors were open to the problems of the world. In Stiglitz's own words, 'the intellectually most formative experiences occurred during the three years 1960–1963 I spent at Amherst college.'[6]

Although Stiglitz was interested in literature and social sciences, he majored in physics and 'enjoyed immensely the camaraderie of the physics students as we strove to solve the hard problems that were assigned to us'.[7] This enabled Stiglitz to develop his interest and his capacities in mathematics, which he used later to deal with 'important social problems'.

Stiglitz in the Neoclassical Stream

Stiglitz sometimes seeks to present himself as the first to draw attention to some of the dysfunctions of capitalism in the 1970s. He attended college in the early 1960s, when proponents of mathematical economics had just about eliminated the 'institutionalists' that had reigned on campuses up to the 1950s. Kenneth Arrow and Gerard Debreu's recent demonstration that the model of a pure (or perfect) competitive economy has at least one solution – called 'equilibrium' and characterized by the equality of supply and demand for all goods and services – represented a landmark mathematical achievement for this camp. It was nonetheless something of an exaggeration, for Stiglitz. In his Nobel autobiography he claims that,

> With the competitive equilibrium models which represented the prevailing paradigm when we went to graduate school, it seemed to say that unemployment didn't exist, that issues of efficiency and equity could be neatly separated, so that economists could neatly set aside problems of inequality and poverty as they went about their business of designing more efficient economic systems.[8]

At that time most economists in fact had a Keynesian, pessimistic vision of the spontaneous evolution of capitalism. The self-described Keynesians played an important role in several U.S. administrations, both Republican and Democrat. They were almost hegemonic in universities, particularly at the Massachusetts Institute of Technology (MIT), where Stiglitz finished his studies. Few were those who contested the policies implemented by Roosevelt during the New Deal (such as the 1935 Social Security Act). Such policies were extended in 1965 with the advent of Medicare (social insurance) and Medicaid (medical insurance). In the 1970s President Nixon proposed a system with full national coverage (one far more ambitious than President Obama's Affordable Care Act of 2010), but the Congress approved only a few amendments (increasing benefits to vulnerable categories of the population).

Starting from the early 1950s, it also became common to distinguish 'macroeconomists' and 'microeconomists'. The former claimed to use Keynes's ideas to construct models of the economy as a whole, sufficient to predict the impact of various monetary, budgetary or mixed policies implemented by states. The microeconomists proposed to go back to the foundations of (neoclassical) theory, as they had been conceived by William Stanley Jevons and Léon Walras in the late nineteenth century, and sought to deduce 'laws' from the rational behaviour of individuals maximizing their individual welfare. This camp included several economists with experience of wartime economic planning eager to apply – in peacetime – the mathematical techniques they had developed. For them, the 'pure competitive model' of Arrow and Debreu, whose research had been financed by the U.S. Office of Naval Research, showed the way ahead: establish mathematical theorems (in the case of Arrow and Debreu, the existence of at least one equilibrium) from well-defined hypotheses.

These hypotheses are very constraining in the case of the 'pure competitive model', which assumes a centralized system, with a benevolent figure who proposes prices, confronts the supplies and demands of the agents at these prices and who aims at finding the prices that equalize these supplies and demands. This strange figure is called the 'auctioneer' by Stiglitz, 'market participant' by Arrow and Debreu, 'price caller' by Walras and 'market player' by game theoreticians. By a queer twist of fate, however, this model, in which individuals are not permitted to trade directly, has come to serve as the ideal representation of a competitive economy. For most people, including economists, a competitive economy signifies an economy where trade is decentralized. The mathematical requirements are the source of this contradictory presentation. Indeed, if there is no centralization, the supply and demand functions (foundation stones of the theory) are not defined. Neoclassical economists (including Stiglitz) have a very hard time recognizing that the model is presented in a contradictory manner.

Most of the theoreticians who have promoted and developed the 'pure competitive model', such as Tjalling Koopmans, John Hicks, Kenneth Arrow and Frank Hahn, were Keynesians who saw in this model a first and necessarily approximate representation of reality. This model has nonetheless occupied more and more space in university curricula. It has provided a precise framework for microeconomics (that is, general equilibrium) and has successfully colonized all branches of theoretical economics. Because it requires a certain amount of mathematical knowledge, the focus of students and of teachers has tended to concentrate ever-increasingly on technique, rather than on the significance or relevance of the hypotheses of the theoretical models. Thus, the pure competitive model has progressively – and almost by stealth, with hardly any questioning – been adopted, as a representation of an ideal decentralized market economy.[9]

The first generation of economists to cut their teeth on mathematical economics and the Arrow–Debreu model (that is, Stiglitz's generation) rapidly divided into two distinct camps. The distinction was at once both ideological and political.

On the one hand, there were those who considered that the model of pure competition (Arrow–Debreu style) gave a good approximation of reality, or at very least that it was the only model we had to analyse reality.[10] The theoreticians of this camp have concentrated their efforts on macroeconomics, which they wished to give microeconomic foundations. They inspired an ultraliberal branch of economics, which they have called 'new classical economics'. This assumed that the market economy is constantly at perfect competitive equilibrium, without (voluntary) unemployment, with an allocation of resources that would be permanently efficient, if only the state did not intervene. This camp, represented by Robert Lucas and Robert Prescott (winners of the Nobel in 1995 and 2004 respectively), violently attacked Keynesians, and ousted them from many U.S. universities in the 1980s and 1990s.

On the other hand, there were other economists (like Stiglitz) who believed that the Arrow–Debreu model gave only a very approximate vision of markets, owing to the 'imperfections' that occur in reality. These imperfections can take many forms. It is common to consider that they result from frictions or rigidities resulting from factors such as monopolies, unions, or more generally because of the defence of acquired privileges or rents. The economists in this trend are often called 'Keynesians', even if their vision of the world is very far from Keynes's own, where dysfunctions are in the nature of markets themselves. This trend was developed by economists such as Paul Samuelson and James Tobin for the old generation, Paul Krugman and Lawrence Summers for the new. They have devoted their efforts to macroeconomics, and have actively participated in the elaboration of various economic policies.

Yet Stiglitz does not belong to this camp either. He has stayed within the framework that characterizes microeconomics in the Arrow–Debreu tradition, and has searched for the 'imperfections' that impede an efficient allocation of resources. For Stiglitz, these imperfections are not linked to the functioning of the markets, but result from individuals' opportunistic behaviours, in keeping with the methodological individualism claimed by neoclassical economists.

Information Asymmetry and Opportunistic Behaviour

For the Economic Sciences Prize Committee, the 'Akerlof, Spence and Stiglitz' analyses of markets and information asymmetries were considered to be fundamental to modern microeconomic theory. The trio's research has furthered our understanding of phenomena in real markets which could not be fully captured by traditional neoclassical theory.'[11]

These phenomena result from the fact that 'one side of the market has better information than the other.' For example,

> The borrower knows more than the lender about his credit-worthiness; the seller knows more than the buyer about the quality of his car; the CEO and board of a firm know more than the shareholders about the profitability of the firm; insurance clients know more than the insurance company about their accident risk; and tenants know more than the landowner about harvesting conditions and their own work effort.[12]

If one adds, 'the employee knows more than the employer about the quality, or intensity, of his work,' one can say that information asymmetry pertains to almost all aspects of economic life, to the extent that the layman might well wonder what traditional neoclassical theory (which overlooks such asymmetry) is really dealing with. In fact, contrary to what the Committee implied, this theory excludes bilateral relationships between agents, who are assumed to trade only through a 'market' (itself, as we have seen, never properly defined, at least, not without recourse to a mythical figure like the 'auctioneer' or the 'market participant').

It is clear that company managers, landowners, insurers, bankers and buyers of all types of goods have been aware of those things we now call 'asymmetries of information' for a long time, if not forever. They exist, to a greater or lesser degree, every time there is a bilateral, trading relationship. The guarantees imposed by law or specified in private contracts, the multitude of contracts, of guarantees, of deductibles proposed by insurers, or the numerous conditions imposed by bank loans all attest that the phenomenon of information asymmetry is (in practice, at least) well known. One can only wonder why economic theoreticians waited until the 1970s to propose models that take them into consideration, and waited even longer to give them official recognition, in the form of the 2001 Nobel award.

The answer to this question is both methodological and ideological. Methodological because for a model to be accepted officially, it has to satisfy the two conditions imposed by neoclassical theory: first, the individual behaviours have to be represented as the maximization of an objective function (rational choice); second, the model has to have at least one equilibrium (from which no one is supposed to depart) which constitutes a 'solution' of the model.[13] Shifting to ideology, the models have to uphold the commonplace according to which the allocation of resources is efficient if there is 'pure competition', without any imperfections. The Arrow–Debreu model remains the benchmark.

The models of equilibrium with information asymmetry proposed by Akerlof, Spence and Stiglitz satisfy these conditions. This may explain their official recognition in 2001.

Rationality and Equilibrium

The models that earned Stiglitz the Nobel all assume rational behaviour and also include at least one equilibrium, whatever the place, time and circumstances under consideration. In the case of sharecropping in Kenya, which Stiglitz points to as an inspiration, 'The sharecropping contract could be thought of as a combination of a rental contract plus an insurance contract, in which the landlord "rebates" part of the rent if crops turn out badly . . . I analyzed the *equilibrium sharecropping contract*.'[14]

Still in the Kenyan example, after having criticized the model developed by Gary Fields – a scholar working at the Institute of Development Studies in Kenya – for failing to 'provide a *full equilibrium analysis*', Stiglitz proposes his own model in which 'high urban wages attracted workers, and they were willing to risk unemployment for the chance of those higher wages. Here was a simple, *general equilibrium model of unemployment*, but again there was one missing piece: how could you explain the high wages, which were well in excess of the minimum wage. One needed an *equilibrium* theory of wage determination.'[15]

Stiglitz developed this missing theory in a later model, which concerns the relationship between an employer and an employee, under all conditions. It is the 'efficiency wage theory'. The difference in utility between having a job and being unemployed depends on the wage for employed people and on the unemployment rate. This sets the time lapse during which a fired worker can remain unemployed. 'Efficiency' wages are set just high enough that all workers prefer not to shirk. A second key finding of the model is that unemployment always exists in *equilibrium*:

> It might pay firms to pay a higher wage than the minimum necessary to hire labor; such wages I referred to as *efficiency wages*. With efficiency wages, there could exist an equilibrium level of unemployment . . . If all workers are identical, and all firms paid workers the same wage, then if it paid one firm to pay a high wage, it would pay all of them. But if a worker was then fired for shirking, and there was full employment, he could immediately get another job, at the same wage. The high wage would provide

> no incentive. But if there was unemployment, then there was a price for shirking. We showed that *in equilibrium* there *had* to be unemployment: unemployment was the discipline device that forced workers to work.[16]

The equilibrium is also at the centre of the insurer–insured relationship, or of the lender–borrower relationship: 'how did the forces for secrecy and for information disclosure get balanced? What was the *equilibrium* that emerged?' or again: 'Perhaps the hardest problem was *modeling equilibrium*. It was important to think about both sides of the market – employers and employees, insurance company and the insured, lender and borrower.'[17] One can add 'landowner and tenant, seller and buyer'. To prove the existence of an equilibrium and to characterize it is part of the game.

A Reading Grid Valid in All Times and Spaces

In his autobiography, Stiglitz explains that in his youth he noticed that

> The market economy seemed to be plagued by repeated periods of unemployment, and to leave large fractions of the population in poverty. Yugoslavia's system of self-managed firms intrigued me ... economics seemed to provide the tools with which one could analyze these alternative economic systems. A central question was how, and how well, alternative systems addressed the problems of gathering, analyzing, and disseminating information, and making decisions based on imperfect information.'[18]

In the same way, the 'economic tools' can be used to analyse very diverse situations. For example, 'the sharecropping contract [can] be thought of as a combination of a rental contract plus an insurance contract, in which the landlord 'rebates' part of the rent if crops turn out badly' and therefore 'the incentive problems' for the landowner are 'isomorphic to those facing modern corporations, e.g. in providing incentives to their managers'.[19] The problem of the share of the harvest between the land owner and tenant in Kenya (or anywhere and at any time) is similar (isomorphic) to the problem faced by the manager of a 'modern corporation'.

The analysis is universal and is applied by combining the diverse types of markets and contracts, pertaining to all particular cases. The rural organization in developing countries can thus be explained by the interlinks between the credit, labour and land markets. In the simple sharecropping contracts of Stiglitz,[20] the contracts involved shares, fixed payments and plot sizes, and, more generally, optimal payment structures related payments to observables, inputs, processes, outputs. Because what went on in one market affected others, the credit, labour and land markets were interlinked; one could not decentralize in the way hypothesized by the standard perfect information model. The theory thus served as the basis of the *rural organization* in developing countries.[21]

'Markets' are therefore an essential element of Stiglitz's models. Indeed, the word 'market' has several meanings for Stiglitz. For example, when he writes: 'It was important to think about *both sides of the market* – employers and employees, insurance company and the insured, lender and borrower.' The word 'market' is used to designate a bilateral relationship, direct, between two people. Hence one can say that the parties 'conclude a market'.

This relationship generally has an undetermined outcome, since there are infinite ways to share the gain that this exchange generates. In order to suppress indeterminacy, models with asymmetry of information assume the existence of 'markets' which represent the 'pressure of competition' that is held by the other members of society. This assumption enables the suppression of the indeterminacy of the bilateral relationship and the demonstration of the existence of equilibrium. As is almost always the case with formalized models, the 'markets' which are considered assume a very centralized form of organization, where each individual considers that what the others do is given, apart from the person with whom he has a direct, bilateral, relationship (the employee, the insured). There is not a very great difference, from this point of view, between these models (for example, a model considering the relationship between employer and employee with information asymmetry) and the model of perfect competition, whose equilibria can always serve as a benchmark.

Unemployment and 'Shirking'

In a 1984 article entitled 'Equilibrium Unemployment as a Worker Discipline Device', Stiglitz and Carl Shapiro proposed a model where 'the optimal behavior of both employers and employees results in equilibrium unemployment'.[22] A more detailed study of this model, without going into the mathematical details (which are of no interest here), enables us to understand the role it has played later on.

At the beginning of their paper, Shapiro and Stiglitz explain 'the intuition behind [their] result'. That is: 'Under the conventional competitive paradigm, in which all workers receive the market wage and there is no unemployment, the worst that can happen to a worker that shirks on the job is that he is fired. Since he can immediately be rehired, however, he pays no penalty for his misdemeanor. With imperfect monitoring and full employment, workers will choose to shirk.'[23]

The model's premise is thus that 'If the worker performs at the customary level of effort for his job, that is, if he does not shirk, he receives a wage of *w* and will retain his job until exogenous factors cause a separation to occur.'[24] The markets do their job, and all those that aim at working normally at the 'competition' wage, *w*, can do so, and there is full employment and the allocation of resources is efficient.

Unfortunately, there are workers that 'shirk'. To dissuade them, they have to pay a penalty: when worker shirking cannot be detected efficiently, high effort can be induced if workers know that if they are caught shirking, they will pay a penalty that is sufficiently high to make shirking not worthwhile. The penalty in the Shapiro–Stiglitz model is dismissal: a fired worker will spend some time in the unemployment pool before finding another job. If the difference between the utility of having a job and being unemployed is sufficiently high, workers will refrain from shirking.

One could stop here. Everyone understands that the greater the incoveniences of being dismissed, the less the workers are encouraged to 'shirk'. But the merit, at least for neoclassical economists, of Shapiro and Stiglitz's model is to have built a story around this idea. As they say: 'a key contribution of this paper is that punishment associated with being fired is endogenous, as it depends on the equilibrium rate of unemployment'.[25]

The rule of the game is to prove that the model has an equilibrium associated with rational behaviour. But to do so, one has to set up a certain number of elements that enable workers and firms to determine the behaviour that will bring them the maximal satisfaction, or the maximal profit (that is, the rational choice). Shapiro and Stiglitz thus assume that 'the probability *q* for a worker to be caught', 'the probability *a* of acquiring a job while in the unemployment pool' and 'unemployment benefits' are defined and known by all.[26] To use technical terminology, they are exogenous parameters.

On the basis of these elements, each worker calculates his utility expectation: the weighted (by their probabilities) sum of the utilities provided by different possible situations. The worker is more inclined to shirk if, for example, the gap between the unemployment benefit and his salary is narrow. On the contrary, if this gap is big, he will be discouraged from shirking. The firm will also calculate the worker's expected gains, which depends on the expected utility of the unemployed: 'the key market variable which determines individual firm behavior is the expected utility of an unemployed worker.'[27]

Under these conditions 'equilibrium occurs when each firm, taking as given the wages and employment levels at other firms, finds it optimal to offer the going wage rather than a different wage.'[28] If information is not 'perfect' in the employer–employee relationship, it is between firms, since each firm knows the price set by others, and which they consider as given.[29] We are not far from the 'conventional competitive paradigm', with given prices and the 'auctioneer', but we are far away from Kenya, or anywhere else on planet Earth.

How These Models are Used

Theoretical models in economics (especially in microeconomics) play the role of fables, which are supposed to give a lesson and which help to justify this or that economic policy.[30] In the case of Shapiro and Stiglitz's unemployment article, several consequences and lessons are given. The first one is that 'the unemployment benefits (and other welfare benefits) increase the unemployment rate', which is not very original. Here the only thing that changes is the type of incentive. The traditional incentive is replaced by the rise of the incentive to shirk.[31] In both cases, unemployment results from the behaviour of workers.

Depending on the values given to the parameters of the model, one can reach very different conclusions on the type of policy to adopt. If, for example, workers are risk averse, this 'may provide a justification for mandatory minimum benefit levels'.[32] In the case where firms 'can select the monitoring intensity' ('endogenous monitoring'), the state should tax the firms, because the gains obtained by society in saving resources on monitoring (supervision) 'more than offset the loss of reduced unemployment'.[33] In the same way, if firms can choose the turnover rate ('endogenous turnover'), then the state should also tax firms, 'since the turnover rate affects the rate of hiring out of the unemployment pool and hence it affects other firms' no-shirking constraints'.[34]

As Shapiro and Stiglitz observe, depending on the 'circumstances', 'there is scope for government interventions, both with respect to unemployment benefits and taxes or subsidies on monitoring and labor turnover, which can lead (if appropriately designed) to Pareto improvements.'[35] It is up to the government to appreciate these circumstances and to choose the levers that it will use to reach a Pareto improvement: it is not equivalent, for example, to lower the unemployment benefits or to raise the taxes on monitoring or on turnover. Nothing obliges the state to limit itself to the case of a 'Pareto improvement'. Thus, Shapiro and Stiglitz observe that, in their model, taxing profits and using the sums obtained to raise salaries triggers a decrease of (equilibrium) unemployment and therefore an increase in global revenue. Collective welfare increases but it is at the expense of private owners (there is therefore no 'Pareto improvement'). This policy has a redistributive effect, one the state has to endorse (or not).

One can tell similar stories about the relationship between a landowner and a tenant, whether in Kenya or elsewhere, or between an insurer and the insured, or between a lender and a borrower. Each time there is a cheating problem in the bilateral relationship, which needs to be limited by a penalty. The monitoring of this penalty comes at a cost. Each time, asymmetry of information leads to an inefficient allocation of resources, which can be improved by legislation or by the direct intervention of the state through a system of taxes or subsidies. Taking the heterogeneity of agents into account (insurance, for example, may be at 'high' or 'low' risk) enables us to distinguish phenomena like adverse selection, well known from insurers, which can make the allocation of resources particularly inefficient and which calls for multiple forms of 'off-market' interventions.

Stiglitz is particularly well known for his analyses and positions on finance. The purpose of finance is risk sharing, and these risks can be assessed differently by different parties. Information therefore plays a crucial role; the person who is informed has a decisive advantage over one who is not.[36] What is at stake here is not only the efficient allocation of resources, but the survival of entire sections of the system, thanks to the risk of serial bankruptcies, for example. This explains why all financial institutions are subject to the same legislation, which can be more or less severe depending on the times. A movement to lighten regulation began under President Reagan in the 1980s and gained momentum in the 1990s, under Bush and Clinton. The ground was prepared in academe by means of a so-called theory according to which financial markets are 'efficient'. The promoter of this idea was Eugene Fama, who was awarded the Nobel in 2012.[37] This theory is summed up by the sentence, now notorious among economists, that 'A market in which prices at any time "fully reflect" available information is called "efficient".'[38]

In 1980 Grossman and Stiglitz questioned this in an article entitled 'On the Impossibility of Informationally Efficient Markets'. The authors began by making a trivial observation: for prices to reflect information (a firm's healthy or unhealthy situation, say) there has to be at least one person who looks for this information. But because this is costly, it is therefore rational for everyone to wait for the others to do this search, and to reveal the information by their own behaviour (by buying or selling of that firm's shares, for example). If everyone makes the same calculus, no one will look for the information, prices will not reflect information and the allocation of resources will be inefficient.

Economists refer to this as the 'Grossman–Stiglitz paradox'. They therefore emphasize and honour the two economists who played the game and proposed a model whose paradox results from of one of its own theorems. This model gives a precise form, in mathematical language, to the idea that prices 'convey information from the informed to uninformed'. It assumes in particular that 'the informed bid up or down the price of a security in function of the information that they observe' and that 'the price system makes publicly available the information obtained by informed individuals.' 'In general', however, 'it does this imperfectly,' which enables the equilibrium to exist. This is, according to Grossman and Stiglitz, rather 'lucky', because if information were to be perfectly transmitted by prices, equilibrium would not exist.[39]

This model contributes to the debate among neoclassical economists, between the supporters of laissez-faire and the more interventionist 'Keynesians'. The force of the demonstration resides in the fact that Stigtlitz and Grossman take position on the grounds of their enemy, that is, of Robert Lucas, the leader of the 'anti-Keynesians' of the 1980s, yet arrive at the opposite conclusion, merely by adding the hardly substantial hypothesis that the search for information is costly.[40] Despite the fact that 'the model is the simplest one in which prices perform a well-articulated role in conveying information from the informed to the uniformed,' it is difficult to read since it contains heavy mathematics. Its main result is a theorem, whose presentation is quite murky, which establishes that there exist equilibrium prices for securities on the conditions that they 'do not contain information on θ', where θ is a parameter whose value is known only by the 'informed'.[41] We therefore have a very complex formulation of a very simple idea.

Despite this criticism, which emphasizes the incoherence of the efficient market hypothesis, it continues to be presented in textbooks and to be discussed in numerous academic publications, as well as being the object of many empirical 'tests' – even though all serious economists agree that it is devoid of any meaning.[42]

The Stiglitz Paradox

Although Stiglitz gave his Nobel lecture the title 'Information and the Change in the Paradigm in Economics', it is hard to perceive a change of paradigm in his academic publications. Quite the reverse: they all pertain to the dominant paradigm, the neoclassical one, and respect the 'rational behaviour equilibrium' that lies at its centre. Despite his statements, Stiglitz does not seem to be able to depart completely from the benchmark of 'pure competition equilibrium'. He does not seem to fear personal contradiction. In *Whither Socialism?* Stiglitz writes that the Arrow–Debreu model assumes not only that there is 'an auctioneer calling out prices until the market clearing level is attained' but also that 'there is a *complete* set of markets . . . on which not only today's goods and services are traded but on which future goods and services are traded.'[43] Put another way, the auctioneer calls out prices and centralizes agents' supplies and demands, for the entire lifetime of the economy.[44] This does not, however, prevent Stiglitz from writing, a few pages later: 'These results have profound implications, both for economic theory and for the feasibility of the kind of *decentralization* envisaged in the standard neoclassical (Arrow–Debreu) model.'[45] In his textbook *Principles of Economics*, Stiglitz does not say a word about the auctioneer or the assumption of the complete set of markets. He goes so far as to say that the 'competition model gives satisfying results – the forecasts obtained, without being perfect, correspond well to what we effectively observe'.[46] The main theoretical part of this book deals with the 'competition model' and its consequences. All the same, 'On the Central Importance of Competition' is the first of the 'tentative recommendations' that Stiglitz gives in the twelfth chapter of his book *Whither Socialism?*. His words are always inflected by the Arrow–Debreu model and its 'efficient' equilibria. The theme of 'competition' against 'monopolies' and their 'rents' is recurrent in Stiglitz's numerous public communications. His aim is not, however, to challenge the 'competitive model' and the idea of 'market efficiency' that it is associated with, but to show their 'limits'. As he says in a recent (2016) interview: 'Those who have pointed out the markets' limitations have often been attacked as anti-market, against capitalism or favoring large government. That's a mischaracterization of this point of view . . . The goal is to make these markets work better, to support the market system rather than undermine it.'[47] From this point of view, Stiglitz shows no originality: the vast majority of economists, including neoclassical economists, believe that markets have 'limitations' and that the state has to intervene to try to suppress them or to lessen their negative effects. It is true that Stiglitz has systematically studied these limitations in many different types of situations, and this explains why he has become one of the most cited authors of mainstream literature. But at the same time, Stiglitz is a sort of rebel, who denounces repeatedly the injustices and inequalities of societies. This is what has made him popular, and is probably why he figures in a book on Great Economic Thinkers – but this is very far from his academic oeuvre.

Stiglitz vehemently criticizes banks and financial institutions, big pharmaceutical companies, the lobbies that act at all levels – starting with politicians. For him, the fault does not lie so much with markets, but rather with what he calls 'ersatz capitalism'. This can be observed in his 'reply' to Thomas Piketty, another critic of inequalities, albeit one who is far less optimistic about the future evolution of capitalism:

> What we have been observing – wage stagnation and rising inequality, even as wealth increases – does not reflect the workings of a normal market economy, but of what I call 'ersatz capitalism'. The problem may not be with how markets *should* work, but with our political system, which has failed to ensure that markets are competitive, and has designed rules that sustain *distorted markets* in which corporations and the rich can (and unfortunately do) exploit everyone else . . . Piketty's forecast of still higher levels of inequality does not reflect the inexorable laws of economics.[48]

Stiglitz strongly believes that if markets are regulated, if the rules of the game are established through political processes, and if the state intervenes to control imperfections, capitalism should lead to other collective outcomes than the ones recently observed. Unlike many others of his neoclassical peers, Stiglitz has taken a position in favour of precise political measures so as to lessen or contain inequalities, whether on the globalized level or in the U.S. He has recently argued, for example, that

> simple changes – including higher capital-gains and inheritance taxes, greater spending to broaden access to education, rigorous enforcement of anti-trust laws, corporate-governance reforms that circumscribe executive pay, and financial regulations that rein in banks' ability to exploit the rest of society – would reduce inequality and increase equality of opportunity markedly. If we get the rules of the game right, we might even be able to restore the rapid and *shared* economic growth that characterized the middle-class societies of the mid-twentieth century.[49]

Although Stiglitz has actively participated in public debate, and enlightened a number of international and domestic economic issues, his theoretical papers have shed light on the 'imperfections' of a model that doesn't represent any existing economy, nor constitutes an ideal towards which decentralized market economies can look.

REFERENCES

Introduction

1 John Maynard Keynes, *The General Theory of Employment, Interest and Money* (London, 1936), Chapter 24.
2 T. S. Kuhn, *The Structure of Scientific Resolutions*, 2nd edn (Chicago, IL, 1970).
3 Charles Whitworth, ed., *The Political and Commercial Works of that celebrated writer Charles Davenant* (5 vols, London, 1771), vol. I, p. 98.

ONE Adam Smith

1 Adam Smith, *Lectures on Jurisprudence*, ed. R. L. Meek, D. D. Raphael and P. G. Stein [1762–3] (Oxford, 1978), p. 105; Adam Smith, *Correspondence of Adam Smith*, ed. E. C. Mossner and I. S. Ross, *Glasgow Edition of the Works and Correspondence of Adam Smith* (Oxford, 1987), p. 245.
2 Adam Smith, *An Inquiry into the Nature and Causes of the Wealth of Nations* [1776], ed. William B. Todd (Oxford, 1975), p. 648.
3 Ibid., p. 493.
4 Smith, *Correspondence*, p. 192.
5 Mark Blaug, *Economic Theory in Retrospect*, 4th edn (Cambridge, 1982), p. 35.
6 David Gauthier, *Morals by Agreement* (Oxford, 1986), p. 13 (quote); George Stigler, 'Economics or Ethics?', in *Tanner Lectures on Human Values*, ed. S. McMurrin (Salt Lake City, UT, 1981), vol. II, p. 188.
7 Jerry Evensky, '"Chicago Smith" versus "Kirkcaldy Smith"', *History of Political Economy*, XXXVII/2 (2005), pp. 197–203.
8 Jacob Viner, 'Adam Smith and Laissez-Faire', in *Adam Smith, 1776–1926*, ed. J. M. Clark et al. (New York, 1928), pp. 116–20.
9 George Stigler, 'Smith's Travels on the Ship of State', *History of Political Economy*, III (1971), p. 265.
10 Smith, *The Wealth of Nations*, p. 28.
11 Smith, *Correspondence*, p. 68.
12 Adam Smith, *The Theory of Moral Sentiments* [1759], ed. A. L. Macfie and D. D. Raphael (Indianapolis, IN, 1984), p. 22.
13 Ibid., p. 117.
14 Francis Hutcheson, *An Essay on the Nature and Conduct of the Passions and Affections, with Illustrations on the Moral Sense* [1728], ed. Aaron Garrett (Indianapolis, IN, 2002), p. 17.
15 Smith, *Theory of Moral Sentiments*, p. 305.
16 Ibid., pp. 126–7.

17 Ibid., p. 309.
18 Ibid., p. 129.
19 Ibid., p. 84.
20 Ibid., p. 92.
21 Ibid., p. 110.
22 Ibid., p. 234.
23 See Steven L. Kaplan, *Bread, Politics and Political Economy in the Reign of Louis XV* (The Hague, 1976).
24 Smith, *The Wealth of Nations*, pp. 14–15.
25 Ibid., p. 25.
26 Ibid., pp. 26–7.
27 Ibid., p. 37.
28 Ibid., p. 44.
29 Ibid., p. 48.
30 Ibid., p. 82.
31 Ibid., p. 73.
32 Ibid., p. 98.
33 Ibid., pp. 111–13.
34 Blaug, *Economic Theory*, pp. 39–49.
35 James Tobin, 'The Invisible Hand in Modern Macroeconomics', in *Adam Smith's Legacy: His Place in the Development of Modern Economics*, ed. Michael Fry (London, 1992), pp. 122–4.
36 Lawrence E. Klein, 'Smith's Use of Data', in *Adam Smith's Legacy*, ed. Fry, pp. 15–28.
37 Smith, *The Wealth of Nations*, p. 321.
38 Ibid., pp. 324, 308–9.
39 Ibid., p. 324.
40 Ibid., p. 380.
41 Ibid., p. 415.
42 Ibid., pp. 418–19.
43 Ibid., pp. 421, 422.
44 Ibid., p. 456.
45 Emma Rothschild, *Economic Sentiments: Adam Smith, Condorcet, and the Enlightenment* (Cambridge, MA, 2001), pp. 135 (ironic), 137 (trinket).
46 Smith, *Theory of Moral Sentiments*, p. 87.
47 Ibid., pp. 183–4.
48 Karl Marx, *Economic and Philosophic Manuscripts of 1844*, trans. Martin Mulligan (Moscow, 1959), p. 63.
49 Smith, *The Wealth of Nations*, pp. 781–2.
50 Ibid., p. 785.
51 Patricia Werhane, *Adam Smith and His Legacy for Modern Capitalism* (Oxford, 1991), pp. 134–6.
52 Smith, *Theory of Moral Sentiments*, p. 213.
53 Ibid., p. 216.
54 Jean-Jacques Rousseau, *The Social Contract and Discourses* [1762], trans. G.D.H. Cole (London, 1973), p. 116.
55 Smith, *Theory of Moral Sentiments*, p. 216.
56 Ibid., pp. 86–7.

TWO David Ricardo

1 Richard F. Teichgraeber III, '"Less abused than I had reason to expect": The Reception of *The Wealth of Nations* in Britain', *Historical Journal*, XXX/2 (1987), p. 351.
2 David Ricardo, *On the Principles of Political Economy and Taxation* [1817] (London, 1911).
3 D. P. O'Brien, *The Classical Economists* (Oxford, 1978), p. xii.
4 Accominotti and Flandreau counsel that Ricardo would have opposed bilateral treaties. Olivier Accominotti and Marc Flandreau, 'Bilateral Treaties and the Most-Favored-Nation Clause: The Myth of Trade Liberalization in the Nineteenth Century', *World Politics*, LX/2 (2008), pp. 147–88.
5 Adam Smith, *The Wealth of Nations, Books I–III* [1776] (London, 1986), pp. 109–17.
6 'It is not from the benevolence of the butcher, the brewer, or the baker that we expect our dinner, but from their regard to their own interest,' ibid., p. 119.
7 Ricardo, *Principles*, p. 125.
8 Eric Roll, *A History of Economic Thought*, 5th edn (London and Boston, 1992), p. 131.
9 Ricardo, *Principles*, pp. 126–33.
10 Perhaps it is not a coincidence that Ricardo chose Portugal and England given his family history.
11 The famous economist Paul Samuelson was once asked to name one proposition in the social sciences that was both true and non-trivial. He named Ricardo's theory of comparative advantage. Costinot and Donaldson note that the theory may be mathematically true, but that it may not be empirically valid. See Arnaud Costinot and Dave Donaldson, 'Ricardo's Theory of Comparative Advantage: Old Idea, New Evidence', *American Economic Review*, CII/3 (2012), pp. 453–8.
12 John Maynard Keynes is the subject of a later chapter. His concept of a demand-deficient economy would fit this situation.
13 David Ricardo, *Essay on the Funding System* (London, 1820).
14 More recently, Robert J. Barro attempted to build a more formal model using the assumption of rational expectations. His work reinvigorated the debate surrounding Ricardian equivalence. See Robert J. Barro, 'Are Government Bonds Net Wealth?', *Journal of Political Economy*, LXXXII/6, pp. 1095–117.
15 Hansard, 'Agricultural Distress, House of Commons Debate 30 May 1820, vol. 1 cc. 635–93', www.hansard.millbanksystems.com, accessed 15 August 2016.
16 Hansard, 'Agricultural Distress', p. 675.
17 Ibid.
18 David Ricardo, *The Works and Correspondence of David Ricardo*, vol. I: *On the Principles of Political Economy and Taxation*, ed. Piero Sraffa with the collaboration of M. H. Dobb (Cambridge, 1951), p. 67.
19 Jacob H. Hollander, *Centenary Estimate* (New York, 1968), p. 13.
20 For instance, *The Wealth of Nations* was a course text for a political economy course at the College of William and Mary from 1784 onwards.

On average only 23 students per year attended the college in the last decades of the eighteenth century. Teichgraeber, 'Reception', p. 344.

21 Teichgraeber, 'Reception', pp. 350–51.
22 Hollander, *Centenary Estimate*, p. 20.
23 Terry Peach, *Interpreting Ricardo* (Cambridge, 1993).
24 Ibid.
25 Malthus, although an Anglican, was sent to undertake some of his education within a 'Dissenting Academy'. Patricia James, *Population Malthus: His Life and Times* (Oxford, 2006), p. 19. The Dissenters or non-Conformists were Protestants who would not conform to the teaching of the established Church of England. Quakers were non-Conformists so both Malthus and Ricardo had links to non-Conformism. I am indebted to Emma Clery for her knowledge of Malthus's educational background.
26 J. R. McCulloch, *The Works of David Ricardo with a Notice of his Life and Writings of the Author* (London, 1871), p. xvii.
27 David Ricardo, *The Works and Correspondence of David Ricardo*, vol. VI: *Letters, 1810–1815*, ed. Piero Sraffa with the collaboration of M. H. Dobb (Cambridge, 1951), p. 340.
28 At this time, many normative arguments proceeded from ideas about the correct social order as ordained by the Almighty. Notably, theological arguments and biblical quotations could be used to condemn the financial sector, but also to support the institution of slavery. For arguments about the financial sector see Roll, *History of Economic Thought*, pp. 31–41. For an example of Christian support for slavery, see Travis Glasson, '"Baptism does not bestow Freedom": Missionary Anglicanism, Slavery, and the Yorke-Talbot Opinion, 1701–30', *William and Mary Quarterly*, LXVII/2 (2010), pp. 304–7. It cites George Berkeley, philosopher and bishop, and his views on the requirement of slaves to remain obedient to the existing order. Berkeley apparently believed that 'the laws of God and nature must be obeyed.'
29 O'Brien, *Classical Economists*, p. 69.
30 Ibid., pp. 37–8. Notably, Peach has argued against the 'Corn Model' approach to Ricardo's work. See Peach, *Interpreting Ricardo*, pp. 1–6. Sraffa had argued that Ricardo had 'formulated a literal corn model, with corn comprising the inputs and outputs in the agricultural sector, implying the determination of the rate of profit as a ratio of corn quantities'. Andrew Glyn, 'The Corn Model, Gluts and Surplus Value', *University of Oxford Department of Economic Discussion Paper*, CXCIV (Oxford, 2004), pp. 1–3.
31 O'Brien, *Classical Economists*, p. 41.
32 Ricardo, *Letters*, pp. 212–36.
33 Ibid., p. xiii.
34 Ricardo, *Principles*, p. x.
35 Ricardo, *Letters*, p. xvii.
36 Ibid., pp. xxi–xxii.
37 McCulloch, *Works of David Ricardo.*
38 Ibid., p. v.
39 Roll, *History of Economic Thought*, p. 155.
40 Quoted ibid.

41 Quoted ibid.
42 Ricardo, *Letters*, pp. xiii–xli.
43 Terry Peach, 'Ricardo, David (1772–1823)', www.oxforddnb.com, 16 August 2016.
44 Hollander, *Centenary Estimate*, p. 28.
45 Ibid., p. 29.
46 Ibid., p. 32. Garraway's was situated in Exchange Alley (now known as Change Alley) where much share-trading took place. A carved stone sign marks its position today. The sign also incorporates Thomas Gresham's symbol of a grasshopper. Gresham founded the Royal Exchange where Abraham was a broker.
47 Peach, *Interpreting Ricardo.*
48 Hollander, *Centenary Estimate*, p. 34.
49 Abraham Gilam, 'A Reconsideration of the Politics of Assimilation', *Journal of Modern History*, L/1 (1978), p. 103.
50 Ibid., p. 104.
51 Quakers were often conflated with other groups, including Cromwell's Puritans, who were seen to be disloyal to the monarch and the state. The 'Friends' themselves had sometimes disrupted Anglican church services or been openly critical of the elite. Richard L. Greaves, 'Seditious Sectaries or "Sober and Useful Inhabitants"? Changing Conceptions of the Quakers in Early Modern Britain', *Albion*, XXXIII/1 (2001), pp. 24–50.
52 Gilam, 'Reconsideration of the Politics of Assimilation', p. 105.
53 'The struggle for civil rights for English Jews took place during the years 1830–60 and generated a substantial public debate'. Ibid., p. 104.
54 Heinz D. Kurz and Neri Salvadori, *The Elgar Companion to David Ricardo* (London, 2015), p. 222.
55 Ibid.
56 Hansard, 'Bank of England – Resumption of Cash Payments, House of Commons Debate 25 May 1819, vol. 40 cc. 750–800', www.hansard.millbanksystems.com, accessed 16 August 2016.
57 Brian Cathcart, *The News from Waterloo: The Race to Tell Britain of Wellington's Victory* (London, 2015).
58 Brian Cathcart, 'Nathan Rothschild and the Battle of Waterloo,' *Rothschild Archive Review of the Year* (2013), pp. 11–18.
59 'Schumpeter', 'Conflicts of Interest', www.economist.com, 27 January 2011.
60 Waterloo teeth were dentures made from the teeth of men who had fallen at Waterloo. Their teeth were hacked out by battlefield scavengers and sold to dentists. Gareth Glover, *Waterloo: Myth and Reality* (Barnsley, 2014), p. 202.
61 In other words, he was helping the government to finance the war.
62 Cathcart, *News from Waterloo.* Eagles were military standards.
63 Gatcombe Park is now owned by the Queen's only daughter, Princess Anne. The spelling seems to have originally been Gatcomb.
64 Ricardo's will states that he was resident in Grosvenor Square and Gatcomb (or Gatcombe) Park. National Archives, PROB 11/1676/151. 1823.
65 Joseph A. Schumpeter, *History of Economic Analysis* (New York, 1954), p. 472. The health resort in question was Bath.

66 Hollander, *Centenary Estimate*, p. 12.
67 Ricardo, *Principles*, p. 7.
68 Ibid., pp. 7–13.
69 Say's law is known to undergraduate economists by the simplification that 'supply creates its own demand'. Producers of a good will sell it and then use their income to buy other goods elsewhere. Say supported a laissez-faire approach to the market as the 'law' states that general oversupply or gluts cannot occur. The details are a little more complicated in Say's own writings, but this is the basic idea.
70 The Physiocrats were French economic thinkers writing before Adam Smith. Roll, *History of Economic Thought*, pp. 111–20.
71 Ibid., pp. 114–15.
72 Ibid., pp. 158–62.
73 Ricardo, *Principles*, p. 11.
74 G.S.L. Tucker, 'Ricardo and Marx', *Economica*, XXVIII/111 (1961), pp. 252–3.
75 George J. Stigler, 'Ricardo and the 93% Labor Theory of Value', *American Economic Review*, XLVIII/3 (1958), p. 357.
76 Christian Gehrke, 'The Ricardo Effect: Its Meaning and Validity', *Economica*, LII/277 (2003), p. 143.
77 Hansard, 'Resumption of Cash Payments'.
78 Roll, *History of Economic Thought*, pp. 175–7.
79 Thomas Robert Malthus, *An Essay on the Principle of Population* (London, 2001), p. 54.
80 Sheilagh Ogilvie, '"Whatever is, is right"? Economic Institutions in Pre-industrial Europe', *Economic History Review*, LX/4 (2007), pp. 649–84. Ogilvie noted that this is an 'urban myth' and that Carlyle was in fact arguing in favour of the reintroduction of slavery (which is truly dismal).
81 Malthus, *Essay on the Principle of Population*, p. 87.
82 Ibid., p. 18.
83 Ricardo, *Letters*, pp. 118–20. Ricardo wrote to Malthus in 1811 that he 'had a bed always at your disposal'. Ricardo had sent Malthus a manuscript with a request that 'should you be so engaged that you cannot devote your attention to it . . . use no ceremony with me, but return the MS [manuscript] by the coach.' Ricardo, *Letters*, pp. 60–61. There are other pleasing instances of the closeness between the two. For example, Malthus ends one letter with 'The bell rings I must finish Ever truly Yours T R Malthus' and another with 'I am interrupted by the Postman and must conclude.' Ricardo, *Letters*, pp. 223–5.
84 Ibid., p. 90.
85 Ibid., p. 178.
86 Ibid., p. 179.
87 Ricardo, *Principles*, p. 23.
88 Gary M. Anderson, David M. Levy and Robert D. Tollison, 'The Half-Life of Dead Economists', *Canadian Journal of Economics*, XXII/1 (1989), p. 177.
89 Royal Economic Society, 'Current Topics: Ricardo Bicentenary', *Economic Journal*, LXXXII/372 (1972), pp. 1019–20.
90 Ibid.
91 There were of course handbooks regarding how to trade in stocks. See, for instance, Thomas Mortimer, *Every Man His Own Broker, or, A Guide to*

Exchange-Alley (London, 1761). Ricardo was attempting something much greater than a mere instructional manual for budding investors.

92 David Ricardo, *The Works and Correspondence of David Ricardo* (11 vols), ed. Piero Sraffa with the collaboration of M. H. Dobb (Cambridge, 1951–73).

93 A. Heertje, D. Weatherall and R. W. Polak, 'An Unpublished Letter of David Ricardo to Francis Finch, 24 February 1823', *Economic Journal*, XCV/380 (1985), pp. 1091–2.

94 S. G. Checkland, 'Essays in Bibliography and Criticism: XIX. David Ricardo', *Economic History Review*, IV/3 (1952), p. 372.

95 'Memoranda of Convictions, General' held at Gloucestershire Archives Q/PC/2/48/A/36.

96 Ricardo, *Letters*, p. 340.

97 Ibid., p. 312.

THREE John Stuart Mill

1 On Smith and Ricardo, see chapters in this volume. Jeremy Bentham (1748–1832) was the highly eccentric English founder of British utilitarianism. The Anglican Reverend Thomas Robert Malthus (1766–1834) was the famous author of *An Essay on the Principle of Population*. On James Mill, see below.

2 For a more extensive exploration of both the roots and intellectual offspring of Mill's political economy of progress, see Joseph Persky, *The Political Economy of Progress: John Stuart Mill and Modern Radicalism* (New York, 2016). For a broad treatment of Mill as a political economist, see Samuel Hollander, *John Stuart Mill: Political Economist* (Singapore, 2015).

3 First and foremost by Mill himself in his *Autobiography* (1871), which ranks as one of the most riveting examples of the genre: Mill, *Autobiography*, in *The Collected Works of John Stuart Mill*, ed. John Robson and Jack Stillinger (Toronto, 1981), vol. I. For a good recent biography, see Richard Reeves, *John Stuart Mill: Victorian Firebrand* (London, 2007). Bruce Mazlish, in *James and John Stuart Mill: Father and Son in the Nineteenth Century* (New York, 1975), puts forward an interesting psychohistory of Mill and his father. While somewhat speculative, it is suggestive in its attempts to link Mill's economics to his childhood and early adult experiences.

4 Mazlish, *James and John Stuart Mill*, p. 353.

5 Mill, *Autobiography*, p. 7.

6 Mill, *Early Draft* [of his autobiography], in *The Collected Works of John Stuart Mill*, ed. John Robson and Jack Stillinger (Toronto, 1981), p. 6.

7 Mill, *Autobiography*, p. 53.

8 Mill, *Early Draft*, p. 52.

9 Ibid., p. 612.

10 One possible explanation is offered by Robson. Mill wrote much of the *Autobiography* after he had married Harriet Taylor, a marriage his mother and the rest of his family found difficulty with. Robson, *The Collected Works*, p. xvii.

11 Mill, *Autobiography*, p. 9.

12 Ibid., pp. 23, 25.
13 Ibid., p. 33.
14 Ibid., p. 35.
15 Ibid., p. 37. Mill is honest enough to admit that 'various persons' thought him 'greatly and disagreeably self-conceited' (p. 37). In his early draft he also noted that his mother 'taxed' him with not showing proper respect to his elders, but 'for her remonstrances I never had the slightest regard'. Mill, *Early Draft*, p. 36.
16 Or again: 'Think (he used to say) of a being who would make a Hell – who would create the human race with the infallible foreknowledge, and therefore with the intention, that the great majority of them were to be consigned to horrible and everlasting torment.' Mill, *Autobiography*, p. 43.
17 Ibid., p. 83.
18 On this incident see Dudley Miles, *Francis Place: The Life of a Remarkable Radical, 1771–1854* (New York, 1988), p. 149.
19 Mill, *Autobiography*, p. 137.
20 Ibid., pp. 137–9.
21 Mazlish goes a good deal further, seeing Mill's existential crisis as an intense Oedipal crisis. Mazlish, *James and John Stuart Mill*, pp. 206–10.
22 Mill, *Autobiography*, 166–7.
23 For an excellent discussion of Mill's approach to autonomy and self-development, see Wendy Donner, *The Liberal Self: John Stuart Mill's Moral and Political Philosophy* (Ithaca, NY, 1991).
24 Mill comments that during his depressive periods (they did not end with his first crisis, but apparently abated) 'the doctrine of what is called Philosophical Necessity weighed on my existence like an incubus'. Mill concludes that 'we have real power over the formation of our own character; that our will by influencing some of our circumstances can modify our future habits or capabilities of willing'. Mill, *Autobiography*, p. 169.
25 For a highly readable treatment of Mill's relation to Harriet Taylor (as well as chapters on several other eccentric Victorian couples) see Phyllis Rose, *Parallel Lives: Five Victorian Marriages* (New York, 1983). Surprisingly, the Mill–Taylor relationship is also the subject of a major work by Friedrich Hayek, *John Stuart Mill and Harriet Taylor* (Chicago, IL, 1951).
26 According to Rose 'it seems to have been a sincere interest in women's rights that brought Mrs. Taylor and Mill together.' Rose, *Parallel Lives*, p. 291. Throughout the 1830s and '40s Harriet's husband tolerated and even financially supported the relationship, which she maintained was non-sexual.
27 Mill, *Autobiography*, p. 257.
28 Ibid., p. 254.
29 Ibid., p. 255.
30 Peter Nicholson, 'The Reception and Early Reputation of Mill's Political Thought', in *The Cambridge Companion to Mill*, ed. John Skorupski (Cambridge, 1998).
31 Ibid.
32 Persky, *Political Economy of Progress*, pp. 169–71.
33 For example, consider Robert Owen, the Welsh socialist pioneer and

founder of cooperatives, on the topic of competition. He held that competition produced 'waste of capital and labour'. But these were 'small evils compared to the extent of injurious feeling, violent passions, vices, and miseries unavoidably attendant on a system of individual competition'. Robert Owen, *Manifesto of Robert Owen*, 6th edn (London, 1840), p. 47.

34 Mill, *Principles*, p. 794.

35 Ibid., p. 201. In this speculation, Mill fully anticipates the position of the radical 'luck egalitarians'. See Joseph Persky, 'Utilitarianism and Luck', *History of Political Economy*, XLV/2 (2013), pp. 287–309.

36 Mill, *Principles*, p. 208.

37 Ibid., p. 207.

38 Ibid., p. 707.

39 Adam Smith, *An Inquiry into the Nature and Causes of the Wealth of Nations* [1776] (New York, 1937), Book 2, Chapter Three.

40 Notice that this definition shares with Smith a 'material fallacy'. By contrast, Marx argues that any labour on which a capitalist can make a profit should be considered productive: see discussion in Helen Boss, *Theories of Surplus and Transfer* (Boston, MA, 1990), pp. 83–6 and 92–6. Thus a musical troupe putting on performances for profit are viewed as productive by Marx, but not by Mill and Smith. In the mid-nineteenth century the difference between these two definitions would not have been quantitatively significant.

41 Mill, *Principles*, p. 411. Mill, here, fully anticipates Marx's division of the working day – a point Marx never acknowledges. Indeed, Marx maintained a deep hostility towards Mill. Early in the twentieth century, the Russian Ladislaus Bortkiewicz argued, 'one will not go wrong if one connects the ill will which Marx display towards Mill, with the circumstance that Mill had basically anticipated Marx's theory of surplus value.' Quoted in Samuel Hollander, *The Economics of John Stuart Mill* (Toronto, 1985), pp. 341–2.

42 Mill, *Principles*, p. 740.

43 Ibid., p. 757.

44 John Stuart Mill, *The Subjection of Women* [1869], in *The Collected Works of John Stuart Mill – Essays on Economics and Society Part II*, ed. John M. Robson (Toronto, 1984), vol. XXI, p. 298.

45 Mill, *Principles*, p. 740.

46 Ibid., p. 736.

47 Ibid., p. 738.

48 Again, the parallels to Marx are very strong. Marx, too, had a list of 'counteracting tendencies' to the tendency for the profit rate to fall. That list very much resembled Mill's. See Bernice Shoul, 'Similarities in the Work of John Stuart Mill and Karl Marx', *Science and Society*, XXIX/3 (1965), pp. 270–95.

49 Jean Charles Leonard de Sismondi (1773–1842) was a Swiss economist (and historian) who, although not a socialist, pioneered the theory of overproduction.

50 Mill, *Principles*, p. 741.

51 Ibid., p. 743.

52 Ibid., p. 746.

53 Ibid., p. 752.
54 Ibid., p. 754.
55 Ibid., p. 762.
56 Ibid.
57 Ibid., p. 767.
58 Ibid., p. 768.
59 Ibid.
60 Ibid., p. 763.
61 Ibid., p. 766.
62 Ibid., p. 769.
63 Charles Babbage, *On the Economy of Machinery and Manufacturing* [1835], 4th edn (New York, 1963), p. 251.
64 For a discussion of late nineteenth-century support for profit sharing and an associated reluctance to endorse Mill's broader schemes of cooperation, see Joseph Persky, 'Producer Co-operatives in Nineteenth-century British Economic Thought', *European Journal of the History of Economic Thought*, XXIV/2 (2017), pp. 319–40.
65 Mill, *Principles*, p. 775.
66 In a sense, Mill here anticipates Keynes's prediction of the 'euthanasia of the rentiers' as interest rates fall towards minimal levels. John Maynard Keynes, *The General Theory of Employment, Interest and Money* (New York, 1936), chapter 24.
67 Mill, *Principles*, p. 792.
68 Ibid.
69 Ibid., pp. 793–4.
70 For a discussion of Schumpeter's position that argues he may have overstated Mill's contribution see Michael Bradley, 'John Stuart Mill's Demand Curves', *History of Political Economy*, vol. XXI/1.
71 John Chipman, 'A Survey of the Theory of International Trade: Part 1, The Classical Theory', *Econometrica*, XXXIII/3 (1965), p. 486. Again, the extent of Mill's originality is questioned by some. See Andrea Maneschi, 'John Stuart Mill's Equilibrium Terms of Trade: A Special Case of William Whewell's 1850 Formula', *History of Political Economy*, XXXIII/3 (2001), pp. 609–25.
72 Thomas Sowell, *On Classical Economics* (New Haven, CT, 2006), p. 32; J. Bradford DeLong, 'This Time, It Is *Not* Different: The Persistent Concerns of Financial Macroeconomics', in *Rethinking the Financial Crisis*, ed. Alan Blinder, Andrew Loh and Robert Solow (New York, 2012), p. 17.
73 David Levy, *How the Dismal Science Got Its Name: Classical Economics and the Ur-Text of Racial Politics* (Ann Arbor, MI, 2001). But note that Mill comes in for serious criticism for his role in British imperialism in India. For a cautious defence of Mill's role in India see Mark Tunick, 'Tolerant Imperialism: John Stuart Mill's Defense of British Rule in India', *Review of Politics*, LXVIII/4 (2006), pp. 586–611.
74 Robert Ekelund Jr and Douglas Walker, 'J. S. Mill on the Income Tax Exemption and Inheritance Taxes: The Evidence Reconsidered', *History of Political Economy*, XXVIII/4 (1996), pp. 559–81.
75 Hayek traced Taylor's influence to the character of Mill's own education. In an essay Hayek chose not to publish, he engages in a bit of psychological speculation as to the source of Taylor's influence:

'Probably by the education given him by his father in his early youth Mill's character was so formed that he stood in need of someone whom he could adore and to whom he could ascribe all possible perfection. Behind the hard shell of complete self-control and strictly rational behaviour there was a core of a very soft and almost feminine sensitivity, a craving for a strong person on whom he could lean, and on whom he could concentrate all his affection and admiration.' Quoted in Bruce Caldwell, 'Hayek on Mill', *History of Political Economy*, XL/4 (2008), p. 699. (Notice Hayek's characterization of Mill's personality as 'almost feminine' echoes the widespread nineteenth-century caricature of a feminized Mill.) Caldwell presents a balanced discussion of Hayek's views of Mill and Taylor.

FOUR Karl Marx

1 Francis Wheen, *Karl Marx: A Life* (New York, 1999), p. 1.
2 Ibid., p. 13.
3 Ibid., pp. 16–17.
4 Karl Marx, 'Afterword to the Second German Edition', in *Capital: A Critique of Political Economy, volume I* [1887] (Moscow, 1977), p. 28.
5 Karl Marx, 'Economic Manuscripts of 1857–58 [*Grundrisse*]', in *Karl Marx Frederick Engels Collected Works*, vol. XXVIII: *Marx: 1857–1861* (Moscow, 1986), p. 38.
6 Marx, 'Afterword to the Second German Edition', p. 28.
7 Tatyana Vasilyeva, 'Preface', in *Karl Marx Frederick Engels Collected Works*, vol. XXVIII: *Marx: 1857–1861*, p. xi.
8 Marx, 'Economic Manuscripts of 1857–58 [*Grundrisse*]', p. 37.
9 Ibid., p. 40.
10 Ibid., pp. 43–4.
11 Ibid., p. 40.
12 David McLellan, *Karl Marx: His Life and Thought* (New York, 1973), pp. 56, 59.
13 Frederick Engels, 'The Condition of the Working Class in England: From Personal Observation and Authentic Sources', in *Karl Marx Frederick Engels Collected Works*, vol. IV: *Marx and Engels: 1844–1845* [1845] (Moscow, 1975), p. 331.
14 McLellan, *Karl Marx*, p. 63.
15 Ibid., p. 98.
16 Ibid., pp. 105–6.
17 Velta Pospelova, 'Preface', in *Karl Marx Frederick Engels Collected Works*, vol. III: *Marx and Engels: 1843–1844* (Moscow, 1975), p. xvi.
18 István Mészáros, *Marx's Theory of Alienation* (London, 1970), p. 217.
19 Marx, 'Economic and Philosophic Manuscripts of 1844' [1844], in *Karl Marx Frederick Engels Collected Works*, vol. III: *Marx and Engels: 1843–1844*, pp. 276–7.
20 Lawrence Krader, *The Ethnological Notebooks of Karl Marx* (Assen, 1974); Marx, *Capital: A Critique of Political Economy, volume III* [1894], in *Karl Marx Frederick Engels Collected Works* (New York, 1998), vol. XXXVII, p. 818.
21 Engels, 'Dialectics of Nature' [1882], in *Karl Marx Frederick Engels Collected Works, Frederick Engels: Anti-Dühring, Dialectics of Nature* (Moscow, 1987), vol. XXV, pp. 452–9; ibid., p. 458.

22 Marx, 'A Contribution to the Critique of Political Economy' [1859], in *Karl Marx Frederick Engels Collected Works*, vol. XXIX: *Marx: 1857–1861* (Moscow, 1987), p. 275.
23 Marx, 'Economic and Philosophic Manuscripts of 1844', p. 271.
24 Ibid., p. 275, italics in original; ibid., p. 277, italics in original.
25 Ibid., p. 272, italics in original.
26 Ibid., p. 273.
27 Marx, *Capital: A Critique of Political Economy, volume I* [1887] (Moscow, 1977), p. 77.
28 Ibid., p. 76.
29 Marx, 'Economic and Philosophic Manuscripts of 1844', pp. 274–5.
30 Ibid., p. 277.
31 Ibid., p. 278.
32 Ibid., p. 279, italics in original.
33 Peter Dickens, *Society and Nature: Towards a Green Social Theory* (Philadelphia, 1992); István Mészáros, *Marx's Theory of Alienation* (London, 1970); Bertell Ollman, *Alienation: Marx's Conception of Man in Capitalist Society* (London, 1976); Sean Sayers, *Marx and Alienation: Essays on Hegelian Themes* (New York, 2011); Dan Swain, *Alienation: An Introduction to Marx's Theory* (London, 2012).
34 Al Gini, *My Job, My Self: Work and the Creation of the Modern Individual* (New York, 2000), p. 55.
35 Marx, 'Economic and Philosophic Manuscripts of 1844', p. 278, italics in original.
36 Ibid., p. 273, italics in original.
37 Vasilyeva, 'Preface', pp. xii, xiv.
38 Marx, 'Afterword to the Second German Edition', pp. 22–3.
39 Engels, 'Preface to the Third German Edition', in *Capital: A Critique of Political Economy, volume I* [1887] (Moscow, 1977), p. 32.
40 Marx, *Capital: A Critique of Political Economy, volume I*, p. 44.
41 Ibid., p. 46; ibid., p. 48.
42 Ibid., pp. 44–5, 46.
43 Ibid., p. 46.
44 Ibid., p. 66.
45 Ibid.
46 Ibid., pp. 66–7.
47 David Ricardo, 'On the Principles of Political Economy and Taxation' [1821], in *The Works and Correspondence of David Ricardo*, ed. Piero Sraffa and M. H. Dobb (London, 1962), p. 275.
48 Marx, *Capital: A Critique of Political Economy, volume I*, pp. 106–8.
49 Ibid., p. 146.
50 Ibid., p. 149.
51 Ibid., p. 558.
52 Ibid., p. 151.
53 Ibid., pp. 85f.
54 Engels, 'Preface', in *Karl Marx Frederick Engels Collected Works, Karl Marx: Capital: A Critique of Political Economy, volume III* [1894] (New York, 1998), vol. XXXVII, pp. 12–13; Karl Marx, *Capital: A Critique of Political Economy, volume I*, pp. 156, 159.

55 Adam Smith, *An Inquiry into the Nature and Causes of the Wealth of Nations*, ed. William B. Todd (Oxford, 1975), p. 83.
56 Marx, *Capital: A Critique of Political Economy, volume I*, pp. 164–6.
57 Ibid., pp. 167–8.
58 Ibid., p. 208.
59 Ibid., p. 209.
60 Ibid.
61 Ibid., p. 222.
62 Marx, *Capital: A Critique of Political Economy, volume III*, p. 230.
63 Marx, *Capital: A Critique of Political Economy, volume I*, pp. 225, 232–3.
64 Ibid., pp. 252–3.
65 Ibid., pp. 256–7.
66 Jill Andresky Fraser, *White-Collar Sweatshop: The Deterioration of Work and Its Rewards in Corporate America* (New York, 2001), p. 20.
67 Ibid., p. 24.
68 Ibid., p. 42.
69 Ibid., pp. 18–19.
70 Marx, 'Theses on Feuerbach' [1844], in *Karl Marx Frederick Engels Collected Works,* vol. V: *Marx and Engels: 1845–1847* (New York, 1976), p. 5, italics in original.
71 McLellan, *Karl Marx: His Life and Thought*, pp. 154, 172.
72 Ibid., p. 177.
73 Marx and Engels, 'Manifesto of the Communist Party', p. 487.
74 Marx, *Capital: A Critique of Political Economy, volume I*, p. 585; Marx and Engels, 'Manifesto of the Communist Party', p. 488.
75 Ibid., pp. 516, 714.
76 Marx and Engels, 'Manifesto of the Communist Party', p. 519.
77 Marx, *Capital: A Critique of Political Economy, volume I*, p. 715.
78 Marx and Engels, 'Preface to the 1872 German Edition of the Manifesto of the Communist Party' [1872], in *Karl Marx Frederick Engels Collected Works,* vol. XXIII: *Marx and Engels: 1871–1874* (Moscow, 1988), pp. 174–5.
79 McLellan, *Karl Marx: His Life and Thought*, p. 188.
80 Ibid., pp. 190, 194.
81 Ibid., p. 198.
82 Ibid., p. 221.
83 Ibid., p. 225.
84 Marx, 'The Eighteenth Brumaire of Louis Bonaparte' [1852], in *Karl Marx Frederick Engels Collected Works,* vol. XI: *Marx and Engels: 1851–1853* (Moscow, 1979), p. 103.
85 Ibid., p. 128.
86 Marx, 'Inaugural Address of the Working Men's International Association' [1864], in *Karl Marx Frederick Engels Collected Works,* vol. XX: *Marx and Engels: 1864–1868* (Moscow, 1985), p. 12.
87 Marx and Engels, 'Manifesto of the Communist Party', p. 505.
88 Marx, 'Economic and Philosophic Manuscripts of 1844', p. 295.
89 Marx, 'Critique of the Gotha Program' [1875], in *Karl Marx Frederick Engels Collected Works,* vol. XXIV: *Marx and Engels: 1874–1883* (Moscow, 1989), p. 87.
90 Marx, 'Economic and Philosophic Manuscripts of 1844', p. 313.
91 McLellan, *Karl Marx: His Life and Thought*, pp. 264–5.

92 Ibid., pp. 330–31.
93 Ibid., pp. 284–5.
94 Ibid., pp. 242, 280, 282.
95 Ibid., p. 360.
96 Paul Thomas, *Karl Marx and the Anarchists* (Boston, MA, 1980), pp. 256, 260–61.
97 McLellan, *Karl Marx: His Life and Thought*, p. 341.
98 Paul Baran and Paul Sweezy, *Monopoly Capital: An Essay on the American Economic and Social Order* (New York, 1966); Immanuel Wallerstein, *The Modern World-System I: Capitalist Agriculture and the Origins of the European World-Economy in the Sixteenth Century* (New York, 1974).
99 Samir Amin, *Capitalism in the Age of Globalization* (London, 1997), pp. 95–7.
100 Joseph Stiglitz, *Globalization and Its Discontents* (New York, 2002), p. 217.
101 Ibid.
102 Marx, *Capital: A Critique of Political Economy, volume I*, p. 50.
103 Ibid., p. 173.
104 Ibid., pp. 474–5.
105 Marx, *Capital: A Critique of Political Economy, volume III*, p. 103.
106 Ibid., p. 799.
107 John Bellamy Foster, Brett Clark and Richard York, *The Ecological Rift: Capitalism's War on the Earth* (New York, 2010).
108 Nicholas Georgescu-Roegen, *The Entropy Law and the Economic Process* (Cambridge, MA, 1971), p. 283.
109 Ibid., p. 304.
110 Paul Prew, 'The 21st Century World-Ecosystem: Dissipation, Chaos, or Transition?', in *Emerging Issues in the 21st Century World-System: New Theoretical Directions for the 21st Century World-System*, ed. Wilma A. Dunaway (Westport, CT, 2003), vol. II, pp. 203–19; Robert Biel, *The Entropy of Capitalism* (Boston, MA, 2012).
111 Marx, *Capital: A Critique of Political Economy, volume III*, p. 871.

FIVE Alfred Marshall

1 Beatrice Webb, *My Apprenticeship*, p. 415. Alfred never gained great popularity in his college and at the university because of 'his authoritarian streak in dealing with colleagues particularly when he himself was in a position of authority; his vanity; his false modesty and egoistical self-centredness'. Peter Groenewegen, *A Soaring Eagle: Alfred Marshall, 1842–1924* (Aldershot, 1995), p. 766. He was substantially misogynistic and particularly ruthless with some of them (as Harriet Martineau, Beatrice Potter and Helen Bosanquet) but a careful, effective and stimulating teacher with his students, especially those who, for him, were one step ahead.
2 Alfred Marshall to J. N. Keynes, 4 August 1892, quoted in Groenewegen, *Soaring Eagle*, p. 23.
3 Nineteenth-century British philosophy, following the Scottish tradition, was largely focused on mental philosophy (or psychology), considered 'the queen of sciences'. W. Hamilton, *Lectures on Metaphysics and Logic*

1870–4, ed. H. L. Mansel and J. Veitch (Edinburgh, 1877), vol. I, p. 19. The Grote Club was a Cambridge philosophy discussion group, founded by John Grote, Professor of Moral Philosophy at Cambridge University and Fellow of Trinity College.

4 These annotations are still preserved in the archive of the Marshall Library of Economics in Cambridge; on these subjects Marshall published some early writings on economics: 'Review of Jevons' *Theory of Political Economy*', *Academy*, April 1872; 'Mr Mill's Theory of Value', *Fortnightly Review* (1876); *The Pure Theory of Foreign Trade and Domestic Value* (for private circulation, 1879). J. Whitaker, *The Early Economic Writings of Alfred Marshall*, 2 vols (London, 1975).

5 John K. Whitaker, *The Correspondence of Alfred Marshall, Economist* (Cambridge, 1996), vol. II, p. 285.

6 For instance, Charles Booth, Thomas Brassey, Edwin Chadwick, Henry Fawcett, Beatrice Potter, George Bernard Shaw, Sydney Webb and others.

7 John M. Keynes, *Official Papers by Alfred Marshall* (London, 1926), p. 205. Marshall was deeply involved with the Poor Law reform participating in the Royal Commission on the aged poor and several interventions on issues of poverty.

8 Alfred Marshall, 'Where to House the London Poor' [1884], in Arthur Pigou, ed., *Memorials of Alfred Marshall* (London, 1925), pp. 144–5.

9 Whitaker, *Correspondence*, p. 399.

10 Marshall 'Lectures to Women' [1873], in *Lectures to Women*, ed. Raffaelli Tiziano, Rita MacWilliams Tullberg and Eugenio Biagini (Aldershot, 1995), p. 106; Alfred Marshall, 'Social Possibilities of Economic Chivalry' [1907], in Pigou, *Memorials of Alfred Marshall*, pp. 323–46.

11 Alfred Marshall, 'Lectures to Women', p. 106.

12 Ibid., p. 119.

13 Alfred Marshall, 'The Future of the Working Classes' [1873], in Pigou, *Memorials of Alfred Marshall*, pp. 103 and 107.

14 Alfred Marshall, 'fragment' [1922], in Pigou, *Memorials of Alfred Marshall*, p. 367.

15 Rita McWilliams Tullberg, 'Marshall's "tendency to socialism"', *History of Political Economy*, VII/17 (1975), pp. 75–111.

16 Marshall, 'Social Possibilities of Economic Chivalry', p. 334.

17 Alfred Marshall, *Industry and Trade* (London, 1919), p. vii.

18 Notes of these lectures taken by Mary Paley and revised by Marshall are included in *Lectures to Women*.

19 Alfred Marshall, *Principles of Economics* [1890], 8th edn (London, 1920), p. 1.

20 Ibid., pp. 26–7.

21 Ibid., p. 14.

22 Ibid.

23 Thorstein B. Veblen, 'The Preconceptions of Economic Science III', *Quarterly Journal of Economics*, XIV (1900), pp. 240–69.

24 Marshall, *Principles of Economics* (London, 1920), p. v.

25 Alfred Marshall, 'The Present Position of Economics' [1885], in Pigou, *Memorials of Alfred Marshall*, p. 153.

26 Moreover, 'they did not see that the poverty of the poor is the chief cause of the weakness and inefficiency which are the causes of their poverty.' Marshall, *Principles of Economics*, pp. 762–3.

27 Marshall to Ludwig Darmstädter, 27 October 1910, in Whitaker, *Correspondence*, vol. III, p. 269.
28 Marshall to William A. S. Hewins, 29 May 1900, in Whitaker, *Correspondence*, vol. II, p. 280.
29 Claude Guillebaud, *Alfred Marshall Principles of Economics, Ninth (Variorum) Edition*, (London, 1961), vol. II, p. 768; Marshall, 'The Present Position of Economics', p. 166.
30 Marshall, *Principles of Economics*, p. 781.
31 Ibid., p. 850.
32 Ibid., p. 366.
33 Ibid.
34 Ibid.
35 Whitaker, *Early Economic Writings of Alfred Marshall*, vol. II.
36 Ibid., p. vii.
37 Ibid., p. vi.
38 Ibid.
39 In the preface, Marshall writes: '[This book] is an attempt to construct on the lines laid down in Mill's *Political Economy* a theory of Value, Wages and Profits.'
40 John Maynard Keynes, 'Alfred Marshall', in *Essays in Biography* (London, 1924), p. 201.
41 Neil Hart, *Equilibrium and Evolution: Alfred Marshall and the Marshallians* (London, 2012), p. 86.
42 Marshall, *Principles of Economics*, pp. 315–16, 367.
43 Neil Hart, *Equilibrium*, p. 90.
44 Marshall, *Principles of Economics*, p. 807.
45 Marshall to Charles W. Eliot, 3 September 1895, in Whitaker, *Correspondence*, vol. II, p. 129.
46 Marshall, *Principles*, p. xii.
47 Schumpeter, 'Alfred Marshall's *Principles*: A Semi-centennial Appraisal', *American Economic Review*, XXXI/2 (1941), pp. 237–8.
48 Joan V. Robinson notes: 'When I came up to Cambridge, in 1922, and started reading economics, Marshall's *Principles* was the Bible, and we knew little beyond it. Jevons, Cournot, even Ricardo, were figures in the footnotes.' Robinson, *Collected Economic Papers* (Oxford, 1951), vol. I, p. vii.
49 Paul Samuelson, 'Monopolistic Competition Revolution', in *Monopolistic Competition Theory: Studies in Impact. Essays in Honor of Edward H. Chamberlin*, ed. R. E. Kuenne (New York, 1967), p. 112.
50 Alfred Marshall, 'Distribution and Exchange', *Economic Journal*, VIII [1898], p. 52.
51 Marshall, *Industry and Trade*, p. 6.
52 Groenewegen, *Soaring Eagle*, p. 715; Keynes, *Essays in Biography*, p. 230.
53 Alfred Marshall, *Money, Credit and Commerce* (London, 1923), p. vi.
54 Groenewegen, *Soaring Eagle*, pp. 193–203; Whitaker, *Early Economic Writings of Alfred Marshall*, sec. 3.4 and vol. III; also Whitaker, *Correspondence*, vol. II, pp. 36–84.
55 Marshall to Alfred W. Flux, 8 March 1898, in Whitaker, *Correspondence*, vol. II, pp. 227–8.
56 Tiziano Raffaelli, *Marshall's Evolutionary Economics* (London, 2003), p. 49.
57 Marshall, *Principles of Economics*, p. 43.

58 Brian Loasby, *Knowledge, Institutions and Evolution in Economics* (London, 1999).
59 Katia Caldari, 'Alfred Marshall's Critical Analysis of Scientific Management', *European Journal of the History of Economic Thought*, XIV/1 (2007), pp. 55–78.
60 Marco Dardi, 'Alfred Marshall's Partial Equilibrium: Dynamics in Disguise', in *The Economics of Alfred Marshall. Revisiting Marshall's Legacy*, ed. Richard Arena and Michel Quéré (London, 2003), pp. 84–112; Katia Caldari, 'Marshall and Complexity: A Necessary Balance between Process and Order', *Cambridge Journal of Economics*, XXXIX/4 (2015), pp. 1071–85.
61 Marshall, *Principles of Economics*, p. 139.
62 Ibid., p. 461.
63 Marshall, 'The Present Position of Economics', p. 154; Marshall, 'Distribution and Exchange', p. 42.
64 Marshall, *Principles of Economics*, pp. xiv and 772.
65 Marshall, 'Distribution and Exchange', p. 43.
66 Marshall refers to the important contributions given to biological perspective by Auguste Comte, Charles Darwin and particularly Herbert Spencer: Marshall, *Principles of Economics*, p. ix and app. C, and Whitaker, *Early Economic Writings*, vol. II, p. 385; Marshall, 'Distribution and Exchange', p. 42.
67 Marshall, *Principles of Economics*, p. 249.
68 Ibid.
69 Ibid., p. 173.
70 Katia Caldari, 'Alfred Marshall's Idea of Progress and Sustainable Development', *Journal of the History of Economic Thought*, XXVI/4 (2004), pp. 519–36.
71 J. M. Keynes, *Official Papers of Alfred Marshall* (London, 1926), p. 358.
72 Marshall, 'Social Possibilities of Economic Chivalry', p. 333.
73 Ibid., p. 336.
74 Ibid., p. 338.
75 Alfred Marshall's archive, Folder 5.26.
76 Ibid., Folder 5.37.
77 Ibid.
78 Ibid., Folder 5.36.
79 Groenewegen, 'Marshall on Taxation', in *Alfred Marshall in Retrospect*, ed. R. McWilliams Tullberg (Aldershot, 1990), p. 91.
80 Ibid.
81 Keynes, *Official Papers*, p. 338.
82 Alfred Marshall, 'National Taxation after the War', in *After-War Problems*, ed. W. H. Dawson (New York, 1917), p. 319.
83 Ibid., p. 322.
84 Ibid., p. 326.
85 Marshall to Eli Filip Heckscher, 28 January 1916, in Whitaker, *Correspondence*, vol. III, p. 328.
86 Keynes, *Official Papers*, p. 361; Marshall to the editor of *The Times*, 13 November 1909, in Whitaker, *Correspondence*, vol. III, pp. 235–6.
87 Groenewegen, *Soaring Eagle*, pp. 557–8.

SIX Joseph Schumpeter

1 Joseph A. Schumpeter, 'Theoretical Problems of Economic Growth' [1947], in *Essays on Entrepreneurs, Innovations, Business Cycles, and the Evolution of Capitalism*, ed. Richard V. Clemence (New Brunswick, NJ, 1989), pp. 238–9.

2 Joseph A. Schumpeter, Preface to the Japanese edition of *Theorie der wirtschaftlichen Entwicklung* [1937], in *Essays*, p. 166.

3 Joseph A. Schumpeter, 'The Creative Response in Economic History' [1947], in *Essays*, p. 222.

4 Joseph A. Schumpeter, 'The Instability of Capitalism' [1928], in *Essays*, p. 72.

5 For Schumpeter's biography see Esben Sloth Andersen, *Joseph A. Schumpeter: A Theory of Social and Economic Evolution* (Basingstoke, 2011) and Richard Swedberg, *Joseph A. Schumpeter: His Life and Work* (Cambridge, 1991), on which I draw.

6 Joseph A. Schumpeter, *Das Wesen und der Hauptinhalt der theoretischen Nationalökonomie* (Leipzig, 1908).

7 Joseph A. Schumpeter, *Theorie der wirtschaftlichen Entwicklung* (Leipzig, 1912).

8 Joseph A. Schumpeter, 'Epochen der Dogmen- und Methodengeschichte' [1914], trans. by R. Aris as *Economic Doctrine and Method: An Historical Sketch* (London, 1954).

9 Joseph A. Schumpeter, 'Das Sozialprodukt und die Rechenpfennige: Glossen und Beiträge zur Geldtheorie von heute' [1917], trans. as 'Money and the Social Product', *International Economic Papers*, VI (1956), pp. 148–211; Schumpeter, *Die Krise des Steuerstaates* [1918], trans. as 'The Crisis of the Tax State', reprinted in *The Economics and Sociology of Capitalism*, ed. Richard Swedberg (Princeton, NJ, 1991), pp. 99–140; Schumpeter, 'Zur Soziologie der Imperialismen' [1919], trans. as 'The Sociology of Imperialisms', reprinted in *Economics and Sociology*, pp. 141–219; Schumpeter, 'Sozialistische Möglichkeiten von heute', *Archiv für Sozialwissenschaft und Sozialpolitik*, XLVIII (1920), pp. 305–60; Schumpeter, 'Die sozialen Klassen im ethnisch homogenen Milieu' [1927], trans. as 'Social Classes in an Ethnically Homogeneous Environment', reprinted in *Economics and Sociology*, pp. 230–83; Schumpeter, 'Gustav v. Schmoller und die Probleme von heute', *Schmollers Jahrbuch für Gesetzgebung, Verwaltung und Volkswirtschaft*, L (1926), pp. 337–88; Schumpeter, *The Theory of Economic Development: An Inquiry into Profits, Capital, Credit, Interest, and the Business Cycle* (Cambridge, MA, 1934).

10 Joseph A. Schumpeter, *Business Cycles: A Theoretical, Historical, and Statistical Analysis of the Capitalist Process* (New York, 1939); Schumpeter, *Capitalism, Socialism and Democracy* (New York, 1942); Schumpeter, *History of Economic Analysis* (London, 1954).

11 See especially Richard R. Nelson and Sidney G. Winter, *An Evolutionary Theory of Economic Change* (Cambridge, MA, 1982).

12 Schumpeter, *Wesen und Hauptinhalt*, p. 7.

13 See Yuichi Shionoya, *Schumpeter and the Idea of Social Science: A Metatheoretical Study* (Cambridge, 1997), pp. 91–123.

14 Schumpeter, *Wesen und Hauptinhalt*, p. 86.

15 See Esben Sloth Andersen, *Schumpeter's Evolutionary Economics: A Theoretical, Historical and Statistical Analysis of the Engine of Capitalism* (London, 2009), pp. 3–4.
16 See Mário Graça Moura, 'Schumpeter's Conceptions of Process and Order,' *Cambridge Journal of Economics*, XXXIX (2015), pp. 1137–8.
17 Schumpeter, *The Theory*, pp. 80, 33.
18 Ibid., p. 76.
19 Joseph A. Schumpeter, 'Economic Theory and Entrepreneurial History' [1949], in *Essays*, p. 258; Schumpeter, 'The Creative Response', p. 223.
20 Schumpeter, *The Theory*, p. 64, n. 1, emphasis removed.
21 Schumpeter, *Cycles*, p. 103.
22 Schumpeter, 'The Creative Response', p. 224.
23 Schumpeter, *The Theory*, pp. 85, 84–5, 80.
24 Ibid., pp. 69–73, 116.
25 Schumpeter, *Cycles*, p. 117.
26 Ibid., p. 129.
27 Ibid., p. 125.
28 Ibid., p. 98.
29 Joseph A. Schumpeter, 'The Analysis of Economic Change' [1935], in *Essays*, p. 139.
30 Schumpeter, *The Theory*, p. 66.
31 Schumpeter, *Cycles*, pp. 131, 135.
32 Ibid., p. 137.
33 Schumpeter, *The Theory*, p. 245.
34 Schumpeter, *Cycles*, p. 146.
35 Ibid., p. 145.
36 Ibid., p. 147 n. 1.
37 Ibid., p. 149.
38 Ibid., p. 155.
39 Ibid., p. 173.
40 Joseph A. Schumpeter, 'The Explanation of the Business Cycle' [1927], in *Essays*, p. 41.
41 See Alan W. Dyer, 'Schumpeter as an Economic Radical: An Economic Sociology Assessed', *History of Political Economy*, XX (1988), pp. 27–41. See also Graça Moura, 'Schumpeter's Conceptions', pp. 1133–6, on which I draw extensively.
42 Schumpeter, 'Classes', pp. 273, 274.
43 Ibid., p. 273.
44 Ibid., pp. 277–8.
45 Ibid., p. 274.
46 Ibid., p. 242.
47 Ibid., p. 253.
48 Schumpeter, *Cycles*, p. 103.
49 Schumpeter, *The Theory*, p. 86.
50 Schumpeter, 'The Instability', p. 70.
51 Schumpeter, 'Entrepreneurial History', p. 261.
52 Schumpeter, 'The Instability', p. 71.
53 Schumpeter, *Capitalism*, pp. 82, 83.
54 Ibid., p. 86.
55 Ibid., pp. 84–5.

56 Ibid., p. 87.
57 Ibid., pp. 91, 102.
58 Ibid., p. 101.
59 Ibid., p. 134.
60 See Mário Graça Moura, 'Schumpeter and the Meanings of Rationality', *Journal of Evolutionary Economics*, XXVII (2017), pp. 129–31.
61 Schumpeter, *Capitalism*, pp. 123, 124.
62 Ibid., p. 127.
63 Ibid., pp. 124, 127.
64 Ibid., pp. 142, 157.
65 Ibid., p. 143.
66 Ibid., p. 167.
67 Ibid., p. 172.
68 Schumpeter, *History*, pp. 886–7.
69 Ibid., p. 12.
70 Ibid., p. 15.
71 Joseph A. Schumpeter, 'Science and Ideology' [1949], in *Essays*, pp. 272–86.
72 Schumpeter, *History*, p. 34.
73 Ibid., p. 38.
74 Ibid., pp. 42–3.
75 Ibid., p. 827.
76 Schumpeter, *Wesen und Hauptinhalt*, pp. 33–4.
77 Schumpeter, *History*, p. 242.
78 Ibid., p. 969.
79 Ibid., p. 242.
80 Ibid., pp. 472, 473, 668.
81 Ibid., p. 754.

SEVEN John Maynard Keynes

1 Quoted in Robert Skidelsky, *Keynes: A Very Short Introduction* (Oxford, 2010), p. 2.
2 Quoted in Angus Burgin, *The Great Persuasion* (Cambridge, MA, 2015), p. 62
3 Quoted in Skidelsky, *Keynes*, p. 2.
4 Quoted in Burgin, *The Great Persuasion*, p. 28.
5 Ibid.
6 Paul A. Samuelson, 'Lord Keynes and the General Theory', *Econometrica*, XIV/3 (1946), p. 187.
7 Lorie Tarshis, student in Cambridge in the 1930s. Quoted in Skidelsky, *Keynes*, p. 2.
8 David Bensusan-Butt, economics student in Cambridge in the 1930s. Quoted ibid.
9 A summary of what was happening in global markets during the lifetime of Keynes (as well as before and after) can be found in Victoria N. Bateman, *Markets and Growth in Early Modern Europe* (London, 2011), Chapter One.
10 Timothy J. Hatton and Jeffrey G. Williamson, *Migration and the International Labour Market* (London, 1994), p. 4.

11 Michael Edelstein, *Overseas Investment in the Age of High Imperialism: The United Kingdom, 1850–1914* (New York, 1982), p. 3.
12 John Maynard Keynes, 'Proposals for the Reconstruction of Europe' [1919], reprinted in *Collected Writings*, 30 vols (London, 1971–89), vol. IX, p. 20.
13 On Keynes and the British economy between the wars, see Nicholas H. Dimsdale, 'Keynes on Interwar Economic Policy', in *Keynes and Economic Policy*, ed. Walter A. Eltis and Peter J. N. Sinclair (London, 1988). Also Michael Stewart, *Keynes and After* (Bungay, 1986), Chapters Three to Six.
14 Keynes, *Collected Writings*, vol. XVII, pp. 372–3.
15 Excerpt from Victoria N. Bateman, *Markets and Growth in Early Modern Europe* (London, 2011), Chapter One.
16 Barry Eichengreen, *Golden Fetters: The Gold Standard and the Great Depression, 1919–1939* (Oxford, 1992).
17 A readable and more extensive account of Keynes's theory than can be provided in this chapter, including Keynes's concepts of effective demand and the multiplier, can be found in Stewart, *Keynes and After*, Chapter Four. For a more technical guide to Keynes's economics, see Roger E. Backhouse and Bradley W. Bateman, *The Cambridge Companion to Keynes* (Cambridge, 2006). Recent scholarly discussion of Keynes can be found in Philip Arestis, Meghnad Desai and Sheila Dow, *Money, Macroeconomics and Keynes: Essays in honour of Victoria Chick* (Oxford, 2002), and Steven Kates, ed., *What's Wrong With Keynesian Economic Theory?* (Cheltenham, 2016). On Keynes's work in the context of the Global Financial Crisis, see Robert Skidelsky, *Keynes: The Return of the Master* (London, 2009).
18 John Maynard Keynes, *General Theory of Employment, Interest and Money* (London, 1936), Chapter One, reprinted in *Collected Writings*, vol. VII.
19 John Maynard Keynes, *General Theory of Employment, Interest and Money* (London, 1936), Chapter Twelve, reprinted in *Collected Writings*, vol. VII.
20 Irving Fisher, 'The Debt-deflation Theory of Great Depressions', *Econometrica*, I/4 (1933), pp. 337–57.
21 Hyman P. Minsky, *Stabilizing an Unstable Economy* (Yale, 1986). For a recent readable account of the work of Minsky, see L. Randall-Wray, *Why Minsky Matters: An Introduction to the Work of a Maverick Economist* (Princeton, NJ, 2015).
22 The reasons are briefly discussed in Burgin, *The Great Persuasion*, p. 29.
23 Quoted ibid.

EIGHT Friedrich Hayek

1 'The [Austrian] cost-of-living index, which had risen [from a base of 100 in 1914] to 1,640 by November 1918, and had gone up to 4,922 by January 1920; by January 1921 it had increased to 9,956; in January 1922 it stood at 83,000; and by January 1923 it had shot up to 1,183,600.' Richard Ebeling, 'The Great Austrian Inflation', www.fee.org, 1 April 2006.
2 Erwin Dekker, *The Viennese Students of Civilization: The Meaning and Context of Austrian Economics Reconsidered* (Cambridge, 2016).
3 Bruce Caldwell, *Hayek's Challenge* (Chicago, IL, 2004), pp. 135–7.
4 Friedrich Hayek, *Hayek on Hayek* (Chicago, IL, 1994), p. 48.
5 Carl Menger, *Grundsätze der Volkswirtschaftslehre* (Vienna, 1871).
6 Caldwell, *Hayek's Challenge*, pp. 136–40.

7 In his work on cognitive psychology, Hayek argued that the capacity to form such theories, which need not be explicitly stated or written down, was selected through evolution. Species without this trait are unable to learn from experience and, naturally, do not survive long. Hayek, *The Sensory Order: An Inquiry into the Foundations of Theoretical Psychology* [1952] (Chicago, IL, 1999).

8 Friedrich Hayek, *The Counter-revolution of Science: Studies on the Abuse of Reason* [1952] (Indianapolis, IN, 1979).

9 Though Carl Menger was the unquestioned father of the Austrian School, Wieser and his brother-in-law, Böhm-Bawerk, did more than even Menger to promote the ideas of the Austrian School to the wider world.

10 Caldwell, *Hayek's Challenge*, pp. 143–4.

11 Ludwig von Mises, 'Economic Calculation in the Socialist Commonwealth' [1920], in *Collectivist Economic Planning*, ed. F. A. Hayek (London, 1935), p. 92.

12 Ibid., pp. 97–8, 107–9.

13 Friedrich Hayek, 'Ludwig von Mises' [1981], ed. Peter G. Klein, in *The Collected Works of F. A. Hayek*, vol. IV: *The Fortunes of Liberalism*, ed. Stephen Kresge (Chicago, IL, 1992), p. 136.

14 Ibid., p. 151.

15 Friedrich Hayek, *Monetary Theory and the Trade Cycle* [1929], ed. Hansjörg Klausinger, in *The Collected Works of F. A. Hayek*, vol. VII: *Business Cycles, Part I*, ed. Bruce Caldwell (Chicago, IL, 2012), pp. 49–165.

16 Bruce Caldwell, 'Introduction', in *The Collected Works of F. A. Hayek*, vol. IX: *Contra Keynes and Cambridge*, ed. Bruce Caldwell (Chicago, IL, 1995), pp. 19–21.

17 Hayek, *Monetary Theory and the Trade Cycle*, pp. 137–40.

18 Ibid., p. 131.

19 Ibid., p. 143.

20 Caldwell, 'Introduction', p. 21.

21 The debate has re-entered the public consciousness in the last decade thanks to the so-called 'Great Recession' and a pair of highly entertaining YouTube videos pairing (actors portraying) Hayek against Keynes in a rap battle. See 'Fear the Boom and the Bust' and 'Fight of the Century', www.econstories.tv

22 Caldwell, 'Introduction', pp. 2–3.

23 John Maynard Keynes, *A Treatise on Money* (London, 1930).

24 Friedrich Hayek, 'The Economics of the 1930s as Seen from London', in *The Collected Works of F. A. Hayek*, vol. IX (Chicago, IL, 1995), p. 60.

25 Friedrich Hayek et al., *Collectivist Economic Planning*, ed. F. A. Hayek (London, 1935).

26 Ibid., p. 233.

27 Ibid., p. 238.

28 Friedrich Hayek, *The Road to Serfdom: Text and Documents – The Definitive Edition*, in *The Collected Works of F. A. Hayek*, vol. II, ed. Bruce Caldwell (Chicago, IL, 2007).

29 Ibid., pp. 59–60.

30 Ibid., pp. 134–70.

31 On the circumstances of the composition of *The Road to Serfdom* and its reception, see Bruce Caldwell, 'Editor's Introduction', pp. 1–33.

32 Friedrich Hayek, 'Economics and Knowledge' [1936], in *The Collected Works of F. A. Hayek*, vol. xv, *The Market and Other Orders*, ed. Bruce Caldwell (Chicago, IL, 2014), pp. 57–77.
33 Hayek, 'Economics and Knowledge', p. 73.
34 Friedrich Hayek, 'The Use of Knowledge in Society' [1945], in *The Collected Works of F. A. Hayek*, vol. xv, pp. 93–104. In 2011 'The Use of Knowledge in Society' was named among the top 20 articles published in the first 100 years of the *American Economic Review*. '100 Years of the American Economic Review: The Top 20 Articles', pubs.aeaweb.org, February 2011.
35 Hayek also considered (and rejected) the possible superiority of planning by monopolized industries. Hayek, 'The Use of Knowledge in Society', p. 94.
36 Hayek, 'The Use of Knowledge in Society', pp. 95–6.
37 Ibid., pp. 99–100.
38 Friedrich Hayek, 'The Meaning of Competition' [1948], in *The Collected Works of F. A. Hayek*, vol. xv, pp. 105–16.
39 Friedrich Hayek, 'Competition as a Discovery Procedure' [1968], in ibid., pp. 304–13.
40 Friedrich Hayek, *The Sensory Order: An Inquiry into the Foundations of Theoretical Psychology* (Chicago, IL, 1999 [1952]).
41 Examples of natural spontaneous orders can be found in the structural features of crystals, biological evolution, ecosystems, the formation of stars, galaxies and perhaps even the universe itself, that is, wherever an *undesigned* pattern is discovered in nature.
42 Hayek left Chicago for the University of Freiburg in 1962, then left Freiburg for Salzburg in 1968, only to return to Freiburg for good in 1977.
43 Friedrich Hayek, 'Degrees of Explanation' [1955], in *The Collected Works of F. A. Hayek*, vol. xv, pp. 195–212.
44 Friedrich Hayek, 'The Theory of Complex Phenomena' [1964], in *The Collected Works of F. A. Hayek*, vol. xv, pp. 257–77. Other sciences of complex phenomena include cognitive psychology (Hayek, *The Sensory Order*), 'cybernetics, the theory of automata or machines, general systems theory, and perhaps also communications theory' (Hayek, 'Degrees of Explanation', p. 211), as well as linguistics (Hayek, 'The Theory of Complex Phenomena', p. 270), geology, evolutionary biology and the branches of astrophysics that investigate the formation of stars and galaxies (Friedrich Hayek, 'Notes on the Evolution of Systems of Rules of Conduct' [1967], in *The Collected Works of F. A. Hayek*, vol. xv, p. 287).
45 Friedrich Hayek, 'Kinds of Rationalism' [1965], in *The Collected Works of F. A. Hayek*, vol. xv, pp. 39–53.
46 Vernon Smith, *Rationality in Economics: Constructivist and Ecological Forms* (New York, 2008).
47 Friedrich Hayek, 'The Pretence of Knowledge' [1975], in *The Collected Works of F. A. Hayek*, vol. xv, pp. 371–2.
48 In a *New Yorker* article titled 'After Communism', published in 1990, the socialist economist Robert Heilbronner famously admitted that 'Mises was right' all along about the problems of economic calculation in a planned socialist economy. David Boaz, 'The Man Who Told the Truth', reason.com, 21 January 2005.

49 Hayek, 'Kinds of Rationalism', p. 49.
50 For example, T. W. Hutchison, *The Politics and Philosophy of Economics: Marxians, Keynesians, and Austrians* (Oxford, 1981), Chapter Seven; B. Caldwell, 'Hayek's Transformation', *History of Political Economy*, xx/4 (1988), pp. 513–41; S. Fleetwood, *Hayek's Political Economy: The Socio-economics of Order* (London, 2013); N. J. Foss, 'More on "Hayek's Transformation"', *History of Political Economy*, xxvii/2 (1995), pp. 345–64; J. Friedman, 'Hayek's Two Epistemologies and the Paradoxes of His Thought', *Critical Review*, xxv/3–4 (2013), pp. 277–304.
51 Friedrich Hayek, 'The Dilemma of Specialization' [1955], in *Studies in Philosophy, Politics, and Economics* (Chicago, IL, 1967), p. 123.

NINE Milton Friedman

1 Quoted in *The Encyclopedia of Libertarianism*, ed. Ronald Hamowy (London, 2008), p. 197.
2 Beatrice Cherrier, 'The Lucky Consistency of Milton Friedman's Science and Politics, 1933–1963', in *Building Chicago Economics*, ed. Robert Van Horn, Philip Mirowski and Thomas A. Stapleford (Cambridge, 2011), p. 341.
3 Lenny Ebenstein, *Milton Friedman: A Biography* (New York, 2007), pp. 6–7.
4 Cherrier, 'The Lucky Consistency', p. 341.
5 Milton Friedman, 'Preface, 1982', in *Capitalism and Freedom* (Chicago, 1982), p. ix.
6 Joel Mokyr, *A Culture of Growth* (Princeton, NJ, 2016).
7 Deirdre McCloskey, *The Rhetoric of Economics* (Madison, WI, 1985).
8 An alternative hypothesis suggests that Friedman was an 'intellectual for hire', becoming increasingly laissez-faire in response to monetary incentives. See Rob Van Horn and Philip Mirowski, 'The Rise of the Chicago School of Economics and the Birth of Neoliberalism', in *The Road from Mont Pelerin: The Making of the Neoliberal Thought Collective*, ed. Philip Mirowski and Dieter Plehwe (Cambridge, MA, 2009), pp. 139–78. However, Bruce Caldwell disagrees. See Bruce Caldwell, 'The Chicago School, Hayek, and Neoliberalism', in *Building Chicago Economics*, pp. 301–34.
9 In Milton Friedman, *Essays in Positive Economics* (Chicago, 1953), pp. 3–43; this was a method in which one would not have to concern oneself with the realism of assumptions: all that mattered was the accuracy of the predictions of a model, something that could be validated with data.
10 For a recent discussion, see Uskali Maki, *The Methodology of Positive Economics* (Cambridge, 2009). Also Victoria Bateman, 'Classical Liberalism: The Foundation for a New Economics', *Critical Review*, xxviii (2016), pp. 450–54.
11 Friedman did, however, acknowledge that there was always going to be a fly in the ointment. Statistically, one can never 'prove' a hypothesis, only 'reject' it, whilst economic evidence can often be ambiguous or somewhat difficult to interpret. This means that the choice between rival theories will inevitably require something other than evidence, which, as Valeria Mosini discusses, marks 'a dis-analogy with the natural sciences'. Valeria Mosini, *Reassessing the Paradigm in Economics* (Oxford, 2012), p. 22.

12 Quoted from Maki, *The Methodology of Positive Economics* (back cover). For a discussion of the associated controversy, see Mosini, *Reassessing the Paradigm in Economics*, pp. 19, 37. Also, J. Cunningham Wood and R. N. Wood, eds, *Milton Friedman: Critical Assessments* (London, 1990).

13 John Stuart Mill, 'On the Definition of Political Economy; and on the Method of Investigation Proper to it', in J. S. Mill, *Essays on Some Unsettled Questions of Political Economy* (London, 1844); Gunnar Myrdal, *Value in Social Theory: A Selection of Essays on Methodology* (New York, 1958); Max Weber, 'The Meaning of 'ethical neutrality' in Sociology and Economics' [1949], in *Methodology of Social Sciences*, ed. and trans. Edward A. Shils and Henry A. Finch (New Brunswick, NJ, 2011), pp. 1–47; Joseph A. Schumpeter, *History of Economic Analysis* (Oxford, 1954); John Neville Keynes, *The Scope and Method of Political Economy* (London, 1891). The fact that Friedman did not seem to acknowledge or engage with this long and established literature did not work in his favour. Also see the more recent work of the Critical Realism School.

14 Gunnar Myrdal, *Objectivity in Social Research* (New York, 1969), p. 51.

15 Cherrier, 'The Lucky Consistency', pp. 343–5, 354, 362. Cherrier also notes that Friedman ascribed 'the survival of his parents, poor Jewish emigrants . . . to the American free enterprise system', p. 341. In *Reassessing the Paradigm in Economics,* Mosini considers both the internal and external validity of Friedman's 'positive economics' claim. Internally, she notes a lack of logical consistency – that Friedman's conclusions often were not arrived at in the rigorous manner that he suggested and were not always amenable to testing. As we will see in regard to his monetary economics, Friedman faced numerous empirical criticisms.

16 John R. Commons, 'Institutional Economics', in *American Economic Review,* XXI (1931), p. 648. Quoted and further discussed in Bo Sandelin, Hans-Michael Trautwein and Richard Wundrak, *A Short History of Economic Thought* (Oxford, 2014), pp. 73–6.

17 Victoria Bateman, *The Sex Factor* (Cambridge, 2019).

18 Avner Offer, 'Self-interest, Sympathy and the Invisible Hand: From Adam Smith to Market Liberalism', *Economic Thought,* I/2 (2012), pp. 1–14.

19 Mosini, *Reassessing the Paradigm in Economics,* p. 74.

20 On the question of where Hayek positioned himself relative to other liberals, see Caldwell, 'The Chicago School, Hayek, and Neoliberalism', in *Building Chicago Economics*, p. 316.

21 Ibid., p. 315.

22 Friedman, 'Preface, 1982', *Capitalism and Freedom.*

23 John Maynard Keynes, *The General Theory of Employment, Interest and Money* (London, 1936), Chapter 24.

24 Victoria Bateman, 'Economists get too much Credit – and Blame', *Bloomberg View,* 23 February 2017; Victoria Bateman, 'Free Trade's Critics were once its Champions', *Bloomberg View,* 6 October 2016, www.bloomberg.com/view/articles.

25 Milton Friedman, 'Lange on Price Flexibility and Employment: A Methodological Criticism', *American Economic Review,* XXXVI/4 (1946), p. 618.

26 Milton Friedman, 'Have Monetary Policies Failed?', *American Economic Review,* LXII/2, (1972), pp. 11–18. On the two very different economic

responses to the notion that the economy is very complicated (the 'cloud-makers' versus the 'over-simplifiers') see Thomas Mayer, 'The Structure of Monetarism', in *A Macroeconomic Reader*, ed. Brian Snowdon and Howard Vane (London, 1997), p. 204.

27 For other predecessors to Friedman's monetarism, see Sandelin et al., *A Short History of Economic Thought*, pp. 86–7. By the time he set to work on monetary matters in the middle of the twentieth century, Friedman was also joined by leading monetary theorists Karl Brunner (who himself coined the term 'monetarism') and Allan Melzer and, later, by Harry Johnson and David Laidler.

28 In the textbook IS-LM Model, Keynesians can be thought of as emphasizing the instability of the IS curve whilst monetarists emphasized the instability of the LM curve.

29 Milton Friedman, 'The Quantity Theory: A Restatement', in *Studies in the Quantity Theory of Money*, ed. Milton Friedman (Chicago, IL, 1956).

30 Milton Friedman and Anna Schwartz, *A Monetary History of the United States* (Princeton, NJ, 1963). Economic historian Nuno Palma analyses the effect of money on the economy for a longer time span than did Friedman, and finds significant effects: Nuno Palma, 'Money and Modernization: Liquidity, Specialization, and Structural Change in Early Modern England', *European University Institute Working Paper*, XI (2016); Nuno Palma, 'The Existence and Persistence of Liquidity Effects: Evidence from a Large-scale Historical Natural Experiment', GGDC *Research Memorandum*, CLVIII (2016).

31 Barry Eichengreen, *Golden Fetters* (Oxford, 1995), also provides an explanation of the Great Depression based on monetary tightness, but within a much more global context and conditioned by the fixed exchange regime of the time, the Gold Standard. Numerous competing explanations of boom and bust abounded during Friedman's lifetime. In response to the Great Depression, the League of Nations had initiated a project that tasked researchers with investigating all possible causes of the business cycle, leading to the publication of Gottfried Haberler, *Prosperity and Depression* (Geneva, 1937). Theories considered included monetary causes, over-investment, psychology, the harvest, maladjustment and under-consumption. Friedman's 'Permanent Income Hypothesis', which provides an alternative to Keynes's Consumption Function and distinguished between permanent and transitory income, was used by Friedman to help 'defeat' both the notion that the economy could settle into an under-consumption equilibrium and that fiscal expansion would have a significant multiplier effect, Cherrier, 'The Lucky Consistency', p. 347. According to Friedman, this was his 'best purely scientific contribution'. However, recent evidence has turned against the Permanent Income Hypothesis, providing greater room for Keynes. See Noah Smith, 'Economists Give Up on Milton Friedman's Biggest Idea', *Bloomberg View*, www.bloomberg.com, 26 July 2016.

32 Milton Friedman, 'Statement on Monetary Theory and Policy', in *Employment, Growth and Price Levels, Hearings Before the Joint Economic Committee, 1st session, 25–28 May 1959* (Washington, DC, 1959), pp. 144–5. Quoted in Brian Hillier, *The Macroeconomic Debate* (Oxford, 1991), p. 59.

33 According to Friedman, an expansion of the money supply could

boost the economy in the short run, but only as a result of workers overestimating the 'real' value of their wages as prices and wages start to increase in the economy in response to the increasing money supply: workers observe that their money wages have increased, but have not yet factored in that the prices of the good they purchase have also increased, meaning that they are incentivized to work longer and harder, generating the extra output that creates boom time conditions. Hence the notion that workers are 'fooled' by monetary stimulus, but that this cannot last indefinitely, meaning that in the longer run, monetary stimulus cannot result in higher levels of output and lower levels of unemployment. The Phillips Curve trade-off is only a short-run phenomenon.

34 This vein of thinking later developed into a debate on 'rules versus discretion', albeit with roots that go back to James Angell many years earlier. By having their hands tied, economists came to believe that policymakers would be able to achieve a more favourable result. This was one case in which less choice was better than more.

35 Friedman also questioned the power of fiscal policy by employing his Permanent Income Hypothesis. See Noah Smith, 'Milton Friedman's Cherished Theory is Laid to Rest', *Bloomberg View*, bloomberg.com, 12 January 2017. The theory of Ricardian Equivalence has also been employed to reject the effectiveness of fiscal policy.

36 Robert Lucas and Thomas Sargent, 'After Keynesian Macroeconomics', in *After the Phillips Curve: Persistence of High Inflation and High Unemployment* (Boston, MA, 1978), p. 49.

37 See Mosini, *Reassessing the Paradigm of Economics*, who suggests that the problems of the 1970s can be seen not as a failure of Keynesian economics but of departure from Keynes's ideas; Yanis Varoufakis notes that the Bretton Woods system was a compromise which, as a result, lacked Keynes's automatic recycling of surpluses, leading to its ultimate undoing. Yanis Varoufakis, *And The Weak Suffer What They Must* (London, 2016).

38 Named after the then Chairman of the Federal Reserve, Paul Volcker, who raised interest rates to around 20 per cent in an effort to tackle inflation.

39 See Daniel J. Hammond, *Theory and Measurement* (Cambridge, 1996), p. 211: 'Even though they were widely credited with revitalising monetary economics . . . Friedman and Schwartz laboured from the beginning to the end of their collaboration under a cloud of professional doubt. The doubt was concerning the scientific credibility of their techniques, and thus of their results . . . They were charged with treating money as the cause when it was in fact the effect and of treating it as the sole cause when it was at most one of many causes.' Peter Temin also questions whether Friedman was free from initial bias, noting in regard to his monetary view of the Great Depression that Friedman and Schwartz's *A Monetary History* 'assumes the conclusion and describes the Depression in terms of it; it does not test it or prove it at all'. Peter Temin, *Did Monetary Forces Cause the Great Depression?* (New York, 1976), pp. 15–16. Given Friedman's emphasis on method (see Section 1), this is particularly unsatisfying.

40 Hyman Minsky, 'A Theory of Systematic Fragility', in *Financial Crises: Institutions and Markets in a Fragile Environment*, ed. E. I. Altman

and A. W. Sametz (New York, 1977), p. 152. Minsky was particularly concerned with the way in which a shift towards a Friedman-style monetary policy based on controlling money by controlling reserves, acting through open market operations, reduced the Central Bank's traditional ability to examine and supervise the loan books of commercial banks – loan books that they were previously forced to 'open up' if they wanted to borrow reserves at the discount window. In the words of L. Randall Wray, 'if the Fed had been watching bank balance sheets closely in the early to mid-2000s, it would have seen all the trashy assets they were accumulating.' Randall L. Wray, *Why Minsky Matters: An Introduction to the Work of a Maverick Economist* (Princeton, NJ, 2016).

41 This eradicated the systematic error that plagued Friedman's adaptive expectation formation process.

42 Robert Leeson and Warren Young, 'Mythical Expectations', in *The Anti-Keynesian Tradition*, ed. R. Leeson (New York, 2008), pp. 101, 106.

43 Keynes, *A Treatise on Money* (New York, 1930). Though by contrast with Friedman, Keynes adopted a Wicksellian (not Fisherite) approach.

44 Keynes, *General Theory*, Chapter Twelve.

45 Gianni Vaggi and Peter Groenewegen, *A Concise History of Economic Thought* (New York, 2003). On the technical difference between Friedman and Keynes in regard to liquidity preference see D. E. Laidler, 'Monetarism: An Interpretation and Assessment', *Economic Journal*, XCI/361 (1981), pp. 1–28.

46 Whilst Classical economists supposed that the interest rate adjusted to equilibrate saving and investment, hermetically sealing the economy at the natural rate, Keynes argued that the interest rate was instead equilibrating money supply and money demand, where the latter involves a demand for liquidity ('liquidity preference'). See Sandelin et al., *A Short History of Economic Thought*, pp. 88–9, for more detail.

47 In regard to Knight's distinction between measured risk and uncertainty, Friedman was certainly clear: 'I do not believe it is valid,' quoted in Mosini, *Reassessing the Paradigm of Economics*, p. 129; Friedman's conception of the Quantity Theory of Money with a stable money demand function implies a stable demand side for the economy. See Thomas Mayer, 'The Structure of Monetarism' [1975], reprinted in *A Macroeconomic Reader*, ed. Snowdon and Vane, pp. 180–216 (at p. 187), who also notes that 'one can be a Keynesian in one's basic theory, and, at the same time, accept the monetarist position that the private sector is . . . stabler than the private and government sectors combined [that is, that government intervention can increase rather than decrease instability]. Admittedly, it is much harder to see how a quantity theorist could believe in the instability of the private sector.'

48 Friedman, *Capitalism and Freedom*, p. 131.

49 Also see Morris M. Kleiner and Alan B. Krueger, 'Analyzing the Extent and Influence of Occupational Licensing on the Labor Market', *Journal of Labor Economics*, XXXI/2 (2013), pp. S173–S202.

50 Mark Pennington, *Robust Political Economy* (Cheltenham, 2011); Mark Steckbeck and Peter J. Boetke, 'Turning Lemons into Lemonade: Entrepreneurial Solutions to Adverse Selection Problems in E-Commerce', in *Markets, Information and Communication: Austrian Perspectives on the*

Internet Economy, ed. Jack Birner and Pierre Garrouste (New York, 2004).

51 More recently, tax credits and a 'basic income guarantee' have come to the fore in policy circles and can be seen to follow in the tradition of Friedman.

52 Friedman, *Capitalism and Freedom*, Chapter One.

53 Friedman and Rose Friedman, *Free to Choose* (New York, 1980).

54 For a critique of Friedman's work from a left-of-centre perspective, including for its neglect of power relations, see E. K. Hunt and Mark Lautzenheiser, *History of Economic Thought: A Critical Perspective* [1949] (London, 2011).

55 On the former, see Victoria Bateman, *Markets and Growth in Early Modern Europe* (London, 2011). On the latter, see Darren Acemoglu, Jacob Moscona and James Robinson, 'State Capacity and American Technology: Evidence from the 19th Century', *American Economic Review*, CVI/5 (2016), pp. 61–7; Alex Marshall, *The Surprising Design of Market Economies* (Austin, TX, 2012); Mariana Mazzucato, *The Entrepreneurial State* (London, 2011).

56 Acemoglu et al., 'State Capacity and American Technology'; Matthew Andrews, Lant Pritchett and Michael Woolcock, *Building State Capability: Evidence, Analysis and Action* (Oxford, 2017); Timothy Besley and Torsten Persson, 'The Origins of State Capacity: Property Rights, Taxation and Politics', *American Economic Review*, XCIX/4 (2009), pp. 1218–44; Mark Koyama and Noel Johnson, 'States and Economic Growth: Capacity and Constraints', *Explorations in Economic History*, LXIV/2 (2017), pp. 1–20.

57 Robert H. Frank, *The Darwin Economy: Liberty, Competition, and the Common Good* (Princeton, NJ, 2012); W. Brian Arthur, *Increasing Returns and Path Dependence in the Economy* (Ann Arbor, MI, 1994); Paul David, 'Clio and the Economics of QWERTY', *American Economic Review*, LXXII/2 (1985), pp. 332–7.

58 George A. Akerlof and Robert J. Shiller, *Phishing for Phools: The Economics of Manipulation and Deception* (Princeton, NJ, 2015).

59 Avner Offer, 'Why has the Public Sector Grown so Large in Market Societies?', *University of Oxford Discussion Papers in Economic and Social History*, XLIV (2002), p. 2.

60 Bradford J. Delong, 'A Brief History of Inequality', www.weforum.org, 28 July 2016.

61 Avner Offer, 'A Warrant for Pain: Caveat Emptor vs. the Duty of Care in American Medicine', *University of Oxford Discussion Papers in Economic and Social History*, CII (2012), p. 15.

62 Victoria Bateman, 'Classical Liberalism: The Foundation for a New Economics', *Critical Review*, XXVIII (2016), pp. 440–60; Victoria Bateman, 'We need a Sexual Revolution in Economics', *The Guardian*, 2 June 2015.

63 This section largely draws on Bateman, 'Classical Liberalism: The Foundation for a New Economics', pp. 454–6, and Bateman, *Economics Has a Sex Problem* (2019); Avner Offer, 'Between the Gift and the Market: The Economy of Regard', *Economic History Review*, L/3 (1997), pp. 450–76; Marilyn Waring, *If Women Counted: A New Feminist Economics* (New York, 1988).

64 Avner Offer, 'The Economy of Obligation', *University of Oxford Discussion Papers in Economic and Social History*, CIII (2012), pp. 4–5.

65 Tine De Moorvand and Jan Luiten Van Zanden, 'Girl Power: The European Marriage Pattern and Labour Markets in the North Sea region in the Late Medieval and Early Modern Period', *Economic History Review*, LXIII/1, (2010), pp. 1–33; Bateman, *Economics Has a Sex Problem* (2019).

66 It should, however, be noted that twentieth-century welfare states have not always supported women's participation in paid work. See Lynn P. Cooke, *Gender-Class Equality in Political Economies* (Oxford, 2011); Gosta Esping-Anderson, *Incomplete Revolution: Adapting Welfare States to Women's New Roles* (Cambridge, 2009).

67 On the controversy surrounding Friedman, see Hammond, 'Markets, Politics, and Democracy at Chicago: Taking Economics Seriously', in *Building Chicago Economics*, ed. Van Horn, Mirowski and Stapleford.

68 Paul Romer, 'Mathiness in the Theory of Economic Growth', *American Economic Review*, CV/5 (2015), pp. 89–93.

69 Friedman's emphasis on learning lessons from economic history and using empirical evidence was prescient. Even if the lessons he drew were not always the right ones, economics would benefit from a more fruitful interchange between theory and history – albeit one that goes in both directions, rather than running singly from theory to history. In Friedman's own words, economic history provides 'precisely the kind of evidence that we would like to get by "critical" experiments if we conduct them'. See Milton Friedman, 'Price, Income and Monetary Changes in Three Wartime Periods', *American Economic Review*, XLII/2 (1952), p. 612.

70 Jonathan D. Ostry, Prakash Loungani and Davide Furceri, 'Neoliberalism: Oversold', *Finance and Development*, LIII/2 (2016), pp. 38–41.

71 John A. Allison, *The Financial Crisis and the Free Market Cure* (New York, 2012).

72 The inadequacies of the post-Friedman monetary policymaking approach are becoming clear: the general neglect of the money supply in favour of using interest rates, when, behind the scenes, that money supply was ballooning; the way in which the most popular measure of inflation, the consumer price index, neglected the fact that property prices were racing ahead of other prices in the economy, meaning that inflation was not as 'low' as it seemed; the monetary ease that has followed 2008 and its potentially adverse longer-run consequences.

TEN John Forbes Nash Jr

1 Sylvia Nasar, *A Beautiful Mind: The Life of Mathematical Genius and Nobel Laureate John Nash* (New York, 1998). This chapter draws much on Nasar's book.

2 See 'The Medal for the Sveriges Riksbank Prize in Economic Sciences in Memory of Alfred Nobel', www.nobelprize.org.

3 John Nash, 'Ideal Money', *Southern Economic Journal*, LXIX/1 (2002), pp. 4–11.

4 Gonçalo L. Fonseca, 'John F. Nash', *History of Economic Thought*, www.hetwebsite.net, accessed 19 February 2018.

5 Johann von Neumann, 'Zur Theorie der Gesellschaftsspiele', *Mathematische Annalen*, X (1928), pp. 295–320. Other precursors had been Antoine-Augustin Cournot and Ernest Zermelo.

6 Ibid., p. 295, trans. Karen Horn.
7 Johann von Neumann and Oskar Morgenstern, *Theory of Games and Economic Behavior* (Princeton, NJ, 1943).
8 Nash, 'Non-cooperative Games', dissertation, University of Princeton, NJ, 1950.
9 Roger Myerson, *Game Theory: Analysis of Conflict* (Cambridge, MA, 1991), p. 105; Roger Myerson, 'Nash Equilibrium and the History of Economic Method', *Journal of Economic Literature*, XXXVII (1999), p. 1067.
10 Nasar, *A Beautiful Mind*, p. 32.
11 Eric T. Bell, *Men of Mathematics* (New York, 1937).
12 Nasar, *Beautiful Mind*, pp. 61–3.
13 John Milnor, 'The Game of Hex', in *The Essential John Nash*, ed. Harold W. Kuhn and Sylvia Nasar (Princeton, NJ, 2002), pp. 31–3.
14 John Nash, 'The Bargaining Problem', *Econometrica*, XVIII/2 (1950), pp. 155–62.
15 John F. Nash Sr and John F. Nash Jr, 'Sag and Tension Calculations for Wire Spans Using Catenary Formulas', *Electrical Engineering*, LXIV/12 (1945), pp. 984–7.
16 Neumann and Morgenstern, *Theory of Games*.
17 Nash, 'Two-person Cooperative Games', *Econometrica*, XXI/1 (1953), pp. 128–40.
18 Luitzen Brouwer, 'Über Abbildungen von Mannigfaltigkeiten', *Mathematische Annalen*, LXXI (1911), pp. 97–115; Shizuo *Kakutani*, 'A Generalization of Brouwer's Fixed Point Theorem', *Duke Mathematical Journal*, VIII/3 (1941), pp. 457–9. We will spare the reader the intricacies of these mathematical tools.
19 A facsimile has been reproduced in *The Essential John Nash*, ed. Kuhn and Nasar, pp. 53–84.
20 Nash, 'Non-cooperative Games', *Annals of Mathematics*, LIV (1951), pp. 286–95.
21 Ibid., p. 286.
22 Myerson, 'Nash Equilibrium', pp. 1069–70.
23 Albert W. Tucker, 'A Two-person Dilemma – The Prisoner's Dilemma', UMAP *Journal* (1950), reprinted in Philipp D. Straffin, 'The Mathematics of Tucker – A Sampler', *Two-year College Mathematics Journal*, XIV/3 (1983), pp. 228–32.
24 See 'Game theory', www.hetwebsite.net, accessed 19 February 2018. See this site also for an excellent brief summary of the developments and ramifications in game theory. For an easy-access didactic introduction with more detail, see Marilu Hurt McCarty, *The Nobel Laureates* (New York, 2001), pp. 311–48.
25 R. Duncan Luce and Howard Raiffa, *Games and Decisions* (New York, 1957).
26 Harold W. Kuhn, 'Extensive Games and the Problem of Information', in *Contributions to the Theory of Games*, ed. Harold W. Kuhn and Alfred W. Tucker (Princeton, NJ, 1953), pp. 193–216.
27 Reinhard Selten, 'Spieltheoretische Behandlung eines Oligopolmodells mit Nachfrageträgheit', *Zeitschrift für die gesamte Staatswissenschaft*, CXXI (1965), pp. 301–24, 667–89.
28 Reinhard Selten, 'Reexamination of the Perfectness Concept for

Equilibrium Points in Extensive Games', *International Journal of Game Theory*, IV (1975), pp. 25–55.

29 John Harsanyi, 'Games with Incomplete Information Played by Bayesian Players', *Management Science*, XIV (1967/68), pp. 159–82, 320–34, 486–502.

30 Adam Smith, *An Inquiry into the Nature and Causes of the Wealth of Nations*, ed. R. H. Campbell and A. S. Skinner (Oxford, 1976).

31 Myerson, 'Nash Equilibrium', p. 1078.

32 Nash, 'Real Algebraic Manifolds', *Annals of Mathematics*, LVI (1952), pp. 405–21.

33 See 'A Brief History of RAND', www.rand.org, accessed 18 February 2018.

34 Nasar, *Beautiful Mind*, p. 105.

35 Interview with Kenneth J. Arrow in Karen Horn, *Roads to Wisdom, Conversations with Ten Nobel Laureates in Economics* (Cheltenham, 2009), p. 76.

36 Nash, 'C1-isometric Imbeddings', *Annals of Mathematics*, LX (1954), pp. 383–96; Nash, 'The Imbedding Problem for Riemannian Manifolds', *Annals of Mathematics*, LXIII (1956), pp. 20–63.

37 Nash, 'Autobiographical Essay', in *Les Prix Nobel*, ed. Nobel Foundation (Stockholm, 1994).

38 See Horn, *Roads to Wisdom*, pp. 19–25.

39 Neumann and Morgenstern, *Theory of Games*.

40 See Nasar, *Beautiful Mind*, pp. 356–73; Avner Offer and Gabriel Söderberg, *The Nobel Factor* (Princeton, NJ, 2016).

41 Personal communication, 20 August 2006.

42 See the website of the Abel Prize, www.abelprize.no.

ELEVEN Daniel Kahneman

1 Tim Adams, 'This Much I Know: Daniel Kahneman', *The Guardian*, www.theguardian.com, 8 July 2012.

2 David Shariatmadari, 'Daniel Kahneman: "What would I eliminate if I had a magic wand? Overconfidence"', *The Guardian*, www.theguardian.com, 18 July 2015.

3 Adams, 'This Much I Know'.

4 Daniel Kahneman, 'Daniel Kahneman – Biographical', *The Sveriges Riksbanks Prize in Economic Sciences in Memory of Alfred Nobel 2002*, www.nobelprize.org.

5 Ibid.

6 Amos Tversky and Daniel Kahneman, 'Belief in the Law of Small Numbers', *Psychological Bulletin*, LXXVI/2 (1971), pp. 105–10.

7 Daniel Kahneman and Amos Tversky, 'On the Reality of Cognitive Illusions', *Psychological Review*, CIII (1996), pp. 582–91.

8 Kahneman, 'Biographical', www.nobelprize.org.

9 Ibid.

10 Ibid.

11 D. Kahneman and E. E. Ghiselli, 'Validity and Non-linear Heteroscadastic Models', *Personnel Psychology*, XV (1962), pp. 1–11.

12 D. Kahneman and J. Beatty, 'Pupil Diameter and Load on Memory', *Science*, CLIV/3756 (1966), pp. 1583–5.

13 Kahneman, 'Biographical', p. 8.

14 Ibid., pp. 9–10.
15 Amos Tversky and Daniel Kahneman, 'Belief in the Law of Small Numbers', *Psychological Bulletin*, LXXVI/2 (1971), pp. 105–10.
16 Amos Tversky and Daniel Kahneman, 'Judgement under Uncertainty: Heuristics and Biases', *Science*, CLXXXV/4157 (1974), pp. 1124–31.
17 D. Kahneman, P. Slovic and A. Tversky, *Judgement under Uncertainty: Heuristics and Biases* (Cambridge, 1982); Daniel Kahneman and Amos Tversky, *Choices, Values and Frames* (Cambridge, 2000).
18 Daniel Kahneman and Amos Tversky, 'Prospect Theory – An Analysis of Decision under Risk', *Econometrica*, XLVII/2 (1979), pp. 263–92.
19 Tversky and Kahneman, 'Belief in the Law of Small Numbers'.
20 See Amos Tversky and Daniel Kahneman, 'Loss Aversion in Riskless Choice: A Reference Dependent Model', *Quarterly Journal of Economics*, CVII/4 (1991), pp. 1039–61.
21 See R. H. Thaler, ed., *Quasi Rational Economics* (New York, 2000); R. H. Thaler, ed., *Advances in Behavioural Finance* (New York and Princeton, NJ, 2005), vol. II.
22 R. H. Thaler, A. Tversky, D. Kahneman and A. Schwartz, 'The Effect of Myopia and Loss Aversion on Risk Taking: An Experimental Test', *Quarterly Journal of Economics*, CXII (1997), pp. 647–61.
23 See Amos Tversky and Daniel Kahneman, 'Advances in Prospect Theory: Cumulative Representation of Uncertainty', *Journal of Risk and Uncertainty*, V (1992), pp. 297–323.
24 G. Gigerenzer, *Gut Feelings: The Intelligence of the Unconscious* (London, 2007).
25 H. A. Simon, 'A Behavioural Model of Rational Choice', *Quarterly Journal of Economics*, LXIX (1955), pp. 99–118.
26 Adams, 'This Much I Know'.
27 J. Gots, 'Hire Thine Enemy: Daniel Kahneman on Adversarial Collaboration, The Big Think', www.bigthink.com, accessed 19 February 2018.
28 See I. Bateman, D. Kahneman, A. Munro, C. Starmer and R. Sugden, 'Is There Loss Aversion in Buying? An Adversarial Collaboration,' *Working Paper – Centre for Social and Economic Research on the Global Environment* 1 (2003), pp. 1–39; D. Kahneman and G. Klein, 'Conditions for Intuitive Expertise: A Failure to Disagree', *American Psychologist*, LXIV/6 (2009), pp. 515–26; A. Mellers, R. Hertwig and D. Kahneman, 'Do Frequency Representations Eliminate Conjunction Effects? An Exercise in Adversarial Collaboration', *Psychological Science*, XII (2001), pp. 269–75; and T. Gilovich, V. H. Medvec and D. Kahneman (1998), 'Varieties of Regret: A Debate and Partial Resolution', *Psychological Review*, CV (1998), pp. 602–5.
29 'Daniel Kahneman Facts', www.nobelprize.org.
30 R. H. Thaler, 'Toward a Positive Theory of Consumer Choice, *Journal of Economic Behavior and Organisation*, XXXIX (1980), pp. 36–90.
31 Kahneman, (2002), 'Biographical', www.nobelprize.org.
32 Adams, 'This Much I Know'.

TWELVE Amartya Sen

1 Amartya Sen, *Poverty and Famines* (Oxford, 1981), pp. 80 (quote), 58.
2 Ibid., p. 66.
3 Ibid., pp. 96, 105, 139.
4 Ibid., p. 152.
5 Ibid., p. 13.
6 Amartya Sen, 'Social Choice Theory: A Re-examination' [1975], in *Choice, Welfare and Measurement* (Cambridge, MA, 1997), pp. 158–200.
7 Amartya Sen, *Commodities and Capabilities* (Oxford, 1999), p. 2.
8 Lionel Robbins, 'Interpersonal Comparisons of Utility: A Comment,' *Economic Journal*, XLVIII (1938), p. 637.
9 Shatakshee Dhongde and Prasanta K. Pattanaik, 'Preference, Choice, and Rationality: Amartya Sen's Critique of the Theory of Rational Choice in Economics,' in *Amartya Sen*, ed. Christopher W. Morris (Cambridge, 2009), p. 21.
10 Amartya Sen, 'Description as Choice' [1979], in *Choice, Welfare, and Measurement*, p. 442.
11 Robert Sugden, 'Welfare, Resources, and Capabilities: A Review of *Inequality Reexamined* by Amartya Sen,' *Journal of Economic Literature*, XXXI (1993), p. 1950.
12 Amartya Sen, 'The Impossibility of Being a Paretian Liberal' [1970], in *Choice, Welfare and Measurement*, pp. 285–90.
13 Amartya Sen, *On Economic Inequality*, enl. edn (Oxford, 1997), p. 75.
14 Ibid., p. 170.
15 Ibid., p. 76.
16 Amartya Sen, 'Equality of What?' [1980], in *Choice, Welfare and Measurement*, p. 366.
17 For Rawls's defence see his 'Social Unity and Primary Goods', in *Utilitarianism and Beyond*, ed. Amartya Sen and Bernard Williams (Cambridge, 1982), pp. 159–85.
18 Jean Drèze and Amartya Sen, *India: Economic Development and Social Opportunity* (Delhi, 1995), p. vii.
19 Ibid., pp. 64, 78.
20 Ibid., pp. 67, 8 (quote).
21 Amartya Sen, *Development as Freedom* (Oxford, 1999), p. 11.
22 Albert O. Hirschman, *The Passions and the Interests: Political Arguments for Capitalism before its Triumph* (Princeton, NJ, 1977).
23 Amartya Sen, 'Albert Hirschman', *Moneta e Credito*, LXVII (2014), p. 163.
24 Sen, *Development as Freedom*, p. 294.
25 Ibid., pp. 6–7.
26 Ibid., p. 151.
27 Drèze and Sen, *India*, p. 156.
28 Amartya Sen, 'Missing Women,' *British Medical Journal*, CCCIV (1992).
29 Sen, *Development as Freedom*, pp. 197–8.
30 Drèze and Sen, *India*, p. 127.
31 Adam Smith, *An Inquiry into the Nature and Causes of the Wealth of Nations* [1776], ed. William B. Todd, in *The Glasgow Edition of the Works of Adam Smith*, ed. R. H. Campbell and A. S. Skinner (Oxford, 1975–87), p. 456.

32 Drèze and Sen, *India*, p. 257.
33 Ibid., pp. 157, 159 (quote).
34 Amartya Sen, 'The Possibility of Social Choice', Nobel Lecture, www.nobelprize.org, 8 December 1998.
35 Sen, *Development as Freedom*, p. 203.
36 Amartya Sen, *The Idea of Justice* (London, 2009), p. xvi.
37 Ibid., pp. 16 (quote), 21.
38 Ibid., p. 105.
39 Ibid., pp. 70, 123, 140.
40 Ibid., p. 141.
41 Sen, *Development as Freedom*, pp. 96–7.
42 Sugden, 'Welfare, Resources, and Capabilities', p. 1951.
43 Amartya Sen, *Inequality Reexamined* (New York, 1992), p. 81.
44 Sugden, 'Welfare, Resources, and Capabilities', p. 1953.
45 Robert Sugden, 'Review of *Commodities and Capabilities*', *Economic Journal*, XCVI (1986), p. 821. For a similar critique, see Emmanuelle Bénicourt, 'Amartya Sen: un bilan critique,' *Cahiers d'économie politique*, I (2007), pp. 65–7.
46 Dan Usher, 'Review of *Commodities and Capabilities*,' *Canadian Journal of Economics*, XX (1987), p. 199.
47 Morris, 'Introduction', in *Amartya Sen*, p. 8.
48 Sen, *Development as Freedom*, p. 8.
49 Adam Smith, *The Theory of Moral Sentiments* [1759], ed. A. L. Macfie and D. D. Raphael, in *Glasgow Edition of the Works*, p. 82.

THIRTEEN Joseph Stiglitz

1 He had only worked for the public sector until then. On this matter, one can relate to Steve Sailer's amused commentary, '"Incentives Matter", Except to Economists', www.vdare.com, 14 January 2014.
2 Economic Sciences Prize Committee, 'Markets with Asymmetric Information' (Stockholm, 2001), p. 10.
3 Ibid., p. 9.
4 Joseph Stiglitz, 'Joseph E. Stiglitz – Biographical', *The Sveriges Riksbank Prize in Economic Sciences in Memory of Alfred Nobel 2001*, www.nobelprize.org, accessed 22 February 2018.
5 Ibid.
6 Ibid.
7 Ibid.
8 Ibid.
9 In advanced books, neoclassical theoreticians – including Stiglitz – do not hesitate to talk about centralization or even of 'planners' but that does not prevent them from nurturing the idea (especially in textbooks) that this model represents an ideal market economy.
10 According to the 'floor lamp principle', in darkness, one looks for a lost object where there is light, since it is vain to try to look for it elsewhere.
11 Economic Sciences Prize Committee, 'Markets with Asymmetric Information'.
12 Ibid.

13 Sometimes, when there are information asymmetries, there is no equilibrium (there are no exchanges). The aim of the modellist is then to propose measures that can enable the equilibrium to exist (guarantees and various forms of monitoring, for example).
14 Joseph Stiglitz, 'Information and the Change in the Paradigm in Economics', *Nobel Lecture 2001*, p. 10, my italics. www.nobelprize.org.
15 Ibid., p. 8, my italics.
16 Ibid., pp. 8–9, Stiglitz's italics.
17 Ibid., p. 10, my italics.
18 Stiglitz, 'Joseph E. Stiglitz – Biographical'.
19 Stiglitz, 'Information and the Change in the Paradigm in Economics', p. 10.
20 Joseph Stiglitz, 'Incentives and Risk Sharing in Sharecropping', *Review of Economic Studies*, XLI (April 1974), pp. 219–55.
21 Stiglitz, 'Information and the Change in the Paradigm in Economics', pp. 500–501, Stiglitz's italics.
22 C. Shapiro and J. Stiglitz, 'Equilibrium Unemployment as a Worker Discipline Device', *American Economic Review*, LXXIV/3 (1984), pp. 433–44.
23 Ibid., p. 433.
24 Ibid., p. 435.
25 Ibid., p. 433.
26 Ibid., p. 435.
27 Ibid., p. 437.
28 Ibid.
29 At equilibrium, unemployment is involuntary in the sense that the workers are disposed to work at the prevailing wage level, or even at the 'competition' wage level (inferior to the former), but cannot because a promise, even sincere, not to shirk would not be credible. They therefore have to wait until fate changes their situation (with the probability q).
30 Macroeconomics, whose starting point is empirical relationships rather than axioms, aims at being more directly operational – and less normative, even if one of its objectives is to guide collective decisions.
31 Shapiro and Stiglitz, 'Equilibrium Unemployment', p. 434.
32 Ibid., p. 441.
33 Ibid.
34 We are in the presence of what economists call 'negative externalities': when employing workers, a firm affects the situation of other firms, who are constrained to increase their salary to compensate for the decrease of penalty associated with shirking, because of the diminution of unemployment.
35 Improvement that benefited some, if not of all, without penalizing anyone.
36 There is therefore a process of insider trading, which penalizes the person who, in the stock exchange, proceeds to operate on the basis of information that has not yet been made public.
37 Yet, because of its vagueness, the Nobel Prize Committee avoids talking about this. Cautiously, the Prize committee has also awarded the prize to Robert Shiller, who denies its validity. B. Guerrien and O. Gün, 'Efficient

Market Hypothesis: What are We Talking About?', *Real World Economic Review*, LVI (2011), paecon.net.

38 E. Fama, 'Efficient Capital Markets: A Review of Theory and Empirical Work', *Journal of Finance*, XXV/2 (1970), p. 383.

39 S. Grossman and J. Stiglitz, 'On the Impossibility of Informationally Efficient Markets', *American Economic Review*, LXVI/2 (1980), pp. 393–408 (at p. 393).

40 They call to mind an 'information market' that their 'pro-market' adversaries cannot contest.

41 The theorem is presented as follows: If $(\theta^*, \varepsilon^*, x^*)$ has a nondegenerate joint normal distribution such that θ^*, ε^* and x^* are mutually independent, then there exists a solution to $\gamma X_l (P_\gamma (\theta,x), \theta) + (1 - \gamma) X_U(P_\gamma (\theta,x); P_\gamma^*) = x$ which has the form $P_\gamma(\theta,x) = a_1 + a_2 w_\gamma(\theta,x)$, where a_1 and a_2 are real numbers which may depend on γ, such that $a_2 > 0$ (if $\gamma = 0$, the price contains no information about θ). Grossman and Stiglitz, 'On the Impossibility of Informationally Efficient Markets', p. 397.

42 Fama has admitted that these tests are in fact on two joint hypotheses and that they therefore cannot enable someone to decide between either one.

43 Joseph Stiglitz, *Whither Socialism?* (Cambridge, MA, 1994), p. 16.

44 Arrow and Debreu suppose that there exist goods which are 'conditional' to the realization of an infinite number of 'states of nature', themselves independent of the actions of agents. This weighs heavily in the task of the auctioneer, who has to propose prices and elaborate conditional contracts with agents, without fundamentally modifying the model itself.

45 Stiglitz, *Whither Socialism?*, p. 60 (my italics).

46 Ibid., p. 27.

47 Stiglitz, 'When markets aren't perfect, governments can help', cbsnews.com, 3 May 2016.

48 Stiglitz, *The Great Divide* (New York, 2015), p. 125.

49 Ibid.

FURTHER READING

Introduction

Backhouse, R. E., *Founder of Modern Economics: Paul A. Samuelson*, vol. I: *Becoming Samuelson, 1915–1948* (Oxford, 2017)

Coffman, D., A. Leonard and L. Neal, *Questioning Credible Commitment* (Cambridge, 2013)

Janeway, W. H., *Doing Capitalism in the Innovation Economy: Markets, Speculation and the State* (Cambridge, 2012)

Jolink, A., and J. Van Daal, *The Equilibrium Economics of Léon Walras* (Routledge, 2002)

Jones, D. S., *Masters of the Universe: Hayek, Friedman, and the Birth of Neoliberal Politics* (Princeton, NJ, 2014)

McCormick, T., *William Petty and the Ambitions of Political Arithmetic* (Oxford, 2009)

Patalano, R., and S. A. Reinert, eds, *Antonio Serra and the Economics of Good Government* (London, 2016), pp. 112–42

Rothschild, E., *Economic Sentiments: Adam Smith, Condorcet and the Enlightenment* (Cambridge, MA, 2013)

Scazzieri, R., A. Sen and S. Zamagni, eds, *Markets, Money and Capital: Hicksian Economics for the Twenty First Century* (Cambridge, 2008)

Stern, P. J., and C. Wennerlind, eds., *Mercantilism Reimagined: Political Economy in Early Modern Britain and its Empire* (Oxford, 2013)

Wennerlind, C., *Casualties of Credit: The English Financial Revolution, 1620–1720* (Cambridge, MA, 2001)

Yamamoto, K., *Taming Capitalism before its Triumph: Public Service, Distrust and 'Projecting' in Early Modern England* (Oxford, 2018)

ONE Adam Smith

Conlin, Jonathan, *Adam Smith* (London, 2016)

Evensky, Jerry, *Adam Smith's Moral Philosophy* (Cambridge, 2005)

Haakonssen, Knud, *The Science of a Legislator: The Natural Jurisprudence of David Hume and Adam Smith* (Cambridge, 1981)

—, ed., *The Cambridge Companion to Adam Smith* (Cambridge, 2006)

Hanley, Ryan Patrick, *Adam Smith and the Character of Virtue* (Cambridge, 2009)

Hirschman, Albert O., *The Passions and the Interests* (Princeton, NJ, 1977)

Hont, Istvan, and Michael Ignatieff, eds, *Wealth and Virtue* (Cambridge, 1983)

Phillipson, Nicholas, *Adam Smith: An Enlightened Life* (London, 2010)

Rasmussen, Dennis C., *The Problems and Promise of Commercial Society: Adam Smith's Response to Rousseau* (Philadelphia, PA, 2008)
Schabas, Margaret, *The Natural Origins of Economics* (Chicago, IL, 2005)
Smith, Adam, *The Glasgow Edition of the Works and Correspondence of Adam Smith*, ed. R. H. Campbell and A. S. Skinner (Oxford, 1975–87)
Werhane, Patricia H., *Adam Smith and His Legacy for Modern Capitalism* (Oxford, 1991)

TWO David Ricardo

Hollander, Jacob H., *David Ricardo: A Centenary Estimate* (New York, 1968)
James, Patricia, *Population Malthus: His Life and Times* (Oxford, 2006)
Kurz, Heinz D., and Neri Salvadori, *The Elgar Companion to David Ricardo* (London, 2015)
Malthus, Thomas Robert, *An Essay on the Principle of Population* (London, 2001)
O'Brien, D. P., *The Classical Economists* (Oxford, 1978)
Peach, Terry, *Interpreting Ricardo* (Cambridge, 1993)
—, *David Ricardo: Critical Responses*, 4 vols (London, 2003)
Roll, Eric, *A History of Economic Thought*, 5th edn (London and Boston, MA, 1992)
Schumpeter, Joseph A., *History of Economic Analysis* (New York, 1954)
Sraffa, Piero, and Maurice Herbert Dobb, eds, *The Works and Correspondence of David Ricardo*, 11 vols (Cambridge, 1951–73)

THREE John Stuart Mill

Babbage, Charles, *On the Economy of Machinery and Manufacturing* [1835], 4th edn (New York, 1963)
Boss, Helen, *Theories of Surplus and Transfer* (Boston, MA, 1990)
Caldwell, Bruce, 'Hayek on Mill', *History of Political Economy*, XL/4 (2008), pp. 689–704
Chipman, John, 'A Survey of the Theory of International Trade: Part 1, The Classical Theory', *Econometrica*, XXXIII/3 (1965), pp. 477–519
DeLong, J. Bradford, 'This Time is Not Different: The Persistent Concerns of Financial Macroeconomics', www.equitablegrowth.org, 13 December 2016
Donner, Wendy, *The Liberal Self: John Stuart Mill's Moral and Political Philosophy* (Ithaca, NY, 1991)
Ekelund, Robert, Jr, and Douglas Walker, 'J. S. Mill on the Income Tax Exemption and Inheritance Taxes: The Evidence Reconsidered', *History of Political Economy*, XXVIII/4 (1996), pp. 559–81
Hayek, Friedrich, *John Stuart Mill and Harriet Taylor* (Chicago, IL, 1951)
Hollander, Samuel, *The Economics of John Stuart Mill* (Toronto, 1985)
—, *John Stuart Mill: Political Economist* (Singapore, 2015)
Keynes, John Maynard, *The General Theory of Employment, Interest, and Money* (New York, 1936)
Levy, David, *How the Dismal Science Got Its Name: Classical Economics and the Ur-Text of Racial Politics* (Ann Arbor, MI, 2001)
Maneschi, Andrea, 'John Stuart Mill's Equilibrium Terms of Trade: A Special Case of William Whewell's 1850 Formula', *History of Political Economy*, XXXIII/3 (2001), pp. 609–25

Mazlish, Bruce, *James and John Stuart Mill: Father and Son in the Nineteenth Century* (New York, 1975)
Miles, Dudley, *Francis Place: The Life of a Remarkable Radical, 1771–1854* (Brighton, 1988)
Mill, John Stuart, 'Debating Speeches, 1823–29', in *The Collected Works of John Stuart Mill*, vol. XXVI: *Journals and Debating Speeches*, ed. John Robson (Toronto, 1988)
—, *The Principles of Political Economy with Some of Their Applications to Social Philosophy* [1848], vols II–III of *The Collected Works of John Stuart Mill*, ed. John M. Robson (Toronto, 1965)
—, *On Liberty* [1859], in *The Collected Works of John Stuart Mill*, vol. XVIII: *Essays on Politics and Society Part I*, ed. John M. Robson (Toronto, 1977)
—, *Utilitarianism* [1861], 1871 edition in *Utilitarianism and other Essays*, ed. Alan Ryan (London, 1987)
—, *The Subjection of Women* [1869], in *The Collected Works of John Stuart Mill*, vol. XXI: *Essays on Economics and Society Part II*, ed. John M. Robson (Toronto, 1984)
—, *Land Tenure Reform* [1871], in *The Collected Works of John Stuart Mill*, ed. John Robson (Toronto, 1967), vol. V
—, *Autobiography* [1873], in *The Collected Works of John Stuart Mill*, ed. John Robson and Jack Stillinger (Toronto, 1981), vol. I
—, 'Chapters on Socialism' [1879], originally published in the *Fortnightly Review*, republished in *The Collected Works of John Stuart Mill*, vol. V: *Essays on Economics and Society*, ed. John Robson (Toronto, 1967)
Nicholson, Peter, 'The Reception and Early Reputation of Mill's Political Thought', in *The Cambridge Companion to Mill*, ed. John Skorupski (Cambridge, 1998)
Owen, Robert, *Manifesto of Robert Owen*, 6th edn (London, 1840)
Persky, Joseph, 'Utilitarianism and Luck', *History of Political Economy*, XLV/2 (2013), pp. 287–309
—, *The Political Economy of Progress: John Stuart Mill and Modern Radicalism* (New York, 2016)
—, 'Producer Co-operatives in Nineteenth-century British Economic Thought', *European Journal of the History of Economic Thought*, XXIV/2 (2017), pp. 319–40
Reeves, Richard, *John Stuart Mill: Victorian Firebrand* (London, 2007)
Rose, Phyllis, *Parallel Lives: Five Victorian Marriages* (New York, 1983)
Shoul, Bernice, 'Similarities in the Work of John Stuart Mill and Karl Marx', *Science and Society*, XXIX (1965), pp. 270–95
Smith, Adam, *An Inquiry into the Nature and Causes of the Wealth of Nations* [1776] (New York, 1937)
Sowell, Thomas, *On Classical Economics* (New Haven, CT, 2006)
Tunick, Mark, 'Tolerant Imperialism: John Stuart Mill's Defense of British Rule in India', *Review of Politics*, LXVIII (2006), pp. 586–611

FOUR Karl Marx

Braverman, Harry, *Labor and Monopoly Capital: The Degradation of Work in the Twentieth Century* (New York, 1974)

Cox, Oliver C., *Caste, Class, and Race: A Study in Social Dynamics* (New York, 1959)
Du Bois, W.E.B., *Writings* (New York, 1986)
Engels, Frederick, *The Condition of the Working Class in England* [1845] (Moscow, 1973)
Foster, John Bellamy, Brett Clark and Richard York, *The Ecological Rift: Capitalism's War on the Earth* (New York, 2010)
Galeano, Eduardo, *Open Veins of Latin America: Five Centuries of the Pillage of a Continent* (New York, 1973)
Georgescu-Roegen, Nicholas, *The Entropy Law and the Economic Process* (Cambridge, MA, 1971)
Marx, Karl, *The Economic and Philosophic Manuscripts of 1844* (New York, 1971)
—, *Grundrisse* [1857–8] (New York, 1973)
—, *Capital: A Critique of Political Economy*, vol. I [1867] (New York, 1977)
—, *Capital: A Critique of Political Economy*, vol. II [1885] (New York, 1981)
—, *Capital: A Critique of Political Economy*, vol. III [1894] (New York, 1981)
McLellan, David, *Karl Marx: His Life and Thought* (New York, 1973)
Mészáros, István, *Beyond Capital* (London, 1995)
Wallerstein, Immanuel, *World-Systems Analysis: An Introduction* (Durham, NC, 2004)

FIVE Alfred Marshall

Arena, Richard, and Michel Quéré, *The Economics of Alfred Marshall: Revisiting Marshall's Legacy* (London, 2003)
Belussi, Fiorenza, and Katia Caldari, 'At the Origin of Industrial District: Alfred Marshall and the Cambridge School', *Cambridge Journal of Economics*, XXXIII/2 (2009), pp. 335–55
—, 'The Lancashire Industrial District: Its Rise, Prosperity and Decline in the Analysis of British Economists', in *Marshall, Marshallians and Industrial Economics*, ed. Tiziano Raffaelli, Tamotsu Nishizawa and Simon Cook (Abingdon, 2011), pp. 135–62
Caldari, Katia, and Fabio Masini, 'The Limits of Growth: Alfred Marshall and the British Economic Tradition', in *Marshall and Schumpeter on Evolution*, ed. T. Nishizawa and Y. Shionoya (Cheltenham, 2008), pp. 166–87
—, 'Pigouvian vs Marshallian Tax: Market Failure, Public Intervention and the Problem of Externalities', *European Journal of the History of Economic Thought*, XVIII/5 (2011), pp. 715–32
Caldari, Katia, and Tamotsu Nishizawa, 'Marshall's Ideas on Progress: Roots and Diffusion', in *The Dissemination of Economic Ideas*, ed. Heinz Kurz, Tamotsu Nishizawa and Keith Tribe (Aldershot, 2011), pp. 125–57
—, 'Marshall's "Welfare Economics" and "Welfare": A Reappraisal Based on his Unpublished Manuscript on Progress", *History of Economic Ideas*, XXII/1 (2014), pp. 51–67
Raffaelli, Tiziano, Giacomo Becattini and Marco Dardi, eds, *The Elgar Companion of Alfred Marshall* (Cheltenham, 2006)
Raffaelli, Tiziano, and Katia Caldari, eds, *The Impact of Alfred Marshall's Ideas: The Global Diffusion of his Work* (Cheltenham, 2010)
Whitaker, John K., 'What Happened to the Second Volume of the *Principles*? The Thorny Path to Marshall's Last Books', in *Centenary Essays on Alfred Marshall*, ed. J. K. Whitaker (Cambridge, 1990)

SIX Joseph Schumpeter

Andersen, Esben Sloth, *Joseph A. Schumpeter: A Theory of Social and Economic Evolution* (Basingstoke, 2011)
Schumpeter, Joseph A., *The Theory of Economic Development: An Inquiry into Profits, Capital, Credit, Interest, and the Business Cycle* (Cambridge, MA, 1934)
——, *Business Cycles: A Theoretical, Historical, and Statistical Analysis of the Capitalist Process* (New York, 1939)
——, *Capitalism, Socialism and Democracy* (New York, 1942)
——, *History of Economic Analysis* (London, 1954)
——, *Essays on Entrepreneurs, Innovations, Business Cycles, and the Evolution of Capitalism*, ed. Richard V. Clemence (New Brunswick, NJ, 1989)
——, *The Economics and Sociology of Capitalism*, ed. Richard Swedberg (Princeton, NJ, 1991)
Swedberg, Richard, *Joseph A. Schumpeter: His Life and Work* (Cambridge, 1991)

SEVEN John Maynard Keynes

Backhouse, Roger E., and Bradley W. Bateman, *The Cambridge Companion to Keynes* (Cambridge, 2006)
Eltis, Walter A., and Peter J. N. Sinclair, *Keynes and Economic Policy* (London, 1988)
Moggridge, D., *Maynard Keynes: An Economist's Biography* (London, 1995)
Peden, G. C., *Keynes, the Treasury and British Economic Policy* (Basingstoke, 1988)
Skidelsky, Robert, *Keynes: The Return of the Master* (London, 2009)
——, *Keynes: A Very Short Introduction* (Oxford, 2010)
——, ed., *The Essential Keynes* (London, 2015)
Stewart, Michael, *Keynes and After* (London, 1986)

EIGHT Friedrich Hayek

Burczak, Theodore, *Socialism after Hayek* (Ann Arbor, MI, 2006)
Caldwell, Bruce, *Hayek's Challenge* (Chicago, IL, 2004)
Dekker, Erwin, *The Viennese Students of Civilization: The Meaning and Context of Austrian Economics Reconsidered* (Cambridge, 2016)
Hayek, F. A., *The Collected Works of F. A. Hayek* (19 vols) ed. Bruce Caldwell
——, *Contra Keynes and Cambridge*, ed. Bruce Caldwell (Chicago, IL, 1995), vol. IX
——, *Socialism and War: Essays, Documents, Reviews*, ed. Bruce Caldwell (Chicago, IL, 1997), vol. X
——, *The Sensory Order: An Inquiry into the Foundations of Theoretical Psychology* [1952] (Chicago, IL, 1999), vol. XIV
——, *The Road to Serfdom: Text and Documents – The Definitive Edition* (Chicago, IL, 2007), vol. II
——, *Business Cycles*, ed. Hansjörg Klausinger (Chicago, IL, 2012), vols VII–VIII
——, *The Market and Other Orders*, ed. Bruce Caldwell (Chicago, IL, 2014), vol. XV
Lavoie, Don, *Rivalry and Central Planning* (New York, 1985)

White, Lawrence H., *The Clash of Economic Ideas: The Great Policy Debates and Experiments of the Last Hundred Years* (New York, 2012)

NINE Milton Friedman

Allison, John A., *The Financial Crisis and the Free Market Cure* (New York, 2012)
Bateman, Victoria, 'Classical Liberalism: The Foundation for a New Economics', *Critical Review*, XXVIII/3–4 (2016), pp. 440–60
Burgin, Angus, *The Great Persuasion: Reinventing Free Markets since the Great Depression* (Cambridge, MA, 2015)
Caldwell, Bruce, 'The Chicago School, Hayek, and Neoliberalism', in *Building Chicago Economics*, ed. Van Horn, Robert, Philip Mirowski and Thomas A. Stapleford (Cambridge, 2011), pp. 301–34
Cherrier, Beatrice, 'The Lucky Consistency of Milton Friedman's Science and Politics, 1933–1963', in *Building Chicago Economics*, ed. Rob van Horn, Philip Mirowski and Thomas A. Stapleford (Cambridge, 2011), pp. 335–67
Ebenstein, Lenny, *Milton Friedman: A Biography* (New York, 2007)
Friedman, Milton, *Essays in Positive Economics* (Chicago, IL, 1953)
—, *Capitalism and Freedom* (Chicago, IL, 1962)
—, and Rose Friedman, *Free to Choose* (New York, 1980)
Hammond, Daniel J., 'Markets, Politics, and Democracy at Chicago: Taking Economics Seriously', in *Building Chicago Economics*, ed. Rob van Horn, Philip Mirowski and Thomas A. Stapleford (Cambridge, 2011), pp. 36–66
Horn, Rob Van, and Philip Mirowski, 'The Rise of the Chicago School of Economics and the Birth of Neoliberalism', in *The Road from Mont Pelerin: The Making of the Neoliberal Thought Collective*, ed. Philip Mirowski and Dieter Plehwe (Cambridge, MA, 2009), pp. 139–78
Laidler, D. E., 'Monetarism: An Interpretation and Assessment', *Economic Journal*, XCI/361 (1981), pp. 1–28
Ostry, Jonathan D., Prakash Loungani and Davide Furceri, 'Neoliberalism: Oversold', *Finance and Development*, LIII/2 (2016), pp. 38–41
Romer, Paul, 'Mathiness in the Theory of Economic Growth', *American Economic Review*, CV/5 (2015), pp. 89–93
Smith, Noah, 'Milton Friedman's Cherished Theory is Laid to Rest', *Bloomberg View*, 12 January 2017
Waring, Marilyn, *If Women Counted: A New Feminist Economics* (New York, 1988)
Wood, J. Cunningham, and R. N. Wood, eds, *Milton Friedman: Critical Assessments* (London, 1990)
Wray, L. Randall, *Why Minsky Matters: An Introduction to the Work of a Maverick Economist* (Princeton, NJ, 2016)

TEN John Forbes Nash Jr

Binmore, Ken, *Playing for Real*, Oxford (2007)
Myerson, Roger, *Game Theory: Analysis of Conflict* (Cambridge, MA, 1991)
Nasar, Sylvia, *A Beautiful Mind: The Life of Mathematical Genius and Nobel Laureate John Nash* (New York, 1998)
Nash, John, 'Equilibrium Points in n-person Games', *Proceedings of the National Academy of Sciences*, XXXVI (1950), pp. 48–9

——, 'The Bargaining Problem', *Econometrica*, XVIII/2 (1950), pp. 155–62
——, 'Non-cooperative Games', *Annals of Mathematics*, LIV (1951), pp. 286–95
——, 'Two-person Cooperative Games', *Econometrica*, XXI/1 (1953), pp. 128–40
——, and Lloyd S. Shapley, 'A Simple Three-person Poker Game, Contributions to the Theory of Games', *Annals of Mathematic Studies*, XXIV (1950), pp. 105–16
Van Damme, Eric, and Jorgen W. Weibull, 'Equilibrium in Strategic Interaction: The Contributions of John C. Harsanyi, John F. Nash, and Reinhard Selten', *Scandinavian Journal of Economics*, XCIV/1 (1995), pp. 15–40
Weintraub, E. Roy, 'Toward a History of Game Theory', *History of Political Economy*, XXIV (1992), supplement

ELEVEN Daniel Kahneman

Adams, Tim, 'This Much I Know: Daniel Kahneman', *The Guardian*, www.theguardian.com, 8 July 2012
Baddeley, Michelle, *Behavioural Economics: A Very Short Introduction* (2017)
Barberis, N. C., 'Thirty Years of Prospect Theory in Economics: A Review and Assessment', *Journal of Economic Perspectives*, XXVII/1 (2013), pp. 173–96
Kahneman, Daniel, *Attention and Effort* (Englewood Cliffs, NJ, 1973)
——, 'Daniel Kahneman – Biographical', *The Sveriges Riksbanks Prize in Economic Sciences in Memory of Alfred Nobel 2002*, www.nobelprize.org
——, *Thinking, Fast and Slow* (New York and London, 2011)
——, and Amos Tversky, 'Prospect Theory – An Analysis of Decision under Risk', *Econometrica*, XLVII/2 (1979), pp. 263–92
Lewis M., *The Undoing Project: A Friendship that Changed Our Minds* (New York, 2016)
Shariatmadari, D., 'Daniel Kahneman: "What would I eliminate if I had a magic wand? Overconfidence"', interview in *The Guardian*, www.theguardian.com, 18 July 2015
Thaler, R. H., A. Tversky, D. Kahneman and A. Schwartz, 'The Effect of Myopia and Loss Aversion on Risk Taking: An Experimental Test', *Quarterly Journal of Economics*, CXII (1997), pp. 647–61
Tversky, A., and D. Kahneman, 'Judgement under Uncertainty: Heuristics and Biases', *Science*, CLXXXV (1974), pp. 1124–31

TWELVE Amartya Sen

Morris, Christopher W., ed., *Amartya Sen* (Cambridge, 2009)
Nussbaum, Martha, and Jonathan Glover, eds, *Women, Culture and Development: A Study of Human Capabilities* (Oxford, 1995)
Sen, Amartya, *Poverty and Famines: An Essay on Entitlement and Deprivation* (Oxford, 1981)
——, *On Economic Inequality*, enl. edn (Oxford, 1997)
——, *Choice, Welfare and Measurement* (Cambridge, MA, 1997)
——, *Development as Freedom* (Oxford, 1999)
——, *Commodities and Capabilities* (Oxford, 1999)
——, *The Idea of Justice* (London, 2009)
——, and Jean Drèze, *India: Economic Development and Social Opportunity* (Delhi, 1995)

——, and Bernard Williams, eds, *Utilitarianism and Beyond* (Cambridge, 1982)
Sugden, Robert, 'Welfare, Resources, and Capabilities: A Review of *Inequality Reexamined* by Amartya Sen,' *Journal of Economic Literature*, XXXI (1993), pp. 1947–62

THIRTEEN Joseph Stiglitz

Economic Sciences Prize Committee, 'Markets with Asymmetric Information' (Stockholm, 2001)
Fama E., 'Efficient Capital Markets: A Review of Theory and Empirical Work', *Journal of Finance*, XXV/2 (1970), pp. 383–417
Grossman, S., and J. Stiglitz, 'On the Impossibility of Informationally Efficient Markets', *American Economic Review*, LXVI/2 (1976), pp. 246–53
Guerrien, B., and O. Gün, 'Efficient Market Hypothesis: What are We Talking About?', *Real World Economic Review*, LVI (2011), pp. 19–30
Sailer, S., '"Incentives Matter," Except to Economists', www.vdare.com, 14 January 2014
Shapiro, C., and J. Stiglitz, 'Equilibrium Unemployment as a Worker Discipline Device', *American Economic Review*, LXXIV/3 (1984), pp. 433–44
Stiglitz J., *Whither Socialism?* (Cambridge, MA, 1994)
——, 'Information and the Change in the Paradigm in Economics', *American Economic Review*, XCII/3 (June 2002), pp. 460–501
——, *The Great Divide* (New York, 2015)
——, 'Joseph E. Stiglitz – Biographical', *The Sveriges Riksbank Prize in Economic Sciences in Memory of Alfred Nobel 2001*, www.nobelprize.org, accessed 22 February 2018

LIST OF CONTRIBUTORS

Jonathan Conlin is Senior Lecturer in Modern History at the University of Southampton. He has published biographies of Calouste Gulbenkian and Adam Smith, the latter for Reaktion's Critical Lives series. His other books include *Evolution and the Victorians* (2014) and *Tales of Two Cities* (2013), a comparative history of Paris and London.

Michelle Baddeley is the Director (Academic) and Research Professor at the Institute for Choice, Sydney – University of South Australia and Honorary Professor, UCL Institue for Global Prosperity, University College London. She has a Bachelor of Economics (First Class Honours) and BA (Psychology) from the University of Queensland, and a Masters/PhD (Economics) from the University of Cambridge. She specializes in behavioural economics, applied macroeconomics and development economics. She has written many papers and her recent books include *Behavioural Economics: A Very Short Introduction* (2017), *Behavioural Economics and Finance* (2013) and *Copycats and Contrarians: Why We Follow Others . . . and When We Don't* (2018).

Victoria Bateman is Fellow in Economics at Gonville and Caius College, University of Cambridge. She is author of the book *Markets and Growth in Early Modern Europe* (2016); writes regular economic commentary, including for *UnHerd*, *Bloomberg View* and *CapX*; and has contributed articles to *The Guardian*, the *Times Higher Education Supplement*, *The Conversation* and *The Telegraph*. She has appeared on the BBC (Radio 4, World Service and *Newsnight*), discussing everything from Brexit to welfare reform, as well as making a public call for a sexual revolution in economics. Her latest book is titled *The Sex Factor* (2019).

Emmanuelle Bénicourt is Senior Lecturer in Economics at the University of Picardie Jules Verne, where she is a member of the CRIISEA (Centre de Recherche sur les Institutions, l'Industrie et les Systèmes Economiques d'Amiens) research network. Her doctoral thesis ('École des Hautes Études en Sciences Sociales', 2005) considered Amartya Sen's role in shaping the United Nations Development Programme and the World Bank's analyses of poverty and development. This research led her to address Sen's critiques of Rawls and of utilitarianism, and, more broadly, the socio-political roles performed by economic theories. Her books include *La théorie économique néoclassique* (2008), written in collaboration with Bernard Guerrien. She contributes regularly to online reviews, including *la vie des idées*.

Katia Caldari is Associate Professor in Economics at the University of Padova, Department of Economics and Management 'M. Fanno'. She has a PhD in History of Economic Thought from the University of Florence, Italy. She has been visiting scholar at Cambridge University and collaborates with the Universities of Pisa, Florence, Rome, Sophia-Antipolis (Nice) and Hitotsubashi University (Tokyo). Her main interests regard analysis of some topics of economic theory (equilibrium, expectations, distribution, planning); history of economic thought (particularly Alfred Marshall and François Perroux) and economic methodology; international economics (financial crises, international trade, globalization, growth and development); and industrial economics (industrial districts).

D'Maris Coffman is a Professor of Economics and Finance of the Built Environment at UCL Bartlett, UK and Director of the Bartlett School of Construction and Project Management. Prior to this D'Maris was a Leverhulme/Newton Trust Early Career Fellow at the History Faculty of the University of Cambridge and Fellow and Director of the Centre of Financial History at Newnham College. Her historical work is primarily on the relationship between public finance and private capital markets in eighteenth- and nineteenth-century Europe, and related histories of early modern economic policymaking. From 2012 to 2018, she sat on the Council of the Economic History Society.

Mário Graça Moura is an Associate Professor of Economics at the Faculty of Economics of the University of Porto (FEP-UP) and a researcher at the Centre for Economics and Finance at UP (cef.up). He was educated at the University of Porto and the University of Cambridge. His research interests are in the history and methodology of economics. He has published articles on Schumpeter in the *Cambridge Journal of Economics, The European Journal of the History of Economic Thought* and the *Journal of Evolutionary Economics.*

Karen Horn teaches the history of economic thought at the universities of Berlin (Humboldt), Erfurt and Siegen. She serves as editor-in-chief for *Perspektiven der Wirtschaftspolitik*, a scholarly journal published by the German Economics Association. Her research focuses on Adam Smith, Friedrich Hayek, James M. Buchanan and the German 'Ordoliberals'. Earlier in her career, she was an economic policy editor at the *Frankfurter Allgemeine Zeitung*, and head of the Berlin office of IW Köln, a large economic research institute. She has authored several books, including *Roads to Wisdom: Conversations with Ten Nobel Laureates* (2009) and *Hayek für jedermann* (2013).

Helen Paul is an economic historian based in the University of Southampton's economics department. Her book *The South Sea Bubble* is an economic history of the famous financial crash of 1720. She has written about how financial crises were depicted and understood by a contemporary audience. She also researches female entrepreneurship in the early modern period. She holds degrees from Oxford and St Andrews and is currently Honorary Secretary of the Economic History Society.

Joseph Persky is Professor of Economics at the University of Illinois at Chicago's College of Liberal Arts and Sciences. He recently authored *The Political Economy of Progress: John Stuart Mill and Modern Radicalism.* Persky has a long-standing interest in the southern United States and is the author of *The Burden of Dependency: Colonial Themes in Southern Economic Thought.* He acts as the informal editor of the *Retrospectives* section of the American Economics Association's *Journal of Economic Perspectives.* Persky has also written extensively on the distributional implications of urban and regional economic growth and is a Research Associate at the Economic Policy Institute.

Paul Prew is an Associate Professor at Minnesota State University, Mankato where he teaches courses on theory, environment and globalization. While his area of specialization is the political economy of the environment, he has collaborated with others in the areas of philanthropy, race and perceptions of police, genocide and pedagogy. Owing to his volunteer work for local non-profits and dedication to social justice on campus, Dr Prew received the Diversity Champion, Community Peace Maker and Global Citizen awards at his university. He is currently serving as treasurer of the Marxist Section of the American Sociological Association.

Scott Scheall is a Lecturer with Arizona State University's College of Integrative Sciences and Arts. He received his PhD in philosophy from Arizona State in 2012. Scott is a former Research Fellow with Duke University's Center for the History of Political Economy and a former Postdoctoral Fellow with the F. A. Hayek Program for Advanced Study in Philosophy, Politics and Economics at George Mason University. Scott is co-editor of *Research in the History of Economic Thought and Methodology.* He has published extensively on the history and methodology of the Austrian School of economics.

ACKNOWLEDGEMENTS

Emmanuelle Bénicourt

I would like to thank Bernard Guerrien for being a source of inspiration, for his insights and constant critical comments. He has undeniably influenced my understanding of economic theories. I would also like to thank Jon Conlin for his remarks and comments on this essay.

D'Maris Coffman

I would like to thank Professors Jonathan Steinberg, Roberto Scazzieri and Alberto Quadrio Curzio for encouraging my interests in the histories of economic thought and economic analysis.

Jonathan Conlin

I would like to thank the following for their constructive comments and suggestions, without which the volume (and in particular my own chapters) would be much the poorer: Roger Backhouse, Nicholas Cron, Martin Daunton, Jerry Evensky, Ben Hayes, Adam Ostaszewski, Margaret Schabas and Richard Toye. I salute Alastair Paynter for his hard work preparing the manuscript for submission.

Mario Graça Moura

I am grateful to Jonathan Conlin, Diogo Lourenço and Francisco Nunes Pereira for their comments and suggestions. Cef.up is financed by the European Regional Development Fund through COMPETE 2020 – Programa Operacional Competitividade e Internacionalização (POCI) – and by Portuguese public funds through FCT (Fundação para a Ciência e a Tecnologia) in the framework of the project POCI-01-0145-FEDER-006890.

Helen Paul

I would like to thank John Aldrich and Emma Clery for their invaluable help.

Paul Prew

I would like to thank John Bellamy Foster, Brett Clark, Matt Vidal, Jonathan Conlin and Thomas Hoerber for their helpful comments on my draft. For invigorating my interest in Marx, I am eternally indebted to Wilma Dunaway and Donald Clelland. They offered up their home and library so that I could learn, and so that we could discuss, into the wee hours of the morning, the breadth of Marx's work and Marxist scholarship in general.

Scott Scheall

Many thanks to Jonathan Conlin, editor of this volume, for the opportunity to contribute, and to Bruce Caldwell, for suggesting my name to Jonathan as a potential author of the Hayek chapter.